RAVEL
Man and Musician

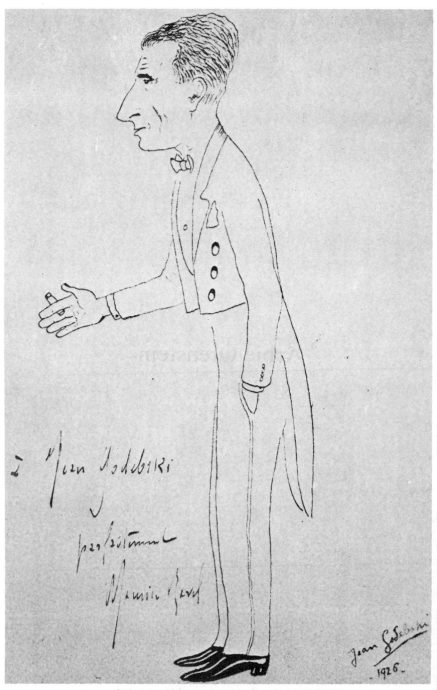

Caricature of Maurice Ravel by Jean Godebski (1926)

RAVEL
Man and Musician

Arbie Orenstein

Dover Publications, Inc., New York

The Andrew W. Mellon Foundation, through a special grant, assisted in the original publication of this book.

Published in Canada by General Publishing Company, Ltd., 30 Lesmill Road, Don Mills, Toronto, Ontario.
Published in the United Kingdom by Constable and Company, Ltd., 3 The Lanchesters, 162-164 Fulham Palace Road, London W6 9ER.

This Dover edition, first published in 1991, is an unabridged, slightly corrected republication of the edition originally published by Columbia University Press, New York, in 1975. The Catalogue of Works and the Selected Bibliography have been updated.

Manufactured in the United States of America
Dover Publications, Inc., 31 East 2nd Street, Mineola, N.Y. 11501

Library of Congress Cataloging-in-Publication Data

Orenstein, Arbie.
    Ravel : man and musician / Arbie Orenstein.
        p.   cm.
    "This Dover edition . . . is an unabridged, slightly corrected republication of the edition originally published by Columbia University Press, New York, in 1975. The catalogue of works and selected bibliography have been updated"—Copr. p.
    Includes bibliographical references and index.
    ISBN 0-486-26633-8 (pbk.)
    1. Ravel, Maurice, 1875-1937. 2. Composers—France—Biography. I. Title.
[ML410.R23073   1991]
780'.92—dc20   91-2789
[B]   CIP
                                       MN

For my Parents and my Wife

Contents

Preface   xv
Acknowledgments   xvii
Introduction   1

PART I   BIOGRAPHY AND CULTURAL BACKGROUND

1   1875–1889   Earliest Years and Youth   7
2   1889–1905   Adolescence and Maturity at the Conservatoire   13
3   1905–1914   From the Sonatine to the Trio   47
4   1914–1921   The War and Its Aftermath   71
5   1921–1928   New Trends in the 1920s   82
6   1928–1937   Concluding Years   94
Epilogue   A Portrait of the Man   110

PART II   THE ART OF MAURICE RAVEL

7   Musical Aesthetics   117
8   Ravel's Musical Language   130
9   The Creative Process   207
Conclusion   217
Appendix A   Catalogue of Works   219
Appendix B   Historical Recordings (1912–1939), compiled by
   Jean Touzelet   247
Selected Bibliography   271
Index   279

Illustrations

Caricature of Maurice Ravel by Jean Godebski (1926). Printed with the kind permission of the artist   *frontispiece*

Plates following page 218

1 Copy of the birth certificate of Joseph Maurice Ravel. Autograph in the Town Hall of Ciboure, France

2 At the Conservatoire, c. 1894. Photograph in the Music Division of the Bibliothèque Nationale

3 Ravel's formal debut as a composer. Program in the Music Division of the Bibliothèque Nationale

4 A program of modern music given by Ricardo Viñes. Program in the Music Division of the Bibliothèque Nationale

5 Letter from Ravel to Mme René de Saint-Marceaux, written August 20, 1898. Autograph in the private collection of B. de Saint-Marceaux

6 Ravel's transcription of an opera by Delius, *Margot la Rouge*, p. 1. Printed with the kind permission of the Frederick Delius Trust, London

7 Georges d'Espagnat, "Réunion de musiciens chez M. Godebski," 1910. Painting in the Bibliothèque de l'Opéra; photo Bibliothèque de l'Opéra

8 Declaration of copyright of several works by Ravel. Printed with the kind permission of the Société des Auteurs, Compositeurs, et Editeurs de Musique, France

9 Founding committee of the Société Musicale Indépendante. Photograph in the Music Division of the Bibliothèque Nationale

10 Inaugural recital of the Société Musicale Indépendante, April 20, 1910. Program in the Music Division of the Bibliothèque Nationale

11 Le Belvédère
The salon. Photo Ariel Temporal
The composer's desk in the study. Photo Ariel Temporal
A view from the balcony. Collection of the author
The front of the house. Collection of the author
The back of the house. Collection of the author
Plaque on front of the house. Collection of the author

12 The study at Le Belvédère. Photo Ariel Temporal

13 Recital in Houston, Texas, April 6, 1928. Printed with the kind permission of Rice University

14 Lecture-recital in Houston, Texas, April 7, 1928. Printed with the kind permission of Rice University

15 A family portrait, c.1886; Edouard, Mme Ravel, Maurice, and Joseph Ravel. Collection Marcelle Gerar
Ravel, c.1902. Collection Marcelle Gerar
Ravel, c.1907. Collection Marcelle Gerar
Ravel, c.1911. Collection of the author

16 c.1925: Ravel in the garden at Montfort l'Amaury. Collection Marcelle Gerar
1928: Le Havre. The return from the United States. Collection Marcelle Gerar
Fall, 1937. With Mme Jacques Meyer and Jacques Février. Photograph in the Music Division of the Bibliothèque Nationale

17 A graphic interpretation of Ravel's art, by Jacques Devigne. Reproduced with the kind permission of the artist and the Société des Auteurs, Compositeurs, et Editeurs de Musique, France. Copyright 1973, Société de la Propriété Artistique et des Desseins et Modèles. Photo Séeberger

18 *Ballade de la Reine morte d'aimer*, p. 1 of the autograph. Copyright 1975, Editions Salabert & A.R.I.M.A.

19 *Sérénade grotesque,* p. 1 of the autograph. Copyright 1975, Editions Salabert & A.R.I.M.A.

20 *Chanson du rouet,* p. 7 of the autograph. Copyright 1975, Editions Salabert & A.R.I.M.A.

21 Overture to *Shéhérazade,* p. 1 of the autograph. Copyright 1975, Editions Salabert & A.R.I.M.A.

22 *Alcyone* (1902), cantata for the Prix de Rome, p. 50. Autograph in the Music Division of the Bibliothèque Nationale

23 *Alyssa* (1903), cantata for the Prix de Rome, p. 78. Autograph in the Music Division of the Bibliothèque Nationale

24 *L'Heure espagnole,* Paris, Opéra-Comique, November 7, 1945. Décor by Mme Suzanne Roland-Manuel. Photo Bibliothèque de l'Opéra *Daphnis et Chloé,* Paris, Opéra, 1958. Décor by Marc Chagall. Photo Bibliothèque de l'Opéra

25 *L'Enfant et les sortilèges,* Paris, Opéra, May 17, 1939. Décor and costumes by Paul Colin. Photos Bibliothèque de l'Opéra

26 Two versions of the opening six measures of *La Cloche engloutie.* Sketches in the private collection of Mme Alexandre Taverne

27–28 Sketches of the first movement of the Sonatine, pp. 1 and 2. Sketches in the private collection of Mme Alexandre Taverne

29–31 *Jeux d'eau,* pp. 4, 5, and 7 of the autograph. Autograph in the Music Division of the Bibliothèque Nationale

32 *Daphnis et Chloé,* p. 102. Original ending of the piano edition (1910). Score in the Music Division of the Bibliothèque Nationale. Autorisation Durand & Cie, Editeurs-propriétaires, Paris

Preface

RESEARCH ON THE LIFE and works of Maurice Ravel has made some important progress in the course of the past sixty years. The first biography of the composer, written by his colleague Roland-Manuel, appeared in 1914, and the author's subsequent work constitutes an excellent and indispensable foundation. Together with a number of personal recollections by colleagues, two important issues of *La Revue Musicale,* and in recent years, a continually growing list of biographical and analytic studies, it would appear that Ravel's career and œuvre have been exhaustively analyzed. Furthermore, it has been categorically asserted that he bequeathed neither any sketches nor any further compositions worthy of publication. Therefore, it would appear, outside of a fresh summary and evaluation, there is little new to be said at this point marking the centenary of the composer's birth. The facts, however, are quite otherwise. With regard to Ravel's music, nine compositions have been recovered which were thought to be lost or destroyed. These compositions are part of a huge collection of holographs and sketches which were bequeathed to Edouard Ravel, and which are presently in the private collection of Madame Alexandre Taverne. Together with another important collection of autographs and sketches in the Robert Owen Lehman Foundation, the result is some 1700 pages of manuscripts which have remained completely unknown until now. The new compositions, which are presently being edited for publication, range from a few overly derivative works to some important achievements. Undoubtedly, the composer's rigorously self-critical attitude was largely responsible for their suppression. In any event, it is clear that many aspects of Ravel's work stand in need of total revision. With regard to the composer's correspondence, of which some 1500 unpublished letters exist in various public and private collections in the United States and Europe, it may be asserted that he wrote considerably more than is generally assumed, and although some important work has been done in this area, a great deal remains to be done. If the ensuing pages will lead to increased insight into Ravel's career and achievement, I will feel amply rewarded.

ARBIE ORENSTEIN

Queens College
Flushing, N.Y.
March, 1975

Note to the Dover Edition

This book was first published in a hardcover edition by Columbia University Press in 1975. The text of this paperback edition is unaltered, except for a few corrections. In addition, the Catalogue of Works (Appendix A) and the Selected Bibliography have been updated in light of recent scholarship.[1]

Particular thanks are due to Mr. Mark Stevens for his meticulous editing of this book.

ARBIE ORENSTEIN

The Aaron Copland School of Music
Queens College
Flushing, N.Y.
March, 1991

---

[1] See A. Orenstein, *A Ravel Reader* (New York: Columbia University Press, 1990).

Acknowledgments

IN THE COURSE of preparing this book over the past decade, I have been assisted by several foundations and a myriad of individuals and institutions. Three years of full-time research in Europe were made possible by grants from the Institute of International Education, the National Endowment for the Humanities Younger Humanist Fellowship, and the City University of New York Faculty Research Award Program, to whom I wish to express my deep gratitude. No acknowledgment could adequately describe my indebtedness to the late Roland-Manuel, and to Manuel Rosenthal, two of Ravel's distinguished disciples, whose unique insights have proven to be of irreplaceable value. This book could not have been successfully completed without the kind cooperation of the late Alexandre Taverne and of Madame Taverne, the present inheritor of the estate of Maurice Ravel. I also wish to thank Jean Touzelet, who diligently compiled the list of historical recordings found in Appendix B; René Dommange, President, and the staff of Durand and Company for their excellent cooperation; the music staff of the Bibliothèque Nationale, and particularly François Lesure for his many kindnesses and the benefit of his wise counsel; my former professors at Columbia University, Paul Henry Lang, Edward A. Lippman, and the late William J. Mitchell, who have read this manuscript at various stages in its development.

The following individuals, colleagues and acquaintances of Maurice

Ravel, have kindly granted me one or more personal interviews, and in many cases have communicated unpublished materials in their private collections: Marie Olénine d'Alheim, Ernest Ansermet, Alexandre Arnoux, Louis Aubert, Georges Auric, Marguerite Babaïan, Jane Bathori, Lennox Berkeley, Nadia Boulanger, Henri Busser, Monsieur and Madame Robert Casadesus, Madame Raymond Charpentier, Claude Dauphin, René Dumesnil, Prince Jean-Louis de Faucigny-Lucinge, Jacques Février, Madame Lucien Garban, Marie-Thérèse Gauley, Marcelle Gerar, Henri Gil-Marchex, Jean Godebski, Maurice Goudeket, Madeleine Grey, Arthur Hoérée, Madame Jacques Ibert, Madame Désiré-Emile Inghelbrecht, Madame G. Jean-Aubry, Madame D. Jobert-Georges, Tristan Klingsor, Yvonne Lefébure, Léon Leyritz, Madame Maurice Maréchal, Marcel Mihalovici, Paul Paray, Vlado Perlemuter, Marc Pincherle, Claude Roland-Manuel, Gustave Samazeuilh, Henri Sauguet, Martial Singher, Alexandre Tansman, Beveridge Webster, and Jean Wiener.

For assistance of various sorts, I am grateful to Madame E. Alekseyva, Madame Ernest Ansermet, Pierre Bernac, Elaine Brody, Lionel Carley, Jacques Chailley, Madame Sylvie Chevalley, Madame J. Colomb-Gérard, Doda Conrad, Madame Piero Coppola, Robert Cosse, Marcel Dietschy, Elisabeth Dunan, Louis Durey, Philippe Entremont, Madame Isabel de Falla, Vladimir Fédorov, Nicole Felkay, Eric Fenby, Mrs. Rudolph Ganz, Yves Gérard, Claude Gitteau, Dr. A. Hauriou, François Heugel, W. J. van Hoboken, Vladimir Jankélévitch, Yves Koechlin, Leo Kraft, Lily Laskine, Jean Leduc, Dr. Robert Le Masle, Jean-Jacques Lemoine, Georges Léon, Edward Lockspeiser, Marc Loliée, Madame Alice Mallet, Darius Milhaud, Paul Morand, G. Morssen, Jean-Michel Nectoux, Marc Perrin, Pierre Renaudin, Ariel Temporal, Jean-Loup Temporal, Daniel Velez, and Ursula Vaughan Williams. For permission to reproduce or quote unpublished documents, I thank Editions Salabert & A.R.I.M.A., Jacques Devigne, Madame Fauré-Frémiet, Jean Godebski, Madame Nina Goubisch, Editions Durand, Madame J.-M. Riéra, France's Société des Auteurs, Compositeurs, et Editeurs de Musique (S.A.C.E.M.) and Société de la Propriété Artistique et des Desseins et Modèles (S.P.A.D.E.M.), B. de Saint-Marceaux, and E. Nussy Saint-Saëns. My sincerest thanks to all of the publishers and individuals who allowed me to study the autographs in their private collections, and whose names appear in Appendix A. I am indebted to the staffs of the Pierpont Morgan Library, the Music Division of the Library of Congress, and the Bibliothèque de l'Opéra for their assistance, and the publishers of *The Musical Quarterly, The Music Forum,* and the *Revue de Musicologie* for permission to quote from my articles which have appeared in these publications. Also, Columbia University for permission to quote from my unpublished doctoral dissertation, "The Vocal Works of Maurice Ravel" (1968), the editors of *La Revue Musicale* for permission to quote from back issues, and Rice University for permission to quote extensively from Ravel's speech entitled "Contemporary Music," which appeared in the Rice Institute Pamphlet of April, 1928. In addition, to those individuals who preferred to remain anonymous, and to all those who assisted in many different ways, I express my esteem and gratitude. Finally, to my favorite typist and research assistant, my wife Mina, my heartfelt thanks for her patience and understanding.

RAVEL
Man and Musician

Introduction

THE LIFETIME of Maurice Ravel (1875–1937) was marked by phenomenal scientific and technological progress, coupled with conspicuous political instability. The concluding decades of the nineteenth century witnessed the discoveries of Thomas Edison and Alexander Bell, the first automobiles, Marconi's wireless, the founding of immunology, and Freud's *Studies in Hysteria*. The opening of the twentieth century saw the invention of the airplane, the discovery of vitamins, and the work of Einstein and Planck. Following the upheaval of World War I, the first sound motion pictures appeared, the neutron and the positron were revealed, and penicillin was discovered. During this period, European history continued to focus upon fragile political alliances and conflicting colonial interests. In France, the Third Republic (1870–1940) was born following a humiliating defeat in the Franco-Prussian War. The Dreyfus affair, which had marked political and racial overtones, separated Frenchmen into opposing camps and led to the separation of Church and State. At the dawn of the twentieth century, France was plagued by strikes and labor unrest, together with several crises with Germany over Morocco, which came to a head in 1911. All of this paled, however, in comparison with World War I. Ravel volunteered to serve his country during the war and personally witnessed its horrors. From August, 1914, until November, 1918, Europe exhausted itself in slaughter, and it has been estimated that half the Frenchmen between the ages of

1

twenty and thirty-two were killed in the war, which claimed some ten million lives, together with twenty million wounded. Even as the conflict continued, the Russian revolution broke out, and between 1917 and 1919, it has been estimated that twenty-five million persons died as a result of a worldwide epidemic of influenza. In 1920, a sobered and hopeful world community founded the League of Nations in Geneva, and eight years later some sixty nations signed the Kellogg-Briand pact, which outlawed war as an instrument of national policy. The postwar years witnessed widespread economic depression and unabated Germanophobia in France. The fragile peace following World War I was jostled by the rise of Mussolini and the Third Reich and was finally smashed in 1939. Thus, the war to end all wars proved to be but a prelude to an even greater carnage.

Despite its political turmoil and agony, the Third Republic witnessed a remarkable flowering of the arts. It was Nietzsche who observed that the Franco-Prussian War appeared to have unleashed France's creative spirit, and during Ravel's lifetime, French painting, literature, and music overtook German hegemony, and Paris became the cultural and artistic capital of Europe. It was the home of Debussy, Fauré, and Poulenc, Matisse, Renoir, and Rodin, Mallarmé, Proust, and Gide, and was an adopted home of Stravinsky, Prokofiev, Falla, Picasso, Modigliani, Wilde, and Stein. Moreover, there was a striking cross-fertilization of the arts, as painters, writers, and musicians freely exchanged views, much to their mutual benefit. Monet's *Impression: Soleil levant* (1872) gave rise to the term impressionism, which was coined by a hostile critic. The impressionists went outdoors in order to experience life and nature firsthand, and their shimmering canvases captured the interplay of light and water, the rhythm of waves and clouds, and the beauty of the French countryside. They also frequented cafés and theaters and captured the sadness, charm, and carefree quality of Parisian life. Between 1874 and 1886, the impressionists frequently exhibited their works together, and after much hostile criticism and ridicule, their art was finally acclaimed by the public. During the first decade of the twentieth century, Matisse led *Les Fauves,* with their experimentation and violent color, and Picasso inaugurated cubism with *Les Demoiselles d'Avignon.* In 1910, the Futurist movement in Italy issued its manifesto, which rejected the past and glorified the machine, while in Munich, Kandinsky began to paint in a completely nonobjective style. Throughout Europe, the depersonalization and futility of World War I resulted in widespread pessimism and escapism.

The short-lived Dadaist movement extolled anti-art and nonsense (Tzara, Picabia) and was soon followed by Surrealism, whose strange visions were influenced by psychoanalytical theories (Breton, Apollinaire, Dalí). Symbolism developed at about the same time as Impressionism, and was largely a reaction against the Parnassian school led by Leconte de Lisle. With Baudelaire and Wagner as their spiritual precursors, the Symbolists stressed the musical qualities of poetry (Verlaine) and achieved greater fluidity by freeing French verse from the strict Alexandrine (Henri de Régnier). Between 1880 and 1894, Mallarmé held his well-known "Tuesdays" at his apartment on rue de Rome, and influenced Claudel, Gide, and Valéry, among many others.

Ravel followed contemporary political developments and artistic trends as a keenly interested observer. His personal world, of course, centered about music: he composed, corrected his manuscripts and proofs, attended rehearsals, served on music juries, heard innumerable concerts, advised many young composers, and performed as pianist and conductor in his own concert engagements. He grew up in the post-Wagnerian epoch in France, which produced a fascinating juxtaposition of widely differing aesthetics, encompassing the subtle lyricism of Fauré, the neoclassical art of Saint-Saëns, and the pioneering work of Erik Satie, who was to influence Debussy and Ravel as well as Poulenc and Milhaud. The influential Vincent d'Indy modeled his art on the works of Beethoven, Wagner, and Franck, while Debussy's shimmering *Prélude à l'Après-midi d'un faune* opened up many fresh directives, and formed a striking counterpart to the achievements of Monet and Verlaine. In addition to the French composers Paul Dukas, Déodat de Séverac, Albert Roussel, and Florent Schmitt, the magnet of Paris attracted Alfredo Casella, Georges Enesco, Manuel de Falla, and Igor Stravinsky, whose career was launched by Diaghilev's Ballet Russe. Furthermore, Richard Strauss, Mahler, and Rimsky-Korsakov came to Paris to conduct their works, and a healthy artistic interchange developed, particularly between French and Russian musicians. Following the war, a heterogeneous group of French composers was dubbed *Les Six,* and important developments took place in Hungary (Bartók and Kodály), England (Vaughan Williams), and Spain (Falla and Turina), while in Vienna, Arnold Schoenberg painstakingly arrived at the abolition of tonality. At the same time, the foundation was laid for an important school of American music, as many young American composers came to Paris to study with the distinguished pedagogue Nadia Boulanger. As the towering figure of Claude Debussy dominated the French musical scene from the turn of the twentieth century until his death in 1918, it was Ravel who was internationally regarded as France's leading musical spokesman following the war. In a career extending over some four decades, from the 1890s to the 1930s, Ravel worked slowly and wrote relatively little, but made distinguished contributions to the literature of the piano, the French art song, chamber music, opera, the orchestra, and ballet. From our vantage point, it is evident that his art was an important contribution to a brilliant epoch in French cultural history.

PART I

Biography and Cultural Background

CHAPTER ONE

1875-1889
Earliest Years and Youth

There is a history in all men's lives.
SHAKESPEARE, *King Henry IV, Part II*

Time is a sort of river of passing events, and strong is its current; no sooner is a thing brought to sight than it is swept by and another takes its place, and this too will be swept away.

MARCUS AURELIUS, *Meditations*

THE CITY OF PARIS has been called the jewel of Europe, and for many centuries its unique charm and beauty have elicited the admiration of artists, poets, scholars, and travellers. The French capital has paid homage to its many distinguished visitors and residents by naming streets in their honor, and thus one may stroll through the Place Chopin, along avenue Victor Hugo, avenue Mozart, rue Claude Debussy, or avenue Maurice Ravel, to name but a few. In addition, sprinkled throughout Paris are many plaques which bear silent witness to important developments in the city's cultural history. At the Montmartre restaurant Auberge de la bonne franquette, a visitor may learn that between 1850 and 1900 this establishment was frequented by Pissarro, Degas, Sisley, Van Gogh, Toulouse-Lautrec, Cézanne, Monet, Renoir, and Zola. A plaque is affixed to the residence at 58 rue Cardinet, where Claude Debussy lived when he completed *Pelléas et Mélisande,* and at 4 avenue Carnot, a moment's walk from the Arc de Triomphe, the passerby may read that Maurice Ravel lived in this building between 1908 and 1917, and here he composed *Daphnis et Chloé.* It was in Paris that Ravel's ideas and personality were molded, and many of the places associated with his career may still be visited. At the offices of Durand and Company, 4 place de la Madeleine, he often visited his editor, and here many of his manuscripts were deposited. The Théâtre du Châtelet, Salle Pleyel, and the Opéra are some of the concert halls which saw the premières of his works, and they still play an active role in the city's musical life.

Although Paris was the artistic hub of Ravel's career, he frequently left the bustling capital to return to his tranquil birthplace in France's Basque territory. Located at the southwestern tip of France, the tiny village of Ciboure is just across the bay from Saint-Jean-de-Luz, and is a short distance from the Spanish border. Here, at 12 rue du Quai, Joseph Maurice Ravel was born at 10 p.m. on March 7, 1875. The following day the infant's birth was duly recorded at the town hall of Ciboure, thus producing the first document to bear his name (see Plate 1). His parents, Marie Delouart (1840–1917), of Basque origin, and Pierre Joseph Ravel (1832–1908), a Swiss civil engineer, were married in Paris on April 3, 1873. Born of Catholic parents, the infant was baptized at the local parish church of Saint Vincent, and some three months later the Ravel family moved to Paris, where a second son, Edouard (1878–1960), was born. He was to follow in his father's footsteps as an engineer.

Maurice Ravel's attachment to his mother was undoubtedly the deepest emotional tie of his entire life. Among his earliest memories were the Spanish folk melodies sung to him by his mother, and through her, he inherited a love of the Basque country, its people, and its folklore, as well as a deep sympathy for the music of Spain. Manuel de Falla commented on the *Rapsodie espagnole* as follows:

> The rhapsody surprised me by its Spanish character. . . . But how could I explain the subtly authentic Hispanic quality of our musician, knowing, by his own admission, that he had but neighboring relations with our country, being born near its

frontier? I rapidly solved the problem: Ravel's Spain was a Spain ideally presented by his mother, whose refined conversation, always in excellent Spanish, delighted me, particularly when she would recall her youthful years spent in Madrid.[1]

Madame Joseph Ravel was a devoted wife and mother, who appears to have been somewhat of a freethinker. When an old friend of the family attempted to "convert" her, Maurice explained the outcome as follows: "Mama cooled this noble zeal considerably by stating that she would prefer to be in hell with her family, rather than in heaven all alone." [2] Madame Ravel took particular pride in her elder son's achievements, and on June 8, 1912, she shared a box at the Théâtre du Châtelet with her sons, Maurice Delage, Florent Schmitt, and Igor Stravinsky, as the Ballets Russes presented a new work, *Daphnis et Chloé*. Ravel venerated his mother, and her death proved to be a blow from which the composer never fully recovered.

The origins of the Ravel family have been traced back to Collonges-sous-Salève, a village in France's Haute-Savoie. During the latter part of the eighteenth century there lived in this village one François Ravex or Ravet,[3] and it appears that the name Ravel came about from a subsequent misreading of the final *t* in Ravet.[4] His son, Aimé Ravel, was born in Collonges-sous-Salève in 1800, but moved to Versoix, in the canton of Geneva, and later became a Swiss citizen. Pierre Joseph Ravel, the father of the composer, was born in Versoix in 1832. He was one of five children, and his younger brother Edouard was a gifted painter. Pierre Joseph was an obedient, sensitive child, and although he was to pursue a career as an engineer, the father of Maurice Ravel was keenly interested in music. In 1845, this engaging thirteen-year-old schoolboy wrote to his mother as follows:

Dear Mama

I forgot to ask you when you visited if you would agree to allow me to study music because M. Angelin told us that the music teacher will be coming next week and I would indeed be happy if you would kindly allow me to learn because it would give me much pleasure, my dear Mama. I had said that I would like to play

[1] Falla, "Notes sur Ravel," trans. Roland-Manuel, *La Revue Musicale* (March, 1939), p. 83.

[2] Autograph letter to Ida Godebska, dated July 19, 1911, in the private collection of Jean Godebski. The letter is partially printed in Chalupt and Gerar, *Ravel au miroir de ses lettres* (Paris, 1956), p. 92.

[3] It appears that the name was written both ways and that both spellings were pronounced identically.

[4] See Roland-Manuel, *A la gloire de Ravel* (Paris, 1938), p. 14.

the flute but was told that this would give me a stomach ache so I would prefer to play the trumpet if you would be so kind. Next week we will also begin drawing which will give me much pleasure. . . . Adieu, dear Mama, I embrace you with all my heart. Adieu

Your respectful son
Joseph Ravel [5]

The young man did study music and acquired an excellent background. Joseph Ravel possessed an inventive, inquisitive mind; he played a pioneering role in the developing automobile industry, and shortly after the Franco-Prussian War, we find him in Spain, involved in railroad construction. In Aránjuez, he met Marie Delouart, who was to become his wife. Joseph Ravel frequently took his sons to visit factories of all sorts, and both youngsters were fascinated with the innumerable machines they saw. In July, 1905, while vacationing with friends in Germany, the elder son of Joseph Ravel wrote to his close friend Maurice Delage:

> This is Haum, a gigantic foundry in which 24,000 men work day and night . . . Towards evening we went down to see the factories. How can I tell you about these great smelting castles, these incandescent cathedrals, and the wonderful symphony of travelling belts, whistles, and terrific hammerblows in which you are submerged? And everywhere the sky is a scorching deep red . . . How much music there is in all this!—and I certainly intend to use it. [6]

In 1928, the composer took time out from a whirlwind concert tour of North America to visit the Ford motor plant in Detroit and described it in glowing terms to his brother. Thus, from his father Ravel appears to have inherited a fascination with mechanical objects of all sorts, as well as a healthy, open-minded curiosity about all aspects of life.

The Ravels were a liberal, sensitive, and devoted couple, and it appears that Maurice was the favorite of his mother, while Joseph Ravel held a special affection for his younger son Edouard. The family's means appear to have been modest but adequate, and when it became clear that the elder child would pursue a career in music, he received unqualified encouragement and support. Thus, Maurice Ravel was fortunate enough to have a happy childhood, and there was to be no Schumannesque crisis over a

[5] Unpublished letter, dated December 12, 1845, in the private collection of Mme Alexandre Taverne.

[6] Chalupt and Gerar, *Ravel au miroir de ses lettres,* p. 38. From his description, Ravel undoubtedly had in mind *La Cloche engloutie* (The Sunken Bell), a projected opera in five acts which was to remain incomplete, although parts of it were used in *L'Enfant et les sortilèges.*

choice of career: it was to be music from the very beginning, and the only problem was whether he would pursue a career as a concert pianist or as a composer.

In May, 1882, shortly after his seventh birthday, Maurice took his first piano lesson with Henry Ghys, who observed that his young pupil appeared to be "intelligent." [7] Charles-René, a pupil of Léo Delibes, gave the youngster his first lessons in harmony, counterpoint, and composition, and among his earliest essays were several pieces for the piano: variations on a chorale by Schumann, the first movement of a sonata, and variations on a theme from Grieg's *Peer Gynt*. Some of this music has been recovered,[8] and it bears out Charles-René's contention that his pupil's conception of music was "natural for him, and not, as with so many others, the result of effort." [9] Following Henry Ghys, Emile Decombes, a professor at the Conservatoire, was the young musician's second piano teacher, and on June 2, 1889, twenty-four of his pupils, among them Reynaldo Hahn and Alfred Cortot, performed excerpts from various piano concerti in a recital at Salle Erard. Maurice played an excerpt from Moscheles's Third Concerto, thus marking his earliest known public performance. At this time, an important international exposition was being held in Paris, commemorating the centenary of the French revolution. For this distinguished event, in which some fifty countries participated, a bold edifice was specially constructed, which has been called the world's first modern building, and which has since become a symbol of the French capital. Under the shadow of the Eiffel Tower, a host of French musicians discovered Javanese gamelans, Annamite dancers, and gypsy orchestras. As part of the festivities, Rimsky-Korsakov conducted two programs of lesser-known works by Russian composers. The fourteen-year-old student was captivated by this unprecedented

[7] Henry Ghys (1839–1908) is chiefly remembered today as the composer of the *Air Louis XIII*. In his library at Montfort l'Amaury, Ravel preserved a copy of this composition with the following dedication: "transcribed specially for four hands, for his little pupil Maurice Ravel, by his professor Henry Ghys, Paris, August 30, 1882."

[8] The autographs are in the private collection of Mme Alexandre Taverne. The Grieg and Schumann pieces each consist of a theme and two variations, based respectively upon "The Death of Ase," and the chorale "Freue dich, O meine Seele," Opus 68. Part of the Grieg work has been published in my article, "Maurice Ravel's Creative Process," *Musical Quarterly* (Oct. 1967), Plate I, opposite p. 478.

[9] Roland-Manuel, *A la gloire de Ravel*, p. 27. The Grieg and Schumann variations exhibit some awkward writing for the keyboard, together with nineteenth-century chromaticism, and a gentle, spontaneous lyricism.

cornucopia and was to retain a lifelong interest in Russian and oriental music.

It appears that Ravel's formal education was restricted to his music lessons. While indicating some natural talent as a composer, he was usually reluctant to practice the piano, and an occasional parental bribe was required to keep him at the keyboard when it would have been more inviting to play in the streets of Montmartre.[10] He was, however, determined to pursue a musical career, and in November, 1889, he passed the entrance examination of the Paris Conservatoire. As it turned out, his long apprenticeship was largely marked by one academic failure after another. On the other hand, his career as a student was one of immense growth, and it was against the backdrop of the Conservatoire that Maurice Ravel was to pass from adolescence to maturity.

[10] Upon arriving in Paris, the Ravel family lived at 40 rue des Martyrs, in the Montmartre section. They moved quite often, and we later find them at 73 rue Pigalle (1888), 15 rue Lagrange (1896), 7 rue Fromentin (1899), 40 bis rue de Douai (April, 1901), and 19 boulevard Pereire (September, 1901). In 1905, the Ravels moved to the Parisian suburb of Levallois Perret (rue Chevalier, now 16 bis rue Louis Rouquier).

CHAPTER TWO

1889-1905
Adolescence and Maturity at the Conservatoire

*I am pleased to acknowledge that I owe to André Gédalge the most valuable ele-
ments of my technique. As for Fauré, his advice as an artist gave me encouragement
of no less value.*

MAURICE RAVEL

*He is, moreover, very complicated, there being in him a mixture of Middle Ages
Catholicism and satanic impiety, but also a love of Art and Beauty which guide him and
which make him react candidly.*

RAVEL AT THE AGE OF TWENTY-ONE, AS DESCRIBED BY RICARDO VIÑES

THE VOLUMINOUS RECORDS of the Paris Conservatoire are now permanently
housed in France's National Archives, and amid the countless listings of
professors, singers, instrumentalists, and composers, one will occasionally
encounter the name of Joseph Maurice Ravel. It is thus possible to trace his
activities as a student and learn, for example, in which classes he was
enrolled, the results of his examinations, and the reports of his professors.
His career at the Conservatoire officially began on November 4, 1889, as six

13

faculty members, headed by the director Ambroise Thomas, auditioned forty-six pianists. Of the forty-six young aspirants, only nineteen were accepted as students, and of these, seven were admitted to the preparatory division and twelve went directly into the advanced piano classes. The fourteen-year-old Ravel performed an excerpt from a Chopin concerto and was placed in the preparatory piano division by unanimous verdict. Thus, his technique and interpretation, although not outstanding, appear to have indicated promise, and he was enrolled in the class of Eugène Anthiôme. In January and June, 1890, the young pianist took his biannual examinations, in which he performed a Chopin Polonaise and the finale of a concerto by Mendelssohn. Professor Anthiôme observed that his pupil was "rather gifted" and would progress well with serious effort. In the final competition of the academic year, held on July 10, 1890, Maurice was awarded a second prize, and thus his initial year at the Conservatoire was rather successful. The following year witnessed a similar pattern of examinations and a final competition. For his examinations, Ravel performed Schumann's Sonata in G minor [1] and a sonata by Hummel and was awarded first prize in the July, 1891, competition. As a result, in the fall of 1891 he advanced to the piano class of Charles de Bériot (see Plate 2), and at the same time he entered the harmony course of Emile Pessard. He was to remain in these courses for almost four years, from November, 1891, until July, 1895. At first, Professor Pessard found his student to be "a rather good harmonist," who had some "natural ability." Soon after, however, it appears that Maurice arrived late to class, and although "very gifted," he was also "somewhat heedless" with regard to his work. Reading between the lines of Professor Pessard's reports, one gets the impression that Ravel quickly assimilated everything the good professor had to teach and was captivated by harmonies which were far in advance of those taught in class. Nevertheless, on the basis of his examinations, he was allowed to compete for the harmony prize in 1893, 1894, and 1895. [2] Failing to win a prize in three consecutive years of competition, as required by the bylaws of the Conservatoire, Ravel was dismissed

---

[1] On Feb. 15, 1892, he participated in an all-Schumann program at the Salle Erard, performing the Andante and Variations for Two Pianos with Henry Ghys. The program included the Piano Quartet in E♭, and the Sonata in F♯ Minor, which was performed by Ghys.

[2] The assignments are notated utilizing four clefs (soprano, alto, tenor, and bass), and consist of harmonizing a given bass and a given melody. The harmonies suggest early- to mid-nineteenth-century practice, with much chromaticism and some enharmonic passages. (Autographs in the National Archives, AJ^{37}204,^{68}.)

from his harmony course in July, 1895. If his rapport with Professors An-thiôme and Pessard was cordial but reserved, it was quite otherwise with Professor Charles de Bériot, who elicited a warm response from his pupil. For his biannual keyboard examinations, Maurice performed the following works: Mendelssohn's Capriccio in B minor, concerti by Grieg and Saint-Saëns, Chopin's Ballade in F minor, Schumann's *Fantaisie,* a scherzo by Weber, an étude by Chopin, and the *Allegro symphonique* by Mathias, a professor at the Conservatoire. The following comments are taken from Professor Bériot's reports.

Work	Ravel's age	Critique
Mendelssohn: Capriccio in B minor	16	Very good musical organization. He also seems to me to be a good worker, which only the future will indicate.
Chopin: Ballade in F minor	18	A good pupil, plays with feeling and warmth, but not always with full control.
Schumann: *Fantaisie,* Op. 17	18	A great deal of temperament, but a tendency to pursue big effects. Needs to be held in check.
Weber: Scherzo	19	Talent, warmth, overly enamored of violence. Intermittent work.
Chopin: Etude	19	Spirited performance, communicative, on condition it does lapse into exaggeration. Works *without excess.*
Mathias: *Allegro symphonique*	20	Very good progress. Spirited temperament.

Thus, it appears that Ravel performed nineteenth-century music in a spirited, highly emotional manner. He was capable of performing well when he practiced, but when he did not, which was often the case, his playing appears to have exasperated Professor Bériot. As a result of repeated failures to win the piano prize Maurice was dismissed from his class in July, 1895. Deeply upset by his failures in harmony and as a pianist, Ravel abruptly quit the Conservatoire. Although eligible to study solfeggio or participate in the chamber music classes, for whatever reason he chose not to do so. It was possibly at this juncture that piano lessons were continued privately with Santiago Riéra. In an unpublished diary, the Spanish pianist noted that he had taught several good students, among them Maurice Ravel and Lemaire.[3] Although the diary is undated, it is known that the lessons extended over a period of two years, and they undoubtedly included a wide variety of Spanish music.

If Ravel's career as a student may be traced through the records of the Conservatoire, his private activities are perhaps best described in the extraordinary journal of Ricardo Viñes (1876–1943). The boys had met in 1888, and Ricardo was at first struck by his friend's long, shoulder-length hair. Both youngsters were blessed with an insatiable curiosity, and while their mothers conversed in Spanish, they played through an imposing variety of music at the keyboard, ranging from Mozart, Mendelssohn, and Franck, through Rimsky-Korsakov, Balakirev, Borodin, Glazunov, Chabrier, and Satie. The boys had passed the Conservatoire's entrance examination on the same day, and Ricardo was Professor Bériot's star pupil. After classes, the boys would take long walks, or play games of all sorts, copy out poetry, make drawings, attend concerts, or visit art galleries. They were particularly attracted to the music of Wagner and the Russian school, and the writings of Baudelaire, Mallarmé, Poe, Villiers de l'Isle-Adam, Huysmans, and Verlaine. On August 15, 1892, the young pianists spent virtually the entire day at the keyboard, "experimenting with new chords." The results of these and other discoveries were later revealed in the "Habanera" for two pianos, in which Ravel boldly affirmed his predilection for subtle and sophisticated harmonies. In February, 1893, the two young men were ushered into the home of Emmanuel Chabrier and performed the *Trois Valses romantiques* for their author. The meeting made a lasting impression on Ravel, who later described Chabrier as "the most profoundly personal, the most French of our composers." [4] About the same time, Joseph Ravel introduced his son to Erik Satie, who was leading a Bohemian life in Montmartre and playing the piano at the Café de la Nouvelle Athènes. Satie's colorful personality and unorthodox music made a strong impression on Ravel, who later described his colleague's influence as follows:

Another significant influence, somewhat unique, and deriving at least partially from Chabrier, is that of Erik Satie, which has had appreciable effect upon De-

---

[3] Diary in the private collection of Mme J.-M. Riéra. On the basis of two unpublished letters from Ravel to his former teacher, it is clear that a cordial relationship existed between them.

[4] Ravel, "Fervaal—Poème et musique de Vincent d'Indy," *Comœdia Illustré* (Jan. 20, 1913), p. 362.

bussy, myself and indeed most of the modern French composers. Satie was possessed of an extremely keen intelligence. His was the inventor's mind par excellence. He was a great experimenter. His experiments may never have reached the degree of development or realization attained by Liszt; but, alike in multiplicity and importance, these experiments have been of inestimable value. Simply and ingeniously Satie pointed the way, but as soon as another musician took to the trail he had indicated, Satie would immediately change his own orientation and without hesitation open up still another path to new fields of experimentation. He thus became the inspiration of countless progressive tendencies; and while he himself may, perhaps, never have wrought out of his own discoveries a single complete work of art, nevertheless we have today many such works which might not have come into existence if Satie had never lived.[5]

While studying with Professors Bériot and Pessard, Ravel wrote his earliest compositions. He acknowledged the influence of Chabrier on the *Sérénade grotesque* (c. 1893, piano) and that of Satie on the *Ballade de la Reine morte d'aimer* (c. 1893, voice and piano, poem by Roland de Marès).[6] Following his break with the Conservatoire, a steady stream of compositions came from Ravel's pen, many of which were to remain virtually unknown during his lifetime. In August, 1895, he completed *Un Grand Sommeil noir* (voice and piano, poem by Verlaine), but subsequently refused to allow its publication. As a result, the song first appeared posthumously. The composer's first work of major importance, the "Habanera" for two pianos, was completed in November, 1895. Although unpublished in its original form, the piece was later transcribed for orchestra and is now well known as the third movement of the *Rapsodie espagnole*. The "Habanera" proved to be the first of many essays in a Spanish idiom, and its harmonic subtlety bears a distinctly personal imprint. Completed in the same month as the "Habanera," the *Menuet antique* turned out to be Ravel's first published work. Strange as it may seem today, these early compositions were regarded as bold, avant-garde works, as may be observed in Alfred Cortot's perceptive portrait of the twenty-year-old musician:

[5] Ravel, "Contemporary Music," *Rice Institute Pamphlet,* 15 (April, 1928), 131–45. The original French version of this remarkable speech, the only formal lecture on music that Ravel ever gave, has not yet been found. The speech was originally printed in English and has been reprinted with an introduction by Bohdan Pilarski, "Une Conférence de Maurice Ravel à Houston," *Revue de Musicologie,* 50 (Dec., 1964), 208–21. This article will be referred to as "Contemporary Music," and the pagination of the *Rice Institute Pamphlet* will be used.

[6] See below, pp. 139–40. An incomplete setting of Verlaine's *Le Ciel est, par-dessus le toit* (c. 1892) has been printed in my article, "Some Unpublished Music and Letters by Maurice Ravel," *The Music Forum,* 3 (1973), 291–334.

Ravel's first essays in composition for the piano date from his student days. His fellow students, of whom I was one, soon discovered the signs of an uncommonly strongly marked musical talent in this slightly bantering, intellectual, and somewhat distant young man, who read Mallarmé and visited Erik Satie. And if we allowed ourselves some reservations with regard to his abilities as a virtuoso, we were always delighted, between two lessons, to play to one another a few measures of highly audacious music, about which we always agreed on one point at least—they must have been taken from one of Ravel's latest compositions.[7]

Ravel was indeed a "somewhat distant young man," for outside of a few close schoolmates such as Ricardo Viñes and Marcel Chadeigne, he generally maintained an air of cool detachment. A certain bantering humor and a deliberate attempt at mystification helped him to keep others at a distance, and this aspect of his personality appears to indicate the influence of Satie. Rather than to Satie's Bohemianism, however, the young composer was attracted to Baudelaire's description of the dandy, who was supposed to exhibit simplicity and elegance in grooming and to carry out a dignified quest for beauty. Thus, Ravel gave careful attention to his grooming and wardrobe, and discussed the colors of his ties and shirts with the utmost seriousness. Behind this mask, he was attracted to things which were complex and even contradictory, and was oriented toward all that was "poetry, fantasy, precious and rare, paradoxical and refined." [8] This description, by Ricardo Viñes, offers an important clue to the elegance, refinement, and preciosity underlying many of Ravel's early compositions. Another important observation is found in Viñes's journal entry dated November 1, 1896: "He is, moreover, very complicated, there being in him a mixture of Middle Ages Catholicism and satanic impiety, but also a love of Art and Beauty which guide him and which make him react candidly." The "mixture of Middle Ages Catholicism and satanic impiety" is not a reference to religion, but rather to Ravel's strong acceptance of artistic tradition coupled with a thirst for individual exploration and innovation. Above all, he was sensitive, indeed hypersensitive, to artistic beauty, and this ideal was to remain his continual guide. Thus, by his early twenties, Ravel's personality was rather firmly set in its own paradoxical way. Apparently distant and reserved, he was in fact fun-loving and sensitive, with a mischievous sense

[7] Cortot, *La Musique française de piano,* 2 (Paris, 1932), 23.

[8] Viñes, "Des Souvenirs d'enfance et d'adolescence," *La Revue Musicale* (Dec., 1938), p. 165.

of humor all his own. His intellectual abilities focused upon the ¿ knowledge of French literature was unusually sophisticated for one so young. As a composer, he was confident in his abilities, hardworking, and extremely self-critical. It was probably during his two-and-one-half-year absence from the Conservatoire that Ravel made the crucial decision to devote himself to composition. By now, any hopes he might have entertained for a career as a concert pianist were thoroughly dashed, not only by Ricardo Viñes, but by a number of highly gifted pianists at the Conservatoire. In December, 1896, two songs were completed, *Sainte* (poem by Mallarmé) and "D'Anne jouant de l'espinette" (poem by Marot). Indicating the spiritual influence of Satie, *Sainte* remained in its composer's portfolio until 1907, when it was published by Durand. Like the *Menuet antique,* the setting of "D'Anne jouant de l'espinette" conjures up a past epoch, in this case the Renaissance.

In 1897 two compositions were completed which until now have remained unknown: a Sonata for violin and piano in one movement, and a piece for two pianos, "Entre cloches." Although nothing is known about the origin of the sonata, the music appears to indicate the dual influence of Fauré and César Franck. The work was probably performed at the Conservatoire by Georges Enesco and the composer, and for whatever reason it was never heard of again. "Entre cloches" was appended to the "Habanera," and both pieces were now jointly entitled *Sites auriculaires.*[9] In the fall of 1897 Ravel was offered a music professorship in Tunisia, but he turned it down in order to resume his studies at the Conservatoire. On January 28, 1898, he entered the composition class of Gabriel Fauré, while at the same time he was studying counterpoint and orchestration privately with André Gédalge. "I am pleased to acknowledge that I owe to André Gédalge the most valuable elements of my technique. As for Fauré, his advice as an artist gave me encouragement of no less value." [10] Although the compositions of André Gédalge have fallen into neglect, he was nonetheless a distinguished pedagogue who influenced many composers, among them, Arthur Honegger, Jacques Ibert, Darius Milhaud, and Florent Schmitt. In a brief homage written in 1926, Ravel commented: "You may not realize every-

[9] See below, pp. 142–43, and pp. 144–45.

[10] Roland-Manuel, "Une Esquisse autobiographique de Maurice Ravel," *La Revue Musicale* (Dec., 1938), p. 20. This important article will be referred to as the "Autobiographical Sketch."

thing that Gédalge meant to me: he taught me to realize the possibilities and structural attempts which may be seen in my earliest works. His teaching was of unusual clarity: with him, one understood immediately that *technique* is not simply a scholastic abstraction.'' [11]

Gédalge stressed the supremacy of the melodic line and based his teaching on the works of Bach and Mozart, all of which would influence Ravel profoundly. The cordial, liberal atmosphere of Fauré's class has been compared to that of Mallarmé's salon, and the composer of *La Bonne Chanson* discreetly guided the careers of Georges Enesco, Charles Koechlin, Raoul Laparra, and Roger-Ducasse, among many others. Fauré's modesty and sensitivity won him the admiration of all his students, and he followed Ravel's career with keen interest. Ravel reciprocated this affection, and dedicated *Jeux d'eau* and the String Quartet "to my dear teacher Gabriel Fauré."

Ravel's first year in Fauré's class was marked by extraordinary accomplishment. He completed two important songs, *Chanson du rouet* (poem by Leconte de Lisle), and *Si morne!* (poem by Emile Verhaeren), as well as his first work for orchestra, the overture to *Shéhérazade*. [12] In addition, with Fauré's encouragement and assistance, Ravel made his formal debut as a composer. On March 5, 1898, Marthe Dron and Ricardo Viñes performed *Sites auriculaires* at a concert of the Société Nationale de Musique, [13] in a program which included Vincent d'Indy's Second String Quartet and Roger-Ducasse's Three Etudes for Piano Four Hands (see Plate 3). The pianists performed from manuscript, a common practice of the day. It appears that their rendition of the "Habanera" was successful, but the rapid passages of "Entre cloches" proved to be a virtual disaster, with many chords, which should have been performed in alternation, played simultaneously. The resulting cacophony turned out to be the first of many stormy premières in

[11] *La Revue Musicale* (March 1, 1926), p. 255. Gédalge first joined the Conservatoire faculty in 1905, and his *Traité de la fugue* was used as the standard text for the study of counterpoint.

[12] It is probable that the songs were performed at the salon of Mme René de Saint-Marceaux. See below, pp. 145–47; for the overture to *Shéhérazade,* see pp. 147–49.

[13] Under the leadership of Romain Bussine and Camille Saint-Saëns, the Société Nationale was founded shortly after the Franco-Prussian War. Faithful to its motto, *Ars Gallica* (French Art), the society introduced and gave frequent performances of works by Saint-Saëns, Franck, Chausson, Duparc, Chabrier, Fauré, d'Indy, Debussy, Ravel, and a host of other French composers. Now over one hundred years old, the Société Nationale continues to participate in French musical life.

Ravel's career. Although critical opinion of the music was divided, the title appears to have elicited universal condemnation and derision. The critic of *Le Temps*, Pierre Lalo,[14] mockingly called it "simple," while Pierre de Bréville, writing in the *Mercure de France*, appeared nonplussed and annoyed. After praising the "Habanera," he asked, "But why did Mr. Ravel entitle these short pieces *Sites auriculaires?*" The title is indeed bizarre, and it probably derives from the influence of Satie. It suggests an interest in synesthesia, and may be explained as follows: Ravel originally envisioned three places (sites), which were to be visited, or comprehended, as it were, by means of the ear (auricular). The first piece, "Habanera," suggests a Hispanic landscape, and the second piece "Entre cloches," evokes an unspecified site, engulfed in bells. The spiritual influence of Edgar Allan Poe is apparent in this work, and the composer's fascination with bells, clocks, and chimes extended throughout his career. (A third piece was projected, "Nuit en gondoles," suggesting a setting in Venice. Perhaps a barcarolle rhythm would have been employed, but this must remain conjectural, for as far as can be ascertained, the piece was not even partially sketched.) In April, 1898, Ricardo Viñes performed the *Menuet antique* as part of a series of recitals devoted to contemporary music (see Plate 4). The twenty-two-year-old pianist was well on his way to a brilliant career, in which he single-handedly introduced virtually all of the keyboard works of Debussy and Ravel, as well as a remarkable variety of contemporary music.

In the late 1890s, Fauré began to take his composition students to the home of Madame René de Saint-Marceaux, who frequently performed their vocal works. Amidst a congenial atmosphere of musicians, writers, and artists who caricatured the musicians as they performed, Fauré frequently presided at the keyboard, and among the guests one might encounter Pierre de Bréville, Debussy, Vincent d'Indy, or André Messager. Ravel attended many of these soirées and participated in the informal performances of contemporary music. It was here that he met Colette for the first time, and she later recalled his distant, detached air. Madame de Saint-Marceaux confirmed this view, and in an unpublished diary, she recalled Ravel's reaction to her performance of the Marot epigrams. "Is he pleased to hear his music? One can't tell. What a strange chap. Talented, with so much mischievous-

---

[14] The son of Edouard Lalo, Pierre Lalo (1866–1943) was the chief music critic of *Le Temps* from 1898 until shortly before his death. A collection of his articles is found in *De Rameau à Ravel* (Paris, 1947).

ness." This "mischievous" quality of Ravel, his ironic, cool humor, is found in an unpublished letter written to Madame de Saint-Marceaux during the summer of 1898, when he was engaged as a pianist in the casino at Granville. Although admittedly one of the most curious letters he ever wrote, it does afford excellent insight into the personality of the twenty-three-year-old composer (see Plate 5).

Saturday the 20th [August, 1898]

Madame

The little symbolist, very happy that you deign to occupy yourself a bit with his music, deeply regrets to have perpetrated no new vocal work in recent days. Some may believe that remorse overwhelms him. Not he, unfortunately, for he is incorrigible and quite ready to do nothing about it. While waiting, he is doing a bit of fugue and a lot of bicycling. He will take the liberty of addressing to you his latest composition, which dates from at least two months ago, and which by chance is singable.

As for the bizarre contexture of certain phrases, I strongly suspect that the musical Alcibiades wished them to be so.

Pardon him Madame, and kindly accept his most respectful homage.

Maurice Ravel

Hôtel du Nord   Granville [15]

Ravel's other activities at Madame de Saint-Marceaux's soirées included improvising at the keyboard, either as the poet André Beaunier read verses translated from the Greek or as the young American Isadora Duncan performed interpretive dances.[16] He also attended the elegant salon of Princess Edmond de Polignac, who commissioned the *Pavane pour une Infante défunte.* The striking popularity of the *Pavane* surprised its composer, and he later criticized it in the course of a concert review, calling attention to the "excessive influence of Chabrier" and its "rather poor form." In 1899, in addition to the *Pavane,* for piano, a second poem by Marot was

[15] Autograph in the private collection of B. de Saint-Marceaux. The vocal work in question is *Chanson du rouet,* the manuscript of which bears the date June 2, 1898. If the "musical Alcibiades" bears any reference to the Athenian statesman, Ravel may have compared himself, as it were, to a musical lawgiver, in order to justify certain "bizarre" liberties.

[16] An unknown work by Ravel entitled *La Parade* appears to have been written for interpretive dancing in the home. Based on a scenario by Antonine Meunier of the Opéra, the work consists of several dances for the piano (two marches, two waltzes, and a mazurka). Probably written in the late 1890s, the music is unusually diatonic and is of purely academic interest. (MS. 16939, Music Division of the Bibliothèque Nationale.)

set, "D'Anne qui me jecta de la neige." This song was appended to the setting of "D'Anne jouant de l'espinette," and the songs were jointly entitled *Epigrammes de Clément Marot.*

During the winter of 1898–99, at a Saturday morning dress rehearsal of the Concerts du Conservatoire, Ravel was introduced to Jane Bathori,[17] who was to become one of his most faithful interpreters. Like Ricardo Viñes, Madame Bathori was able to master the most complex contemporary scores almost instantaneously. Not only did she première *Noël des jouets,* the *Histoires naturelles, Trois Poèmes de Stéphane Mallarmé,* the *Chansons madécasses,* and *Rêves,* but in her brilliant career which spanned some four decades, she interpreted the vocal works of virtually every important French composer from the late 1890s until the outbreak of World War II. The critic Georges Jean-Aubry succinctly summarized Madame Bathori's vital contribution by calling her "modern French song incarnate."

On Saturday evening, May 27, 1899, the venerable Société Nationale presented its 278th concert. The program included first performances of works by Ravel, Charles Koechlin, Sylvio Lazzari, J. Guy Ropartz, Isaac Albéniz, and Ernest Chausson, as well as compositions by Pierre de Bréville, César Franck, and Fauré. The first work on the program was an orchestral overture entitled *Shéhérazade.* One can imagine Ravel's nervousness as he conducted his first orchestral work in front of his colleagues and teachers, as well as the public and critics. Following the performance, the reaction of the audience was mixed: some whistled loudly (to express disapproval), while others applauded with gusto. In a letter to Florent Schmitt, written some two weeks after the performance, Ravel summed up his impressions of the evening:

> Koechlin's piece was very successful, as we expected; its effect is truly charming, and it was the part of the concert which seemed to me to be the most felicitous. That's no doubt why G. V. devoted only three lines to him. As this . . . (choose the epithet) stated very accurately, *Shéhérazade* was strongly booed. They applauded also, and in all honesty I must admit that the applauders were more numerous than the protestors, because I was called back twice. Moreover, d'Indy, whose behaviour toward me was first-rate, was delighted that people could still become impassioned about anything. As far as I could judge from the podium, I

[17] The stage name of Jeanne-Marie Berthier (1877–1970). Mme Bathori has written two books, *Conseils sur le chant* (1929), and *Sur l'interprétation des mélodies de Claude Debussy* (1953).

was satisfied with the orchestration. It was generally found to be picturesque: the *Ménestrel* even called it "curious." [18]

Actually, the reviewer of the *Ménestrel* was somewhat more critical, observing that the "curious" orchestration did not conceal the overture's imperfections.

The critic Henri Gauthier-Villars (referred to as G. V. by Ravel), who is now chiefly remembered as Colette's first husband, wrote the following stinging critique:

A jolting debut: a clumsy plagiarism of the Russian school (of Rimsky faked by a Debussyian who is anxious to equal Erik Satie) disaffects the audience, which, irritated besides by the aggressive bravos of a bunch of young claques, protests and boos. Why this cruelty? I regret it with regard to young Ravel, a mediocrely gifted debutant, it is true, but who will perhaps become something if not someone in about ten years, if he works hard.[19]

The most extensive critique of the overture to *Shéhérazade* appeared in *Le Temps* on June 13, 1899. Pierre Lalo's carping review was to be the first of many attacks on Ravel's music, and the critic and composer were to be at swords' points for some three decades.

Finally, two scores of special importance: *Shéhérazade,* a fairy-tale overture, by M. Maurice Ravel, and Psalm 136, for chorus and orchestra, by M. Guy Ropartz. M. Maurice Ravel is a young student at the Conservatoire, and his colleagues and professors speak very highly of him. One of his pieces was heard recently, which bears this simple title: *Sites auriculaires;* the music was not at all unworthy of the title. *Shéhérazade* is explained in a program note as follows: 'This piece is intended to serve as an introduction to a fairy-tale opera inspired by the Thousand and One Nights. Composed according to the classical structure of the overture, it is preceded by an introduction in which the theme of *Shéhérazade,* played by an oboe, is repeated by the horns and trumpets. The overture, properly speaking, then begins: 1st part—Initial theme in B minor; development. Episodic theme (muted trumpets), leading to the second theme (in F# major), inspired by a Persian melody. Conclusion of the 1st part. 2nd part—Development of the four themes. Pedal point based on the expanded initial theme. 3rd part—Return of the first and second themes, heard simultaneously. Return of the introduction, which serves as the coda.' Doesn't this prose immediately suggest the notion that this work is clearly constructed, composed with vigor and directed with certitude? You would be wrong to believe it too blindly; and if you're looking in the music for every-

[18] Chalupt and Gerar, *Ravel au miroir de ses lettres,* p. 19. The letter is dated "Friday the 9th," and was written on June 9, 1899.

[19] Gauthier-Villars, *Garçon l'audition!* (Paris, 1901), p. 125.

thing that the program note indicates, you will have great difficulty in perceiving it. The 'developments' above all are so inaudible, that one would be tempted to think that M. Ravel were speaking of them ironically. In reality, *Shéhérazade* is composed of a series of very brief fragments, without natural connections between them, and attached to each other by extremely weak bonds. You have ten measures, or fifteen, or thirty, which seem to present an idea; then brusquely, something else happens, and then something else again. You don't know where you're coming from, or where you're going. If this is what M. Ravel believes to be an overture 'composed according to the classical plan,' one must admit that M. Ravel has a great deal of imagination. With regard to structure, or the lack thereof, his style recalls that of M. Grieg, even more, M. Rimsky-Korsakov or M. Bala-kirev. One sees the same incoherence in the overall structure and in the tonal relations; but these qualities, already quite striking in the models, are carried to excess by the student, who lacks, moreover, the semipopular spontaneity of the Norwegian, as well as the glitter and color of the Russians. However, one should not think that *Shéhérazade* is a score without merit. The harmonic workmanship is extremely curious, excessively, no doubt: here M. Ravel is obviously undergoing the dangerous influence of a musician whom one should esteem but not imitate, M. Claude Debussy. But the orchestration is replete with ingenious novelties and piquant effects of timbre. From all of this an artist may emerge. One hopes that M. Ravel will not scorn unity, and will think more often of Beethoven.

The *Psalm* by M. Guy Ropartz does not resemble *Shéhérazade* at all. It is a very considerable work, truly classical by the clarity of its structure and the solidity of its architecture; rest assured that its 'developments' do not have to be mentioned in the program: they are self-evident.

Whether or not one accepts Lalo's critique, it does contain a number of important observations. With regard to Ravel, it appears that he was somewhat of a celebrity at the Conservatoire and a leader of his generation. The program note which Lalo cited is of particular interest, since it undoubtedly was written by Ravel, and it bespeaks the same clarity and simplicity found in all of the composer's subsequent comments on his art. In addition to finding the harmonies "curious," Lalo suggested that Ravel's music was influenced by the art of Claude Debussy, a charge which was to be vigorously supported and vociferously denied during the course of the first decade of the twentieth century. Thus, from the very beginning of his career, Ravel's name was linked with that of Debussy. In conclusion, as he thought the overture lacking in structural coherence, Lalo suggested that the young composer "think more often of Beethoven." This advice would be emphatically rejected. Many years after completing the overture, Ravel asserted that it was poorly constructed, with enough whole-tone scales to last him a lifetime.

In addition, he observed that it was rather strongly dominated by the influence of Russian music.[20] Ultimately, the overture to *Shéhérazade* shared the same fate as *Sites auriculaires:* after one performance it was never heard again during the composer's lifetime.

At the Conservatoire, students in the composition course studied fugue as part of their curriculum, and in July, 1899, Ravel entered the required fugue competition for the first time. Together with five other students, however, he did not submit his work. Although the motive behind this unusual withdrawal is obscure, it appears that a considerable amount of friction existed between Ravel and Théodore Dubois, who became director of the Conservatoire upon the death of Ambroise Thomas in 1896. In January, 1900, as a preparatory exercise for the Prix de Rome, a cantata was submitted, *Callirhoé,* which was not awarded a prize. In a revealing letter to the Romanian composer D. Kiriac, who had been a fellow student in Fauré's class, Ravel explained as follows:

> . . . I am preparing, indeed, for the Prix de Rome, and have seriously begun work. The fugue is beginning to come rather easily, but I am quite uneasy with regard to the cantata. For the January examinations I had patiently elaborated a scene from *Callirhoé,* the music of which was rather dull, prudently passionate, and with a degree of boldness which was accessible for these gentlemen of the Institute. As for the orchestration, Gédalge found it skillful and elegant. All of this ended up in a miserable failure. As Fauré tried to reassure me, Monsieur Dubois assured him that he was deceiving himself with regard to my musical nature. What is disturbing is that the criticisms were not addressed to my cantata, but indirectly to *Shéhérazade,* at whose performance, you may recall, the director was present. Will it be necessary to struggle for 5 years against this influence? I'm very sure that I will never have the courage to maintain the same attitude until the end.[21]

Thus, we see a sharp conflict, not unlike a generation gap, between the young, avant-garde composer, and the highly conservative director. As it turned out, Ravel competed for the Prix de Rome on five occasions, dutifully writing "dull" and "accessible" music, but he was never to receive the first prize.

On January 27, 1900, the *Epigrammes de Clément Marot* were performed at a Société Nationale recital by M. Hardy-Thé, with the composer at the piano. Programmed between d'Indy's *Tableaux de voyage* and Bach's

[20] Roland-Manuel, *A la gloire de Ravel,* p. 44.

[21] Letter dated March 21, 1900, printed in Brailoiu, *Patru muzicanţi francezi* (Bucharest, 1935), p. 32. The manuscript of *Callirhoé* has not been preserved.

Chromatic Fantasy and Fugue, which were performed by pianist Blanche Selva, the songs were on the whole well received. With his customary verbal virtuosity, Willy (Henri Gauthier-Villars) found them "agréables sans plus, ne Ravèlent pas un tempérament bien personnel. Attendons." [22]

In May, 1900, Ravel entered the Prix de Rome competition for the first time. His candidacy was short-lived, for after submitting a fugue and a choral piece, *Les Bayadères,* he was promptly eliminated in the preliminary round. [23] A more serious setback occurred in July, when he entered the fugue competition for the second time. His work was given a zero by Théodore Dubois, together with the following comment: "Impossible, owing to terrible inaccuracies in writing." [24] Having failed to win a prize in two consecutive fugue competitions, as required by the regulations of the Conservatoire, Ravel was expelled from his composition class. One can only imagine his dismay and disappointment, particularly in light of Fauré's enthusiastic support. Furthermore, he was making excellent progress under Fauré's tutelage, as the following class reports indicate.

Date of report	Ravel's age	Comments
June 16, 1898	23	A gifted and assiduous student. Not yet sufficiently advanced for the fugue [competition] (1st year).
January 13, 1899	23	Very intelligent, very gifted, but too recherché, overly refined. An assiduous student.
June 13, 1899	24	Finely gifted, but still not set in his aspirations, which are rather confused for the moment. He is, however, gaining in maturity.
January 18, 1900	24	Very artistic temperament, less exclu-

[22] "Pleasant, nothing more, not unRaveling a very personal temperament. Let's wait." Gauthier-Villars, *Garçon l'audition!,* p. 274.

[23] The "Autobiographical Sketch" does not mention this initial participation in the Prix de Rome. The official register containing Ravel's entry is found in the National Archives, and the autographs of all of his Prix de Rome essays are found in the Music Division of the Bibliothèque Nationale.

[24] National Archives, AJ[37], 204,[31]. Ravel's fugue does indeed contain several academic infractions, such as hidden octaves, parallel fifths and parallel octaves. Outside of one obvious blunder in harmony, it is on the whole a dry-as-dust textbook fugue. It may be pointed out in passing that each candidate's entry was numbered, and the signature following the entry remained covered until the final vote was taken by number.

		sively attracted than before by pursuit of the excessive. Notable maturity.
June 16, 1900	25	Very good student, hardworking and punctual. Musical nature very taken with innovation, with a disarming sincerity!

Here we must speculate and ask whether Fauré found *Sainte* "too recherché" and "overly refined." Were Ravel's "rather confused aspirations" revealed in the Sonata for Violin and Piano, or perhaps in the overture to *Shéhérazade?* Did the *Pavane pour une Infante défunte* or the *Epigrammes de Clément Marot* indicate "notable maturity"? At any event, Fauré's final class report offers a perspicacious description of his twenty-five-year-old student, whose artistic sincerity and propensity for innovation were to remain unaltered throughout his lifetime. Although expelled from his composition class in July, 1900, Ravel was allowed to participate in Fauré's class as an auditor. Listed in the Conservatoire's registry as a "former student," he remained an auditor until 1903, when he broke with the Conservatoire for the last time.

About 1900, the nucleus was formed of a group of enthusiastic devotees of the arts who were to call themselves the *Apaches*. The name was coined by Ricardo Viñes, and rather curiously it refers to underworld hooligans. To some extent the young men considered themselves "artistic outcasts"—constantly defending what they considered to be important, whether or not the public agreed. The *Apaches* were ardent supporters of *Pelléas et Mélisande* during its stormy infancy and faithfully attended innumerable recitals of contemporary music. With the distaff element strictly excluded, the group met far into the night, discussing painting, declaiming poetry, and performing new music. The coterie met fairly regularly until the outbreak of World War I, and it was an extremely important influence upon Ravel. Not only were his own intellectual horizons broadened, but it was at the *Apaches* meetings that he met many of his future collaborators and lifelong friends. Among the members of the group were the poets Tristan Klingsor and Léon-Paul Fargue, painters Paul Sordes and Edouard Benedictus, the Abbé Léonce Petit, the conductor Désiré-Emile Inghelbrecht, the decorator Georges Mouveau, pianists Marcel Chadeigne and Ricardo Viñes, and the composers André Caplet, Maurice Delage, Manuel de Falla, Paul Ladmirault, Florent Schmitt, and Déodat de Séverac. Other members of the group included the critics Michel D. Calvocoressi, Magnus Synnestvedt, and Emile Vuillermoz, the Spanish mathematician Joaquín Boceta, the aviator

Maurice Tabuteau, and Ravel's close friends Pierre Haour and Lucien Garban. In 1909, a young Russian musician briefly joined the group, Igor Stravinsky. The group usually met on Saturday evenings, either at the studio of Paul Sordes on rue Dulong, at the home of Tristan Klingsor on avenue du Parc Montsouris, or at the apartment of Maurice Delage on rue de Civry. The *Apaches* had their own secret theme song (the opening of Borodin's Second Symphony), their own nicknames (Ravel was called "Rara"), and even their own phantom member "Gomez de Riquet," a character invented by Ravel as a pretext for leaving a tedious rendezvous or a dull evening party. It would be difficult to recapture the great excitement and unbounded enthusiasm of the *Apaches* meetings. Léon-Paul Fargue wrote that "Ravel shared our predilections, our weaknesses, our manias for Chinese art, Mallarmé, Verlaine, Rimbaud and Corbière, Cézanne and Van Gogh, Rameau and Chopin, Whistler and Valéry, the Russians and Debussy." [25] Amid this warm atmosphere of mutual encouragement, Ravel first performed his *Jeux d'eau,* "Oiseaux tristes," and the Sonatine. Fargue's matinal arrivals at the meetings, generally about 1:00 a.m., signaled the closing of the piano lid, but the discussions would continue with renewed vigor. In addition to setting poems by Klingsor (*Shéhérazade*) and Fargue (*Rêves*), Ravel gave composition lessons to Delage, who remained one of his closest friends for some thirty-five years. Lucien Garban was to become the chief proofreader at Durand and Company, and Calvocoressi's fluent knowledge of Greek led to the creation of the *Cinq Mélodies populaires grecques.* In addition to writing important articles and books in English and French, he became the chief music critic of *Comœdia Illustré* and persuaded Ravel to join the staff of the magazine. As a result, we have a permanent record of some of the composer's relatively rare comments on his art.

In addition to these important expanding horizons of personal relationships, Ravel occasionally attended the Tuesday receptions of the *Mercure de France,* and through his friendship with Misia Godebska,[26] he became associated with the literary milieu of *La Revue Blanche.* In these

[25] Fargue, "Maurice Ravel," *Plaisir de France* (August, 1936), p. 15.

[26] This remarkable woman was highly esteemed by Mallarmé, and her portrait was painted by Renoir. She was married three times: her first husband was Thadée Natanson, cofounder of *La Revue Blanche;* her second husband was Alfred Edwards, the wealthy and influential publisher of *Le Matin;* finally, she married the Spanish painter José-Maria Sert. Her salons continually attracted the most talked-about personalities of the day. Ravel dedicated "Le Cygne" and *La Valse* to her, and was also particularly close to the family of her brother, Cipa Godebski.

circles, he would meet Henri de Régnier, Thadée and Alexandre Natanson, Paul Valéry, Léon Blum, Claude Terrasse and Franc-Nohain.

The musical scene in which the *Apaches* actively participated was one of striking diversity. While the Société Nationale presented a wide variety of contemporary French music, the Société des Concerts du Conservatoire, founded in 1828, generally performed works from Bach through Wagner. Owing to important advances in musicology, the vast treasures of Gregorian chant and Renaissance and Baroque music became accessible and were featured at the important concerts of the Schola Cantorum, directed by Vincent d'Indy. In the opera house and the concert hall Wagner reigned supreme, and virtually every aspect of French cultural life felt the striking impact of the Bayreuth master. In addition to the ever popular French operetta, the operas of Massenet, Meyerbeer, Mozart, Puccini, and the nineteenth-century Italian school were frequently heard, and in 1904 the 1000th performance of *Carmen* was given at the Opéra. The Concerts Colonne, Lamoureux, and Pasdeloup,[27] frequently programmed works by Beethoven and Wagner and generally emphasized the music of the Viennese Classical school and the Romantic era. Among the many outstanding younger recitalists one could hear Pablo Casals, Mischa Elman, Arthur Rubinstein, or Jacques Thibaud.

Ravel's activities at the turn of the century focused upon Fauré's class, attending concerts, *Apaches* meetings, as well as middle-class and upper-class salons. The richness of French musical life may be seen in the fact that two distinct schools of composition were vying with each other for musical leadership. The older school consisted of César Franck's followers headed by Vincent d'Indy, whereas the leader of the newer, progressive element was Claude Debussy. The musical polemics which raged back and forth were outdone only by the trial of Alfred Dreyfus, and in the course of an article written in 1913, Ravel pleaded for moderation, noting that "it no longer suffices to lament the aesthetics of the older masters, or to feign incomprehension, anger, or hilarity as regards the pursuits of the younger

[27] In 1873, the Concerts Colonne were founded by Jules-Edouard Colonne (1838–1910), who was succeeded by Gabriel Pierné. At the Concerts Colonne, Richard Strauss conducted his *Symphonia Domestica* in March, 1906; Debussy premièred *La Mer* in 1908; and Mahler led his Second Symphony in April, 1910. The Concerts Lamoureux were founded in 1881 by Charles Lamoureux (1834–99), who was succeeded by Camille Chevillard, and in 1861 Jules-Etienne Pasdeloup founded the orchestra bearing his name. Following World War I, Ravel's works were frequently performed at these concerts, which still play an active role in Parisian musical life.

composers: old and young are contemporaries.'' In addition to the heated battles of the critics, French audiences did not hesitate to jeer or applaud during performances of contemporary music, and a veritable combative spirit filled the concert halls.

During the first two decades of the twentieth century, Vincent d'Indy (1851–1931) was perhaps the most influential musician in France. Together with Charles Bordes and Alexandre Guilmant, he was one of the founders of the Schola Cantorum, and became director of the school in 1904. Among the many distinguished musicians who studied at the Schola Cantorum were Isaac Albéniz, Paul Dukas, Albert Roussel, and Déodat de Séverac. Through his many pupils, d'Indy's doctrines were taught throughout France, and as far away as South America. His theories, which were based upon the music of Beethoven, Franck, and Wagner, combined solid classical development, cyclical structures, and an aesthetic based on Christian faith, love, and mysticism. Debussy, on the other hand, did not teach in any institution, his musical aesthetics were less doctrinaire and more intuitive than d'Indy's, and his compositions were considerably freer with regard to structure and harmony. Ravel was immediately classified as a follower of Debussy, and this may partially explain why his music was usually poorly received by the audiences of the Société Nationale, which was the stronghold of the conservative d'Indy faction. Although Ravel's personal rapport with d'Indy was cordial, he repudiated his aesthetics and did not care for his music. D'Indy, in turn, had little sympathy for Ravel's music, which he found to be overly refined, pithy, and lacking in genuine emotion and structural coherence.

About 1925, Ravel was planning to write two short books, one dealing with orchestration and the other explaining the nature of his relationship with Debussy. Georges Auric had been asked to assist with the writing, and an editor was waiting for the manuscripts. Unfortunately, both projects came to nought. Ravel probably would have mentioned the circumstances, still unknown, under which he was introduced to Debussy. The composers had many common acquaintances in the 1890s, among them Fauré, Satie, and Chausson, and their professional and social engagements overlapped to some extent. Ravel was Debussy's junior by some twelve-and-one-half years, and like many younger musicians, he looked up to Debussy as the leading French composer of his day. As a young man, Ravel was profoundly moved by the *Prélude à l'Après-midi d'un faune,* which appeared to open up innumerable unexplored horizons. It appears that Debussy was present at the

31

première of *Sites auriculaires* and was sufficiently interested in the new work to ask Ravel for the manuscript. In 1900, Debussy invited Raoul Bardac, Lucien Garban, and Ravel to his home, and played excerpts from *Pelléas et Mélisande* for them, and Ricardo Viñes relates that on November 30, 1901, he came to Debussy's home and found Ravel there. Viñes performed *Pour le piano* at this meeting, and Debussy expressed satisfaction with his interpretation. During the stormy infancy of *Pelléas et Mélisande,* which dramatically catapulted Debussy's career into the limelight, he must have been gratified to learn of Ravel's support, and thus, for a number of years, the two composers were on cordial but not intimate terms. They possessed widely divergent personalities, and perhaps at best their relationship would have remained one of distant cordiality. Yet, as it turned out, they were eventually made to be estranged by their respective supporters and by the many music critics who ceaselessly pitted the merits of one composer against the other. Pierre Lalo harped on the point that Ravel was merely a clever imitator of Debussy, while M. D. Calvocoressi and Jean Marnold defended Ravel's originality in their articles. In 1910, the critic Gaston Carraud observed that, although there remained a difference, it now appeared that Debussy's music was beginning to resemble Ravel's. In addition to this confusing state of affairs, questions of priority were continually raised: did Ravel's "Habanera" influence Debussy's "Soirée dans Grenade," or did *Jeux d'eau* influence "Jardins sous la pluie"? Ravel acknowledged the spiritual influence of Debussy on his String Quartet and the song cycle *Shéhérazade,* but took issue with Pierre Lalo concerning the priority of *Jeux d'eau.* Writing in *Le Temps,* Lalo asserted that following Chopin, Schumann, and Liszt, Debussy had "created a new manner of writing for the keyboard, a special style of particular virtuosity." Ravel's reply to this statement was published in *Le Temps* on April 9, 1907:

> I would like to call your impartial attention to the following point. You dwell upon a rather special type of writing for the piano, whose invention you ascribe to Debussy. *Jeux d'eau* appeared at the beginning of 1902, however, when there were only Debussy's three pieces *Pour le piano,* for which, I do not need to tell you, I have the warmest admiration, but which, from a purely pianistic point of view, did not contain anything new. I hope you will excuse this legitimate claim.

Ravel's claim is indeed legitimate, and it is now evident that each composer was influenced to some extent by the other, and each was keenly aware of the other's achievements. Although Ravel had reservations with regard to

Debussy's art, he candidly acknowledged his elder colleague's towering stature, and on one occasion he unequivocally called him "the most phenomenal genius in the history of French music. . . . His genius was obviously one of great individuality, creating its own laws, constantly in evolution, expressing itself freely, yet always faithful to French tradition. For Debussy, the musician and the man, I have had profound admiration, but by nature I am different from Debussy . . ." [28] On the other hand, Debussy was critical of the *Histoires naturelles* and appears to have been disturbed by his younger colleague's successes. The composers thus became estranged, entangled in an atmosphere of rivalry, partially of their own doing, but largely fueled by their overly zealous supporters.

In January, 1901, Ravel returned to Fauré's class as an auditor. He competed unsuccessfully for the composition prize, submitting a Prelude and Fugue which has not been preserved. In addition to working with Raoul Bardac on a transcription of Debussy's *Nocturnes* for two pianos, he was preparing once again for the Prix de Rome. [29] This time, it turned out that he was a serious contender for the Grand Prix, and we may now examine his candidacy in greater detail. The competition was conducted in two stages.

---

[28] "Contemporary Music," p. 139.

[29] On the third day of Pluviose in the year XI, corresponding to the 28th day of January, 1803, the French Republic formally established the Grand Prix de Rome in musical composition. The purpose of the prize was to further the artistic development of talented young composers by means of a state subsidy. Between 1803 and 1863, the Prix de Rome was administered by the Institut de France, and for a short period (1864–71) the Paris Conservatoire was responsible for conducting the competition. Finally, in 1871, by presidential decree, the Prix de Rome was to be under the aegis of France's Académie des Beaux-Arts, a division of the Institut de France. Among the distinguished recipients of the award were Berlioz (1830), Gounod (1839), Bizet (1857), Massenet (1863), Debussy (1884), Florent Schmitt (1900), and Jacques Ibert (1919). Unfortunately, a long list of prize winners could also be made, consisting of composers such as Rifaut (1821), Barbereau (1824), Kunc (1902), and Gallois (1905), none of whom are even listed in the most authoritative biographical dictionaries. The Grand Prix de Rome was awarded in painting, sculpture, architecture, engraving, and composition. All contestants were required to be French citizens, either by birth or naturalization, and had to be under thirty years of age by January first of the year of the competition. The winner of the Grand Prix was assured a modest stipend for four years. The first two years were to be spent at the Medici Villa in Rome, the third year in Germany or Austria, and the fourth year in Rome or Paris. During these four years, the composer was expected to complete chamber and orchestral works, choral music, and so on. Following this period, the composer could be supported for several more years by a private foundation. Thus, winning the Grand Prix could mean a minimum of four and a maximum of seven years of untroubled artistic growth, coupled with special opportunities for the performance of one's compositions.

The preliminary round, which was held to eliminate less qualified candidates, consisted of writing a four-part fugue based on a given subject, and setting a short text for mixed chorus and orchestra. These two assignments had to be completed within a week. Some twenty candidates generally entered the preliminary round, and usually five or six were allowed to go on and compete for the coveted first prize. The second and final round of the competition was extremely grueling. Held at the Compiègne Palace, the finalists were now isolated in their studios for an entire month and were required to set an extended cantata text for several solo voices and orchestra. The following schedule of events indicates the manner in which the competition was conducted.

The 1901 Prix de Rome

Date	Event	Place
May 4–10	Preliminary round (fugue and choral piece)	Compiègne Palace
May 11	Judgment of the preliminary round	The Conservatoire
May 16	Judgment of the cantata texts	The Conservatoire
May 17	Final competition—choice of the cantata text	The Conservatoire
May 18–June 17	Final round (setting of the cantata text)	Compiègne Palace
June 28	Preparatory judgment—performance of all the cantatas	The Conservatoire
June 29	Final judgment—announcement of awards	The French Institute
October 19	Performance of the prize-winning cantata	The French Institute

This schedule was repeated with clocklike regularity, and thus in May and June 1901, 1902, and 1903, we find Ravel occupied with his Prix de Rome essays. In 1901, after completing the fugue and choral piece, he set the required cantata text, *Myrrha,* by Fernand Beissier.[30] The story takes place in Nineveh in 795 B.C., and the dramatis personae are Sardanapalus, the king of Nineveh, Myrrha, a Greek slave, and Bélésis, high priest of the Baal

---

[30] The president of France's Society of Authors, Composers, and Publishers of Music for some forty years, Fernand Beissier (1856–1936) wrote about three hundred works in many genres, including novels, vaudeville, and operetta libretti.

cult. The king's overthrow is imminent, but Myrrha urges him to escape with her. Bélésis intercepts the fleeing couple, and convinces the king that he must face his inexorable defeat. Myrrha chooses to share Sardanapalus's fate, and the text concludes as they mount a funeral pyre together:

> Sur vos ailes d'or, ô célestes flammes,
> Venez nous ravir au divins séjours,
> Et dans votre vol emportez nos âmes
> Vers l'éternité des pures amours! [31]

Unfortunately, the text is but a pale imitation of its model, *Sardanapalus,* by Lord Byron.

On Friday evening, June 28, 1901, the finalist's cantatas were performed at the Conservatoire, and the jury evaluated the work of Albert Bertelin, André Caplet, Gabriel Dupont, Aymé Kunc, and Maurice Ravel. The following day the jury pondered its verdict, and among the nine judges were Théodore Dubois, Charles Lenepveu, Massenet, and Saint-Saëns. The first question to be decided was whether or not to award the Grand Prix. As five judges were in favor (with four opposed), it was decided to grant the prize. On the first ballot, Caplet received three votes, Dupont two, Ravel one, and there were three zeros (signifying an abstention). As no candidate received the required majority of five votes, a second ballot was held. Caplet received three votes, Dupont three, Ravel one, and there were two zeros. Accordingly, a third ballot was held, in which Caplet received four votes, Dupont two, Ravel one, and there were two zeros. The president, Saint-Saëns, then called for more discussion, and following that, a fourth ballot was held, which produced results identical with the third. Finally, on the seventh ballot, Caplet received four votes, together with five zeros, and it was decided not to award the Grand Prix. For the second prize, Caplet won on the first ballot, and Dupont was awarded the third prize on the first ballot. Ravel then received honorable mention (eight votes and one zero), and the jury observed that his setting of *Myrrha* was distinguished by its "melodic charm" and its "sincerity of dramatic sentiment." [32] The voting was not

[31] On your golden wings, o celestial flames,
   Come and delight our heavenly sojourn,
   And in your flight transport our souls
   Toward the eternity of pure love!

[32] Quoted from the unpublished minutes of the Académie des Beaux-Arts, housed in the archives of the Institut de France.

quite finished, however, as the full committee of the Académie des Beaux-Arts, consisting of twenty-one members, finally decided to award the Grand Prix. The net result of the ensuing discussion was that each prize winner advanced one degree: Caplet was awarded the Grand Prix, and Dupont received the second prize. Ravel's third prize turned out to be his sole award in five years of Prix de Rome competition.[33] In a letter to Lucien Garban, the composer summed up his views of the 1901 Prix de Rome:

Let's chat a bit about the competition: Caplet's prize surprised everyone. His cantata was certainly one of the most mediocre, as a composition, I mean, but its orchestration was quite remarkable. Almost everyone here would have given me the first prize. (Massenet even voted for me every time). A rather curious thing was disclosed to me: I possess a melodic tap at a place which you will not permit me to designate more clearly, and music flows from it effortlessly. This gracious metaphor comes from your dear teacher X. Leroux, who together with Vidal was very enthusiastic on my behalf. I was even assured—I shudder as I relate—that Lenepveu praised my cantata very much, but not to the point of preferring it to that of his own pupil. You will say to me, 'Why didn't you obtain the grand prix'? Who would have believed it? My orchestration played this nasty trick on me. Although my composition was among the first to be finished, it happened that my orchestration was begun late, and there remained very little time for it. It turned out to be done somewhat too hastily. I'll have to begin all over again, that's all.[34]

An important event was to occur some eight months after the 1901 competition, which would have a profound effect on Ravel's future as a contestant: *Jeux d'eau* was published by E. Demets, and the powerful voice of Saint-Saëns promptly judged it to be total cacophony. This opinion was undoubtedly shared by many of the highly conservative jury members, and Ravel must have realized that his chances of any future academic success were now virtually nil.[35]

During their meeting in November, 1901, one wonders if Ravel showed Debussy his most recent composition, *Jeux d'eau*. In this work, the twenty-

[33] Saint-Saëns was particularly impressed with Ravel's cantata, and in an unpublished letter to Charles Lecocq, dated July 4, 1901, he observed that "the third prize winner, whose name is Ravel, appears to me to be destined for an important career." The winner of the Grand Prix, André Caplet (1878–1925), was a gifted conductor and composer and a close associate of Debussy.

[34] Autograph letter dated July 26, 1901, in the private collection of Mme Lucien Garban. The letter is partially printed in Roland-Manuel, *A la gloire de Ravel,* p. 47.

[35] In Jan., 1902, Ravel again competed unsuccessfully for the composition prize, submitting a cantata, *Semiramis,* which has not been preserved. At this time, he was giving private lessons in harmony and composition for the modest fee of twenty francs a lesson.

six-year-old composer opened up fresh paths in writing for the keyboard, combining sweeping virtuosity with the refined tinting of impressionism, and a personal blend of structural clarity with subtle chords of the seventh and ninth. Ravel explained that his composition was "inspired by the sound of water, and the music of fountains, cascades, and streams," and he later returned to the "music" of water in the *Miroirs* and *Gaspard de la nuit*. When Ricardo Viñes premièred the *Pavane pour une Infante défunte* and *Jeux d'eau* at a Société Nationale recital in April, 1902, it was perhaps inevitable that musicians and critics would compare the two works. The prevailing opinion was that the *Pavane* was elegant and charming, but *Jeux d'eau* was thought to be cacophonic and overly complicated. It now appears that the *Pavane* is a minor work, as the composer himself acknowledged, while *Jeux d'eau* is firmly established as an important landmark in the literature of the piano.

On April 30, 1902, Ravel attended the première of *Pelléas et Mélisande* at the Opéra-Comique, and during the following two months his activities centered about the Prix de Rome. As in 1901, he was a finalist, and set the cantata text *Alcyone,* by Eugène and Edouard Adénis.[36] Based on Ovid's *Metamorphoses,* the plot describes the tragic love of Queen Alcyone and King Céyx. In an orchestral interlude which depicts the queen's dream, the king is drowned in a shipwreck: "Alcyone! Alcyone! Aimée! Aimée! Adieu!" Céyx's shade tells the queen that he has perished, and when some fishermen enter with the king's remains, Alcyone utters a horrible shriek and falls dead on her husband's body. Although the bathos of the text was reasonably well matched by Ravel's Wagnerian orchestration, the Grand Prix was awarded to Aymé Kunc,[37] and the remaining prizes went to Roger-Ducasse and Albert Bertelin. During the remainder of 1902, Ravel was occupied with a commission from Frederick Delius, and by December he had completed two movements of a string quartet. Delius had unsuccessfully entered an opera, *Margot la Rouge,* in a competition sponsored by the Italian publisher Sonzogno, and soon after, Ravel accepted a flat fee for arranging a piano-vocal score from the original orchestral version (see Plate 6). The

[36] Eugène Adénis-Colombeau (1854–1923) and his brother Edouard (1867–1952) frequently collaborated in writing plays (*Les Noces de Panurge,* 1910), as well as cantatas for the Prix de Rome.

[37] A student of Charles Lenepveu, Aymé Kunc competed for the Prix de Rome in 1898, 1899, 1900, and 1901, before he won the Grand Prix in 1902. He began his musical studies at the conservatory in Toulouse and later became the director of that institute.

project was handled with customary meticulousness, as is evident from this extract of an unpublished letter:

St.-Jean-de-Luz, Friday, October 3, [1902]

My dear Delius,

You will receive by the same mail the transcription of *Margot*. I am keeping the full score for a few more days in order to make the changes we agreed upon. . . . As regards the music, I have corrected obvious mistakes (omitted accidentals, etc.). I have transcribed literally certain doubtful passages, and will discuss these with you later, except for several measures (scene five—"Why Confide These Things in Me"), which seemed obscure, and which I have left blank. . . . Please write to me at the same address, 41 Gambetta Street, as soon as you have received the score. See you soon, my dear friend.[38]

In January, 1903, the first movement of the String Quartet was submitted for the composition prize. Although the essay elicited some favorable comment, one judge found it laborious, and Théodore Dubois observed that it "lacked simplicity." Owing to this academic failure, Ravel was expelled from the Conservatoire for the last time. In 1903, in addition to his fourth fruitless candidacy for the Prix de Rome, he completed the String Quartet and the song cycle *Shéhérazade.* The cantata text, *Alyssa,* by Marguerite Coiffier,[39] deals with the time-honored conflict between love and duty. The young Irish chief Braïzyl is ready to follow Alyssa, a fairy, into her domain, until Le Barde, a sword bearer, tells him that his people are engaged in a life and death struggle. After some hesitation, Braïzyl chooses the path of duty, and leaves Alyssa to fight for his people.

LE BARDE: Votre peuple crie: Au secours!
ALYSSA: Et moi, moi, déjà tu m'oublies? Que t'importe, insensé! La guerre et ses horreurs, le monde et ses folies, si peu de gloire et tant de sang versé!
BRAÏZYL: J'ai mon peuple à défendre!
ALYSSA: Tu pars! . . . et tu m'aimais!
BRAÏZYL: Je sauve mon pays! [40]

---

[38] Autograph in the collection of the Frederick Delius Trust, London.

[39] She appears to have been an amateur, who occasionally sent her verses to the juries of various competitions.

[40] LE BARDE: Your people cry out for help!
  ALYSSA: And I, have you forgotten me? Of what consequence is it to you, o madman! War and its horrors, the world and its folly, so little glory and so much blood spilled forth!
  BRAÏZYL: I have my people to defend!
  ALYSSA: You are leaving! . . . and you loved me!
  BRAÏZYL: I must save my country!

Viewing the cantata texts in retrospect, it is obvious that their jejune plots of love, passion, and glory were thoroughly removed from Ravel's literary sensibilities. He was thus caught in a dilemma: while he found the texts so pretentious as to be amusing, he was yet required to set them in a serious manner. The Grand Prix was given to Raoul Laparra,[41] with the other prizes awarded to Raymond Pech and Paul Pierné.

While working on *Shéhérazade,* Ravel completed the first movement of a sonatine for piano, and set "Manteau de fleurs," a poem by Paul Gravollet.[42] At the suggestion of Calvocoressi, the first movement of the Sonatine was submitted in a competition sponsored by the *Weekly Critical Review.* The competition was canceled, however, as the review rapidly approached financial collapse, and the remaining movements of the Sonatine were completed in 1905. The poetry of Paul Gravollet has remained obscure with good reason, and "Manteau de fleurs" proved to be a rare lapse in Ravel's fastidious selection of texts for musical adaptation. The poet's lack of inspiration appears to have been compensated by considerable acumen in practical matters. On one occasion, he sent his poems to the leading French composers of the day, and managed to convince twenty-two of them to set his work. The result was an undistinguished collection of songs entitled *Les Frissons,* published by Hamelle.[43]

Although Ravel's String Quartet is now a standard work in the chamber music repertory, while it was being written it gave rise to many conflicting opinions. As we have observed, the first movement was not considered worthy of the composition prize, and Fauré found the last movement too short. It has been claimed that Debussy wrote to Ravel, urging him not to change one note of the Quartet, but this letter has not yet come to light. Following the first performance, by the Heymann quartet on March 5, 1904, the critics were sharply divided. Pierre Lalo observed that "in its harmonies and successions of chords, in its sonority and form, in all the elements which it

---

[41] A student of Fauré, Raoul Laparra (1876–1943) was a gifted composer who is largely remembered for his operas, among them *La Habanera* (1908) and *L'Illustre Fregona* (1931). According to an entry in Ricardo Viñes's journal, Ravel believed that Roger-Ducasse should have been awarded the Grand Prix. It is of interest to observe that Ravel did not consider his own cantata worthy of the Grand Prix.

[42] The stage name of Paul Barthélémy Jeulin (1863–1936). In addition to performing secondary roles at the Comédie Française, he wrote several plays and collections of poetry.

[43] See *Les Frissons* (Paris: J. Hamelle, 1906). Among the collection of twenty-two songs are Caplet's *Dans la fontaine,* Debussy's *Dans le jardin,* d'Indy's *Mirage,* and Henri Busser's *Les Roses pleurent.*

contains and in all the sensations which it evokes, it offers an incredible resemblance with the music of M. Debussy." On the other hand, Jean Marnold, writing in the *Mercure de France,* praised the new work, and boldly asserted that "one should remember the name of Maurice Ravel. He is one of the masters of tomorrow." [44]

In discussing the *fin de siècle* in France, Tristan Klingsor observed that "the Orient was in the air, through Bakst, Rimsky-Korsakov, and Doctor Mardrus, who translated the *Thousand and One Nights."* The song cycle *Shéhérazade* was Ravel's second encounter with oriental fantasy, and the significant interrelationship between the overture to *Shéhérazade* and its homonymous song cycle will be discussed later. The earliest verses of Tristan Klingsor [45] appeared in *La Revue Blanche, La Plume,* and the *Mercure de France,* and in 1903 he completed a collection of one hundred poems entitled *Schéhérazade.* The title was taken from Rimsky-Korsakov's orchestral suite, and the collection centers about the Orient and its kaleidoscopic lure. Born just one year apart, Ravel and Klingsor had spent many evenings together discussing music and poetry with their fellow *Apaches* members, and at the composer's request, the poet declaimed "Asie," "La Flûte enchantée," and "L'Indifférent" for him. Thereupon, Ravel went into his customary isolation when composing, reappearing to request some minor changes in the text of "Asie," to which the poet agreed.[46] On May 17, 1904, the Société Nationale presented its final concert of the season. It proved to be a busy evening for Alfred Cortot, who participated as composer (*Intermèdes*), pianist (works by Franck and others), and conductor (*Shéhérazade*). The new song cycle, which was sung by soprano Jane Hatto of the Opéra, was favorably received,[47] and Vincent d'Indy judged it to be Ravel's best composition to date.

[44] *Mercure de France* (April, 1904), p. 251. Marnold was an ardent supporter of Ravel, and soon became a trusted friend.

[45] The pseudonym of Arthur Justin Léon Leclère (1874–1966), French poet, painter, art critic, and composer.

[46] Ravel was perturbed that Jane Hatto would be required to sing "En conservant comme Sindbad ma vieille pipe arabe de temps en temps entre mes lèvres," and he suggested that the pipe be replaced by an Arabic cup, as follows: "En elevant comme Sindbad ma vieille tasse arabe de temps en temps jusqu'à mes lèvres."

[47] At the première, "La Flûte enchantée" was sung first, followed by "L'Indifférent" and "Asie." Louis Laloy praised the "finesse" and "exquisite lightness of touch" found in the song cycle, and stressed the independence of Ravel's musical personality from that of Debussy. See *Revue Musicale,* 4 (June 1, 1904), 290.

The genesis of the *Cinq Mélodies populaires grecques* may be traced to a lecture which the French musicologist Pierre Aubry planned to give on the songs of oppressed peoples (Greeks and Armenians). He asked Calvocoressi to select some Greek songs for illustrative purposes, and after making his choice, Calvocoressi taught them phonetically to the singer Louise Thomasset, who agreed to perform them on short notice, but wished, however, to have piano accompaniments for the melodies. The critic thereupon turned to Ravel, who wrote accompaniments to five melodies within some thirty-six hours, thus marking his first venture into the realm of folklore. The melodies were selected from two sources: Hubert Pernot's *Chansons populaires de l'Île de Chio,*[48] and Pericles Matsa's *Chansons* (Constantinople, 1883). Of the five songs performed by Mlle Thomasset two ("Quel Galant m'est comparable," and "Chanson des cueilleuses de lentisques"), were later incorporated into the *Cinq Mélodies populaires grecques,* while the other songs remained unpublished, as Ravel found their accompaniments "too brief." [49] As a result, three other melodies were later set from the Pernot collection and were performed by Marguerite Babaïan [50] at a lecture-recital given by Calvocoressi.

In June, 1904, Ricardo Viñes introduced Ravel to Ida and Cipa Godebski, who were soon to become two of the composer's closest confidants. Their modest apartment on rue Saint-Florentin soon attracted the *Apaches* and many who were prominent in the arts: Jean Cocteau, Paul Valéry, André Gide, Valéry Larbaud, Satie, Roussel, Casella, Pierre Bonnard, and Georges d'Espagnat (see Plate 7). Ravel would soon be a frequent visitor to the Godebski's country home "La Grangette" ("The Little Barn"), at Valvins, a short distance from Fontainebleau, and here he would complete *Ma*

---

[48] Together with Paul Le Flem, Pernot spent the summers of 1898 and 1899 collecting folk melodies on the island of Chios, off the western coast of Asia Minor. See Hubert Pernot, *Rapport sur une mission scientifique en Turquie* (Paris: Imprimerie Nationale, 1903).

[49] These three songs, which have not been recovered, were set from the Matsa collection: "A vous, oiseaux des plaines," "Chanson de pâtre épirote," and "Mon Mouchoir, hélas, est perdu." See Calvocoressi, "Correspondances," *La Revue Musicale* (Jan., 1939), p. 17.

[50] As Ravel admired Mlle Babaïan's interpretations of the songs, he subsequently set a sixth Greek melody for her, *Tripatos*. Together with Jean Périer, Mlle Babaïan coauthored a book on the teaching of voice, entitled *Mes Exercises* (Paris: Senart, 1917), and in 1935, she wrote a second didactic work, *Airs de chasse à l'usage des chanteurs* (Paris: Leduc). She frequently sang rarely heard Armenian, Greek, and Russian songs as musical illustrations in lecture-recitals. Among the distinguished lecturers she appeared with were Pierre Aubry, Henry Expert, Louis Laloy, André Pirro, and Romain Rolland.

Mère l'Oye, which was dedicated to the Godebski children Mimie and Jean.[51]

On March 7, 1905, Ravel celebrated his thirtieth birthday. In his student days he had grown a mustache, to which were added side-whiskers and a dark, neatly trimmed beard. Coupled with his simple, but fashionable wardrobe, his taut frame and short height, he was already a well-known figure in Parisian musical life. Despite the strong reservations of Théodore Dubois and many professors at the Conservatoire, the strenuous criticisms of Pierre Lalo, and the largely negative opinions of Vincent d'Indy and his followers, Ravel had made his reputation as the leading composer of his generation and was generally considered the foremost successor to Debussy. At this point, he was encouraged by Debussy himself and was supported by Fauré, André Gédalge, and several important music critics. The fifth and final episode in Ravel's fruitless attempts to win the Prix de Rome produced one of the most spectacular scandals in the annals of the Conservatoire. Having failed to win the first prize in four consecutive attempts, he probably concluded that it would be futile to try again, and did not compete in 1904. Now at the age limit of thirty, for whatever reason, he decided to compete, and this time was eliminated in the preliminary round, the jury solemnly declaring that the composer of *Jeux d'eau,* the String Quartet, and *Shéhérazade* lacked the technical proficiency to be a finalist in the competition. His disqualification was not only hotly debated by music critics, but the ensuing *affaire Ravel* turned out to be front-page news in the French dailies.[52] In a letter to Paul Léon, director of the Académie des Beaux-Arts, Romain Rolland eloquently summed up the views of many impartial observers:

Friday, May 26, 1905

Dear Sir:

I read in the papers that there is no *affaire Ravel.* I believe it my duty to tell you (in a friendly way and just between ourselves) that this question exists, and can not be evaded. In this *affaire* I am personally entirely disinterested. I am not a friend of Ravel. I may even say that I have no personal sympathy with his subtle and refined art. But justice compels me to say that Ravel is not only a student of promise—he is already one of the most highly regarded of the young masters in our school, which does not have many. I do not doubt for an instant the good faith

[51] Jean Godebski possessed some two hundred postcards and letters from Ravel to his parents. They are now in the Pierpont Morgan Library.

[52] See *Le Matin,* May 21 and 22, 1905.

of the judges. I do not challenge it. But this is rather a condemnation for all time of these juries; I can not comprehend why one should persist in keeping a school in Rome if it is to close its doors to those rare artists who have some original-ity—to a man like Ravel, who has established himself at the concerts of the Société Nationale through works far more important than those required for an examina-tion. Such a musician did honor to the competition; and even if by some unhappy chance, which I should find it difficult to explain, his compositions were or seemed to have been inferior to those of the other contestants, he should neverthe-less have been rewarded outside of the competition. It is a case rather analogous to that of Berlioz. Ravel comes to the competition for the Prix de Rome not as a pupil, but as a composer who has already proved himself. I admire the composers who dared to judge him. Who shall judge them in their turn? Forgive me for mix-ing into an affair that does not concern me. It is everyone's duty to protest against a decision which, even though technically just, harms real justice and art, and since I have the pleasure of knowing you, I feel I should give you—I repeat, en-tirely between ourselves—the opinion of an impartial musician.

N.B. Isn't there any way for the State (without going against its decision) at least to prove its interest in Ravel?[53]

Other observers, however, ventured to impugn the jury's integrity, and another scandal erupted when it was disclosed that all of the six finalists were pupils of the same professor of composition—Charles Lenepveu. Ravel protested that Lenepveu, a professor of composition at the Conservatoire, was concomitantly allowed to be a member of the jury. In addition, a peti-tion was circulated which formally protested the jury's selection of the final-ists. In attempting to defend himself from a barrage of verbal attacks, Le-nepveu insisted that the competition had been properly and fairly conducted and claimed that it was perfectly legal for a professor of composition at the Conservatoire to be a member of the Prix de Rome jury. In addition, he stated that the finalists were selected unanimously by the other judges and his personal vote was merely an additional confirmation of the jury's deci-sion. For once, Pierre Lalo strongly defended Ravel's position. After calling Lenepveu a "poor musician," and "the author of several paltry works," the critic wrote about Ravel: "I have often spoken about him; and almost always with a mixture of criticism and praise, the criticism having a particu-lar severity. It is precisely because M. Ravel has unusual qualities that I grant him his shortcomings. I hope that he corrects them; nevertheless, were

[53] Marguerite Long, "Souvenir de Maurice Ravel," *La Revue Musicale* (Dec., 1938), pp. 173–74.

he to correct nothing at all, he would be a *musician,* a genuine musician, and one of the leaders of his generation.'' [54] In addition to the personal charges and countercharges, the entire curriculum of the Conservatoire was sharply attacked,[55] and among the concrete results of the scandals were the resignation of Théodore Dubois as director, and his replacement by Gabriel Fauré. Several faculty members submitted their resignations as well.

One must differentiate clearly between two decisions made by the jury. The first was to eliminate Ravel in the preliminary round, while the second was to award all the prizes to Lenepveu's pupils. Although both verdicts evoked vigorous opposition, the latter appears particularly objectionable, and despite Lenepveu's assertions to the contrary, an impartial observer will find it difficult to believe that the jury arrived at its decision in a scrupulous manner. Although Ravel's elimination has been explained by all commentators as a personal expression of the jury's hostility, an impartial study of his fugue and choral piece shows considerable justification for his disqualification. In addition to numerous minor errors in the choral piece, *L'Aurore,* one passage contains seven consecutive measures of parallel octaves between the soprano and bass parts—a blatant infraction of traditional four-part writing which any first-year student at the Conservatoire would have eschewed.[56] Moreover, in what appears to be a gesture of defiance, the fugue, like *Jeux d'eau,* ends on a chord of the major seventh (which was corrected by a member of the jury). When viewing these obvious academic blunders, the jury must have assumed that Ravel was either not taking his work seriously or was disdainful of them. Both assumptions appear to have been correct. Thus, the long, simmering feud between the headstrong revo-

[54] *Le Temps,* July 11, 1905. Lalo did not mention Lenepveu by name, but the reference to him was unequivocal.

[55] Calvocoressi wrote that the Conservatoire was ''little more than a stronghold of time-worn conventions and blind prejudices. The one object of its curriculum (apart from the instrumental classes, which were excellent), was to turn out composers of conventional operas and operettas'' (*Musicians Gallery,* p. 19). Pierre Lalo observed that the Conservatoire taught its students their craft, but did not teach them their art. They were taught rules and formulas, but possessed no musical culture whatsoever. See *Le Mercure Musical* (Oct. 1, 1905), p. 398. Louis Laloy suggested that it was time to abolish the absurd notion that the Conservatoire's primary purpose was to produce opera singers and composers of operettas. In a scathing attack, he noted the resignation of two well-known ''comedians'' and trusted that they would be replaced by ''musicians.'' See *Le Mercure Musical* (Oct. 15, 1905), p. 453.

[56] The passage is printed in *The Music Forum,* 3 (1973), 306–07.

Yacht
Aimée

Figure 1

Figure 2

lutionary and the highly conservative jury members finally came to an unexpected and dramatic denouement.

During this stormy juncture, Ravel accepted an invitation from Alfred and Misia Edwards to join them aboard their luxurious yacht *Aimée* for an extended vacation in Belgium, Holland, and Germany. Just before leaving Paris, he completed the *Introduction et Allegro,* which had been commissioned by the Maison Erard.[57] Once aboard the yacht *Aimée,* the Edwardses and their guests began to relax in a carefree atmosphere of comradery. During the voyage, Ravel observed the monogram of Misia Edwards (see Fig. 1) which he soon adapted for his personal stationery and his printed scores (see Fig. 2). Some high points of the itinerary included Liège, Amsterdam, and Frankfurt. Ravel was particularly impressed by the factories in the Belgian and German industrial zones,[58] the Dutch countryside with its famous windmills, the zoo and aquarium in Amsterdam, Goethe's birthplace in Frankfurt, and the paintings of Franz Hals, Rembrandt, and Velásquez. Following this well-deserved rest, the composer rejoined his family and friends in Paris, and in the summer of 1905, he wrote to Madame de Saint-Marceaux, summing up his mood with unusual candor.

Morgat, August 23, 1905

Dear Madame, ...

I see from your questions that the letter I addressed to you from Dordrecht shared the fate of many others. In it, I told you about the beginning of a magnifi-

[57] In a letter to Jean Marnold, the composer explained that "a week of continuous work and three sleepless nights" enabled him to finish the piece "for better or worse." The *Introduction et Allegro* is dedicated to M. A. Blondel, the director of the Erard Company, which supplied the Conservatoire with its harps and pianos.

[58] See his letter to Maurice Delage on p. 10.

cent voyage through Belgium, Holland, and the banks of the Rhine up to Frankfurt, through rivers, canals, and seas, in the yacht of my friends, the Edwardses. I saw unforgettable things in this marvelous situation. During all of this time, I didn't compose two measures, but I was storing up a host of impressions, and I expect this winter to be extraordinarily productive. I have never been so happy to be alive, and I firmly believe that joy is far more fertile than pain. It's an opinion as valid as any other. We'll see this winter if I was mistaken. While awaiting the pleasure of bringing you the fruit of these considerable labors, I would be very happy to hear from you.[59]

Ravel's letter reaffirms his marked ability to judge himself impartially, and his observation that ''joy is far more fertile than pain'' offers an important clue to his personal and artistic make-up. As it turned out, not only was the winter of 1905 rich in achievement, but the period preceding World War I proved to be the most intensely productive in his entire career.

[59] Autograph in the private collection of B. de Saint-Marceaux.

CHAPTER THREE

1905-1914
From the Sonatine to the Trio

Wednesday, May 22, 1907
Dinner at Marnold's home with Ravel. . . . I appreciated Ravel a great deal.
He is intelligent, open, and natural in everything he says. He judges himself and
others with a strong desire for impartiality and a clear-sightedness which is quite
rare in an artist.

ROMAIN ROLLAND, JOURNAL

Over the last weeks we have had an almost uninterrupted succession of con-
certs, gala performances, musical evenings, and dinners. Never in Paris has there
been such an eventful season.
LETTER, ROMAIN ROLLAND TO SOFIA B. GUERRIERI-GONZAGA, MAY 31, 1907

THE 1905 PRIX DE ROME scandal marked a definite turning point in Ravel's career. Gone forever were the academic fugues, dull cantatas, and sterile battles with conservative and reactionary juries. Looking back upon his career, Ravel might well have been amused at its paradoxical aspects. At the Conservatoire, he had received a first prize as a pianist, but never as a composer. Furthermore, some of his most avowed opponents on the Prix de Rome jury had in fact catapulted him to fame and had also caused the collapse of the conservative-reactionary element at the Conservatoire. In the fall of 1905, Gabriel Fauré assumed the directorship of the Conservatoire, and owing to a program of bold reforms, a renewed sense of dedication and enthusiasm filled the classrooms.[1] Ravel now entered into an extended period of intense creativity, completing the Sonatine and *Miroirs* (1905), the *Histoires naturelles* (1906), *L'Heure espagnole* and the *Rapsodie espagnole* (1907), *Gaspard de la nuit* (1908), *Ma Mère l'Oye* (1908–10), *Valses nobles et sentimentales* (1911), *Daphnis et Chloé* (1909–12), *Trois Poèmes de Stéphane Mallarmé* (1913), and the Trio (1914). In addition, he composed a handful of minor works, completed several acts of an unfinished opera, *La Cloche engloutie,* and carried out several transcriptions. During this period, his music began to extend far beyond the confines of the Société Nationale, as the Sonatine was heard in Lyon, the *Rapsodie espagnole* was premièred at the Concerts Colonne, and various works were performed throughout Western Europe, the United States, and North Africa. With the performance of the *Rapsodie espagnole* at an important festival of French music held in Munich (1910), the première of *L'Heure espagnole* at the Opéra-Comique (1911), and the creation of *Daphnis et Chloé* by Diaghilev's Ballets Russes (1912), Ravel's reputation as one of France's leading composers was firmly established. During this period, in the company of Nelly and Maurice Delage, many short trips were taken within France, from the Riviera to Mont-Saint-Michel, and from Alsace-Lorraine to the Basque territory. Ravel also visited Spain, Italy, and Switzerland, and concertized on three occasions in England (1909, 1911, and 1913). In Paris, his social activities included dinners followed by musicales at the homes of Alfred and Misia Edwards, M. D. Calvocoressi, Jean Marnold, Louis Laloy, Magnus Synnestvedt, Edouard Benedictus, and the pianist Jeanne Mortier. In addition, he faithfully attended *Apaches* meetings, the Godebski salon, which moved to new quarters on rue d'Athènes in 1909, and the salons of Princess Edmond de Polignac and Madame de Saint-Marceaux.[2]

---

[1] Although expelled from the Conservatoire in 1903, in a larger sense, Ravel never fully severed his ties. At Fauré's request, he participated in various juries, among them the piano jury and the Prix de Rome, and under Fauré's successor, Henri Rabaud, he continued to serve the Conservatoire until 1933, when poor health forced him to discontinue his activities.

[2] The following extracts from the Journal of Ricardo Viñes indicate some of the music performed at these gatherings. 1) At the salon of Mme de Saint-Marceaux, Jan. 13, 1905: Viñes

On September 16, 1905, Ravel formally authorized the publication of his Sonatine by Durand and Company, and thus began a lifelong relationship with Auguste and Jacques Durand.[3] Soon after, under the auspices of Auguste Durand and Fauré, he became a member of France's Society of Authors, Composers, and Music Publishers, and periodically returned to the society's headquarters in order to copyright his compositions (see Plate 8).

In the early months of 1906, the *Miroirs,* the Sonatine,[4] and *Noël des jouets* were performed in Paris and were generally well received. Each of the five pieces in the piano suite *Miroirs* was dedicated to a fellow *Apaches* member, and on January 6, Ricardo Viñes introduced the work at a recital of the Société Nationale with marked success. From all accounts, the pyrotechnics of "Alborada del gracioso" were performed with consummate skill, and the piece was immediately encored. In the course of an important review, Calvocoressi praised the *Miroirs,* and some of his commentary appears to reflect Ravel's own thinking:

> "Oiseaux tristes" is something extremely new, a rather extended étude (in the sense that painters use this word) and with perfect verity of notation. The same is true of "La Vallée des cloches." On the other hand, "Barque sur l'océan" is a veritable small symphonic poem, constructed very vigorously, and "Alborada" is a scherzo, a big independent scherzo in the manner of Chopin and Balakirev. If I am not mistaken, "Noctuelles" is a sort of étude (this time in the pianistic sense) which is also realized in an extremely fresh manner. . . . But what I find most re-

performs Rimsky-Korsakov's piano concerto accompanied by André Messager, Ravel plays "Oiseaux tristes" and Debussy's *D'un cahier d'esquisses.* 2) At the home of M. and Mme Robert Mortier, June 11, 1907: Viñes and Ravel perform Rimsky-Korsakov's *Antar,* a cousin of Abbé Léonce Petit sings works by Duparc and Ravel, Mme Mortier plays works by Liszt, and Ravel performs his Sonatine. 3) At the home of Magnus Synnestvedt, Jan. 20, 1909: Viñes plays *Gaspard de la nuit,* Debussy's "Poissons d'or" and "Reflets dans l'eau," and Déodat de Séverac performs several of his compositions. 4) At the home of Calvocoressi, March 8, 1912: Among the guests are Siloti, Schmitt, Roussel, and Marguerite Babaïan, who sings. Ravel performs the *Valses nobles et sentimentales.*

[3] An exclusive contract was soon drawn up, in which Durand was to have the right to the first refusal of Ravel's works, and, in turn, the composer was to receive an annuity of 12,000 francs. He explained to Calvocoressi that he preferred an annuity of only 6,000 francs, "so as not to risk feeling compelled to turn out a greater amount of music." Calvocoressi, "When Ravel Composed to Order," *Music and Letters* (Jan., 1941), p. 59.

[4] The Sonatine was premièred in Lyon by Mme Paule de Lestang in March, 1906, and was performed several weeks later at a Société Nationale recital by Gabriel Grovlez. Although well received in Lyon, in Paris some objections were raised with regard to its technical difficulty, and one critic observed that the Sonatine was well written and charming, although lacking in emotion. *Le Mercure Musical* (April 15, 1906), p. 363.

markable in these diverse pieces are their emotional qualities. In "Oiseaux tristes" and "La Vallée des cloches" there is a great depth of feeling, of intimate feeling, totally devoid of grandiloquence. "Barque sur l'océan" is once again beautiful, intense poetry. The "humor," the frank and vivacious fantasy of "Alborada" merit the highest praise.[5]

Pierre Lalo was also favorably impressed, and expressed the hope that the *Miroirs* would be the beginning of a direction toward a "less exterior, more intimate, and more human" art.

In March, 1906, Jane Bathori sang *Noël des jouets* with the composer at the piano, and soon after, she performed the song once again with orchestral accompaniment.[6] Louis Laloy found Ravel's poem "exquisite," and called the new work "a tiny masterpiece." The song marks the composer's initial venture into the pristine realm of childhood.

Ravel's first projected work for the theater was an adaptation of Gerhardt Hauptmann's play *Die versunkene Glocke,* in a French translation by A. Ferdinand Hérold.[7] The libretto of *La Cloche engloutie* is a spiritual descendant of *Der Freischütz,* with a generous supply of forest scenes, elves, nymphs, prayers, incantations, and dances, as well as human and supernatural beings. In a letter to Maurice Delage, written in June, 1906, Ravel could scarcely contain his enthusiasm: "For two weeks I haven't left the grind. I have never worked with so much frenzy. Yes, at Compiègne perhaps, but that was less sportive. It is thrilling to write a work for the theater." On August 20th, in an enthusiastic burst of hyperbole, he wrote once again to his friend: "Would you like an opera in five acts? You will have it within a week!" Ravel continued to work on the opera intermittently, and in January, 1909, a contract stipulating the financial details of forthcoming performances of the work was signed by the composer, Auguste Durand, Hérold, and Hauptmann.[8] As it turned out, the opera was abandoned shortly after the outbreak of World War I.

In the winter of 1906, two fresh projects were completed: an orchestral

---

[5] *Le Courrier Musical* (Jan. 15, 1906), p. 63.

[6] An orchestral holograph of *Noël des jouets,* in the archives of Salabert & Co., is signed by Ravel and bears the following cryptic inscription: "reorchestrated—because of divorce—in December, 1913." The "divorce" apparently refers to a rupture of relations with the publisher A. Z. Mathot, who continually refused to cede the rights of the song to Durand. This reorchestrated version was performed in Lyon, in Jan., 1914.

[7] André Gédalge gave Ravel a letter of introduction to Hérold, and a warm friendship soon developed between the composer and librettist of *La Cloche engloutie.*

[8] The document, dated January 15, 1909, is in the archives of Durand & Co. Durand allotted a fixed sum for each of the following events: 1) delivery of the completed manuscript; 2) the first

transcription of "Une Barque sur l'océan" [9] and a setting of five animal sketches from Jules Renard's *Histoires naturelles*. "The direct, clear language and the profound, hidden poetry of the poems in prose tempted me for a long time. My author's text demanded a particular kind of musical declamation from me, closely related to the inflections of the French language." [10] The composer's "particular kind of musical declamation" turned out to be a novel departure, for in place of traditional melody, he substituted a type of recitative which approximated the inflections of everyday speech. This "musical conversation" exhibits a bold elision of many mute *e*s, a technique frequently encountered in the music hall. It is clear from the *Journal* of Jules Renard that he viewed the entire project of setting the *Histoires naturelles* as quite superfluous. The author, who openly confessed his complete incompetence in musical matters, recorded the following conversation in his *Journal* entry of November 19, 1906:

> Thadée Natanson says to me: A gentleman wishes to set to music several of your *Histoires naturelles*. He is an avant-garde musician who is dependable, and for whom Debussy is already an old fogey. How does that affect you?
> Not at all.
> Now then, it concerns you!
> Not at all.
> What shall I say to him for you?
> Whatever you like. Thank him.
> Wouldn't you like him to play his music for you?
> Oh no, no. [11]

Undaunted by Renard's snub, Ravel personally asked his author to attend the first performance of the *Histoires naturelles*. The *Journal* entry dated January 12, 1907, records this remarkable encounter:

Parisian performance of the opera in a nationally subsidized theater; 3) the twenty-fifth performance in the same theater; 4) the fiftieth performance in the same theater. In addition, the contract stipulated that the fiftieth performance was not to take place more than ten years after the first. For these initial fifty performances, two-thirds of the profits were allotted to Ravel, with the remaining one-third equally divided between Hauptmann and Hérold.

[9] Performed at the Concerts Colonne on Feb. 3, 1907, the transcription was poorly received and was later retracted.

[10] "Autobiographical Sketch," p. 21. My translation is based upon Roland-Manuel's additional comments and corrections in his article, which are inserted in the copy of *La Revue Musicale* belonging to the Bibliothèque Nationale.

[11] It is impossible to know at just what point the confusion arose which resulted in the absurd implication that Ravel considered Debussy "an old fogey." Knowing Renard's passion for precise description, one may assume that Natanson was quoted correctly and that he in turn was simply repeating the musical gossip of the day.

M. Ravel, the composer of the *Histoires naturelles,* dark, rich, and elegant, urges me to go and hear his songs tonight. I told him I knew nothing about music, and asked him what he had been able to add to the *Histoires naturelles.* He replied: I did not intend to add anything, only to interpret them.

But in what way?

I have tried to say in music what you say with words, when you are in front of a tree, for example. I think and feel in music, and should like to think and feel the same things as you. There is instinctive, sentimental music, like mine—naturally you must learn your craft first—and intellectual music, like d'Indy's. The audience this evening will consist mainly of d'Indys; they don't recognize feeling and don't wish to explain it. I take the opposite view, but they must find my work interesting since they admit me. This test tonight is very important for me. In any case I can rely on my interpreter; she is excellent.

Many authors have doubted the authenticity of this passage. Roland-Manuel has claimed that it contains many improbabilities, particularly the phrase in which Ravel describes his music as "instinctive" and "sentimental." However, in comparison with d'Indy's approach to composition, Ravel must have considered his own music freer, both structurally and emotionally. The only unmistakable error in the passage is the description of Ravel as being "rich"—a lapse which is quite understandable in view of his well-trimmed dark beard and his elegant clothing. Other comments in the passage present no problem: probably owing to the fresh directive of the melodic line, Ravel was particularly concerned about the reception of his work, and had the utmost confidence in his interpreter, Jane Bathori. One eyewitness, the composer and theorist Charles Koechlin, recalled that the audience at the Société Nationale recital was scandalized by the declamation, outraged by the rests in "Le Grillon," and one phrase in "Le Martin-Pêcheur,""Ça n'a pas mordu ce soir"(Not a bite this evening), was greeted with jeering laughter. Following the thorough fiasco, vigorous polemics appeared in the music journals and the press. The reactions of several critics could be safely predicted on the basis of their past performances: the humor and subtlety of the *Histoires naturelles* were greeted with approbation by Georges Jean-Aubry, Jean Marnold, M. D. Calvocoressi, and Louis Laloy, and the songs were excoriated by Pierre Lalo, whose critique reflected the view of many musicians:

The idea of setting the *Histoires naturelles* to music is in itself surprising. . . . M. Ravel has not thought so: he has discovered something lyrical in M. Renard's Guinea-fowl and Peacock; in my opinion this subtle musician has never been so completely mistaken. . . . I admit that in other respects his music is well fitted to the text—it is just as precious, just as laborious, just as dry and almost as unmusical; a collection of the most out-of-the-way harmonies, industriously contrived, and the most elaborate and complicated sequences of chords. . . . When our good Chabrier wrote a song about Turkeys and Little Pink Pigs, he did it with gaiety and let himself go; he treated it as a joke. M. Ravel is solemn all the time with his farmyard animals; he doesn't smile, but reads us a sermon on the Peacock and the Guinea-fowl.

Lalo's attack was outdone by Auguste Sérieyx, professor of harmony at the Schola Cantorum, and coauthor with Vincent d'Indy of the imposing *Traité de composition*. Sérieyx viewed the *Histoires naturelles* as little short of a hoax, and claimed that one must "fight mercilessly" to avoid any similar attempts at "musical decomposition." [12] A forward-looking view of the *Histoires naturelles* was expressed by Gaston Carraud, who observed that the songs were simply amusing and original scenes from animal life. He bravely described the polemics as "idiotic," and noted that neither was French art in danger, nor was Salle Erard a temple. Another close observer of Ravel's latest composition was Claude Debussy, who thanked his editor Jacques Durand for a copy of the score: "It's excessively curious! It's artificial and chimerical, somewhat like a sorcerer's house. But 'The Swan,' nevertheless, contains very lovely music." In a letter to Louis Laloy, who had favorably compared the *Histoires naturelles* with Mussorgsky's *Nursery*, Debussy gave a different appraisal:

> But, entre nous, do you sincerely believe in "humoristic" music? First of all, it doesn't exist by itself; it always requires an occasion: either a text or a situation. . . . I agree with you in acknowledging that Ravel is extraordinarily gifted, but what irritates me is his posture as a "trickster," or better yet, as a fakir enchanter, who can make flowers spring out of a chair. . . . Unfortunately, a trick is always prepared, and it can astonish only once. [13]

Following his widely publicized expulsion from the Prix de Rome, and the scandalous reception of the *Histoires naturelles,* whatever one's opinion

[12] *La Revue Musicale de Lyon* (Feb., 1910), pp. 615–16.

[13] Lesure, " 'L'Affaire' Debussy-Ravel," in *Festschrift Friedrich Blume,* pp. 231–34. Ravel was obviously aware of his presumed posture as a "trickster," as he observed in a letter to Jean-Aubry written on March 23, 1907: "I want to tell you how much I am touched by your interest in my music. People strive so much, particularly most recently, to prove to me that I am deceiving myself, or better, that I am attempting to deceive others! At times I cannot help but feel a certain annoyance at this."

about Ravel or his music, he was undoubtedly the most controversial composer of his generation. In February, 1907, the Cercle Musical, an organization devoted to chamber music, presented a program of his works,[14] and soon after, in a flurry of activity, Ravel completed two important works in a Spanish idiom, *L'Heure espagnole,* his first opera, and the *Rapsodie espagnole.* In addition, he wrote three songs, the *Vocalise-Etude en forme de Habanera, Les Grands Vents venus d'outremer* (poem by Henri de Régnier), and *Sur l'herbe* (poem by Verlaine). It was a particularly brilliant season in Paris, with the participation of the leading German and Russian musicians. In May, a festival of Russian music was presented, in which Rimsky-Korsakov and Glazunov conducted their compositions, Chaliapin sang works by Mussorgsky, and Rachmaninov performed as pianist and conductor. Ravel's longstanding interest in Russian music was stimulated by the concerts, and at a banquet in honor of the Russian visitors, the numerous guests included Chaliapin, Diaghilev, Glazunov, Rimsky-Korsakov, and Scriabin, with the French contingent represented by Fauré, d'Indy, Messager, Ravel, and the critics Jules Ecorcheville, Louis Laloy, Lionel de la Laurencie and Romain Rolland. Ravel was also introduced to Richard Strauss and was particularly impressed by *Salome.*

Amid all of this invigorating creativity, the failing health of Joseph Ravel loomed in the background. Anxious to please his ailing father with a successful work for the theater, Ravel put aside *La Cloche engloutie,* and composed *L'Heure espagnole* with furious speed, completing the work at "La Grangette" in October, 1907.[15] This one-act comedy by Franc-Nohain [16] was first performed in 1904 at the Odéon Theater with marked success. Ravel was particularly attracted to its cool, ironic humor and its vivacious language, and he wrote to Franc-Nohain requesting permission to

[14] The program included the String Quartet, the *Histoires naturelles* performed by Mme Bathori and the composer, and the first performance of the *Introduction et Allegro,* which was favorably received.

[15] Shortly after completing the opera, Ravel wrote despondently to Ida Godebska: "Things are not well at home. My father is weakening continually. His mental capacity is at its very lowest: he mixes up everything, and no longer knows where he is at times. I no longer have any hope that he will see my work on stage: he is already too far gone to understand it." (Letter dated Nov. 15, 1907, in the private collection of Jean Godebski.)

[16] The pen name of Maurice-Etienne Legrand (1873–1934). Nohain is the name of a river near Corbigny, the author's birthplace. Franc-Nohain's collection of poems, *Flûtes* (1898), indicates a touch of the charming buffoonery found in the work of Ogden Nash, while *Le Dimanche en famille* (1903) abounds in curious rhymes.

adapt the play. The author, like Jules Renard, was amazed that anyone would consider setting his work to music, but willingly gave his permission. Following the completion of *L'Heure espagnole,* endless difficulties were encountered in having it performed, largely owing to its double entendres. The final decision whether or not to mount the work was in the hands of Albert Carré, the director of the Opéra-Comique. His first verdict was a flat refusal, and it appeared for a while that the opera was destined to remain in its composer's portfolio. Subsequently, Carré promised that it would be performed, but for various reasons the production was continually postponed. In 1908, Durand published the piano-vocal score, and the orchestration was completed one year later. At this time, *L'Heure espagnole* was scheduled to be performed with Strauss's *Feuersnot,* but the production did not materialize. In 1910, fragments of the opera were heard in concert performance with marked success, and in one review, a critic posed the very question which had been disturbing Ravel for three years: "When will *L'Heure espagnole* be performed at the Opéra-Comique?" The publication of the score and the performance of excerpts from the opera were significant factors leading to its ultimate creation. Were it not for the personal intervention of Madame Jean Cruppi, the wife of an influential minister in the French government, all efforts might well have come to nought. Madame Cruppi admired the opera and used her extensive influence to secure its public performance.[17] Nearly four years of haggling drew to a close when *L'Heure espagnole* was finally heard at the Opéra-Comique on May 19, 1911. Ravel had learned an important lesson as a result of the scandal caused by the *Histoires naturelles,* and he was determined to avoid a similar mishap with *L'Heure espagnole.* Not only did both works exhibit a similar type of conversational melodic line, but Franc-Nohain's witty play about the amorous adventures of a clockmaker's wife had been criticized as too risqué for the operatic stage. In an attempt to reassure both public and critics, Ravel wrote a long letter to the editor of *Le Figaro,* which was excerpted in the newspaper on May 17, 1911. Below is the complete text of his statement.

Dear Sir,

What have I attempted to do in writing *L'Heure espagnole?* It is rather ambitious: to regenerate the Italian opera buffa—the principle only. This work is not conceived of in traditional form. Like its ancestor, its only direct ancestor, Mussorgsky's *Marriage,* which is a faithful interpretation of Gogol's play, *L'Heure*

---

[17] *Noël des jouets* and *L'Heure espagnole* were gratefully dedicated to her.

espagnole is a *musical comedy*. Apart from a few cuts, I have not altered anything in Franc-Nohain's text. Only the concluding quintet, by its general layout, its vocalises and vocal effects, might recall the usual repertory ensembles. Except for this quintet, one finds mostly ordinary declamation rather than singing. The French language, like any other, has its own accents and musical inflections, and I do not see why one should not take advantage of these qualities in order to arrive at correct prosody. The spirit of the work is frankly humoristic. It is through the music above all, the harmony, rhythm, and orchestration, that I wished to express irony, and not, as in an operetta, by an arbitrary and comical accumulation of words. I was thinking of a humorous musical work for some time, and the modern orchestra seemed perfectly adapted to underline and exaggerate comic effects. On reading Franc-Nohain's *L'Heure espagnole,* I decided that this droll fantasy was just what I was looking for. Many things in this work attracted me, the mixture of familiar conversation and intentionally absurd lyricism, and the atmosphere of unusual and amusing noises which surround the characters in this clockmaker's shop. Finally, the opportunities for making use of the picturesque rhythms of Spanish music.[18]

Ravel thus forewarned the public, defended his conversational declamation, and explained that his work was nothing more than a musical comedy. Shortly before the première, a special performance of the opera took place at the home of Franc-Nohain. In the presence of Albert Carré and the critic Adolphe Boschot and with Ravel singing and presiding at the keyboard, Franc-Nohain and his wife read through the opera from beginning to end. Although puzzled by the adaptation, which he found to be cacophonous, the librettist agreed to be present at the first performance. The humor of the opera was highlighted even further by its juxtaposition with Massenet's *Thérèse,* based on a conventional plot of intrigue, love, and murder, set during the French Revolution. The reception of *L'Heure espagnole* was mixed: some in the audience were scandalized, some were puzzled, and others were enthusiastic. A few critics observed that Franc-Nohain's witty prose was poorly matched by Ravel's pompous music, while others asserted that the composer's scintillating music was set to a totally insignificant libretto. Emile Vuillermoz was on the whole disappointed:

[18] My translation is based upon Ravel's sketches for his statement, now in the Pierpont Morgan Library. (This statement has been printed with several inaccuracies and omissions in Chalupt and Gerar, *Ravel au miroir de ses lettres,* pp. 60–61.) In one passage, which was subsequently omitted, Ravel observed that he wished to revive "the old Italian opera buffa," and not the French operetta, which he called "light and parodying, at times sentimental."

Ravel knows the unknowable, molds the imponderable, and juggles with atoms and ions. He creates colors and perfumes. He is a painter, goldsmith, and jeweler. Would that he exercise these marvelous talents and let others evoke a smile by means of simple instrumental pleasantries, such as rumblings in the brass instruments or burlesque rejoinders in the contrabassoon—effects catalogued in the music hall a long time ago. . . . Ravel has always dreamed of a musical prosody restoring exactly the rhythm of the word. Already in the *Histoires naturelles,* while using familiar language, the curious elision of mute syllables had stupefied singers. In the course of his new work, the composer pushes this pursuit to its most vigorous consequences. . . . In the name of logic, Ravel removes from the musical language not only its internationalism and its universality, but its simple humanity.[19]

In addition to finding the declamation stiff and distorted, Gaston Carraud called the libretto "mildly pornographic vaudeville," a charge which brought a pointed reply from Franc-Nohain, who observed that his play had been printed in the *Revue de Paris* and had been performed over one hundred times at the Odéon Theater. The critic apologized, admitting that his use of the term was somewhat exaggerated.[20] Although praising the orchestration, Pierre Lalo found the characters totally lacking in vitality. Writing in *Le Figaro,* Gabriel Fauré greeted *L'Heure espagnole* with approbation, noting the originality of its harmony and orchestration, and its excellent interpretation. From all accounts, it appears that two of the principals were outstanding: Jean Périer, who had created the role of Pelléas, gave a sidesplitting portrayal of the muleteer, and François Ruhlmann conducted with exceptional skill. The novelty and difficulty of the score may be seen in the fact that Ruhlmann was given the assignment owing to the inability of the scheduled conductor to perform the work. After several performances, *L'Heure espagnole* promptly vanished from the billboards of the Opéra-Comique and was revived with far greater success at the Opéra following the war.

The final work written in 1907, which may well be called Ravel's "Spanish year," was the *Rapsodie espagnole.* A version for piano four hands was completed by October, and the orchestration was finished the following February. The first performance took place at the fashionable Sunday afternoon Concerts Colonne on March 15, 1908, in a long program, which

---

[19] Vuillermoz, "Les Théâtres," *Revue Musicale de la S.I.M.,* 7 (June 15, 1911), 68.
[20] *La Liberté,* May 24, 1911.

began with the overture to Edouard Lalo's *Le Roi d'Ys,* followed by Schubert's *Unfinished Symphony,* excerpts from Rimsky-Korsakov's opera *La Nuit de Noël,* Fauré's Ballade for Piano and Orchestra, with Alfred Cortot as soloist, the *Rapsodie espagnole,* excerpts from Rimsky-Korsakov's opera *Snégourotchka,* César Franck's *Symphonic Variations,* with Alfred Cortot, and finally, the march from Act Two of *Tannhäuser.* The *Apaches* were in full attendance for this important event, and according to one eyewitness account, following some hissing after the ''Malagueña,'' a booming voice was heard from the balcony: ''Once more, for the public downstairs, which didn't understand!'' After Edouard Colonne obliged, the same voice was heard: ''Tell them it's Wagner and they will find it very good.'' Critical opinion of the *Rapsodie espagnole* was generally favorable. Many observers praised the subtlety and freshness of the orchestration, as well as the picturesqueness of the music, and one critic called the work ''one of the most interesting novelties of this season.'' [21] Minority opinions were voiced by Gaston Carraud, who found the piece ''slender, inconsistent, and fugitive,'' and Pierre Lalo, who called it laborious and pedantic.

In the winter of 1907, with Calvocoressi acting as intermediary, Ravel was introduced to Ralph Vaughan Williams, to whom he gave some lessons in composition and orchestration. The lessons extended over a period of some three months, and consisted mainly of orchestration, either of Ravel's piano music or of works by Rimsky-Korsakov and Borodin. In a letter to Calvocoressi, Vaughan Williams declared: ''I must write you one line to thank you for introducing me to the man who is *exactly* what I was looking for. As far as I know my own faults he hit on them all exactly and is telling me to do exactly what I half felt in my mind I ought to do—but it just wanted *saying.*'' [22] A close friendship soon developed between the composers that extended well into the postwar years.

Between May and September, 1908, Ravel devoted his attention to *Gaspard de la nuit,* a piano triptych based upon the poetry of Aloysius Bertrand (1807–41). Although Maurice Delage was told that the new work would be even more difficult than Balakirev's *Islamey,* which indeed it is, the fact is that Ravel was deeply moved by Bertrand's grotesque, visionary

[21] *Le Figaro,* March 16, 1908. See also *Le Temps,* March 24, 1908, and *La Liberté,* March 17, 1908.

[22] Ursula Vaughan Williams, *R.V.W.: A Biography of Ralph Vaughan Williams* (London: Oxford Univ. Press, 1964), p. 80.

poems, which he had read and reread during his student days. The young man who introduced him to Bertrand's poetry was none other than Ricardo Viñes, who performed the triptych at a Société Nationale recital in January, 1909. The critics were unanimous in lauding Viñes's prodigious technique and interpretation, and the new work was generally well received. Louis Laloy commented enthusiastically on the "inexhaustible richness" of the "unexpected, pleasing, and piquant sonorities," and noted that *Gaspard de la nuit* marked an important advance in Ravel's art. On the other hand, Gaston Carraud grudgingly acknowledged the presence of some emotion in the music, but concluded that the work was little more than a curious and charming trifle.

Following a protracted illness, Joseph Ravel died of a cerebral thrombosis on October 13, 1908. The closely knit family had been living in Levallois Perret since 1905, and now Madame Ravel, Maurice, and Edouard decided to move to a more centrally located apartment. Their choice fell upon 4 avenue Carnot, in the fashionable Seventeenth Arrondissement.

In April, 1909, Ravel concertized abroad for the first time, appearing in London with Florent Schmitt under the auspices of the Société des Concerts Français. Among the works presented were the Sonatine, the Greek folk melodies, and the *Histoires naturelles,* which were favorably received by the London public and press.[23] Upon returning to Paris, Ravel wrote to his hostess, Mrs. Ralph Vaughan Williams:

May 5, 1909

Dear Madame,

Here I am, once again a Parisian: but a Parisian homesick for London. I have never before really missed another country. And yet I had left here with a certain fear of the unknown. In spite of the presence of Delage, in spite of the charming reception of my British colleagues, I should still have felt a real stranger. I needed the warm and sensitive welcome which awaited me at Cheyne Walk to make me feel at home in new surroundings, and to give me a taste of the charm and magnificence of London, almost as if I were a Londoner.[24]

During the remainder of 1909, the *Menuet sur le nom d'Haydn* [25] and *Tripatos* were completed, as well as the orchestration of *L'Heure espagnole.*

---

[23] See *The Times,* April 27, 1909.

[24] Autograph in the British Museum (Add. MS. 50360.)

[25] This short piano piece was commissioned by Jules Ecorcheville, editor of *La Revue Musicale de la S.I.M.,* for a special issue commemorating the centenary of Haydn's death. The

Another preoccupation centered upon a commission from Serge Diaghilev, whose Ballets Russes was making a profound impact upon Parisian musical life.[26] Together with Michel Fokine, Ravel began work on an adaptation of *Daphnis et Chloé,* a pastoral romance attributed to the Greek author Longus (3rd century A.D.). There were many complications, as the composer explained in a letter to Madame de Saint-Marceaux, written in June, 1909. "I must tell you that I've just had an insane week: preparation of a ballet libretto for the next Russian season. Almost every night, work until 3 a.m. What complicates things is that Fokine doesn't know a word of French, and I only know how to swear in Russian. In spite of the interpreters, you can imagine the savor of these meetings." [27]

In the early months of 1910, despite the unusual floods which caused the Seine to overflow its banks, bringing life to a virtual standstill, Ravel managed to continue work on the ballet, and a version for piano was completed in May. In the course of 1911, however, the finale was totally reworked, and the orchestration was completed the following year. Ravel explained that his intention in writing the ballet was to compose "a vast musical fresco, less thoughtful of archaism than of fidelity to the Greece of my dreams, which identifies quite willingly with that imagined and depicted by late eighteenth-century French artists. The work is constructed symphonically according to a strict tonal plan, by means of a small number of motifs, whose development assures the symphonic homogeneity of the work."[28]

Unfortunately, Ravel's conception of Greece was far removed from Leon Bakst's archaic stylization, and the composer was also dissatisfied with Fokine's libretto. In addition to these vexations, Ravel was very late in completing the score, and at one point Diaghilev seriously contemplated cancelling the entire project. After many problems and delays, the première finally took place on June 8, 1912, with the title roles performed by Vaslav Nijinsky and Thamara Karsavina, décor and costumes by Leon Bakst, and

---

other participating composers were Debussy, Paul Dukas, Reynaldo Hahn, d'Indy, and Charles-Marie Widor.

[26] Following the Parisian debut of the Ballets Russes in 1908, in which *Boris Godunov* was performed with Chaliapin in the title role, Diaghilev commissioned works by Stravinsky, Debussy, Ravel, Satie, and Falla. In the 1920s, he mounted ballets by Auric, Milhaud, Poulenc, Prokofiev, Rieti, and Sauguet, who collaborated with Cocteau, Braque, Matisse, Picasso, and Utrillo. Diaghilev's troupe disbanded following his death in 1929.

[27] Autograph in the private collection of B. de Saint-Marceaux.

[28] "Autobiographical Sketch," pp. 21–22.

Pierre Monteux conducting. The program, which was performed but twice, owing to the close of the ballet season, began with *Daphnis et Chloé,* followed by Debussy's *Prélude à l'Après-midi d'un faune,* Weber's *Le Spectre de la rose,* and Rimsky-Korsakov's *Shéhérazade.* Although the critics were sharply divided with regard to the music, it appears from virtually all accounts that the performance was inadequately prepared. During the stormy rehearsals, the dancers apparently encountered considerable difficulty in mastering the $\frac{5}{4}$ meter of the finale, and in his review, Gaston Carraud admitted that he would like to hear the work again, as he viewed the entire production as one of deplorable confusion. Pierre Lalo found Bakst's conception of Greece unintelligible, Fokine's choreography poor, and the music lacking in rhythm. Most critics, however, were very favorably impressed with the brilliant interpretations of Nijinsky and Karsavina, and spoke highly of the music's rhythmic verve, its exquisite plastic beauty, and the brilliant orchestration. Emile Vuillermoz called the new work "a genuine masterpiece," and observed that the Russian season ended in an "apotheosis," thanks to *Daphnis et Chloé.* While working on the ballet, Ravel extracted two orchestral suites from the score, which were heard in the concert hall. In reviewing a performance of the second suite, Vincent d'Indy gave his guarded approval, observing that Ravel's art appeared to be abandoning— for the moment at least—the bibelot and miniature, in order to proceed directly toward music.[29]

While *Daphnis et Chloé* was still in its incipient stage, Ravel decided to break with the Société Nationale and form a new organization devoted to contemporary music. His reasons were explained in a letter to Charles Koechlin, dated January 16, 1909:

Societies, even national, do not escape from the laws of evolution. But one is free to withdraw from them. This is what I am doing by sending in my resignation as a member. I presented 3 works of my pupils, of which one was particularly interesting. Like the others, it too was refused. It didn't offer those solid qualities of incoherence and boredom, which the Schola Cantorum baptizes as structure and profundity. . . . I am undertaking to form a new society, more independent, at least in the beginning. This idea has delighted many people. Would you care to join us? [30]

[29] D'Indy, "Concerts Lamoureux," *S.I.M.* (May 1, 1914), p. 48.
[30] Autograph in the private collection of Yves Koechlin. The piece which Ravel found "particularly interesting" was Delage's *Conté par la mer,* which was soon after performed at a recital of the new organization.

Koechlin did join the new group, whose nucleus consisted of former pupils of Gabriel Fauré, who was elected president (see Plate 9).[31] The opening concert of the Société Musicale Indépendante (S.M.I.) took place at the Salle Gaveau on April 20, 1910 (see Plate 10). For this auspicious event, Ravel performed Debussy's *D'un cahier d'esquisses,* Fauré accompanied Madame Jeanne Raunay in *La Chanson d'Eve,* and *Ma Mère l'Oye* was premièred by two children.[32] Ravel hoped to have his young friends Mimie and Jean Godebski perform the work, but in spite of its relative simplicity, it proved too difficult for them. Following the recital, Ravel wrote to one of his interpreters, Jeanne Leleu, as follows:

> La Grangette, April 21, 1910
>
> Mademoiselle,
> When you will be a great virtuoso and I either an old fogey, covered with honors, or else completely forgotten, you will perhaps have pleasant memories of having given an artist the very rare joy of hearing a work of his, of a rather special nature, interpreted exactly as it should be. Thank you a thousand times for your child-like and sensitive performance of *Ma Mère l'Oye* . . .

At the same time he wrote to Fauré:

> My dear teacher,
> How I would have wished to express my joy to you, yesterday, as deeply as I felt it, after the performance of *La Chanson d'Eve!* I was too moved, and moreover, how to do it amid the jostling? But you certainly understood me. One feels so close at these magnificent moments.[33]

The founding of the S.M.I. marked a distinct turning point in Ravel's career. Not only did he play a leading role in the society's steering committee, but his compositions were now performed before an audience of sympathetic admirers. Above all, the S.M.I. proved to be a healthy competitor of the Société Nationale for some three decades.

[31] The founding committee of the Société Musicale Indépendante consisted of Fauré, Louis Aubert, André Caplet, Jean Huré, Charles Koechlin, Ravel, Roger-Ducasse, Florent Schmitt, and Emile Vuillermoz, with A. Z. Mathot as secretary. The society disbanded in the late 1930s.

[32] The young performers were Jeanne Leleu, who later won the Grand Prix de Rome, and Geneviève Durony. Mlle Leleu was a pupil of Marguerite Long. *Ma Mère l'Oye* was begun in 1908 and completed at "La Grangette" in April, 1910. Although the year of composition is always given as 1908, the autograph is dated April, 1910, and the earliest known letter which mentions the piece also dates from 1910.

[33] Printed with the kind permission of Mme Fauré-Frémiet.

During the remainder of 1910, Ravel orchestrated the *Pavane pour une Infante défunte,* and at the invitation of Madame Marie Olénine d'Alheim,[34] he participated in an international competition sponsored by the Maison du Lied in Moscow. The organization was founded with a threefold purpose in mind: first, to stimulate public interest in folk melodies; second, to increase the repertory of artistically harmonized folk melodies by inviting composers to enter biannual competitions; finally, to encourage young singers by giving them the opportunity to perform folk songs before the public in small recital halls. The seven prizewinning songs were published by P. Jurgenson.

Song	Harmonization [35]
1. Spanish	M. Ravel
2. Russian	A. Olénine
3. Flemish	A. Georges
4. French	M. Ravel
5. Scottish	A. Georges
6. Italian	M. Ravel
7. Hebraic	M. Ravel

Shortly after learning of his quadruple victory, Ravel wrote to Madame Olénine d'Alheim: "By the same mail I am writing to Moscow in order to thank the jury for the pleasant and flattering distinction with which it has honored me. In this regard, I wish to express my sentiments of gratitude to you personally. Indeed, thanks to your kindness, it was possible for me to take part in the competition." [36] The seven winning songs were performed by Madame Olénine d'Alheim in December, 1910, at the Salle des Agriculteurs, a small auditorium in Paris. They were well received, and one critic wrote that when it comes to singing Mussorgsky or folk songs, Madame Olénine d'Alheim is the artist par excellence.

[34] Mme Olénine d'Alheim's official debut took place in Paris in 1896, and for some forty years she specialized in singing the music of Russian composers, particularly Mussorgsky, as well as folk songs from many nations. In 1908, she founded the Maison du Lied with her husband Pierre d'Alheim. A gifted linguist, he carried out many of the organization's translation assignments.

[35] Alexander Olénine, Mme Olénine d'Alheim's brother, was a student of Balakirev. Alexandre Georges (1850–1938) was a minor French composer of the day. Ravel's Russian and Flemish songs have not yet been recovered. On the basis of a sketch, it has been possible to reconstruct his Scottish song. See *The Music Forum,* 3 (1973), 311–14.

[36] Letter dated Nov. 3, 1910, in the Glinka Museum of Musical Culture, Moscow. Printed with the kind permission of Mme Olénine d'Alheim.

In January, 1911, Ravel concertized in England and Scotland, appearing in London, Newcastle, and Edinburgh. The programs generally included works by Franck, Saint-Saëns, and Fauré, and featured the Marot epigrams, the String Quartet, selections from the *Histoires naturelles,* and the *Pavane pour une Infante défunte.* It is clear from the reviews that the thirty-five-year-old musician was considered the most eminent French composer of his generation.[37] At this time, Ravel graciously acknowledged his longstanding indebtedness to Erik Satie by performing several of his piano pieces at an S.M.I. recital, much to the pleasure of his elder colleague. Later in the year, Satie introduced his friend to a young Belgian musician, who had come to Paris to study at the Schola Cantorum. Instead, the young man, Roland-Manuel,[38] began to study with Ravel and soon became one of his closest associates.

On May 9, 1911, the S.M.I. presented an unusual recital, in which the audience was requested to guess the identity of the composers. The fourth item in the program was listed as follows: *Valses nobles et sentimentales,* composed by "X," performed by Louis Aubert. Ravel kept a straight face as many of his admirers jeered at what they assumed to be a hoax of dissonances and wrong notes. When the results of the voting were made public,[39] it became clear that the sophisticated, avant-garde audience was unable to distinguish Debussy from Léo Sachs, or Ravel from Lucien Wurmser. Furthermore, although the authorship of the *Valses nobles et sentimentales* was correctly attributed, many credited the work to Satie or Kodály.

The Program (Composers)	Majority opinion
Quatuor vocal (1) (Léo Sachs)	Théodore Dubois, Léo Sachs
Quatuor vocal (2) (Léo Sachs)	Léo Sachs, Schmitt, Debussy
Trois Poèmes (D.-E. Inghelbrecht)	Inghelbrecht, Debussy

[37] *Newcastle Journal,* Jan. 21, 1911.

[38] The pseudonym of Alexis Manuel Lévy (1891–1966), French musicologist, composer, and critic.

[39] *Le Courrier Musical* (May 15, 1911), p. 365. The interested reader will find a third column of diverse guesses, some of which are even farther from the mark than the majority opinions.

Valses nobles et sentimentales (Maurice Ravel)	Ravel, Satie, Kodály
Poème de pitié (Mariotte)	Jean Huré, Wurmser, Léo Sachs
J'aime l'âne (Fraggi)	Ravel, Koechlin
Quatuor vocal (Busser)	Auber, Saint-Saëns, R. Hahn
Quatuor vocal (Mignan)	Locard, Duparc, Debussy
Quatuor vocal (Léo Sachs)	Schumann
Deux Rondels (Lucien Wurmser)	Wurmser, Ravel
Concert (Couperin)	Rameau, Casella (pastiche)

The experiment was obviously very revealing.

In the early months of 1912, Ravel's orchestral transcriptions of *Ma Mère l'Oye* and *Valses nobles et sentimentales* were mounted as ballets. In addition to writing his own scenarios, the composer attended numerous rehearsals and was intimately involved with all aspects of the productions. *Ma Mère l'Oye* was commissioned by Jacques Rouché, director of the Théâtre des Arts. Performed with choreography by Madame Jeanne Hugard, the ballet was favorably received, and one critic called it ''a triumph of Ravel's elegant, aristocratic, delightful, and somewhat ironic art.'' *Adélaïde, ou le langage des fleurs* (the ballet adaptation of *Valses nobles et sentimentales*), was commissioned by the Russian ballerina Natasha Trouhanova. Orchestrated within two weeks in March, 1912, the ballet was performed in April at the Théâtre du Châtelet. The première was an outstanding event, as four ballets were conducted by their respective composers: *Istar* by Vincent d'Indy, *La Tragédie de Salomé* by Florent Schmitt, *La Péri* by Paul Dukas, and *Adélaïde, ou le langage des fleurs* by Ravel.[40]

Shortly after the creation of *Daphnis et Chloé,* Ravel's health deterio-

---

[40] This performance marked Ravel's first important conducting role since he had led the overture to *Shéhérazade*. Although well received, *Adélaïde* was performed but four times.

rated sharply, largely owing to the exhausting schedule he had maintained over the past year. His illness was diagnosed as incipient neurasthenia, and he returned to "La Grangette" in the summer of 1912 and later went to the Basque territory for a complete rest. His health improved steadily, and by 1913 he was able to resume full activity.

During the opening seasons of the Ballets Russes, in which *The Firebird, Petrushka,* and *Daphnis et Chloé* were presented, Ravel and Stravinsky occasionally attended rehearsals of each other's music. Their cordial relationship was to become even closer when they jointly accepted a commission from Diaghilev to reorchestrate and readapt parts of Mussorgsky's incomplete opera *Khovanshchina.* The composers worked on the assignment in Clarens, Switzerland, during March and April, 1913.[41] In the course of their collaboration, Stravinsky showed his colleague the manuscript of his most recent ballet, *Le Sacre du printemps.* Ravel was extremely enthusiastic, and predicted in a letter to Lucien Garban that the creation of *Le Sacre du printemps* would be an event as important as the première of *Pelléas et Mélisande.* Another score which Ravel discovered at Clarens was Stravinsky's *Poèmes de la lyrique japonaise,* and he expressed considerable interest in the music, as well as its setting for solo voice accompanied by a chamber ensemble. Stravinsky explained that his instrumentation was derived from the score of *Pierrot Lunaire,* which Schoenberg had recently shown him in Berlin. Though unacquainted with Schoenberg's work, Ravel was anxious to exploit its coloristic possibilities and soon completed "Soupir," the first of his *Trois Poèmes de Stéphane Mallarmé.* On April 2, 1913, he wrote enthusiastically to Madame Alfredo Casella about his plan for a "scandalous concert," calling for narrator, voice, piano, string quartet, two flutes, and two clarinets. The compositions suggested were (a) *Pierrot Lunaire* (b) Stravinsky's *Poèmes de la lyrique japonaise,* and (c) his own two Mallarmé poems.[42] At the moment, Ravel observed, he only knew of (a) through hearsay, but felt it important for the S.M.I. to program the work. As for (b), he judged the songs to be worthy of their composer, whom he called a "genius." For the composer of (c), he quipped, consult Pierre Lalo.

[41] The Ballets Russes presented the Rimsky-Korsakov–Ravel–Stravinsky adaptation on June 5, 1913. See p. 242.

[42] At this time, "Surgi de la croupe et du bond" had not yet been projected. Ravel's letter is partially printed in Chalupt and Gerar, *Ravel au miroir de ses lettres,* p. 97. Autograph in the private collection of Mme A. Mallet.

Following his fruitful visit with Stravinsky, Ravel returned to Paris, completed "Placet futile," and attended the stormy première of *Le Sacre du printemps,* which was solemnly declared to be anti-music, hysteria, and barbarism. Soon after, he summered at Saint-Jean-de-Luz, where "Surgi de la croupe et du bond" was completed.

Following the death of Auguste Durand in 1909, Durand and Company initiated a distinguished series of commemorative concerts, which took place between 1910 and 1913. Among the participating composers were Caplet, Debussy, Fauré, d'Indy, Ravel, Saint-Saëns, and Schmitt. Although their personal relationship was strained, Debussy and Ravel appeared on the same program on two occasions,[43] and in 1913, their careers intersected once again owing to an uncanny coincidence. While Ravel was occupied with his settings of Mallarmé's poetry, Debussy was composing his final homage to the poet, the *Trois Poèmes de Stéphane Mallarmé,* and both collections were published by Durand about the same time. It was curious that both composers would independently set three poems by Mallarmé; when two of their three selections turned out to be identical, it was, as Debussy noted with dismay, a "phenomenon of autosuggestion worthy of communication to the Academy of Medicine." Ravel completed his songs before Debussy, and asked Dr. Edmond Bonniot, Mallarmé's son-in-law, for permission to utilize the poet's texts. The men were on friendly terms and the required authorization was granted immediately. A short time later, when Dr. Bonniot was approached by Jacques Durand with a similar request, he agreed to the publication of "Eventail," but refused "Soupir" and "Placet futile," whose rights had just been granted to Ravel. The imbroglio was mentioned in a letter to Roland-Manuel: "We will soon witness a Debussy-Ravel match. The other day, our publisher sent me a desperate letter, because Bonniot had refused the authorization for "Soupir" and "Placet futile" which Debussy had just set to music. I have settled everything." [44] Ravel secured the publications of Debussy's songs by begging Dr. Bonniot to grant Durand the required authorization, a gesture typical of his probity and good will.

While setting the poetry of Mallarmé, Ravel completed two minor

[43] On March 12, 1912, Debussy accompanied Maggie Teyte in the *Fêtes galantes* (2nd series), and Ravel performed *Valses nobles et sentimentales.* On March 5, 1913, Debussy played selections from his *Préludes,* Book Two, and Ravel conducted the *Introduction et Allegro.* Many people had to be turned away from these concerts, which were a brillant success.

[44] Roland-Manuel, *Ravel,* plate opposite p. 121. Letter dated Aug. 27, 1913.

works for the piano, a prelude written for the women's sight-reading competition at the Conservatoire, and two bona-fide pastiches in the style of Borodin and Chabrier. The caricaturing of an author's style was a popular diversion in France, both in the area of music and literature. Alfredo Casella had composed and successfully performed pastiches of Wagner, Brahms, Debussy, and others, and at an S.M.I. recital in December, 1913, he introduced two of his caricatures, based on the music of Ravel and d'Indy, and also premièred Ravel's pastiches of Borodin and Chabrier. Ravel was not present at the performance, as he was appearing in a series of recitals in England sponsored by the Classical Concert Society and the Music Club. By this time, with the exception of *L'Heure espagnole* and *Daphnis et Chloé,* virtually all of his compositions had been performed in England with considerable success.

On January 14, 1914, Ravel's projected "scandalous concert" took place at the S.M.I.: Jane Bathori sang the *Trois Poèmes de Stéphane Mallarmé,* and Stravinsky's *Poèmes de la lyrique japonaise* were performed. There was one significant change: *Pierrot Lunaire* was replaced by Maurice Delage's *Quatre Poèmes hindous.* Performed before a sympathetic audience, the Mallarmé songs were greeted with acclaim. A broader spectrum of opinion was achieved when the songs were first performed in England in March, 1915. The critic of the *Daily Mail* observed that the compositions "are among the most recent and interesting examples of modern song. The tiny orchestra is handled with utmost delicacy and intimacy of expression. . . . Mr. Thomas Beecham conducted and Mme. Jane Bathori-Engel sang the very difficult vocal part with great insight and expressiveness."

On the other hand, the critic of the *Westminster Gazette* called attention to the bewildered but attentive audience, and thus one notes the politeness of English audiences as opposed to French audiences of the time. "An attentive audience listened in absolute bewilderment to some of the strangest exercises in ultramodern cacophony which it would be possible to imagine. . . . Now and then the divergence between the voice part and the accompaniment seemed so pronounced as almost to suggest that Mdme. Bathori-Engel was singing one number while the instrumentalists were playing another." [45]

Commissioned by Nijinsky, Ravel orchestrated Schumann's *Carnaval* and Chopin's *Les Sylphides,* which were performed by Nijinsky's troupe in

[45] *Daily Mail* and *Westminister Gazette,* March 18, 1915.

London's Palace Theatre in March, 1914.[46] Another commission, from Madame Alvina-Alvi, a soprano in the St. Petersburg opera company, led to the setting of two Hebraic melodies, "Kaddisch" and "L'Enigme éternelle," which proved to be Ravel's final setting of folk melodies. Harmonized during April and May, 1914, the songs were performed by Madame Alvina-Alvi accompanied by the composer, at the concluding S.M.I. recital of the 1914 season.

Following the innumerable vexations encountered with the original production of *Daphnis et Chloé,* still another contretemps was to occur when Diaghilev presented the ballet at London's Drury Lane Theatre in June, 1914. The dispute centered about the choral sections, which Diaghilev viewed as an unnecessary additional expense. Ravel insisted they were an important component of the work, but as a compromise, he wrote an alternate orchestral version of the ballet's only solo choral section, with the understanding that the chorus would be utilized in all major productions. The controversy came to a head, when it was disclosed that the London production would take place without the chorus. Ravel was incensed, and protested in an open letter to four London newspapers. In addition, he sent a copy of his statement to Vaughan Williams, asking him to circulate its contents as widely as possible.[47] The letter was printed in the *Morning Post,* together with a reply by Diaghilev.

Paris, June 7

Sir,

My most important work, *Daphnis et Chloé,* is to be produced at the Drury Lane Theatre on Tuesday, June 9. I was overjoyed, and fully appreciating the great honor done to me, considered the event as one of the weightiest in my artistic career. Now I learn that what will be produced before the London public is not my work in its original form, but a makeshift arrangement which I had accepted to write at M. Diaghilev's special request, in order to facilitate production in certain minor centers. M. Diaghilev probably considers London as one of the aforesaid "minor centers," since he is about to produce at Drury Lane, in spite of his positive word, the new version, without choir.

---

[46] In light of this commentary, cf. *The Music Forum,* 3 (1973), 322–27. Following the 1913 Ballets Russses season, Nijinsky broke with Diaghilev and formed his own troupe. Because of sudden illness, however, most of Nijinsky's 1914 London season did not materialize. See below, pp. 241 and 242.

[47] Ravel copied a translation of his statement into English (a language he did not understand), and thus created a curious document. It is reproduced in *The Music Forum,* 3 (1973), 316.

I am deeply surprised and grieved, and I consider the proceedings as disrespectful towards the London public as well as towards the composer.

In his reply, Diaghilev stated that he had recently produced *Daphnis et Chloé* at Monte Carlo without chorus, and was unaware of any protest from the composer. Furthermore, he denied that the alternate orchestral version was intended solely for small theaters. When the chorus had been included in Paris, he continued, its participation was found to be detrimental. Therefore, he concluded, M. Ravel was asked to write a second version. In a long statement to the editor of *Comœdia,* Ravel convincingly exposed Diaghilev's misrepresentations point by point, and observed that henceforth the impresario would be bound by written agreement to include the chorus in all major productions.[48] This apparently was done, and as a result the composer was appeased and continued to write for the Ballets Russes in the postwar years.

As was his custom, Ravel spent the summer months of 1914 in Saint-Jean-de-Luz, taking long walks, swimming, boating, and visiting with friends. He was occupied with two fresh projects, a suite for piano, which advanced rapidly during the month of July, and a trio for piano, violin, and cello, which had been contemplated as early as 1908. The trio was progressing slowly when the stunning disclosure came of mobilization and war with Germany. Many people accepted the news with incredulity, assuming that hostilities would be terminated in short order. As it turned out, the ensuing carnage was to mark the end of an epoch.

[48] *Comœdia,* June 18, 1914.

CHAPTER FOUR

1914-1921
The War and Its Aftermath

I truly suffer from only one thing, not being able to embrace my poor mother . . . Yes . . . there is something else: music. I thought I had forgotten it. Several days ago it returned, tyrannical. I think of nothing else. I'm sure I would have been in a period of full creativity.

LETTER, RAVEL TO ROLAND-MANUEL, JUNE, 1916

I saw a hallucinating thing: a nightmarish city, horribly deserted and mute. . . . Undoubtedly I will see things which will be more frightful and repugnant; I don't believe I will ever experience a more profound and stranger emotion than this sort of mute terror.

POSTCARD, RAVEL TO JEAN MARNOLD, APRIL, 1916

WITH ONE THUNDERCLAP, European life was burst asunder in August, 1914. At the age of twenty, Ravel had been exempted from military service, owing to a hernia and general weakness,[1] but now, aged thirty-nine, he was determined to serve his country. One important reason was that Edouard and vir-

[1] Medical report in the Archives de Paris, DR ¹ 553–1895.

71

tually all of his friends had enlisted. Another significant factor was mentioned in a letter to Cipa Godebski: "And now, if you wish, Vive la France! but, above all, down with Germany and Austria! or at least what those two nations represent at the present time. And with all my heart: long live the Internationale and Peace!" [2] On August 4, the composer described his dilemma in a letter to Maurice Delage:

> If you only knew how I suffer . . . Since this morning and without respite, the same horrible, cruel, idea . . . if I left my poor old mother, it would surely kill her. . . . Yes, I am working [on the Trio] with the sureness and lucidity of a madman. But as I work, something gnaws at me, and suddenly I find myself sobbing over my music! Naturally, when I come down and face my poor mother, I must appear quite calm and even amusing . . . but will I be able to keep it up?
>
> This has been going on for four days, since the tocsin. [3]

Ravel was anxious to complete the Trio before applying for military service and managed to do so with a burst of speed. [4] By September, he was caring for wounded soldiers in Saint-Jean-de-Luz, and one month later he described his activities in a letter to Roland-Manuel:

> What is incredible is the number if not the variety of needs which 40 soldiers can have in the course of one night! I am also writing music: impossible to continue *Zaspiak-Bat*, the documents having remained in Paris. It's a delicate matter to work on *La Cloche engloutie*—this time I think it really is [sunk], and to complete *Wien* [Vienna, the original title of *La Valse*], a symphonic poem. While awaiting the opportunity to resume my old project, Maeterlinck's *Intérieur*—a touching effect of the alliance—I have begun two series of piano pieces: 1) a French suite—no, it isn't what you think: *la Marseillaise* will not be in it, but it will have a forlane and a gigue; no tango, however. 2) a *Romantic Night,* with spleen, infernal hunt, accursed nun, etc. [5]

---

[2] Unpublished letter dated Aug. 20, 1914, in the private collection of Jean Godebski.

[3] Chalupt and Gerar, *Ravel au miroir de ses lettres,* p. 113.

[4] As might be expected, the first performance of the Trio, which took place at an S.M.I. recital in Jan., 1915, went virtually unnoticed. Jean Marnold wrote a long and very favorable review (in *Le Cas Wagner,* Paris: E. Demets, 1918, pp. 63–73), and Gaston Carraud spoke highly of its simplicity and breadth (*La Liberté,* Feb. 2, 1915).

[5] Of the six works, only two were completed following the war: the "French suite," *Le Tombeau de Couperin,* and *La Valse.* (For the remaining works, see pp. 243–44). *Zaspiak-Bat,* a projected piano concerto based upon Basque themes, was contemplated as early as 1906. The title, which means "the seven are one" in Basque, refers to the unity of the four Spanish and the three French Basque provinces. A surviving fragment of Maeterlinck's play *Intérieur* appears to have been written during the early 1890s. See Roland-Manuel, *A la gloire de Ravel,* p. 127.

The Three Songs for Unaccompanied Mixed Chorus, which were composed between December, 1914, and February, 1915, marked Ravel's final adaptation of his own poetry, and proved to be his sole essay in this genre.[6] During this time, the piano works of Mendelssohn were edited for Durand,[7] and in March, 1915, following an unsuccessful attempt to join the Air Force, Ravel managed to enlist in the Thirteenth Artillery Regiment as a truck driver. His vehicle was promptly baptized "Adélaïde," and many letters were proudly signed "Driver Ravel." The driving conditions were exhausting and extremely hazardous, frequently involving the transportation of war materiel at night, under heavy enemy bombardment. Near the front at Verdun, Ravel came within inches of losing his life on several occasions. A less dangerous assignment was described in a postcard to Jean Marnold, written in April, 1916:

The other day, I was assigned one of those "interesting missions" which you have told me you distrust. It consisted of going to X . . . in order to bring back a requisitioned vehicle, abandoned would be more correct. Nothing troublesome happened to me. I did not need my helmet, my gas mask remained in my pocket. I saw a hallucinating thing: a nightmarish city, horribly deserted and mute. It isn't the fracas from above, or the small balloons of white smoke which align the very pure sky; it's not this formidable and invisible struggle which is anguishing, but rather to feel alone in the center of this city which rests in a sinister sleep, under the brilliant light of a beautiful summer day. Undoubtedly, I will see things which will be more frightful and repugnant; I don't believe I will ever experience a more profound and stranger emotion than this sort of mute terror.[8]

A National League for the Defense of French Music, formed in 1916, proposed to ban all music by German and Austrian composers whose works were not yet in the public domain. The league's notice was signed by some eighty French musicians, among them d'Indy and Saint-Saëns. Although its statutes attracted wide support, Ravel refused to join the league, and in a formal reply, he made the following observations.

---

[6] As with the Trio, the première, which took place in Oct., 1917, was scarcely noticed. Georges Auric praised the "simplicity, lightness, and genuinely exquisite poetry" of the songs. *Le Courrier Musical* (Nov. 1, 1917), p. 355.

[7] Because supplies from Germany were cut off several fresh editions were published by Durand, among them the works of Chopin edited by Debussy and those of Schumann edited by Fauré.

[8] Unpublished autograph in the Music Division of the Bibliothèque Nationale, dated April 4, 1916.

June 7, 1916

Gentlemen,

An enforced repose enables me at last to reply to your letter containing the notice and statutes of the National League for the Defense of French Music, which reached me with considerable delay. I beg you to excuse me for not having replied sooner, but my various transfers and active duty have left me very little free time. Excuse me, also, for not being able to subscribe to your statutes; having carefully studied them, and your notice as well, I feel unable to do so. . . . I am unable to agree with you when you assert as a principle that 'the role of the art of music is economic and social.' I have never considered music, or any of the arts, in that light. . . . I do not believe that 'in order to safeguard our national artistic inheritance' it would be necessary to 'forbid the public performance in France of contemporary German and Austrian works not yet in the public domain.' . . .

It would even be dangerous for French composers to ignore systematically the productions of their foreign colleagues, and thus form themselves into a sort of national coterie: our musical art which is so rich at the present time, would soon degenerate, becoming isolated by its academic formulas.

It is of little importance to me that M. Schoenberg, for example, is of Austrian nationality. This does not prevent him from being a very fine musician, whose very interesting discoveries have had a beneficial influence on certain allied composers, and even our own. Moreover, I am delighted that MM. Bartók, Kodály and their disciples are Hungarian, and show it so unmistakably in their music.

In Germany, apart from M. Richard Strauss, there appear to be only composers of secondary rank, whose equivalent could easily be found within France. But it is possible that some young artists may soon be discovered, whom we would like to know more about here . . .

You will observe, Gentlemen, that our views are so disparate, as to make it impossible for me to join your organization.

I hope nevertheless to continue to 'act like a Frenchman' . . .

Very truly yours,
Maurice Ravel [9]

The preceding statement bears witness to Ravel's independent thinking, and to his courage in defending a minority position on what was an explosive emotional issue. In the last analysis, he was convinced that ignoring the artistic achievements of other nations was counterproductive, and that the best way to defend French music would be for French composers to write good music.

Amid the war's hardships, tragedies, and galvanizing experiences, Ravel was obsessed by his mother's failing health and by the frequent lack of news from family and friends. His own health had deteriorated sharply: in

[9] *La Revue Musicale* (Dec., 1938), pp. 70–71.

addition to frequent insomnia and poor appetite, he finally underwent an operation for dysentery in September, 1916. Following a satisfactory convalescence, which was largely spent devouring book after book,[10] Ravel suffered the deepest grief of his entire life: on January 5, 1917, Marie Delouart Ravel died at the age of 76. This tragedy marked a decisive turning point in Ravel's career. Its immediate effect was some three years of virtual silence with regard to composition, and from this point until his swan song, *Don Quichotte à Dulcinée,* only about one composition a year would be completed.

In 1917, Ravel received a temporary discharge from military duty, and in June he was a guest at the home of Monsieur and Madame Fernand Dreyfus[11] at Lyons-la-Forêt, some sixty miles northwest of Paris. In this restful setting, he completed *Le Tombeau de Couperin,* much of which had been written in 1914. Each of the piano suite's six pieces was dedicated to the memory of a fallen comrade in arms. The "Rigaudon," for example, was dedicated to the composer's childhood friends Pierre and Pascal Gaudin, the "Prélude" to Lieutenant Jacques Charlot, a cousin of Jacques Durand, who had transcribed several of Ravel's works, and the "Toccata" to Captain Joseph de Marliave, the husband of Marguerite Long. As *Le Tombeau de Couperin* was being completed, Edouard and Maurice moved out of their apartment on avenue Carnot to share a villa in Saint-Cloud, just outside of Paris, with Monsieur and Madame Bonnet, Edouard's business associates. In 1918, two works were completed, an orchestral transcription of "Alborada del gracioso," which had been commissioned by Diaghilev, and a short musical frontispiece for a book by the Italian poet Ricciotto Canudo.[12] Because of continuing insomnia and fatigue, the opening months of 1919 were spent in the quiet and isolated mountain resort of Mégève, in France's Haute-Savoie. On February 9th, Ravel wrote to Jacques Durand that he felt an "intense

---

[10] Ravel was particularly impressed with Alain-Fournier's *Le Grand Meaulnes,* and for many years he contemplated writing a rhapsody for piano and orchestra, or cello and orchestra, based upon the celebrated novel. It appears that the project was not even partially sketched.

[11] Mme Dreyfus, the mother of Roland-Manuel, was Ravel's "marraine de guerre"—a soldier's correspondent who "adopts" him and mails him gifts, news clippings, and so on.

[12] Ravel and Canudo had met in Paris about 1905 and were to remain on cordial terms well into the 1920s. The composer's library at Montfort l'Amaury contains several works by the poet with personal dedications, among them *Le Livre de l'évolution* (Paris: E. Sansot, 1908), and *Combats d'Orient* (Paris: Hachette, 1917).

need'' to work, but was ''absolutely incapable'' of obeying his impulse. Several days later, he wrote to his editor that he was in an ''indescribable furor''—for two consecutive days he had been seized by a strong desire to work. This proved to be but another false alarm, and the crisis continued.

Following a long delay, the first performance of *Le Tombeau de Couperin* finally took place in Paris on April 11, 1919. Ravel wrote to Jacques Durand that he would be present at the performance, unless an ''earthquake, a new war, or the dissolution of the S.M.I.'' postponed the date once again. The recital marked the composer's first public appearance following the war, and he acknowledged an exceptionally warm ovation. Marguerite Long's interpretation of *Le Tombeau de Couperin* was greeted with enthusiasm, and the entire suite was encored. An orchestral transcription of the work was completed in June, and in September, 1919, Ravel wrote to Vaughan Williams that his stay at Mégève had proved beneficial: ''It is now my morale that must be cared for, and I don't know how to do it. . . . Won't you be coming to Paris soon? I would be very happy to see you after so many terrible years. I was going to go to England next season, but I think it would be preferable to work, if I am still capable of it.'' [13]

At this point Ravel's morale was indeed at its nadir. Unable to compose and haunted by his mother's memory, he was bitter and disillusioned. A generous and timely invitation from A. Ferdinand Hérold enabled him to spend the winter of 1919 at his colleague's country home in Lapras, a village in the Ardèche region, some 350 miles southeast of Paris. Here, in total isolation, Ravel painstakingly began to recapture his former creative enthusiasm. He orchestrated the accompaniments to ''Kaddisch'' and ''L'Enigme éternelle,'' hoping thereby to whet his appetite and stimulate his creative faculties. Soon after, while hard at work on a fresh commission from Diaghilev, Ravel wrote to Roland-Manuel that he was ''waltzing frantically.'' The new work, *La Valse,* had in fact been contemplated in 1906, as an homage to Johann Strauss. After completing two versions of the piece, for piano solo and two pianos, Ravel finished the orchestration in about three months. While working on *La Valse,* he reminisced about his mother, in a remarkably candid letter written to Ida Godebska on December 27, 1919:

I think of those former times at the charming apartment on avenue Carnot, where I was so happy. I think that it will soon be three years that she has died, and my

[13] Vaughan Williams, *R.V.W.: A Biography of Ralph Vaughan Williams,* p. 133.

despair increases from day to day. Since I have begun working again, I am thinking about it more—I no longer have this dear silent presence enveloping me with her infinite tenderness, which was, I see it more than ever, my only reason for living.[14]

On January 15, 1920, the French government's Official Journal published a list of nominations and promotions for the Legion of Honor, and as a matter of course, the list was printed the following day in the French press. Ravel was nonplussed to learn of his nomination as Chevalier of the Legion of Honor, and he created an uproar by refusing to be decorated. "What a ridiculous incident!," he wrote to Roland-Manuel. "Who could have played this joke on me?" No one, in fact, had acted in bad faith. Léon Bérard, the minister of public education, had submitted Ravel's name after being told by a colleague that the award would be accepted. As it turned out, many newspapers supported the composer's position in this new "affaire Ravel," and in a press interview in Saint-Cloud, Edouard Ravel explained that his brother had refused the decoration in principle, as he was opposed to all honorary awards.[15] As a faithful Baudelairean, the composer was well acquainted with a passage from the *Intimate Journals* dealing with the Legion of Honor: "If a man has merit, what is the good of decorating him? If he has none, he can be decorated, since it will give him distinction." In addition, it appears that Ravel still harbored resentment against the very same official circles which had refused him the Prix de Rome on five occasions. On April 2nd, the hotly debated episode was officially closed; Ravel's nomination was formally revoked by André Honnorat, the new minister of public education, and Paul Deschanel, the president of the French republic.

By the spring of 1920, the orchestration of *La Valse* was completed at Lapras, and in April Ravel returned to Paris in order to attend the première of his two Hebraic songs, which were performed by Madeleine Grey, with the Pasdeloup Orchestra conducted by Rhené-Baton. At this time, a preliminary hearing of *La Valse* took place at the home of Misia Sert, in the presence of Diaghilev, several members of his staff, Massine, Poulenc, and Stravinsky. According to Poulenc's eyewitness account, following the two-piano performance by Marcelle Meyer and Ravel, Diaghilev called the work

[14] Autograph in the private collection of Jean Godebski.

[15] See *Le Temps,* April 9, 1920. Despite his refusal of the Legion of Honor, Ravel subsequently accepted many honorary citations.

a "masterpiece . . . but it's not a ballet. It's a portrait of ballet . . . a painting of a ballet." [16] Stravinsky remained silent. Ravel calmly took his manuscript and walked out. This incident marked a permanent rupture of relations between Ravel and Diaghilev. *La Valse* was subsequently performed in the concert hall, where it soon achieved considerable popularity.

By the summer of 1920, Ravel was occupied with two fresh commissions, as he explained in a letter to Roland-Manuel: "Latest news: I am working on an opera with the collaboration of Colette—the definitive title hasn't been decided—and a duo for violin and cello, dedicated to the memory of Debussy." The first movement of the duo, later to be entitled Sonata for Violin and Cello, was commissioned by Henry Prunières, the editor of *La Revue Musicale,* for a special commemorative issue devoted to Debussy.[17] The genesis of the new opera, later entitled *L'Enfant et les sortilèges,* may be traced back to World War I. At that time, Colette agreed to write a libretto for the Opéra, and its director, Jacques Rouché, suggested the names of several possible collaborators. It soon became apparent that Ravel would be the best choice. Colette's imagination was captivated by the project, and although she generally worked slowly, the libretto was completed in less than a week. A copy was sent to Ravel, who was stationed near Verdun, but it was lost in the mail. Finally, in 1918, he received a copy of the libretto, but did nothing with it until the spring of 1920. Concerned about his silence, Colette wrote in the early part of 1919: "Oh! dear friend, when, oh when—the 'Divertissement for my Granddaughter'? [18] Is it true that it's going to be finished? With hope and friendship, Colette de Jouvenel." Replying from Mégève in February, 1919, Ravel apologized for his silence, and pleaded poor health as his sole excuse:

> In fact, I am working already: I am taking notes—without writing any—; I am even thinking of some modifications . . . Don't worry: they're not cuts; on the contrary. For example: couldn't the squirrel's dialogue be developed? Imagine everything that a squirrel could say about the forest, and how that would lend itself to music!

[16] Poulenc, *Moi et mes amis,* p. 179.

[17] *La Revue Musicale,* Dec. 1, 1920. Together with a frontispiece by Raoul Dufy, musical contributions were written by Bartók, Dukas, Falla, Eugene Goossens, Malipiero, Roussel, Satie, Schmitt, and Stravinsky. All of the compositions were performed at an S.M.I. recital on Jan. 24, 1921.

[18] In addition, two other proposed titles were subsequently abandoned: "Divertissement for my Daughter," and "Ballet for my Daughter." See my article, "L'Enfant et les sortilèges: Correspondance inédite de Ravel et Colette," *Revue de Musicologie,* 52, No. 2 (1966), 215–20.

Another thing: what would you think of the cup and teapot, in old black Wedgwood, singing a ragtime? I must confess that the idea of having two negroes singing a ragtime at our National Academy of Music fills me with great joy . . . Perhaps you will object that you're not acquainted with American-negro slang. I don't know a word of English, but I'll do the same as you: I'll manage it. I would be very grateful to have your opinion of these two points.

In her delightful reply, Colette enthusiastically accepted all of Ravel's suggesions. She wrote in part:

Dear Sir,

But certainly a ragtime! But of course negroes in Wedgwood! What a terrific gust from the music hall to stir up the dust of the Opéra! Go to it! . . . Do you know that cinema orchestras are playing your charming Mother Goose Suite while they show American Westerns? If I were a composer and Ravel, I believe I would be pleased to learn that.

And the squirrel will say everything you wish. Does the 'cat' duo, exclusively meowed, please you? We will get some acrobats. Isn't the Arithmetic business a polka? I wish you good health, and shake your hand, with impatience

Colette de Jouvenel

The opening scenes of *L'Enfant et les sortilèges* were sketched in the spacious and elegant château of Ravel's old friend Pierre Haour, at Châteauneuf-en-Thimerais, some sixty miles southwest of Paris. The opera was soon interrupted, however, by a busy schedule of concerts and rehearsals. In October, 1920, several programs were given in Vienna, with the composer participating. In a special program in which Arnold Schoenberg conducted his *Gurrelieder,* Ravel played the two-piano version of *La Valse* with Alfredo Casella, and in another recital he accompanied Marya Freund in the *Histoires naturelles* and the Mallarmé poems. An orchestral concert, conducted by Oskar Fried, was somewhat unusual in that it featured two performances of the *Rapsodie espagnole.* The concerts were greeted with marked acclaim, and in several interviews, Ravel expressed his delight in visiting Vienna, as well as his appreciation of the public's warm reception.[19] He also expressed admiration for the waltzes of Johann Strauss, and praised Franz Lehár's operetta *Die blaue Mazur,* which he heard in Vienna. Back in Paris, the composer attended numerous rehearsals of *Le Tombeau de Couperin,* which was presented with choreography by the Swedish Ballet.[20]

[19] *Neue Freie Presse,* Oct. 29 and 30, 1920.
[20] The ballet was favorably received, and in 1923 Ravel conducted its 100th performance at the Théâtre des Champs Elysées.

In December, 1920, the Lamoureux Orchestra, led by Camille Chevillard, presented the première of *La Valse*. Although the reviews were largely favorable, many critics were confused by the truculence and frenzy of the conclusion. Henry Prunières praised the "inexhaustible verve" as well as the "dazzling orchestration" of the score, and concluded his review by predicting that the composer of *La Valse* would have many "lovely surprises" in store for the public. This observation was probably directed against the musical gossip of the day, which claimed that Ravel's career would be finished following the war. Indeed, while he had remained practically silent for three years, Parisian musical life began to focus upon the avant-garde composers whose works were frequently performed at the Théâtre du Vieux-Colombier between 1917 and 1919. In 1920, six of these young composers were introduced to a critic of *Comœdia* at the home of Darius Milhaud. The critic, Henri Collet, who saw in their work a "magnificent and voluntary return to simplicity," called the group *Les Six*.[21] The name caught on, and as Milhaud observed, *Les Six* were a group whether they liked it or not. Honegger remarked that several other colleagues might have been present at the meeting, thus forming a group of eight or ten composers. "Naturally," he observed, "most of the young composers of the day believed in a necessary reaction against the Debussy-Ravel influence, but each one envisioned it in a different way."[22] In addition to Debussy and Ravel, composers such as Fauré and Roger-Ducasse, whose works were widely performed before the war, were now thought to be overly refined and outdated. In what was perhaps an attempt to align himself with the postwar mood, the enigmatic Erik Satie suddenly turned against his former colleague and benefactor: "Ravel refuses the Legion of Honor," he jibed in the avant-garde pamphlet *Le Coq*, "but all of his music accepts it." Auric, Milhaud, Poulenc, and Jean Cocteau soon adopted an anti-Ravel posture, but a reconciliation with the younger generation came about, largely owing to Ravel's probity, good will, and his extraordinary tact.[23]

[21] *Comœdia*, Jan. 16, 1920.

[22] Luigi Rognoni, "Due colloqui con Arthur Honegger," *L'Approdo musicale*, 19–20 (1965), 132.

[23] See Poulenc, *Moi et mes amis*, p. 177. Ravel had always maintained friendly relationships with Louis Durey, Honegger, and Germaine Tailleferre, and generously assisted them in furthering their careers. In the course of an article in *Les Nouvelles Littéraires* (April 2, 1927), Ravel defended Milhaud's *Les Malheurs d'Orphée*, which had been attacked by Pierre Lalo and, in an unpublished letter to Ravel, Milhaud thanked his elder colleague for his support. (Autograph in the Music Division of the Bibliothèque Nationale.) See Jean Cocteau's conciliatory statement in *La Revue Musicale* (Jan., 1930), p. 16.

Following the war, Ravel had found it impossible to work in Paris, and after a great deal of searching, he finally decided to buy a villa in Montfort l'Amaury, a sleepy village some thirty miles west of the capital. It provided a quiet, country atmosphere conducive for work, with Paris easily accessible by train and bus. The villa, Le Belvédère, turned out to be the composer's final official residence, and it has been preserved exactly as he left it. Now located at 5 rue Maurice Ravel, Le Belvédère is a national museum open to the public. From the balcony of the villa, one sees a sumptuous view of the flowing countryside of the Île-de-France. The library reveals the composer's particular literary taste, which will be discussed later, and one notes a Japanese garden, many Japanese prints, an Arabic coffee set—showing his penchant for the exotic—and finely wrought bibelots, mechanical birds, music boxes, and carved statuettes—showing his predilection for perfectly crafted miniatures of all sorts. The panels in the living room and the friezes in the bedroom were designed and painted by the master of the house, and in the study, adjacent to the Erard piano and the composer's desk, there is a fine portrait of Madame Ravel, done by her brother-in-law Edouard (1885), a portrait of Joseph Ravel (M. Desboutin, 1896), and a painting of Maurice Ravel at the age of eleven (L. Tanzy, 1886) (see Plates 11 and 12). To these small, immaculately polished rooms, which were tended by his faithful housekeeper Madame Reveleau, the composer added his Siamese cats, upon whom he lavished loving attention. Ravel's mischievous humor often came to the fore when guiding his friends through the villa, for when his guests gazed in admiration at a ''rare'' Monticelli, he would enjoy informing them that it was an imitation. Indeed, throughout the villa, one finds a curious combination of rare authenticity and flagrant pastiche side by side, together with an aura of make-believe enchantment, not unrelated to the exoticism of *Shéhérazade* or the childlike humor of *L'Enfant et les sortilèges*. After being extensively remodeled, Le Belvédère was ready for occupancy in May, 1921, a point which ushers in a fresh period in Ravel's career.

CHAPTER FIVE

1921-1928
New Trends in the 1920s

. . . I am happier than you can imagine about the solid position which you occupy and which you have acquired so brilliantly and so rapidly. It is a source of joy and pride for your old professor.

LETTER, FAURÉ TO RAVEL, OCTOBER, 1922

M. Maurice Ravel was most cordially received, as was natural. Since the death of Debussy he has represented to English musicians the most vigorous current in modern French music.

THE TIMES, April 16, 1923

FOLLOWING A DIFFICULT period of postwar adjustment, Parisian musical life gradually returned to its former vigor and diversity. While the Concerts Colonne, Pasdeloup, and Lamoureux continued to emphasize the works of Wagner, Beethoven, Saint-Saëns, Franck, Rimsky-Korsakov, Mozart, Berlioz, Mendelssohn, and Debussy, the S.M.I. played an active role in presenting contemporary music. In addition to festivals of English music (Arnold Bax, Cyril Scott, Vaughan Williams), and American music (George

Antheil, Aaron ᴠopland, Walter Piston, Virgil Thomson), Honegger, Roussel, and Schoenberg participated in special recitals devoted to their works. Under Ravel's leadership as vice president and later as president, the S.M.I. introduced the works of many younger composers, among them Lili Boulanger, Louis Durey, Paul Hindemith, Jacques Ibert, Marcel Mihalovici, Darius Milhaud, Olivier Messiaen, Roland-Manuel, Manuel Rosenthal, Alexandre Tansman, and Joaquín Turina. In addition to the Concerts du Conservatoire and the Société Nationale de Musique, subscription orchestral concerts were led by Vladimir Golschmann, Serge Koussevitzky, and Walther Straram, while at the Théâtre du Vieux-Colombier, Henry Prunières organized important recitals devoted to contemporary chamber music. Among the important ballet companies were the troupe of Ida Rubinstein, the Ballets Russes, and the Swedish Ballet, while many of the concerts organized by Jean Wiener featured avant-garde works and jazz side by side.[1] At the Opéra, the works of Wagner and Meyerbeer were frequently performed, and in 1925, the 1500th performance of Gounod's *Faust* was given.

In the 1920s and 1930s, Ravel divided his time between Montfort l'Amaury, Paris, the Basque country, and his increasingly frequent concert tours. The isolation of Le Belvédère and the tranquillity of Saint-Jean-de-Luz were offset by innumerable social and professional engagements in Paris. Although the *Apaches* were no longer meeting, Ravel kept in touch with many of them and remained particularly close to M. D. Calvocoressi, Maurice Delage, Léon-Paul Fargue, and Lucien Garban. He often visited the Roland-Manuels and the Godebskis,[2] and attended the elite salon of Monsieur and Madame Paul Clémenceau, where one might encounter Albert Einstein, Paul Painlevé, or Stefan Zweig. At the home of Prince Jean-Louis de Faucigny-Lucinge, the composer often enjoyed a convivial dinner and discussion of the arts with younger colleagues, among them Georges Auric, Serge Lifar, Paul Morand, and Francis Poulenc. The 1920s also marked the heyday of Le Bœuf sur le toit, on the fashionable rue Boissy d'Anglas, where the artistic and intellectual aristocracy of Paris gathered. Amid the

---

[1] In Dec., 1921, Ravel and Roussel attended Wiener's opening concert, which consisted of works by Stravinsky and Milhaud. The program began with Billy Arnold's jazz group, and a moment later Roussel stormed out of the hall. Ravel, on the other hand, was delighted with the performance.

[2] In the postwar years, their salon attracted the younger generation, Cocteau, *Les Six,* and Jacques Ibert, as well as many of their old friends. When in Paris, Ravel frequently stayed at the Hotel d'Athènes, just across the street from their apartment.

conversations, the smoke, and the expert jazz renditions of Jean Wiener and Clément Doucet, one might encounter Bartók, Braque, Cocteau, Gide, Max Jacob, Picasso, Prokofiev, or Stravinsky. Ravel spent many evenings there with friends. "I can see him now," Léon-Paul Fargue recalled, "a sort of debonair wizard, buried in his corner at the Grand Ecart or Le Bœuf sur le toit, telling me endless stories which had the same elegance, richness, and clarity as his compositions. He could tell an anecdote as well as he could compose a waltz or an adagio." [3] During the postwar years, Ravel was forced to adjust to a new, uncomfortable situation, one in which he was no longer a member of the avant-garde, but rather a follower of the trends set by Schoenberg, *Les Six,* Prokofiev, and others. The new sounds in the air were those of jazz, polytonality, and atonality, as the lush velvet of impressionism gave way to the hard steel which had been prophesied in *Le Sacre du printemps.* In addition, many composers were turning to a spare texture in a reaction to the mammoth orchestrations of Wagner, Mahler, and Strauss. The postwar years thus presented many fresh challenges. Ravel listened a great deal, absorbed, and composed with difficulty, generally requiring considerably more time for his new works.

By the summer of 1921, Ravel was occupied with rehearsals of *Daphnis et Chloé* and *L'Heure espagnole,* which were reintroduced at the Opéra, thanks to the efforts of Jacques Rouché. Both works fared considerably better with the public and press than did their original productions. At the same time, work was resumed on the Sonata for Violin and Cello, which was finally completed in February, 1922. In January, Ravel interrupted his intensive work on the Sonata in order to attend the Paris première of *Pierrot Lunaire,* performed by Marya Freund, with pianist Jean Wiener, and Darius Milhaud conducting. Although Ravel was favorably impressed, the work engendered a riot, and the police were called in to restore order. On January 30th, he wrote to Calvocoressi: "There is the duo for violin and cello which has been dragging on for a year and a half, and which I decided to finish. Until then, I will not leave Montfort, and will not reply to any of the letters which are accumulating in a majestic pyramid. The day before yesterday it was completed. Only I thought that the scherzo was not what I had wanted, and I began all over again." [4]

Because of a concert engagement in Lyon, Ravel was unable to attend

[3] Fargue, in Vuillermoz et al., *Maurice Ravel par quelques-uns de ses familiers,* p. 159.

[4] Calvocoressi, "Ravel's Letters to Calvocoressi," p. 10.

the première of the Sonata, which took place in Paris on April 6th. The soloists were violinist Hélène Jourdan-Morhange and cellist Maurice Maréchal. The novelty and difficulty of the work were responsible for a performance which apparently included some dissonances not found in the music. In a letter to Madame Jourdan-Morhange, Ravel commented that he was not upset by the news of the "massacre." In addition, he jested, "I have learned of my departure for Africa and of my forthcoming marriage. I don't know which of these events is supposed to precede the other." [5] The reviews of the Sonata were mixed. Writing in *La Républicaine,* Gustave Samazeuilh commented on the "supple imagination" of the first movement, the "surprising verve" of the scherzo and the finale, and the "pure and sustained line" of the third movement. Others, however, were disturbed by the excessively sober instrumentation, and compared the Sonata unfavorably with Ravel's prewar achievements.

The completion of the Sonata for Violin and Cello marked the beginning of an extended creative impasse. During the next two years, outside of several transcriptions, only two compositions were completed, both of which were commissioned for *La Revue Musicale* by Henry Prunières: the *Berceuse sur le nom de Gabriel Fauré* (violin and piano), and a song, *Ronsard à son âme,* composed for an issue commemorating the 400th anniversary of the poet's birth.

In June, 1922, the publisher Jean Jobert wrote to Ravel, asking him to orchestrate Debussy's *Danse* (1890), and "Sarabande" (1901). The composer replied that he would willingly transcribe the pieces, particularly the "Sarabande," but before making a definite commitment, he would seek the authorization of Madame Claude Debussy. The authorization was granted promptly, and the transcriptions were completed in the winter of 1922.

Amid his increasing number of concert tours, Ravel frequently visited England during the 1920s. Georges Jean-Aubry, who was now editor of *The Chesterian,* arranged several concerts in July, 1922, in which the composer participated as pianist and accompanist. In the course of an interview, Madame Robert Casadesus recalled a private musicale which took place at this time, in which Jelly d'Aranyi and Hans Kindler performed the Sonata for Violin and Cello. Late in the evening Ravel asked the Hungarian violinist to play some gypsy melodies. After Mlle d'Aranyi obliged, the composer

---

[5] Chalupt and Gerar, *Ravel au miroir de ses lettres,* p. 192. At the composer's request, the Sonata was performed again at an S.M.I. recital on May 16, 1922.

asked for one more melody, and then another. The gypsy melodies continued until about 5 a.m., with everyone exhausted except the violinist and the composer. That evening was to mark the initial gestation of *Tzigane.*

Following a successful reception in London, Ravel returned to Lyons-la-Forêt, where he completed the orchestration of Mussorgsky's *Pictures at an Exhibition,* which had been commissioned by Serge Koussevitzky.[6] While completing the transcription, he composed a lullaby for Roland-Manuel's son Claude, the *Berceuse sur le nom de Gabriel Fauré,* published in a special issue of *La Revue Musicale* honoring Fauré (October 1, 1922).[7] Fauré was touched by all of the homages and articles, and in a letter to Ravel he wrote in part: "I am thinking of your growth, dear friend, since the Faubourg Poissonnière [the street on which the Conservatoire was located], and I am happier than you can imagine about the solid position which you occupy and which you have acquired so brilliantly and so rapidly. It is a source of joy and pride for your old professor."[8]

Shortly after completing the *Berceuse,* Ravel participated in a festival of contemporary French music held in Amsterdam. A performance of *La Valse* given by the Concertgebouw Orchestra led by Willem Mengelberg was greeted with acclaim, and in another recital, the composer accompanied Claire Croiza in several of his songs. The entire festival, which included works by Debussy, Lili Boulanger, Fauré, Roussel, and Schmitt, was a brilliant success. In November, Ravel participated in a program of his works given in Milan, sponsored by the Italian review *Il Convegno.* The recital, which was enthusiastically received, included the first performances in Italy of the *Berceuse* and the Sonata for Violin and Cello.

Ravel's creative impasse reached its nadir in 1923, when, as far as can be ascertained, he completed nothing more than several initial sketches of a sonata for violin and piano. Following an extended vacation in the Basque territory, he set out in April for Italy, England, and Belgium. In London, he

---

[6] In Paris, and later as conductor of the Boston Symphony Orchestra, Koussevitzky commissioned many outstanding works, among them Honegger's *Pacific 231* and Stravinsky's *Symphony of Psalms.*

[7] Other musical homages were contributed by Fauré's former pupils Georges Enesco, Louis Aubert, Florent Schmitt, Charles Koechlin, Paul Ladmirault, and Roger-Ducasse. The *Berceuse* was introduced by Hélène Jourdan-Morhange and her sister-in-law Mme Raymond Charpentier at an S.M.I. recital on Dec. 13, 1922, in a program which included all of the homages to Fauré published by *La Revue Musicale.*

[8] Autograph dated Oct. 15, 1922, in the Music Division of the Bibliothèque Nationale.

conducted *Ma Mère l'Oye* and *La Valse,* and the following unsigned review appeared in *The Times* on April 16th:

M. Maurice Ravel was most cordially received, as was natural. Since the death of Debussy he has represented to English musicians the most vigorous current in modern French music. To the enterprise, daring and ingenuity common to many of the moderns he brings a graciousness of melody, a refinement of harmony and orchestration, which give his music a personal charm . . . His baton is not the magician's wand of the virtuoso conductor. He just stood there beating time and keeping watch, getting everything into its right place. The orchestra did their very best for him, not because they were charmed into it, but because he showed them so clearly what he wanted each member to play, when, and how. *Ma Mère l'Oye* has never sounded so simple and childlike; the introduction to *La Valse,* with its flitting scraps of waltz rhythm on bassoons and deep-toned instruments, had an unusual clarity, and both pieces were immensely enjoyed.

This review, or a similar one, prompted the following comment, written to Madame Jourdan-Morhange: "According to the newspapers, I am, if not a *great* conductor, at least a *good* one. I didn't expect as much." In another letter written from London, the composer offered the following suggestions for a forthcoming recital in Brussels:

1) The Sonata for Violin and Cello, if, of course, you have artists who have already worked on this piece, my most recent work, which is very difficult.

2) Either the String Quartet or the Trio (piano, violin, cello), without the participation of the author, who would be absolutely incapable of playing the piano part.

3) With a singer whom I would accompany, and several piano pieces which I would perform very badly, it seems to me the program would be complete.[9]

During the 1920s, friends and colleagues occasionally gathered at Le Belvédère for a Sunday afternoon luncheon. Old and new friends mingled in a convivial atmosphere, and the afternoon would often end with a long walk in the nearby Rambouillet Forest, where Ravel was intimately acquainted with every bird call and every byway. The guests included many of the composer's favorite interpreters, pianists Henri Gil-Marchex, Jacques Février, and Robert Casadesus, singers Jane Bathori, Marcelle Gerar, and Madeleine Grey, violinists Hélène Jourdan-Morhange and Jacques Thibaud. There were old friends such as Maurice and Nelly Delage, Ida and Cipa Godebski,

---

[9] Unpublished letter dated April 17, 1923, in the private collection of Jean Touzelet. The addressee of this letter was Désiré Defauw (1885–1960), the Belgian violinist, conductor, and impresario.

Monsieur and Madame Roland-Manuel, and younger musicians Vladimir Golschmann, Arthur Honegger, Jacques Ibert, Manuel Rosenthal, Germaine Tailleferre, and Alexandre Tansman. Other guests included the sculptor Léon Leyritz, whose fine bust of Ravel is found in the Paris Opéra, and the painter Luc-Albert Moreau, the husband of Hélène Jourdan-Morhange, who drew many sketches of the composer.

During the summer of 1923, the initial sketches of a sonata for violin and piano were completed at Le Belvédère, and in October, Ravel concertized in Amsterdam and London.[10] The winter of 1923 found him secluded in Le Belvédère, working on two projects which were completed in January, 1924: an orchestral version of the Hebraic folk song "Mejerke mein Suhn," which had been set in 1910, and *Ronsard à son âme*, published in *La Revue Musicale* (May, 1924).[11] Although *Tzigane* had been gestating for almost two years, the writing was completed in London just a few days before its première on April 26th. The all-Ravel program also featured *Ronsard à son âme*, which was performed by Marcelle Gerar, accompanied by the composer. The audience and the press were enthusiastic: the new song was encored, and from all accounts it appears that Jelly d'Aranyi's dazzling performance of *Tzigane* caused a sensation.[12]

In May, 1924, Ravel concertized in Madrid and Barcelona, marking his first trip beyond the Basque provinces of northern Spain. At the invitation of

[10] At a Ravel festival given in London on Oct. 18, 1923, the following announcement appeared in the program: "Daniel Mayer Company Ltd. beg to announce that they have arranged with M. Maurice Ravel to give a concert of his own works with the composer at the piano at the Aeolian Hall, on January 16 [1924] at 8:30. The first performance in the world will be given on that occasion, if ready, of the composer's new Sonata for Violin and Piano." As we know, the sonata was not ready in 1924, and three more years were to elapse before its completion.

[11] The other composers participating in the homage to Ronsard were Dukas, Roussel, Aubert, Caplet, Honegger, Roland-Manuel, and Delage.

[12] A decidedly minority opinion was voiced by the anonymous critic of *The Times* (April 28, 1924), who wrote in part:

"The *Histoires naturelles* were the most effective, but they are really matter for a super-refined music-hall programme. The new song, which was repeated, proved very jejune.

"The other new work, which had been completed only just in time for the performance, was the *Tzigane* for violin and piano. It is rhapsodical in the literal meaning of the word, being a series of episodes in the Hungarian manner strung together. One is puzzled to understand what M. Ravel is at. Either the work is a parody of the Liszt-Hubay-Brahms-Joachim school of Hungarian violin music and falls into the class of *La Valse*, or it is an attempt to get away from the limited sphere of his previous compositions to infuse into his work a little of the warm blood it needs."

Madrid's Philharmonic Society, he conducted *La Valse* and the transcriptions of Debussy's "Sarabande" and *Danse,* and in another recital, at Madrid's French Institute, he performed several of his piano pieces, sharing the program with Joaquín Turina. Following this brief tour, Ravel returned to Le Belvédère, and by July the orchestration of *Tzigane* was completed. Thanks to the prodding of Raoul Gunsbourg, the director of the Monte Carlo Opera, work on *L'Enfant et les sortilèges* was finally resumed. During a recent visit to Le Belvédère, Gunsbourg explained that *L'Heure espagnole* had been a triumph at Monte Carlo, and he insisted on having a new opera for the coming season. The result of his tenacity and enthusiasm was a formal contract, which stipulated the completion of a new opera by the end of the year. Ravel loathed deadlines, and by the autumn of 1924, he was well behind schedule in keeping his commitment. On September 2nd, he wrote to Jacques Durand: "I am working for Monte Carlo, not without anxiety when I compare what is done and what remains to be done: three scenes on the one hand, and two acts on the other!" On October 13th, he wrote to Ida Godebska: "I'm still hard at work . . . I'm up to the verses 'Wedgwood tea-pot and Chinese cup' which Colette has just sent me." By November, Ravel was working frantically at Le Belvédère: "I'm not budging," he wrote to Marcelle Gerar, "and I'm seeing no one but my frogs, my negroes, my shepherds, and various insects." Despite all his forebodings, Ravel managed to complete the opera with an extraordinary burst of speed and spent the early months of 1925 in Monte Carlo, retouching his score and supervising rehearsals. Although there were many last-minute corrections, the rehearsals progressed satisfactorily, due to the excellence of the performers as well as their enthusiastic reception of the difficult work. Writing to Jacques Durand on March 16th, the composer summed up his impressions as follows:

> Thanks to a marvelous orchestra, which loves the work, and a conductor *the like of whom I have never before encountered,* everything has worked its way out: this evening, a complete run-through. The roles are remarkably performed. Mlle Gaulet [*sic*], the child, looks like a six-year-old, and has a delightful voice. The cat duet will never be meowed better than by Madame Dubois and Warnery, who, moreover, sings the clock's air to perfection.[13]

[13] Autograph in the archives of Durand & Co. Vittorio de Sabata conducted the première of *L'Enfant et les sortilèges,* and the role of the child was sung by Marie-Thérèse Gauley. The opera was presented with a musical comedy in one act, *Un Début,* composed by Philippe Bellenot.

On March 21, 1925, some twenty-five years after Colette and Ravel first met, *L'Enfant et les sortilèges* received its world première. Henry Prunières called the opera "a masterpiece of imagination, fantasy, humor, and sensitivity," and declared it to be a worthy descendant of the eighteenth-century *opéra-ballet*. Following an enthusiastic reception at Monte Carlo, the work encountered a stormy reception at the Opéra-Comique in Paris. *"L'Enfant et les sortilèges* is playing twice a week before a packed but turbulent house," Colette wrote to her daughter. "The partisans of traditional music do not forgive Ravel, the composer, for his instrumental and vocal audacities. The modernists applaud and boo the others, and during the 'meowed' duet, there is a dreadful uproar." [14] The critics were equally divided. Writing in *La Liberté* (February 3, 1926), Robert Dezarnaux observed that the opera "is not convincing. It seems void of music! Why? Because the music never has the opportunity to expand. . . . The rapid succession [of differing styles] bewilders the mind, fatigues the ear—and, what is worse, is not amusing." Writing in *Le Temps* on the same day, Henry Malherbe came to the opposite conclusion:

> The most refined of our contemporary composers and the most penetrating of our authors have united in order to create a work of incomparable enchantment. . . . It is impossible, indeed, to enumerate all the carefully selected riches, all the subtle notations, the rhythmic forms, all the tours de force of this classical and spiritually sensual score, which is so ingeniously reconciled with contemporary taste.

Another favorable review was written by Arthur Honegger, who judged the cat's duet to be the most remarkable section of the score. The reviewer of *Comœdia* (February 2, 1926), appraised Ravel's abilities as follows:

> The agility of his technique dazzles us. A descendant of Couperin, Daquin, Dandrieu, and, in general, of the eighteenth-century French descriptive composers, he is surely considered today among the most essentially French of our masters. A chorus in the second part would be worthy of the most admirable contrapuntists of the Renaissance. Many musicians would wish, however, that his phenomenal facility were always exercised in the domain of sensibility.

A number of critics ventured to suggest that *L'Enfant et les sortilèges* would perhaps lead to further collaboration between Colette and Ravel. As it turned out, the work proved to be the sole collaboration between the artists, and, in addition, it marked the composer's farewell to opera.

---

[14] Printed in the catalogue *Colette*, Paris, Bibliothèque Nationale, 1973, p. 129.

Shortly after the completion of *L'Enfant et les sortilèges,* work was begun on a fresh commission, this one from the United States. Acting on behalf of the distinguished American Maecenas Elizabeth Sprague Coolidge, the cellist Hans Kindler cabled Ravel, requesting a song cycle set to a text of his own choice, with accompaniment, if possible, for flute, cello, and piano. During their student days, Ricardo Viñes had introduced his friend to the writings of the Creole poet Evariste-Désiré de Parny, and Ravel now turned to the *Chansons madécasses* (1787). The proposed instrumentation was willingly accepted, and by the summer of 1925, one of Parny's poems was set for voice and piano. In the fall, the song, "Aoua!," was performed by Jane Bathori and the composer at a recital sponsored by Mrs. Coolidge. As it was about to be encored, a minor composer of the day, Léon Moreau, stood up and shouted that he was leaving the hall, not wishing to hear such a disgraceful anti-colonial text repeated when French soldiers were fighting Abdel-Krim in Morocco! He was unaware, of course, that Parny's text predated the French Revolution. A formal letter of protest was sent to Ravel, who was nonplussed by the entire incident.

During the summer of 1925, several preoccupations disrupted progress on the *Chansons madécasses.* "My work? It's a nasty job," Ravel wrote to Nelly Delage. "I am correcting the orchestral proofs of *L'Enfant.* Although reviewed by a lot of people, there remain ten corrections per page." [15] At this time Ravel seriously contemplated writing an operetta, which he hoped to finish in several months. Unfortunately, the project remained in the planning stages. [16] During the winter of 1925, the composer was supervising rehearsals of *L'Enfant et les sortilèges* at the Opéra-Comique, and in December he wrote to Mrs. Coolidge apologizing for his lateness in completing the *Chansons madécasses.* A forthcoming concert tour was only a delay, he explained, and the commission would be completed upon returning to Montfort l'Amaury. [17] Ravel now set out on an extended tour of Belgium, Germany, Scandinavia (Copenhagen, Stockholm, and Oslo), England, and Scotland. In addition to many concerts of his works, in which he appeared as soloist, accompanist, and conductor, he spent several days in Brussels

[15] In addition to Lucien Garban, Ravel was assisted by his younger colleagues Pierre-Octave Ferroud and Arthur Hoérée.

[16] The text was to be written by Mayrargues, with Maud Loty in the leading role. See Roland-Manuel, *Ravel,* p. 117.

[17] Unpublished letter dated Dec. 19, 1925, in the Music Division of the Library of Congress. The letter indicates that at this stage Ravel was still planning to set only two of Parny's texts.

directing rehearsals of *L'Enfant et les sortilèges*. A number of recitals were presented with the composer's good friends Georges Jean-Aubry, who gave several lectures on contemporary music, and the British singer Louise Alvar. In Copenhagen, on February 2, 1926, Ravel led a performance of Mozart's Fortieth Symphony, thus marking a rare occasion in which he conducted the music of another composer. The performance was greeted with enthusiasm, as was the remainder of the program which consisted of *Ma Mère l'Oye*, the transcriptions of Debussy's "Sarabande" and *Danse, Shéhérazade*, with Mrs. Alvar as soloist, and *La Valse*. Following the concert, at a gala soirée, the composer and his colleagues were introduced to the leading musical personalities in the Danish capital. In several chamber music recitals in England and Scotland, Ravel accompanied some younger colleagues, among them the violinist Zino Francescatti, who performed the *Berceuse* and *Tzigane*. From Glasgow, the composer returned to Brussels in order to attend a special performance of *L'Enfant et les sortilèges*, which took place on March 4th. Following the performance, at the Théâtre Royal de la Monnaie, he appeared on stage and was decorated by the king of Belgium "Chevalier de l'Ordre de Léopold."

Following this highly successful tour, which lasted just over two months, Ravel returned to Le Belvédère, and by April the *Chansons madécasses* were completed. The song cycle was introduced in Paris at the Salle Erard on June 13, 1926, with soloists Jane Bathori, Alfredo Casella, piano, M. Baudouin, flute, and Hans Kindler, cello. The program, which consisted entirely of chamber works commissioned by Mrs. Coolidge, included Ernest Bloch's Suite for Viola and Piano, and Charles Loeffler's *Cantique au soleil,* for soprano and chamber orchestra, which was specially composed for the inauguration of the new music room in the Library of Congress. The *Chansons madécasses* were greeted with acclaim by the audience and by the critics. In a glowing review, Henry Prunières commented upon their wide emotional range, and made the following observation with regard to Ravel:

> of any other important contemporary musician in Europe, who, as much as Ravel, succeeds in transforming himself continually in this manner without apparent crisis. In recent years Ravel's art has become more linear, thinner in texture, more contrapuntal. He condenses his thought in forms of increasingly rigorous simplicity.

The critic summed up by calling the *Chansons madécasses* a "genuine masterpiece." During the remainder of 1926, the Sonata for Violin and Piano approached its concluding stages. At this time, Ravel was giving instruction in composition to Manuel Rosenthal, who was just beginning his career and who soon became an intimate associate. In November, the composer participated in a series of recitals in Switzerland, which were devoted to his works, and in February, 1927, he completed *Rêves* (poem by Léon-Paul Fargue). The song was commissioned by the author Marcel Raval for a special issue of *Les Feuilles Libres* (June, 1927), honoring Fargue.[18]

In the spring of 1927, Jacques Durand presented two recitals of contemporary music, featuring compositions recently published by Durand and Company. The programs included works by Louis Aubert, Gabriel Pierné, Ravel, Roger-Ducasse, Roussel, and Schmitt. Following some four years of intermittent work, the Sonata for Violin and Piano was finally ready and was performed by Georges Enesco and the composer.[19] The reviews were favorable, with most attention focusing upon the second movement, "Blues." The lyricism and simplicity of the first movement, coupled with Enesco's brilliant performance of the finale engendered a long ovation. Just after completing the Sonata, Ravel wrote a short fanfare for a ballet *L'Eventail de Jeanne,* which was commissioned by the Parisian hostess Madame Jeanne Dubost. In all, ten composers contributed to the ballet, which was performed in Madame Dubost's salon with a small orchestra conducted by Roger Désormière.[20] The summer of 1927 found Ravel vacationing at Saint-Jean-de-Luz, and in the fall he made a brief concert appearance in Amsterdam. After several years of intermittent negotiations, an extended concert tour of North America was now fully prepared. In late December, the *S.S. France* sailed from Le Havre, arriving in New York on January 4, 1928. On board was a fifty-two-year-old composer, who was about to discover a new continent, and who would soon plunge into the most exhilarating tour of his entire career.

[18] Other contributors included Federico Mompou, Picasso, and Paul Valéry. *Rêves* was introduced by Jane Bathori and Ravel in March, 1927, and was favorably received. See *Le Ménestrel* (March 25, 1927), p. 137.

[19] The Sonata is dedicated to Hélène Jourdan-Morhange, and Ravel undoubtedly would have wished her to introduce the work. Her brilliant career was tragically cut off by the onset of motor cramps. Because of her friendship with Colette, she became interested in writing and completed an important book of souvenirs, *Ravel et nous*. She also collaborated with pianist Vlado Perlemuter in another work, *Ravel d'après Ravel*. Perlemuter was coached by Ravel, and in 1929 he performed the complete works for piano solo in Paris.

[20] The official première took place in March, 1929, at the Paris Opéra. See below, pp. 238–39.

CHAPTER SIX

1928-1937
Concluding Years

I was forgetting the concert which the Boston Symphony played in New York, devoted to my works. I had to appear on stage: a standing audience of 3500; a tremendous ovation, climaxed by whistling.

LETTER, RAVEL TO HIS BROTHER, JANUARY, 1928

Don't you think this theme has an insistent quality? I'm going to try and repeat it a number of times without any development, gradually increasing the orchestra as best I can.

A COMMENT BY RAVEL ON THE GENESIS OF THE BOLÉRO

RAVEL'S FOUR-MONTH TOUR of the United States and Canada proved to be a phenomenal success. The critics were lavish in their approbation, and the audiences enthusiastic. At an all-Ravel program given by Koussevitzky and the Boston Symphony in Carnegie Hall, the entire audience arose in applause at the composer's appearance. Deeply touched by this spontaneous gesture, Ravel turned to Alexandre Tansman and observed, "You know, this doesn't happen to me in Paris." The tour was arranged largely through the efforts of pianist E. Robert Schmitz, president of the Pro Musica Society, an organization devoted to chamber music.[1] Its numerous chapters were spread throughout the United States, and as he had frequently done in Europe, Ravel performed the Sonatine, or selections from the *Miroirs,* and accompanied his songs. In addition, he appeared as guest conductor of the leading symphony orchestras, among them the Boston, Chicago, Cleveland, New York, and San Francisco. Finally, there were a number of private engagements at various exclusive soirées. Although the itinerary was exhausting, Ravel managed to rest on the long train rides which brought him to some twenty-five cities from New York to California and from Canada to Texas. The final leg of the tour included New Orleans, Houston, Phoenix, Buffalo, New York City, Montreal, and back to New York for embarkation on the *S.S. Paris,* which sailed for Le Havre on April 21. In a colorful letter to his brother, the composer could scarcely contain his enthusiasm:

> The Copley-Plaza, Boston
> January 13, 1928

My dear little Edward,

if I return to Europe alive, it will prove that I am long-lived! In short, until now, I've survived, and my manager assures me that I have gone through the worst. As soon as we arrived in the harbor, a swarm of journalists and cartoonists invaded the boat, with cameras and movie cameras. I had to leave them for a moment in order to see our entry into the port: it was even a bit too late, but splendid all the same. I wasn't even able to practice the piano a little during my stay in New York (4 days which seemed like 4 months). As soon as I settled down at the Langdon Hotel, a little nothing of a hotel which has only 12 stories (I was on the 8th), and delightfully comfortable (an entire apartment), the telephone didn't stop ringing. Every minute they would bring me baskets of flowers, and of the most delicious fruits in the world. Rehearsals, teams of journalists (photographs, movies, caricaturists) relieving one another every hour, letters, invitations to which my manager replies for me, receptions. In the evening, relaxation: dance halls, Negro theaters, gigantic movie houses, etc. I hardly know New York by day, cooped up in taxis in order to go to appointments of all sorts. I was even in a film, with make-up two centimeters thick. . . . I was forgetting the concert which the Boston Symphony played in New York, devoted to my works. I had to appear on stage: a standing audience of 3500; a tremendous ovation, climaxed by whistling. Sunday evening, a private concert and a gallop in evening dress for the train to Boston.

---

[1] The technical matters of itinerary, publicity, and so on, were handled by the Bogue-Laberge concert management in New York, and France's Association Française d'Expansion et d'Echanges Artistiques.

January 14

I continue: I have been relatively undisturbed here during the day between orchestral rehearsals (a marvelous orchestra). The day before yesterday a concert at Cambridge, yesterday at Boston: a triumph (they thought I looked English!) Koussevitzky told me that I was the greatest living French conductor. . . . When I think that I had to conduct the *Rapsodie espagnole* at sight! I'm doing it again tonight, returning immediately to New York for tomorrow's concert, setting out again for Chicago where I will remain a few days, and from there on to Texas. Several free moments have enabled me to write to you; today, no receptions. Those at Cambridge and Boston were less exhausting than the one given by Mrs. Thomas Edison in New York: 2 or 300 persons filing before me and speaking English, more often French (it's amazing how many people speak our language here). As in New York, in the evening, relaxation: dance halls, Chinese theater, etc. Attached are several clippings. Keep them. Affectionately to all, I embrace you

Maurice [2]

Ravel's initial chamber music recital took place at New York's Gallo Theater on January 15. The program included the String Quartet and the Sonatine, which were well known to New York audiences, and the *Introduction et Allegro* and the Sonata for Violin and Piano, which were comparatively unfamiliar. The Sonata was performed by Joseph Szigeti, who made the following perceptive observation: "Ravel was somewhat nonchalant about his piano-playing; 'unconcerned' might better describe his attitude. It was the confidence of the creative artist that determined his stand with respect to our task. It was as if he said: 'What of it, whether we play it a little better, or in a less polished and brilliant fashion? The work is set down, in its definitive form, and that is all that *really* matters.' " [3]

Writing in the *New York Times* on January 16, Olin Downes commented:

Nothing could have been more typical of the precision, economy and refinement of this music than the slight, aristocratic, gray-haired and self-contained gentleman who bore himself with such simplicity on the platform; presenting his music with a characteristic reticence and modesty; well content, as it were, to give an accounting of what he had done, and to leave his listeners to their own conclusions. And, indeed, his achievement speaks for itself.

Never to have composed in undue haste; never to have offered the public a piece of unfinished work; to have experienced life as an observant and keenly in-

[2] Printed in *The Music Forum,* 3 (1973), 332. (Autograph in the private collection of Mme Alexandre Taverne.)

[3] Szigeti, *With Strings Attached,* 2nd ed. (New York: Knopf, 1967), p. 139.

terested beholder, and to have fashioned certain of its elements into exquisite shapes of art that embody the essence of certain French traditions, is a goal worth the gaining. Mr. Ravel has pursued his way as an artist quietly and very well. He has disdained superficial or meretricious success. He has been his own most unsparing critic. The audience was appreciative of the opportunity to welcome the man and the composer.

Among the many highlights of the trip were a visit to the home of Edgar Allan Poe, an excursion to Niagara Falls, and a visit to the Grand Canyon, whose majesty and beauty Ravel found overwhelming. He saw old friends such as Bartók and Varèse and was introduced to literally hundreds of musicians and admirers, among them George Gershwin, Fritz Kreisler, and Paul Whiteman. Several evenings were spent in Harlem listening to jazz with Gershwin and Alexandre Tansman, and in Hollywood Ravel posed for photographs with Douglas Fairbanks and Mary Pickford. He was fascinated by the dynamism of American life, its huge cities, its skyscrapers, and its advanced technology, and was impressed by the Negro spirituals, the jazz, and the excellence of American orchestras.[4] In Houston, at the invitation of the Rice Institute, Ravel gave a public lecture on contemporary music, and one of the topics he discussed was his view of American music (see Plates 13 and 14).

Before closing this short address I wish to say again how very happy I am in visiting your country, and all the more so because my journey is enabling me to become still more conversant with those elements which are contributing to the gradual formation of a veritable school of American music. That this school will become notable in its final evolution I have not the slightest doubt, and I am also convinced that it will realize a national expression quite as different from the music of Europeans as you yourselves are different from them. . . . At all events, may this national American music of yours embody a great deal of the rich and diverting rhythm of your jazz, a great deal of the emotional expression in your blues, and a great deal of the sentiment and spirit characteristic of your popular

[4] In the course of an interview, Ravel's comments were quoted as follows: "Your orchestras are the best anywhere. This is because of their international membership, and the standards of individual excellence demanded of the players. Your brass choirs have the depth and richness of tone that ours lack, because of the prevailing superiority of the instruments themselves and the fact that most of the players of these instruments are Germans. They produce a certain nobility of tone of which musicians of other nations are seldom capable, and when you hear a trumpet it is not a cornet-à-piston. Your wood-wind choirs, in a majority, are predominantly French, and the French wood-wind players are the best in the world." *New York Times,* Feb. 26, 1928.

melodies and songs, worthily deriving from, and in turn contributing to, a noble heritage in music.

The success of Ravel's North American tour brought his international reputation to its zenith. Upon arrival at Le Havre on April 27, he was greeted by Edouard, the Delages, and several other close friends. Following a brief vacation, full activity was resumed. In June, the S.M.I. presented a special Ravel festival with the participation of the composer and several younger colleagues, Madeleine Grey, violinist Claude Lévy, Maurice Maréchal, and the American pianist Beveridge Webster. Soon after, with the efficient planning of Marcelle Gerar, some forty friends and colleagues gathered at Le Belvédère for a Sunday afternoon luncheon to honor the composer's triumphant tour. Ravel was delighted to see so many close friends, and the festivities finally ended in a cabaret about 4 a.m. By this point, invitations of all sorts were pouring in: a concert tour in Spain, a request from Oxford University to accept an honorary doctoral degree, a series of concerts in Holland, a recital of chamber music in Bordeaux. In addition, before leaving for North America, Ravel had promised to complete a ballet for his good friend Ida Rubinstein. Madame Rubinstein requested an orchestral transcription of six pieces from Albéniz's *Iberia,* and the initial sketches of "Rondeña" were under way when, much to his vexation, Ravel was informed that the Spanish conductor Enrique Arbós had already orchestrated the pieces, and copyright laws forbade anyone else from transcribing them. Upon learning about the situation, Arbós graciously offered to renounce his exclusive copyright, and it appeared that the situation was saved. But now Ravel changed his mind and decided it would be more expeditious to orchestrate one of his own compositions. It turned out, finally, that he was to compose an original work. During a brief vacation in Saint-Jean-de-Luz, just before going for a morning swim with Gustave Samazeuilh, Ravel went to the piano and played a melody with one finger. "Don't you think this theme has an insistent quality?" he asked. "I'm going to try and repeat it a number of times without any development, gradually increasing the orchestra as best I can." Returning to Le Belvédère, he began work on this fresh project, which was entitled *Fandango.* The title was soon changed to *Boléro,* and the ballet was completed in about five months. The new work was introduced at the Paris Opéra by Madame Rubinstein's troupe in November, 1928, as Walther Straram conducted a program of music by Bach transcribed by Honegger, and works by Schubert and Liszt orchestrated by Milhaud. Although well received, the *Boléro* was soon to become incredibly popular, much to the surprise of its composer, who predicted that the leading symphony orchestras would refuse to program it.[5] In addition to the nature of the music itself, several factors appear to have contributed to its striking popularity. In January, 1930, Ravel recorded the *Boléro* with the Lamoureux Orchestra, and thereafter he frequently conducted it in the concert hall, with his moderate, quasi-metronomic tempo. Several months later, Arturo Toscanini led the New York Philharmonic in a performance of the work at the Paris Opéra. An uproar occurred when Ravel refused to acknowledge Toscanini's gesture to his box, and in a heated discussion backstage, he told the Maestro that his tempo was ridiculously fast. Toscanini observed that a bolero is not a funeral march and that his interpretation had been awarded a standing ovation by the capacity audience. Although the men eventually shook hands, the *Boléro* had now become a *cause célèbre*. Finally, following many performances on the radio and innumerable transcriptions, in 1934 Paramount released a film entitled *Bolero,* starring Carole Lombard and George Raft, in which the music played an important role. Today, the *Boléro* remains Ravel's most widely known composition.

Shortly after completing the *Boléro,* Ravel participated in a recital of his chamber music at London's Aeolian Hall,[6] and several days later, on October 23, 1928, he appeared in academic garb at Oxford University, which conferred upon him the degree of Doctor of Music, *honoris causa.* Speaking in Latin, the public orator compared his achievements to "colors worthy of Parrhasius," and referred to the composer of *Daphnis et Chloé* as a "charming artist, who persuades all cultured people that Pan is not dead, and that even now Mount Helicon is green." Following the ceremony, the guest of honor conducted the *Introduction et Allegro* before a large gathering, as part of an all-Ravel program given in the Town Hall. In November, together with Madeleine Grey and Claude Lévy, Ravel undertook a hectic tour in Spain, appearing in nine cities within some eighteen days. In addition to an enthusiastic reception in Granada, the composer was pleased to visit with his old friend Manuel de Falla. In Málaga, the audience indicated

[5] According to the contractual arrangements, Ida Rubinstein was given the exclusive right to perform *Boléro* for three years in the theater and one year in the concert hall. Thus, in October, 1929, the work fell into the public domain in the concert hall, and was soon thereafter performed and recorded extensively.

[6] Presented by Gordon Bryan, the recital proved so successful that a second program with the composer's participation was given in Jan., 1929.

its disapproval by exiting discreetly, leaving an empty hall at the conclusion of the recital. Undaunted, Ravel remarked to Madeleine Grey that he appreciated an audience with the courage of its convictions. At the French Embassy in Madrid, the composer lost his place during a performance of the Sonatine, skipping from the exposition of the first movement to the coda of the finale. The audience applauded heartily, much to his delight. Shortly after this tour, Ravel served on the jury of the International Society for Contemporary Music,[7] which met in Geneva, and a brief concert appearance in Bordeaux rounded out a year of extraordinary activity.

In the early months of 1929, Ravel participated in several festivals of his music given in England, Switzerland, and Austria, and following all of these exhausting travels, he looked forward to a long vacation. Still suffering from periodic insomnia, he found it more difficult than ever to undertake fresh projects. Since 1928, a piano concerto had been contemplated, as well as an opera, *Jeanne d'Arc,* based on the novel by Joseph Delteil. Detailed plans for the opera were discussed with Jacques Rouché, and the décor was confided to Jean Hugo, but it appears that the project was not even partially sketched.[8] Much of the summer and fall of 1929 was spent in the Basque country. During this time, the *Menuet antique* was orchestrated and the proofs of the *Boléro* and *Pictures at an Exhibition* were corrected. These projects were carried out in relatively short order, and work was resumed on the piano concerto. The concerto was soon interrupted, however, by a commission from the Austrian pianist Paul Wittgenstein, who had lost his right arm in World War I.[9] Intrigued by the challenge of writing a concerto for the left hand, Ravel completed the work in some nine months.[10] As the concerto approached completion, he paid a brief visit to the Basque country in order to participate in a special festive event. On August 24, 1930, the

[7] Founded in 1922, the society sponsored annual festivals, which offered an important cross section of modern European and American music.

[8] About this time, Ravel contemplated reworking some of the passages of Chabrier's *Le Roi malgré lui,* in order to increase their effectiveness, but the project was not realized.

[9] In addition to his own compositions and arrangements for the left hand, Wittgenstein commissioned works from many composers, among them Benjamin Britten, Hindemith, Prokofiev, and Richard Strauss.

[10] In addition to the concerti, Ravel mentioned a project entitled *"Dédale 39,* which as you can guess is an airplane—and an airplane in *C.* " (Unpublished letter to Manuel de Falla, written in March, 1930.) Another projected work inspired by aviation was to be a symphonic poem, *Icare* (unpublished letter to Manuel Rosenthal). It appears that both works were not even partially sketched.

village of Ciboure honored its distinguished native son with a commemorative plaque placed on his birth house, now on the newly inaugurated Quai Maurice Ravel. The composer was deeply touched by the festivities, which included a pelota match and a special concert of his works, the proceeds of which were donated to charity. The concert included choreographic interpretations of "Alborada del gracioso" and the "Rigaudon" from *Le Tombeau de Couperin,* which were apparently carried out with Ravel's approbation. Just after the completion of the Concerto for the Left Hand, a preliminary hearing of the work took place at Le Belvédère. Unable to perform the solo part as written, Ravel played it with two hands and then played the orchestral part for Paul Wittgenstein. "He was not an outstanding pianist," Wittgenstein recalled, "and I wasn't overwhelmed by the composition. It always takes me a while to grow into a difficult work. I suppose Ravel was disappointed, and I was sorry, but I had never learned to pretend. Only much later, after I'd studied the concerto for months, did I become fascinated by it and realize what a great work it was." [11]

Upon completing the Concerto for the Left Hand, Ravel resumed work on the G major concerto, hoping to finish it within several months. As it turned out, a full year was to elapse before its termination. During this period, in February, 1931, the composer led the Orchestre Symphonique de Paris in *Le Tombeau de Couperin* and *Boléro,* sharing the all-Ravel program with his old friend Pierre Monteux. In March, he participated in another program of his works, a benefit concert for Belgium's disabled war veterans, held in the Palais des Beaux-Arts in Brussels. At an elegant soirée given in his honor, Ravel was introduced to Respighi, and the following day he was the guest of honor at an afternoon tea sponsored by the Society of Phonic Arts and Sciences. In the presence of a large audience, recordings of the *Menuet antique, Introduction et Allegro, La Valse,* and *Boléro* were heard, as well as excerpts from *Shéhérazade, L'Heure espagnole, Ma Mère l'Oye,* and *Daphnis et Chloé.*

As the concerto in G major approached completion, Calvocoressi published the following information communicated to him by the composer:

> Planning the two piano concertos simultaneously was an interesting experience. The one in which I shall appear as the interpreter is a concerto in the truest sense of the word: I mean that it is written very much in the same spirit as those of

[11] Stelio Dubbiosi, "The Piano Music of Maurice Ravel," Diss., New York Univ. School of Education, 1967, p. 132.

101

Mozart and Saint-Saëns. The music of a concerto should, in my opinion, be light-hearted and brilliant, and not aim at profundity or at dramatic effects. It has been said of certain great classics that their concertos were written not "for," but "against" the piano.[12] I heartily agree. I had intended to entitle this concerto "Divertissement." Then it occurred to me that there was no need to do so, because the very title "Concerto" should be sufficiently clear.

The concerto for left hand alone is very different. It contains many jazz effects, and the writing is not so light. In a work of this kind, it is essential to give the impression of a texture no thinner than that of a part written for both hands. For the same reason, I resorted to a style that is much nearer to that of the more solemn kind of traditional concerto.

Not only did Ravel plan to be the soloist in the G Major Concerto but he contemplated a world tour, which would have included Europe, North and South America, and the Orient. Because of his declining health,[13] he conducted the Concerto with Marguerite Long as soloist, and the projected tour was limited to Europe. In November, 1931, the manuscript was given to Madame Long and interpretative details were carefully worked out in the ensuing weeks. The première of the Concerto took place on January 14, 1932, at the Salle Pleyel as part of a Ravel festival. The composer shared the podium with the young Portuguese conductor Pedro de Freitas-Branco, who was making his Parisian debut. The evening was a brilliant success, and the critics were unanimous in their approbation of the Concerto, noting the brilliance of the first movement, the tender poetry of the second, and the dazzling verve of the finale.[14] Emile Vuillermoz tempered his enthusiasm as follows:

> Once again, I wish to protest against the habit, more and more frequently indulged in, of attempting at all costs to bring a composer before the public in a part

[12] Ravel had in mind the concerti of Brahms. See *Daily Telegraph,* July 11, 1931.

[13] In a letter to Henri Rabaud, dated Nov. 20, 1931, Ravel wrote in part: "Kindly excuse me for the Osiris competition: my concerto is finished, and not far from being so myself, I would risk falling asleep at the first candidate. I have been ordered complete rest, and am being treated with injections of serum." (Unpublished autograph in the private collection of Jean Touzelet.)

[14] In a decidedly minority opinion, Henry Prunières took exception to Mme Long's interpretation, suggesting that it was technically correct, but lacked sensitivity and poetry. His negative critique engendered a formal reply from Ravel, who insisted that her interpretation fully revealed his intentions and should be considered a model for future performers. See *La Revue Musicale* (April, 1932), p. 320. As Mme Long subsequently recorded the Concerto, the reader may form his own opinion.

which he is incapable of filling. M. Ravel is continually brought out as a pianist or as a conductor, whilst he cannot possibly shine in either of these two specialities. The Portuguese conductor much more efficaciously presented the works he conducted than did Ravel the scores confided to him. His *Pavane* was unutterably slow, his *Boléro* dry and badly timed. And the accompaniment of the concerto lacked clarity and elasticity. . . .

But there is only praise for the composer of all these delicate, subtle works, the orchestration of which abounds in amusing and profound inventions, and which is really of inimitable originality of writing and of thought. The new concerto is worthy of the other masterpieces that we owe to Ravel. . . . The work is very easy to understand and gives the impression of extreme youth. It is wonderful to see how this master has more freshness of inspiration than the young people of today who flog themselves uselessly in order to try to discover, in laborious comedy or caricature, a humor that is not in their temperament.

Vuillermoz summed up by calling the concert "the finest artistic manifestation of the season." [15] A few days after the concert, disobeying his doctor's orders, Ravel undertook a taxing three-month tour with Marguerite Long, performing the Concerto in some twenty cities, among them Brussels, Vienna, Bucharest, Prague, London, Warsaw, Berlin, Amsterdam, and Budapest. In many cities the finale had to be repeated, because of extended ovations by the large and enthusiastic audiences. In London, Ravel shared the podium with Sir Malcolm Sargent, in Berlin with Wilhelm Furtwängler, and in Bucharest he was received in private audience by the royal family and decorated by the king.

Following this triumphant tour, Ravel returned to the Basque country for an extended rest. Two recent commissions were being contemplated, a ballet for Ida Rubinstein, *Morgiane,* based on the tale of Ali Baba and the Forty Thieves, and music for a film, *Don Quixote,* with Chaliapin in the title role. While only fragmentary sketches of *Morgiane* were committed to paper, the music for *Don Quixote* proved to be the composer's swan song. In the summer of 1932, Ravel began to set three texts by Paul Morand, which were scheduled to be sung by Chaliapin. The composer and author were approached for two main reasons: firstly, for their respective talents, and secondly, of equal importance, as a means of inducing sponsors for the film. By this point, Ravel was internationally regarded as one of Europe's foremost composers. His interest in Spanish music had been amply proven, and for many years he had even been thinking of an opera based on Cervan-

[15] *Christian Science Monitor,* Feb. 13, 1932.

tes' novel. Paul Morand was well-known as a versatile author, a skilled diplomat and world traveller, whose novels captured the subtleties of many cultures with clarity and realism.[16] As Ravel was late in completing his score, the assignment was turned over to Jacques Ibert, who hurriedly composed the background music and five songs for Chaliapin. Thus, Ravel's songs, *Don Quichotte à Dulcinée,* were introduced in the concert hall. Despite serious financial problems, the director, Georg W. Pabst, managed to complete the film, in which Chaliapin towers over the other performers.[17]

In October, 1932, Ravel was involved in a taxi collison in Paris and suffered several facial wounds and chest bruises. Although he endured considerable pain, his condition was not serious, and in December he felt well enough to participate in a concert of his works given in Basel.

The long-awaited Parisian debut of the Concerto for the Left Hand took place on January 17, 1933, with Paul Wittgenstein as soloist and the composer leading the Orchestre Symphonique de Paris. The remainder of the all-Ravel program was conducted by Roger Désormière. Most of the reviews focused upon the new Concerto, which was an instantaneous success. One critic spoke of its "sumptuous richness" and "astonishing variety," while another observed that Wittgenstein's left hand was miraculously transformed into two, one singing and the other accompanying. Henry Prunières called the pianist a "prodigious virtuoso," and summed up as follows:

> Even those, who, as I, admire all of Ravel's achievements, feel a certain regret at so many Pyrrhic victories, and think still in all that the author of *Daphnis* should indeed have been able to let us observe more frequently what he was guarding in his heart, instead of accrediting the legend that his brain alone invented these admirable sonorous phantasmagorias. From the opening measures, we are plunged into a world in which Ravel has but rarely introduced us.[18]

Shortly after their collaboration in Paris, composer and pianist were scheduled to perform the Concerto in Monte Carlo, but owing to his deterio-

[16] Morand has written in virtually every literary genre and was awarded the Prix Combat in 1966. See *Combat* (March 8, 1966).

[17] In the preface to his novel *France la Doulce,* Morand explained that he would describe the "financial jungle" of certain cinematic milieus and emphasized that his account would be understated rather than exaggerated. According to an article in *Paris-Midi* (June 13, 1933), Ravel sued the film company for damages, but apparently nothing came of the matter.

[18] *La Revue Musicale* (Feb., 1933), p. 128. Because of a dispute between pianist and composer over the interpretation of the Concerto, the world première was performed by Wittgenstein in Vienna on January 5, 1932, with Robert Heger conducting the Vienna Symphony Orchestra (see *New York Times,* April 17, 1932).

rating health, Ravel asked Paul Paray to replace him. He was present at the performance, however, and acknowledged an exceptionally warm ovation.

Following many years of periodic insomnia and occasional bouts with neurasthenia, Ravel's health took a sudden turn for the worse during the summer of 1933. While vacationing at Saint-Jean-de-Luz, he found himself incapable of coordinating his motions when swimming and encountered unusual difficulty in writing. The physicians who were consulted spoke of ataxia, the inability to coordinate voluntary muscular movements, and aphasia, involving difficulty in speech and a partial loss of memory. Ravel appeared overworked, exhausted, and, of course, fearful of this ominous development.[19] Following several months of complete rest his condition improved, and in November, 1933, he led the Pasdeloup Orchestra in *Boléro* and the Concerto in G Major with Marguerite Long as soloist. This engagement appears to have marked the composer's final public performance. About this time, he regretfully had to reject a proposal for an extended concert tour in Russia, offered by the Soviet government. By now he was too ill to undertake such an exhausting trip, and thus he was never to visit the country whose music had played such a key role in his artistic development.

Following a difficult winter, Ravel stayed at a Swiss rest home during the early months of 1934. Once again, his health improved slightly, and in a letter to Lucien Garban, he mentioned that he had given the manuscript of *Don Quichotte à Dulcinée* to Martial Singher, and was hoping to conduct the first performance of the song cycle.[20] M. Singher kindly wrote to me as follows:

> Ravel gave me the manuscript of the songs after a lunch in the house of a common friend M. Lacombe, professor of mathematics. . . . To a young singer with only three operatic seasons to his credit, and very little concert experience, it was a staggering and unbelievable event. Previous commitments, and a summer vacation in my home town of Biarritz delayed any action on the songs until the fall. I surrendered the manuscript to Durand publishers, more precisely to M. Garban who seemed to be in charge of its publication, and whom I saw later doing the correcting of the proofs. Very soon (November?) I was called upon to record the songs

[19] Professor Alajouanine, who examined Ravel during the last few years of his life, observed that the composer's ability to understand speech was far superior to his ability to speak or write. As the aphasia progressed, the reading of music became difficult and finally impossible.

[20] Letter dated April 22, 1934 (see Orenstein, *A Ravel Reader,* p. 321). The letter is printed and was written with the assistance of a dictionary. It is one of the last letters that Ravel was able to write.

for "La Voix de son Maître," and the songs were performed directly with orchestra, before being published or performed with the piano arrangement, for that recording. Ravel was present at the recording session and made several remarks about wrong notes, tempi, and dynamics, both for the voice and the instruments. One notation which does not appear in the published songs is a ritardando, in the "Chanson romanesque," on the three eighth notes on the words "dessous le" (blâme) and again on the words "vous bénis" (sant). The song was then called "Chanson romantique," and it is only at the proofs correction that the name was rightly modified. . . . Before the songs were printed, Ravel was gracious enough to ask me whether I would be pleased if he dedicated them to me. Actually blushing, I answered that I had not served him well enough or long enough for deserving such an honor. He laughed lightly and said, "In this case, would you care to choose one of the three songs as being your favorite?" I chose the "Chanson épique," and he decided to dedicate it to me. But he was already unable to write the dedication with his own hand, and I saw my name in print on the song when it was published. He commentated later that "of course, I had chosen the right one!" [21]

The song cycle was introduced in December, 1934, as Paul Paray conducted the Colonne Orchestra in a program of works by Franck, Mozart, and Borodin. Following a performance of Franck's Symphony and several operatic arias sung by Martial Singher, the second part of the program consisted of *Ma Mère l'Oye, Don Quichotte à Dulcinée,* and *La Valse.* The songs were greeted with acclaim, and Ravel was brought on stage to acknowledge an extended ovation. The press was equally enthusiastic, and judging from the lavish encomiums, it appears that his art was now beyond criticism. Thus, if his earliest works were generally greeted with suspicion and hostility, beginning with *Shéhérazade* and the String Quartet, the critics were hopelessly divided. During the postwar years, positive commentary usually outweighed the negative, but following the trip to North America, the scales had totally shifted, and French critics were virtually unanimous in their praise, if not adulation. Ravel's view of critics and criticism was perhaps best summarized in a letter to Charles Koechlin: "I did indeed read the article . . . it's an incoherent chattering, no sillier than so many others. Didn't I represent to the critics for a long time the most perfect example of insensitivity and lack of emotion? That was of no importance. And the success they have given me in the past few years is just as unimportant." [22]

[21] Letter dated Sept. 3, 1965. Printed with the kind permission of Martial Singher.

[22] Unpublished autograph dated Oct. 21, 1924, in the private collection of Yves Koechlin. In the course of an article on Debussy's *Images* (*Les Cahiers d'Aujourd'hui,* Feb., 1913), Ravel

The anguish and tragedy of Ravel's final years were perhaps best explained by the composer when he told Ernest Ansermet that his mind was replete with ideas, but, when he wished to write them down, they vanished. In January, 1935, the composer authorized Durand to publish a statement praising the "pathetic strength" of Nicolas Obouhov's recent work *Le Livre de vie,* and in February, he attended an all-Ravel program given by the Pasdeloup Orchestra conducted by Piero Coppola, with soloists Lily Laskine and Martial Singher. The program included a performance of *Ronsard à son âme,* with orchestral accompaniment. Incapable of notating the score, Ravel had dictated the transcription to Manuel Rosenthal and Lucien Garban. Shortly after the concert, thanks to the behind-the-scenes generosity of Ida Rubinstein, the composer set out on a trip to Spain and North Africa, accompanied by Léon Leyritz. Their itinerary included Madrid, Algeciras, Tangiers, and Marrakech, where they spent three weeks. Ravel was enchanted by the exotic scenery in Morocco, and unexpectedly found himself able to notate several sketches of *Morgiane.* These were to be the very last notes to come from his pen. During the trip, several colorful festivities were given in his honor, and every opportunity was taken to hear Moorish and Arabic music. Amid the exotic scales, quarter tones, and the wail of the muezzin calling the faithful to prayer, Ravel was pleasantly surprised one day to hear a young man whistling the *Boléro.* Following this wonderful voyage, which appeared to spring out of a page from the *Arabian Nights,* the return trip was made through Seville and Cordova. In August, the two companions set out from Saint-Jean-de-Luz for Spain, this time visiting the Cantabrian coast. This trip marked the composer's farewell to Spain, a country he had often called his second musical homeland. Although diverted by these travels, Ravel's condition continued to worsen. His friends watched over him, taking him to concerts and doing their best to keep him occupied. He frequently stayed with Edouard at Levallois Perret, with the Delages, or with Monsieur and Madame Jacques Meyer, and at Le Belvédère Madame Révelot catered to his every wish. Many friends and neighbors came to visit,

---

defended his elder colleague's work, and attacked the criticisms of Gaston Carraud and Pierre Lalo. On another occasion (*Les Nouvelles Littéraires,* April 2, 1927), he summed up his long-standing opposition to Lalo's aesthetics: "Speaking of Debussy's marvelous *Images,* M. Lalo wrote in 1910 that 'there comes a time when these trifles cease to amuse.' At that time M. Lalo tried to crush Debussy under Wagner, as he undertook to crush me under Debussy, and now he is trying to subdue under poor me that charming musician Marcel Delannoy." Ravel went on to support Honegger and Milhaud against Lalo's attacks and called the critic an "amateur."

among them Jacques de Lacretelle, Dr. Robert Le Masle, and Jacques de Zogheb.[23]

Despite the inexorable progress of a debilitating disease, Ravel continued to serve his art well into the last year of his life. In March, 1937, he coached Jacques Février, who was to perform the Concerto for the Left Hand with Charles Münch, and in June he offered counsel to Madeleine Grey and Francis Poulenc, who were soon to perform *Don Quichotte à Dulcinée* at the Salle Gaveau. One of the last concerts Ravel attended was led by Désiré-Emile Inghelbrecht, conducting the Orchestre National. Following a performance of *Daphnis et Chloé,* he began to sob: "I still have so much music in my head," he told Hélène Jourdan-Morhange, "I have said nothing. I have so much more to say."

During the autumn of 1937, Ravel's health declined sharply, and on December 17 he was admitted to the clinic on rue Boileau in Paris. Two days later, a delicate brain operation was performed by the celebrated surgeon Dr. Clovis Vincent.[24] At first, Ravel appeared to rally, but soon after he lapsed into a semi-coma. His long agony came to an end during the early morning hours of December 28, 1937.

The death of Maurice Ravel engendered innumerable expressions of grief, particularly in Europe and North America. Among many others, Milhaud, Prokofiev, and Stravinsky acknowledged the passing of a master musician. A simple burial service took place on December 30th in the presence of a large gathering of friends and colleagues. Led by Edouard Ravel, the mourners included Robert Casadesus, Darius Milhaud, Francis Poulenc, and Igor Stravinsky. A brief eulogy was delivered by the minister of education, Jean Zay, who spoke on behalf of the French government. "If I reflect upon Ravel's message," he observed, "if I evoke the greatest names in our moral and artistic tradition, . . . and ask myself what common characteristic marked these men of genius, and what was the essence of Ravel's genius, I believe I would be correct in stating that it was a supremely in-

[23] During this period, with Ravel's approbation, Manuel Rosenthal transcribed the accompaniments of three of the Greek folk songs. Two of them had been transcribed by Ravel many years before, and it was agreed that a complete set would be useful. Rosenthal also orchestrated the accompaniments of the *Histoires naturelles,* and Ravel observed that he would have carried out these transcriptions himself years ago, but somehow never found the time to do so.

[24] Because of medical ethics, the exact nature of Ravel's malady has remained obscure. It is clear that no tumor was found, and that Dr. Vincent succeeded in equalizing the level of the cerebral hemispheres, one of which had become depressed.

telligent way of looking at things, whether the most passionate or the most pathetic, and subjecting them to the discipline of style.'' [25]

In the sixteenth division of the small cemetery at Levallois Perret, one will find a simple grey granite tomb, with the following inscription:

Joseph Ravel 1832– October 13, 1908
Marie Delouart Ravel 1840– January 5, 1917
Maurice Ravel– composer– 1875– December 28, 1937
Edouard Ravel 1878– April 5, 1960

Edouard Ravel married late in life and left no descendants. With his death, this branch of the Ravel family passed into eternity.

[25] *Le Temps,* Dec. 31, 1937.

EPILOGUE

A Portrait of the Man

Spring: a host of little birds, still awkward, are preparing their recitals.

Everyone has his shortcomings; mine is to act only with complete conscience.

EXCERPTS OF TWO LETTERS FROM RAVEL TO CIPA GODEBSKI

. . . And the ironic and tender heart which beats under the velvet vest of Maurice Ravel.

TRISTAN KLINGSOR

IN THE COURSE of Ravel's lifetime, his music was performed throughout Europe, North and South America, and from North Africa to the Orient. His career intersected with those of many outstanding personalities of the day—Ansermet, Bartók, Casals, Chaliapin, Debussy, Heifetz, Horowitz, Matisse, Monteux, Nijinsky, Picasso, Prokofiev, Schoenberg, Stravinsky, Villa-Lobos—the list could easily be extended. Granted honorary awards and citations by universities, ministers, and kings, Ravel's career was brilliant and rich in achievement. Behind it all lies the essential simplicity yet subtle complexity of the man. The main traits of Ravel's personality were set during his student days and were relatively unaltered in later years. Correct and cool with strangers, he was fun-loving and amusing with friends, optimistic, independent, headstrong, and idealistic. His physical appearance was striking. To Roland-Manuel, Ravel resembled a jockey, to Colette, a squirrel. His short height (about 5 feet, 3 inches), and light frame (about 108 pounds), were notable, as were his taut, bony features, and his gentle, mischievous brown eyes. After experimenting with a mustache, side whiskers, and a full beard, he became clean-shaven about the age of thirty-five, and his dark brown hair slowly changed to silvery white (see Plates 15 and 16). At the time of *Daphnis et Chloé,* Madame Nijinsky described the composer as "a charming young man, always a little extravagantly dressed, but full of gaiety." Indeed, Ravel's dandyism included being up to date with the latest fashions in clothing. He was among the first to wear pastel-colored shirts in France, and on one occasion, a young composer who came for advice was surprised to find him dressed in a white sweater, white pants, white stockings, and white shoes. Beveridge Webster, who met the composer in the 1920s, recalled "a tiny man with an enormous head, a huge nose and an enormous intellect" (see frontispiece). Perhaps the best overall gauge of Ravel's intellectual pursuits may be culled from his personal library at Le Belvédère, which has been preserved exactly as he left it. The library contains about 1,000 volumes and reflects the composer's demanding taste as a bibliophile. There are many rare, beautifully bound editions, among them the complete works of Balzac, Hugo, La Fontaine, Molière, Proust, Racine, and Voltaire. A large part of the library is devoted to memoirs of individuals such as Alexandre Dumas, Casanova, or La Comtesse de Boigne, and many books reflect the composer's interests in gardening, travel, general history, interior decorating, animals, and personal grooming. There are also many books with dedications from colleagues and admirers.[1] Ravel was proud of the French language, and in his articles he wrote with marked clarity and aplomb.[2] Many of his informal letters contain colloquialisms and slang and bespeak the playfulness and ironic humor of the man.

---

[1] Although the library contains a large collection of scores, from Bach through Schoenberg, it has relatively few books on music. Of particular interest are collections of Basque music, Spanish dances, folk melodies from around the world, Negro spirituals, and French operettas, together with many personally dedicated scores from colleagues.

[2] It is a commonly mistaken notion that he was fluent in Basque. He knew some Basque and Spanish, but was fluent only in French, a fact which of course colored all of his reading. His handwriting was angular and sharply chiseled, largely because he held a writing instrument between the second and third fingers of his right hand, pulling it toward himself as he wrote.

Ravel's personal habits have been frequently described by those who knew him. Although a confirmed hermit when composing, he enjoyed Parisian nightlife, the endless discussions in cafés, the lights, the jazz, and the crowds. He was a heavy smoker of Caporal cigarettes and was attracted to stimulating condiments, exotic dishes, cocktails, and fine wines. He was an excellent swimmer and an indefatigable walker. Even during his terminal illness, there was a youthful agility in his step, and the Forest of Rambouillet, the streets of Paris, and large areas of Basque territory held few secrets for him. The composer's meticulous grooming was counterbalanced by a curious disorder in his personal affairs. He was somewhat absent-minded and often lost track of time, particularly in antique shops, when buying gifts, or when examining rare editions for his library. Arriving at "La Grangette" on one occasion, he wrote to Ida Godebska: "I found a pile of invitations here for last week." He was touched by small, thoughtful gestures—a package of cigarettes from Joseph Conrad or a salesgirl in Vienna who insisted on presenting him with a gift portfolio because she played and admired *Jeux d'eau*. A request for a concert tour might receive a tardy answer, but an unknown musician who asked for counsel was sure to receive a prompt, thoughtful reply.[3] Ravel was a great friend of young composers, giving generously of his time, not only in matters of advice, but assisting them in having their works performed and published. In addition to his closest pupils Maurice Delage, Vaughan Williams, Roland-Manuel, and Manuel Rosenthal, whom he enjoyed calling "the school of Montfort," many other composers were assisted, among them Lennox Berkeley, Louis Durey, Marcel Mihalovici, Nicolas Obouhov, Germaine Tailleferre, and Alexandre Tansman.

Relatively little can be said about Ravel's inner life, which he felt to be his own private matter. Although not insensitive to feminine charm and beauty, there was apparently no romantic attachment at any point in his career. His mother was clearly the dominant woman in his life, and in an unusual comment on matrimony, the composer once observed that artists were rarely fit for marriage. "We are rarely normal," he wrote, "and our lives

---

[3] In a letter to a mother who had inquired about musical instruction for her son, Ravel wrote in part: "At first, allow him to assimilate instinctively the elements of music by perfecting himself in the study of an instrument, which will enable him to become acquainted with classical and modern works. Above all, have him continue his academic studies. Today, more than ever, a musician should not be only a musician." A copy of this letter is found in the Fonds Montpensier, Music Division of the Bibliothèque Nationale.

are even less so.'' Like most bachelors, Ravel was fond of animals and adored children. He told the Godebski children enchanting fairy tales and apparently enjoyed playing with their toys as much as they did. His extreme sophistication was curiously combined with childlike enthusiasm and wonder. Ravel was a friend and admirer of Léon Blum and Paul Painlevé, and his political views were socialistic. The one newspaper he subscribed to, *Le Populaire de Paris,* now defunct, was a well-known socialist organ. Although born of Catholic parents and baptized as an infant, the composer appears to have adopted his mother's freethinking attitude toward religion. He was not a practicing Catholic and did not accept the last rites of the Church. Apparently he tended toward agnosticism, relying upon his inner conscience and moral sensitivity.[4] In the 1930s, a number of musicians, refugees from Nazi Germany, found their way to Le Belvédère, where they received both encouragement and financial assistance. This action is characteristic of Ravel, who gave generously to charity and abhorred all racism. Ironically, in the infamous racial publications of the Third Reich, he was listed as being of Jewish origin, since it was assumed that only a Jew could have set Hebraic melodies so perfectly. The question of his Jewish origin had been previously raised in the United States, and in a formal reply to the American impresario Bernard Laberge, the composer observed that his parents were Catholic and he was not a Jew. ''If I were,'' he concluded, ''I would by no means deny it, but I simply wish to re-establish the facts.''

Like any other human being, Ravel had his moods and quirks. He was sensitive about his short height and his limited abilities as a pianist and conductor. If he had a compliment, it was rarely given directly to the person involved. Thus, when Marcelle Gerar went to Le Belvédère for an audition, she was received properly but coolly. Not one comment about her voice or interpretation. Only later, through a mutual friend, did she learn that Ravel was impressed with her ability, and soon after she was asked to concertize with the composer. On the other hand, criticism was given directly to the person involved. ''Your ballet is very bad,'' he told a young composer. ''I tell you this because I know you can do much better.'' His frequently paradoxical way of looking at things was perhaps epitomized in a projected volume on orchestration which was planned with the assistance of Georges

---

[4] Ravel's library contains the Old and New Testaments, as well as a translation of Saint Francis d'Assisi's *I Fioretti,* a work which he particularly admired. Roland-Manuel has mentioned the composer's high regard for Condillac's *Traité des sensations.*

Auric. Ravel was going to present a series of examples with commentary, taken from his own compositions, showing how not to orchestrate by highlighting passages which were bungled!

Behind all the quirks, surprises, and paradoxes of the man lies his unshakable artistic probity and integrity. Ravel believed in his art and fought for it, not in the grand manner of a Berlioz, which he considered grotesque, but in a modest, dignified way. He brought his music before the public and took keen interest in performances of his works both in France and abroad. He was particularly delighted to learn of the marked success of *L'Heure espagnole* at Covent Garden and of Henri Gil-Marchex's successful concert tour of Japan. He stood up to Diaghilev, Toscanini, and anyone else he thought to be misinterpreting his art, and defended the music of Debussy, Stravinsky, and others from the attacks of critics. No doubt Ravel would have wished to compose more, particularly during the postwar years, but he endured extended periods of silence rather than compromise with his ideals. Thus, in the last analysis, the man and his art are one. Ravel's Swiss-Basque heritage and Parisian sophistication, his ironic humor, his fascination with travel and exoticism, his interest in animals and children, and his keen observations of nature are mirrored in his art, as are the disorientation and tragedy of World War I. Behind all of these multifarious threads lies the composer's sovereign conscience, and ''the ironic and tender heart which beats under the velvet vest of Maurice Ravel.''

PART II

The Art of Maurice Ravel

CHAPTER SEVEN

Musical Aesthetics

We should always remember that sensitiveness and emotion constitute the real content of a work of art.

MAURICE RAVEL

That pleasure which is at once the most pure, the most elevating, and the most intense, is derived, I maintain, from the contemplation of the Beautiful.

EDGAR ALLAN POE, *The Poetic Principle*

RAVEL'S VIEWS of the nature and meaning of art were primarily based upon his formative studies at the Conservatoire, his reading of Baudelaire and Poe, and, of course, his personal amalgam of these and other elements. Thanks to the foresight of Roland-Manuel, who acted on occasion as the composer's amanuensis, we possess the following important statement:

Some reflections on music.

I have never felt the need to formulate, either for the benefit of others or for myself, the principles of my aesthetic. If I were called upon to do so, I would ask to be allowed to identify myself with the simple pronouncements made by Mozart on this subject. He confined himself to saying that there is nothing that music can

117

not undertake to do, or dare, or portray, provided it continues to charm and always remains music.

I am sometimes credited with opinions which appear very paradoxical concerning the falsity of art and the dangers of sincerity. The fact is I refuse simply and absolutely to confound the *conscience* of an artist, which is one thing, with his *sincerity,* which is another. Sincerity is of no value unless one's conscience helps to make it apparent. This conscience compels us to turn ourselves into good craftsmen. My objective, therefore, is technical perfection. I can strive unceasingly to this end, since I am certain of never being able to attain it. The important thing is to get nearer to it all the time.

Art, no doubt, has other *effects,* but the artist, in my opinion, should have no other aim.[1]

These remarks are unmistakably French in orientation. Music must "charm" and remain "music"—that is, it need not be philosophy or metaphysics. Ravel thus viewed his role as that of a craftsman arranging tones, rather than a philosopher thinking with tones. With regard to the objective of "technical perfection," Léon-Paul Fargue made the following observation:

One of the most striking traits of this curious Pyrenean was his passion for perfection. This man, who was profoundly intelligent, versatile, precise, extremely well-informed, and who did everything with a facility which was proverbial, had the character and qualities of an artisan. And he liked nothing better than to be compared to one. He liked doing things and doing things well. . . . His passion was to offer the public works which were "finished," polished to the ultimate degree.[2]

How was one to approach the objective of technical perfection? According to Ravel, one submitted to a thorough and rigorous academic training. During his student days, he often cited an apothegm attributed to Massenet: "in order to know one's own craft, one must study the craft of others." At the Conservatoire, he methodically analyzed the standard masterworks of the Baroque, Classical and Romantic periods, and performed a wide variety of nineteenth-century piano music. In later years, the following

[1] Roland-Manuel, "Lettres de Maurice Ravel et documents inédits," *Revue de Musicologie,* 38 (July, 1956), 53. With regard to the "dangers of sincerity," Ravel was critical of those who wrote imperfect works, but claimed that their music was "sincere." For him, sincerity without a thorough mastery of one's craft was a sham. As a young man, Ravel was attracted to paradoxes of all sorts, and in later years he enjoyed exploring the paradoxical aspects of art with colleagues. Although he stated that art was "false" and "a marvelous imposture," this notion must be seen in its proper perspective—namely, that he believed art to be a quest for beauty, rather than truth, an idea derived from the writings of Poe.

[2] Vuillermoz et al., *Maurice Ravel par quelques-uns de ses familiers,* p. 160.

advice was often given to young composers: "If you have nothing to say, you can not do better, until you decide to give up composing for good, than say again what has already been well said. If you have something to say, that something will never emerge more distinctly than when you are being unwittingly unfaithful to your model." [3]

Ravel was convinced that composers should learn their craft like painters—by imitating good models. He did not merely pay lip service to this notion, but throughout his career diligently studied the scores of Mozart, Debussy, Richard Strauss, Chopin, Liszt, Saint-Saëns, and the Russian composers, particularly Mussorgsky. In explaining his own compositions, Ravel attempted to make them appear as simple as possible: this passage is pure Saint-Saëns, he would say, or this harmony was used by Chopin. Indeed, the titles *Jeux d'eau, Valses nobles et sentimentales,* or *La Valse,* indicate the spiritual origin of the music. Yet, as Cocteau pointed out in *Le Coq et l'arlequin,* "an original artist *cannot* copy. Thus, he has only to copy in order to be original." This observation is of crucial importance with regard to Ravel, who found his original path by the age of twenty, and whose music illustrates to some extent Valéry's curious notion that "art should be the pastiche of what doesn't exist."

In explaining what he looked for in a composition, Ravel stressed the key importance of "musical sensitivity," and insisted that "a composer must have something to say." [4] Calvocoressi pointed out that he was particularly attracted to

points of originality in idiom and texture. When calling attention to some beautiful thing, he would often wind up with: 'Et puis, vous savez, on n'avait jamais fait ça!' [And then, you know, that hasn't been done before!] Questions of form seemed to preoccupy him far less. The one and only test of good form, he used to say, is continuity of interest. I do not remember his ever praising a work on account of its form. But, on the other hand, he was very sensitive to what he considered to be defective form. [5]

Ravel's views on composition were further clarified in the lessons he gave to Maurice Delage, Vaughan Williams, Roland-Manuel, and Manuel Rosenthal. He taught mostly by means of conversation and then illustrated his comments at the piano. Pupils were frequently told to model their exer-

---

[3] Vuillermoz et al., p. 145.
[4] Unpublished letter to Jacques Durand dated Feb. 9, 1919.
[5] Calvocoressi, *Musicians Gallery: Music and Ballet in Paris and London,* p. 52.

cises on Mozart's works. However, when teaching Roland-Manuel, who particularly admired Debussy's art, Ravel would pose the following question: in this passage, in an analogous musical context, what would Debussy have done? In teaching counterpoint and fugue, Ravel was punctilious and extremely demanding. The rules had to be rigorously observed, and he would painstakingly ferret out and condemn parallel fifths and octaves, as well as other infractions of contrapuntal law. In teaching orchestration, Strauss's tone poems were stressed as excellent models for imitation and study. Manuel Rosenthal recalled that Ravel's personal copies of these scores had thoroughly blackened page corners, resulting from his frequent study of them. Like his teacher Fauré, Ravel avoided panacea-like formulas. When looking at some of Roland-Manuel's orchestrations, for example, he might suggest that a particular passage could effectively be orchestrated in precisely the opposite manner. When the new assignment was carried out, he would frequently reconsider, and note that the passage was more convincing in its original version! What he desired, above all, was to have the student think for himself and develop along his own path.

In addition to the axioms of imitation as the gateway to mastering one's craft and the objective of technical perfection, Ravel was convinced that a work of art is the product of a composer's individual consciousness, which is inextricably bound to his national heritage:

> . . . in musical treatises there are no such laws as would be of any avail in judging a contemporary musical work of art. Apparently the uselessness of all such arguments must come from the fact that such would-be laws are dealing only with the obvious and superficial part of the work of art without ever reaching those infinitely minute roots of the artist's sensitiveness and personal reaction. The elusive roots, or sources, are often sensed as two in character: one might be called the national consciousness, its territory being rather extensive; while the other, the individual consciousness, seems to be the product of an egocentric process. Both defy classification and analysis as well, yet every sensitive artist perceives the value of their influence in the creation of a real work of art. The manifestation of these two types of consciousness in music may break or satisfy all the academic rules, but such circumstance is of insignificant importance compared with the real aim, namely, fullness and sincerity of expression.[6]

It is apparent that Ravel's "fullness and sincerity of expression" are solidly within French tradition. He told Vaughan Williams that the "heavy con-

[6] "Contemporary Music," p. 132.

trapuntal Teutonic manner'' was not necessary, and that his own motto was ''complex but not complicated.'' Calvocoressi noted that Ravel's preference for writing shorter compositions was due to a ''deliberate, carefully thought-out aesthetic choice,'' and this terseness of logic is characteristic of French art. One also observes emotional reserve rather than expansiveness, elegance and preciosity,[7] humor and tenderness, all of which is underpinned by a marked sensuousness. There is also a less common but distinct thread of drama extending from *Un Grand Sommeil noir, Si morne!*, and *Gaspard de la nuit*, through *La Valse*, the *Chansons madécasses*, and the Concerto for the Left Hand.[8]

Ravel's aesthetic values may be highlighted by a closer examination of his critical opinions. Unfortunately, he wrote relatively little. He was an astute critic, usually indulgent toward others, and most of his comments deal with nineteenth- and twentieth-century music.[9] Although certain contemporaries appear to have been overrated, he immediately recognized the importance of Strauss, Debussy, Vaughan Williams, Falla, Stravinsky, Milhaud, Bartók, Kodály, and Schoenberg, at a time when many of these composers were subjected to the crudest diatribes. Although the monumentality of Bach was unquestioned, serious reservations were held with regard to Beethoven, Berlioz, Brahms, Wagner, Tchaikovsky, Franck, and d'Indy, whose expansive architecture or metaphysical aspirations were far removed from Ravel's personal artistic priorities. In the course of reviewing several concerts given by the Lamoureux Orchestra, Brahms's Symphony in D Major, Franck's Symphony, and d'Indy's symphonic poem *Saugefleurie* were discussed:

> The principle of *genius,* that is, of artistic creation, can be established only by instinct or sensibility. . . . Now, in art, *craft,* in the absolute sense of the word, can not exist. In the harmonious proportions of a work, in the elegance of its ar-

[7] Wallace Fowlie's commentary with regard to the preciosity found in Mallarmé's work is partially applicable to Ravel: ''A poem must, by necessity, impinge upon something. Hence, the impure origin of every poem. The poet is defeated before he begins. He must deceive himself with preciosity, with the exterior and final beauty which conceals a troubled creation.'' *Mallarmé* (Chicago: Univ. of Chicago Press, 1953), p. 19.

[8] The origin of this darker element partially derives from the influence of Poe. In his youth, Ravel was captivated by Poe's writings and particularly by *The Raven* with its obsessive refrain.

[9] It may be added that Ravel's knowledge of European music from Gregorian chant through the seventeenth century appears to have been relatively limited. In addition to a solid command of eighteenth- and nineteenth-century music, he was acquainted with an enormous amount of music written during his lifetime, much of which is now forgotten.

rangement, the role of inspiration is virtually unlimited. The will to develop can only be sterile.

This is what appears most clearly in the majority of Brahms's works. . . . [In the D Major Symphony] the themes bespeak an intimate and gentle musicality; although their melodic contour and rhythm are very personal, they are directly related to those of Schubert and Schumann. Scarcely have they been presented when their progress becomes heavy and laborious. It seems that the composer had been ceaselessly haunted by the desire to equal Beethoven. [Ravel now compares this symphony with Franck's, stating why he is disappointed in both compositions]. Their faults have the same source: a similar disproportion between the themes and their development. With Brahms, a clear and simple inspiration, sometimes playful, sometimes melancholy; learned developments which are grandiloquent, complicated, and heavy. With Franck, melody of an elevated and serene character, bold harmonies of particular richness; but a distressing poverty of form. The structure of the German master is skillful, but one perceives too much contrivance. [With Franck] . . . groups of measures up to entire pages are repeated, transposed textually; he awkwardly abuses out-of-date academic formulas. [After calling Brahms's orchestral technique "brilliant," Ravel points out a number of faults in Franck's orchestration. With regard to *Saugefleurie*], the orchestration is rich and colored, the form is clear. But one discovers in it the disdain of natural harmony, of spontaneous rhythm, of free melody, in one word, of everything not in the domain of pure will. This principle, pushed to its limits, must give as a final result, that musical abstraction, d'Indy's sonata for piano.[10]

The aesthetic distance separating Ravel from Beethoven and Wagner can perhaps be measured only in terms of light-years. "There are in fact only two types of music," Ravel once asserted: "that which pleases and that

[10] *Revue Musicale de la S.I.M.* (March, 1912), pp. 50–51. Continuing the thread from Franck and d'Indy, Ravel once commented upon the "imperfect but genial" songs of Duparc, an observation which might well have summed up his view of Mahler's symphonies. Chausson's *Poème de l'amour et de la mer* was praised for its gentle charm and sensitivity, which were partially marred by confused and clumsy developments. D'Indy's most important pupils were Dukas, Roussel, and Séverac, whose styles and artistic aspirations were naturally far removed from those of Ravel. Although on cordial terms with these composers, it is most likely that his appreciation of their music was limited. In a letter to Cipa Godebski, Ravel summed up his impressions of a concert presented by the Société Nationale on March 13, 1909: "Fugal diversions take the place of craft, themes from *Pelléas* make up for inspiration. And all of this makes a noise! From the gong, the tambourine, snare drum, the glockenspiel, and cymbals used at random. . . . A little music and it would be fine. In all of this Schmitt seems an intrusion: a richness of inspiration, of melody, a sumptuous and delicate orchestration, everything which the others lack! One managed to discern these qualities in spite of a wretched performance and an interpreter with no voice." (Chalupt and Gerar, *Ravel au miroir de ses lettres*, p. 80.)

which is boring." He apparently found much of Beethoven exasperating, if not worse.[11] Ravel never made a pilgrimage to Bayreuth, and although he was overwhelmed by Wagner as a young man, and later called him "a magnificent musician," he was critical of Wagner's thick orchestral texture and believed that Wagnerian influence in France was "pernicious" and would be "disastrous" if unchecked. It is perhaps not surprising that the music of Berlioz, that most atypical of Frenchmen, was held in low regard. While praising his innovative orchestral technique, Ravel often found his harmony clumsy, and once observed that Berlioz was "a genius who couldn't harmonize a waltz correctly."

If the thread from Beethoven through d'Indy was problematic, the line from Mozart through Schubert, Mendelssohn, Bizet, Massenet, Gounod, Chabrier, Saint-Saëns, Satie, and Fauré was closer to Ravel's aesthetic orientation. Mozart was revered above all other composers: the clarity, perfection of workmanship, and the purity of his lyricism, not to mention his prodigious output, struck Ravel as virtually superhuman. He also saw in Mozart's work a striking balance between classical symmetry and the element of surprise, of the unexpected, and this union of symmetry and surprise was to remain a key aspect of his artistic aspirations.[12] Ravel once observed that his own music was "quite simple, nothing but Mozart," a statement which contains a goodly element of truth. The lyricism, elegance, and harmonic subtlety of Schubert were admired, rather than Schubertian "heavenly length," and Mendelssohn's Violin Concerto was regarded as a paragon of perfection, as was Bizet's *Carmen*. Although Ravel's admiration for Saint-Saëns was limited, he nonetheless praised the clarity of his elder

[11] Ravel once told a young colleague that d'Indy's teaching was false because it was based on Beethoven. My teaching, he explained, is based on Mozart. Beethoven's Trio, Opus 97, was judged "annoying," and the *Missa Solemnis* was called an "inferior" work. It should be kept in mind that the music of Beethoven and Wagner was performed incessantly in France during Ravel's lifetime. In a letter to pianist Rudolph Ganz, written in Sept., 1908, the composer observed that he would be pleased to meet the "paradoxical virtuoso" who interested himself in *Gaspard de la nuit*, "at the moment when our national virtuosi insolently persist in revealing the Sonatas of Beethoven." Ravel's complex attitude toward Beethoven and Wagner would appear to combine elements of respect, awe, and jealousy, coupled with marked rejection.

[12] In the *Journaux intimes*, which formed part of Ravel's Baudelairean catechism, the author wrote as follows: "That which is not slightly distorted lacks sensible appeal—from which it follows that irregularity, that is to say, the unexpected, surprise and astonishment, are an essential part and characteristic of beauty."

colleague's orchestration (*Phaéton, La Jeunesse d'Hercule*), as well as his inventiveness within the framework of classical structure.[13] Gounod was regarded as an important precursor of the modern French school, whose vocal works *(Venise, Philémon et Baucis),* had recaptured "the secret of a harmonic sensuousness lost since the French *clavecinistes* of the seventeenth and eighteenth centuries." The tenderness, humor, and spontaneous lyricism of Chabrier strongly impressed the young Ravel, as did the forward-looking harmonies of Satie and the charm and elegance of Massenet.[14] Fauré's songs were thought to be his most important achievement, and Ravel compared their "limpid grace" to the arias of Mozart and their lyricism to the Lieder of Schumann. Among other nineteenth-century composers, Ravel was particularly attracted to the originality and poetry of Chopin,[15] whose lyricism was compared to that of Bellini, and Carl Maria von Weber's operas and Lieder were held in high esteem. Schumann was largely praised for his Lieder and piano music,[16] and Liszt was regarded as an important precursor of far-reaching influence.[17]

[13] Saint-Saëns (1835–1921) viewed the music of Debussy and Ravel as cacophony, an opinion which should be understood in terms of his unusually long career, as well as his fear that their art would lead to a collapse in musical syntax resulting in chaos.

[14] In later years, Ravel acknowledged that Massenet's influential style was overly facile, but he maintained his respect for his elder colleague's orchestration. Ricardo Viñes has commented upon Ravel's youthful attraction to the music of Grieg.

[15] It has been assumed that Ravel's opinions of Chopin were contained in an article he wrote for *Le Courrier Musical:* "Les Polonaises, les Nocturnes, la Barcarolle—Impressions," *Le Courrier Musical* (Jan. 1, 1910), pp. 31–32. Unfortunately, this article is now seen to be unreliable. In an unpublished letter to René Doire, the editor of the magazine, Ravel complained bitterly of the cuts and changes made in his article and stated emphatically that he would have no further dealings with *Le Courrier Musical.* (A copy of the letter is found in the Fonds Montpensier, Music Division of the Bibliothèque Nationale.)

[16] Ravel commented upon the marked individuality of Schumann and Chabrier, which he felt was evident from the very opening measures of their compositions. This, of course, was of great importance, and the transcriptions of *Carnaval* and the *Menuet pompeux* reaffirm his admiration for these composers.

[17] In a review of the tone poem *Les Idéals,* Ravel commented as follows: "Of what importance the shortcomings of this work, or of the entire œuvre of Liszt? Are there not enough good qualities in this tumultuous ebullition, in this vast and magnificent chaos of musical matter, which several generations of illustrious composers have imbibed? It is in large part due to these shortcomings, it is true, that Wagner owes his overly declamatory vehemence, Strauss, his expansive enthusiasm, Franck, the heaviness of his elevation, the Russian school, its occasionally gaudy picturesqueness, and the present French school the extreme coquettishness of its harmonic grace. Yet do not these composers, who are so dissimilar, owe the best of their good qualities to the musical generosity, indeed prodigious, of this great precursor? Within this form, often clumsy, always effusive, doesn't one distinguish the embryo of the ingenious, facile and

It would be difficult to exaggerate Ravel's admiration for the Russian school, particularly for Borodin, Mussorgsky, and Rimsky-Korsakov. While fully aware of the technical deficiencies found in much of their music, their straightforward spontaneity, orchestral color, exoticism, and modality were seen as a fresh direction worthy of emulation, particularly as it offered a strong antidote to Wagnerian influence. The attractive qualities of the Russians were matched to some extent by the Spanish school and the work of Falla, Granados, and Turina was held in esteem. Surveying the contemporary scene in Germany, Italy, Hungary, and England, Ravel pointed out the importance of Strauss, Puccini, Bartók and Kodály, and Vaughan Williams.[18] The achievements of Ernest Bloch, Sibelius, and Gershwin were praised, [19] and the far-reaching significance of Schoenberg and Stravinsky was recognized.[20] Ravel admired the solid craftsmanship found in the work of Schoenberg, Berg, and Webern, an admiration which was reciprocal.[21] With regard to the influence of Schoenberg's discoveries, he noted that

---

limpid development of Saint-Saëns? And the dazzling orchestration, with its powerful yet light sonority, has it not exercised considerable influence on Liszt's most avowed opponents?'' *Revue Musicale de la S.I.M.* (Feb. 15, 1912), p. 63.

[18] Strauss's innovative orchestration was particularly praised (*Salomé*), as well as his comic verve (*Till Eulenspiegel*). Although *Tosca* was admired, Ravel strongly criticized the orchestral and emotional platitudes of the verismo school, finding them a retrogression from earlier nineteenth-century Italian opera. He was pleased with the evolution of Vaughan Williams's career, noting that his former pupil had ''only realized his richness when he learned to be English.''

[19] Bloch was called ''a powerful and passionate nature; a true musician,'' and Sibelius was viewed as ''a magnificent talent—I do not say a supreme artist, but a composer strong in feeling and color and inspired by his vast and sombre north.'' Ravel was attracted to Gershwin's originality, and praised the *Rhapsody in Blue*.

[20] In a review of *Le Rossignol*, which he called a ''masterpiece,'' Ravel commented upon its ''audacious independence of themes, rhythms, and harmonies, whose combination, owing to one of the rarest of musical sensibilities, offers such a fascinating ensemble. Stravinsky's new conception is chiefly attached to the latest style of Arnold Schoenberg. But the latter is harsher, more austere, let us say the word: more cerebral.'' In the course of an interview in 1927, Ravel observed that Stravinsky ''is, happily, never content with his last achievement. He is seeking. His neo-classicism may be somewhat of an experiment, but don't think that Stravinsky has stopped. His last work, ''Oedipus,'' showed that while he plays with old forms, he is actually finding something new.'' *New York Times,* Aug. 7, 1927.

[21] In an interview with the author, Alexandre Tansman recalled Schoenberg's high regard for Ravel's music and Webern's particular admiration for *Ma Mère l'Oye*. In a post card written in August, 1925, Berg told Ravel of his ''great joy'' in hearing his colleague's ''charming'' music once again. This unpublished post card is also signed by Walter Gieseking, Paul Hindemith, Arthur Honegger, and Hermann Scherchen. (Autograph in the private collection of the author.)

we have often heard or read that atonality is a blind alley leading nowhere, but I do not accept the validity of this opinion; because, while as a system it may be so, it certainly cannot be as an influence. In fact, the influence of Schoenberg may be overwhelming on his followers, but the significance of his art is to be identified with influences of a more subtle kind—not the system, but the aesthetic, of his art. I am quite conscious of the fact that my *Chansons madécasses* are in no way Schoenbergian, but I do not know whether I ever should have been able to write them had Schoenberg never written.[22]

Despite Schoenberg's influence, Ravel believed that the main stream of French music would neither follow his path nor rally to the amalgam of French and Germanic elements found in the teaching of d'Indy. Among the younger French composers, he found the work of Milhaud outstanding (*Les Choéphores, Les Malheurs d'Orphée*), and praised the achievements of *Les Six,* Marcel Delannoy, Jacques Ibert, and Henri Sauguet.

Posterity has seen fit to link the names of Debussy and Ravel, and a comparison of their achievements may perhaps best highlight Ravel's individual aesthetic path. Both composers were pianists who were trained at the Conservatoire and whose national inheritance encompassed a millennium of music. Their approbation of Mozart, Chopin, Chabrier, Mussorgsky and the Russians, and their reservations with regard to Beethoven, Wagner, and d'Indy, were on the whole rather similar. They shared common friendships with Satie, Falla, and Stravinsky, and were strongly attracted to Baudelaire, Mallarmé, and Poe. At a rehearsal of Satie's *Parade,* Ravel told Jean Cocteau that he did not understand the technique of a piece "which was not bathed in any sonorous fluid"—an important clue to Ravel's conception of sound. He appreciated the rather thin, dry tone of the Erard piano, whereas Debussy preferred the Bechstein, with its thicker, deep sonority. Despite their common heritage and many points of contact, Ravel claimed that he had followed a direction "opposite to that of Debussy's symbolism." Whereas Debussy's melody is often elliptical, the purity and omnipresence of melody is characteristic of Ravel's art. Both composers boldly extended harmonic practice within the framework of tonality, and although Debussy was generally more adventurous in this area, "Surgi de la croupe et du bond" is perhaps the closest example in the work of either composer of a complete suspension of tonality. The strikingly open structure found in the art of Debussy is offset by his younger colleague's preference for masking the essentially classical outlines of his works. Despite Ravel's profound admiration for Debussy, he was critical of his colleague's treatment of form. In the course of an interview in London, his comments were summarized as follows: "Debussy had shown a *négligence de la forme;* he had achieved through intellectual perception what Chopin had done from inspiration or intuition. Thus, in the larger forms, he showed a lack of architectonic power. In a masterpiece like the *Après-midi d'un faune,* where he achieved perfection, it was impossible to say how it had been built up."[23]

In addition, Ravel was critical of Debussy's orchestration. *"La Mer* is poorly orchestrated,'' he told Henri Sauguet. "If I had the time, I would reorchestrate *La Mer.''* (The project was not carried out.) Details of craftsmanship were of vital concern to Ravel, and he generally found Debussy's treatment of the percussion section weak. Furthermore, he criticized *L'Île joyeuse* as poorly written for the keyboard, calling it an orchestral reduction for the piano. From our vantage point, it is evident that each composer influenced the other to some extent, keeping in mind that once an artist achieves his own personality, external influences are of secondary importance. If *Shéhérazade* and the *Miroirs* indicate the spirit of Debussy, the *Estampes* bespeak the achievements of Ravel. It is possible that the clearer outlines and structures found in Debussy's late works came about through Ravel's influence, and Debussy's call for a thinner, less congested art was taken up by Ravel, *Les Six,* and much of the postwar generation. Ernest Ansermet has recalled a meeting with Debussy in which the composer gave him a score of the *Nocturnes* covered with corrections of all sorts. When asked which ones were valid, Debussy replied, ''I am no longer sure. They are all possibilities. Take this score and use those which seem good to you.'' [24] One could scarcely imagine Ravel making such a statement. For him, there was but one final product—the one which was as perfect as he could make it. In the last analysis, the creative personalities of Debussy and Ravel were widely divergent. Debussy's productivity was effusive, uninhibited, and opened up fresh paths, whereas Ravel's small output, emotional reticence, and innovation within tradition were coupled with an unrivalled technical mastery of his craft.

[23] *Morning Post,* July 10, 1922.
[24] Ansermet, *Entretiens sur la musique* (Neuchatel, 1963), p. 37.

No discussion of Ravel's aesthetics would be complete without commenting upon the decisive importance of Edgar Allan Poe's essays. Poe's marked influence upon modern French literature has frequently been observed, and, among others, Baudelaire and Mallarmé translated his works, which proved to be a revelation for Ravel. In *The Philosophy of Composition,* which the composer read in Baudelaire's translation, *La Genèse d'un poème,* Poe made the following observations:

> I have often thought how interesting a magazine paper might be written by any author who would—that is to say, who could—detail, step by step, the processes by which any one of his compositions attained its ultimate point of completion. . . . Most writers—poets in especial—prefer having it understood that they compose by a species of fine frenzy—an ecstatic intuition—and would positively shudder at letting the public take a peep behind the scenes, at the elaborate and vacillating crudities of thought— . . . at the cautious selections and rejections—at the painful erasures and interpolations. . . . It will not be regarded as a breach of decorum on my part to show the *modus operandi* by which some one of my own works was put together. I select *The Raven* as most generally known. It is my design to render it manifest that no one point in its composition is referable either to accident or intuition—that the work proceeded step by step, to its completion, with the precision and rigid consequence of a mathematical problem.[25]

Ravel saw in this striking defense of objectivity a brilliant balance between the poet's intellect and his emotion, between his craftsmanship and his inspiration. Like his author, Ravel was well aware of the unique and irreplaceable role of inspiration,[26] but almost invariably found it more suitable to discuss technical matters with others, rather than his inner visions, which he felt to be his own private matter. A revealing exception is found in a letter to Roland-Manuel, written on October 7, 1913:

> . . . Just as your letter arrived I was finishing my 3 poems. Indeed, *Placet futile* was completed, but I retouched it. I fully realize the great audacity of having attempted to interpret this sonnet in music. It was necessary that the melodic con-

[25] A somewhat similar defense of objectivity is found in Diderot's *Paradoxe sur le comédien,* which Ravel often praised. In brief, the paradox is that to move an audience, the actor must himself remain unmoved and possess "a cool head, a profound judgment, an exquisite taste—a matter for hard work, for long experience, for an uncommon tenacity of memory."

[26] With regard to the vexing problem of inspiration, Ravel often quoted Baudelaire's aphorism: "Inspiration is decidedly the sister of daily work" (*L'Art romantique*). There was, of course, no simple solution to this question, as he observed in a letter to Jacques Durand, written in June, 1918: "I went through some terrible moments, convinced that I was drained, and that neither inspiration nor even the desire to work would ever return. And then, a few days ago, it reappeared."

tour, the modulations, and the rhythms be as precious, as properly contoured as the sentiment and the images of the text. In spite of that, it was necessary to maintain the elegant deportment of the poem. Above all, it was necessary to maintain the profound and exquisite tenderness which suffuses all of this. Now that it's done, I'm a bit nervous about it.[27]

Ravel's concern to maintain the "profound and exquisite tenderness" of the sonnet is of considerable interest, particularly in view of the fact that he was often maligned as a cerebral contriver of effects—as was Stéphane Mallarmé.

Above all, it is in *The Poetic Principle* that one finds the closest approximation of Ravel's aesthetic:

> *That* pleasure which is at once the most pure, the most elevating, and the most intense, is derived, I maintain, from the contemplation of the Beautiful. In the contemplation of Beauty we alone find it possible to attain that pleasurable elevation, or excitement *of the soul,* which we recognize as the Poetic Sentiment, and which is so easily distinguished from Truth, which is the satisfaction of the Reason, or from Passion, which is the excitement of the heart.

Ravel's art strove neither for passion nor for truth, but rather for the "contemplation of the Beautiful," through the satisfaction of the mind by means of the ear's pleasure. Thus, a final paradox was perfectly stated by Keats, who already knew that by creating his own beauty, Ravel would thereby create his own truth. In addition, with his striving for clarity, balance, and good taste, the composer of *Daphnis et Chloé* created an art which embodies the timeless values of the French nation.

[27] Unpublished autograph in the private collection of Claude Roland-Manuel.

CHAPTER EIGHT

Ravel's Musical Language

As a child, I was sensitive to music—to every kind of music.

MAURICE RAVEL

There is no such thing any longer as an inadmissible chord, or melody, or rhythm—given the proper context, of course. Contemporary practice has firmly established that fact.

AARON COPLAND (1952)

A SURVEY of Ravel's art indicates a small body of music written over a creative period of four decades. There are approximately sixty compositions, of which slightly more than half are instrumental: fifteen pieces and suites for the piano, eight chamber works, six orchestral works, several ballets, and two piano concerti. The vocal music consists of eighteen songs and song cycles with accompaniment for piano, chamber ensemble, or orchestra, several settings of folk melodies, one work for unaccompanied mixed chorus, and two operas. It would be misleading to divide this music into periods of apprenticeship and maturity, for Ravel's earliest compositions were on the whole remarkably characteristic. The "Habanera" and the *Menuet antique* were written by a twenty-year-old student, and with the completion of *Jeux d'eau* at the age of twenty-six, the composer's style was firmly set. These early works indicate many of the trends he would pursue: a predilection for dance rhythms, the music of Spain, archaic pastiche and contemporary impressionistic techniques. Thus, from the outset, Ravel's approach to composition might be called metamorphic—that is, in each new undertaking he would cover fresh ground, placing his personal stamp upon widely differing techniques and idioms.[1] Other compositions indicate his interest in Basque music, oriental exoticism, and American jazz. Ravel's observation that as a child he was sensitive "to every kind of music" offers an important clue to the striking diversity found in his art. Behind all of the multifarious threads lies the composer's personal manipulation of his material.

André Gédalge taught his pupils that melody is the essence of music. "Whatever sauce you put around the melody is a matter of taste," he would say. "What is important is the melodic line, and this doesn't vary." [2] Throughout Ravel's art one finds a clear melodic thread, and he once told Vaughan Williams that in his opinion, there was "an implied melodic outline in all vital music." Perhaps the most characteristic aspect of the Ravelian melody is its mixture of tonality and modality. Found in the work of Chabrier, Satie, and the Russian school, the combination of tonality and modality was in the air in the latter nineteenth century, adding a fresh dimension to the major-minor system. The Dorian mode is frequently used (*Ballade de la Reine morte d'aimer*, or the beginning of the Sonata for Violin and Cello), while the Phrygian is characteristic of Spanish music (*Rapsodie espagnole* and *L'Heure espagnole*). Ravel's frequent adaptation of various defective scales, among them the whole-tone and pentatonic, reflects the spiritual influence of the music performed at the 1889 International Exposition (Overture to *Shéhérazade*, *Tzigane*, or the scherzo in the Piano Concerto for the Left Hand). The melody is generally diatonic, and proceeds by sequential treatment or repetition, rather than by motivic development, and in this respect Ravel's workmanship indicates the spirit of the Russian school rather than Beethovenian architecture. The intervals of the second, fourth, and the fifth are often favored, and the composer's predilection for joining themes which are first presented individually is a feature of his workmanship which may be observed from the *Menuet antique* to the Piano Concerto for the Left Hand. Roland-Manuel has perceptively described Ravel's

---

[1] A somewhat similar outlook may be seen in the work of Copland and Stravinsky.

[2] *La Revue Musicale* (March 1, 1926), p. 257.

lyricism as "supple, but extremely pure, with contours which strongly indicate something Italian, in the sense of the Italianism of Mozart, Schubert, even of Weber, or of Chopin."

Although it is clear that Ravel's harmonic language was considered novel, indeed revolutionary during his day, it now appears to be a logical outgrowth of the rapid evolution of harmony which followed the decisive opening measures of *Tristan und Isolde*.[3] Together with his contemporaries, Ravel exploited unresolved chords of the seventh and ninth, complex harmonies over pedal points, and sonorities based upon the second and the fourth. His adventurous harmonic language is solidly rooted in tonality, with many modal inflections, and some exploitation of bitonality and even atonality. In the prewar compositions, one generally observes a richer texture and harmonic palette, coupled with homophonic writing which bespeaks a close interrelationship between the melody and its underlying harmony, while some of the postwar compositions indicate a more austere harmonic style, coupled with increasing interest in linear motion. The minor and major seventh (or the diminished octave) are perhaps the hallmark of Ravel's harmonic language, appearing from the earliest works through *Jeux d'eau* (E, G♯, B, D♯), *Shéhérazade* (E♭, G♭, B♭, D♭), the *Miroirs* (G♯, B, D, G♮), and later on in the quasi-Schoenbergian suspensions of tonality in the Mallarmé poems and the *Chansons madécasses*. Finally, the lowered seventh step, the "blue" note, will be exploited in the postwar adaptations of jazz. Although Ravel occasionally analyzed his music on a chord-by-chord basis, he was also well aware of larger structural prolongations, as is evident from his analysis of the following passage from the *Valses nobles et sentimentales*. "With regard to unresolved appoggiaturas," he wrote to René Lenormand, "here is a passage which may interest you [see Example 1].[4] This fragment is based upon a single chord [see Example 2], which was al-

---

[3] At the Conservatoire, Ravel mastered the traditional aspects of eighteenth- and nineteenth-century harmony found in Henri Reber's *Traité d'harmonie* (1862), and the supplement to this work by Théodore Dubois (1889).

[4] René Lenormand, *Etude sur l'harmonie moderne* (Paris: Editions Max Eschig, 1913). Although this analysis has always been ascribed to Lenormand, it is in fact Ravel's. (The composer's manuscript is found in the Bibliothèque de l'Opéra.) In his book, Lenormand thanks the composers who clarified their intentions for him, and it turns out that many of the analyses of Ravel's music are those of the composer. With regard to Schoenberg, the author makes the following interesting observation: "We scarcely dare cite M. Arnold Schoenberg of Vienna, whose works we find completely unintelligible."

(Autorisation Durand & Cie, Editeurs-propriétaires, Paris)

Example 1

Example 2

ready used by Beethoven, without preparation, at the beginning of a sonata [Opus 31, No. 3]. Here now is the passage with the appoggiaturas resolved, resolutions which really do not alter anything until measure A. [see Example 1], at which point the chord changes [see Example 3]."

133

Example 3

X   XX   "The *E* does not change the chord. It is a passing note in both cases [see Example 4]":

Example 4

In Ravel's analysis—and here Gédalge's comment about melody is apt—the F in the bass and the $\frac{6}{5}$ above are the "essence" of this passage. Whether an A natural or a C♯ or an E is placed above is a matter of "sauce," and does not alter the fundamental basis of the passage. The preceding commentary may be considered typical of the composer's analytic approach, as he invariably linked his work with the achievements of his predecessors. Thus, the notion of the *Valses nobles et sentimentales* derives from Schubert, the harmony in this passage from Beethoven, and the rhythm from Chopin (Waltz in A♭, opus 42). The passage is of course distinct from all of these sources, and herein lies one of the problematic aspects of Ravel's style—prying apart the craftsman from his model.

Much of Ravel's treatment of rhythm is conditioned by the dance. In 1906, he mentioned the genesis of *La Valse* in a letter to Jean Marnold: "You know of my deep sympathy for these wonderful rhythms, and that I value the joie de vivre expressed by the dance far more deeply than the

Franckist puritanism.'' In addition to the lilting waltz, the graceful minuet, and the colorful rhythms of Basque and Spanish music, Baroque dances are adapted in *Le Tombeau de Couperin,* and *L'Enfant et les sortilèges* is replete with dancing. Rather than incorporate the striking rhythmic innovations found in *Le Sacre du printemps,* Ravel sought rhythmic subtleties within traditional meters. In *Daphnis et Chloé,* and throughout his œuvre, whether the rhythm is virile or caressing, its outlines are generally pointed and precise.

Rather than architectonic in breadth, Ravel's art is essentially that of a miniaturist, who could, on occasion, convincingly fill a large canvas. Even when the canvas is relatively extended, it consists of small brush strokes expertly placed side by side. *Daphnis et Chloé* and *L'Heure espagnole* are unified by the repetition of a small number of motifs, and together with *L'Enfant et les sortilèges,* each work lasts only about one hour, achieving its length by the addition of one relatively short scene or episode to another. Other extended works are frequently unified by means of thematic transformation, which largely bespeaks the spiritual influence of Liszt (the Sonatine, much of the chamber music, *La Valse*). Ravel was frequently content to work within traditional structures (A–B–A, Sonata form), filling them with fresh content, together with his predilection for structural subtleties.[5] To the extent that his chamber music bespeaks a classical orientation, it may be said to derive from the work of Mozart, Mendelssohn, Fauré, and Saint-Saëns. On occasion, however, the treatment of structure is quite innovative (*Miroirs, Gaspard de la nuit*). In sum, the composer's approach to melody, harmony, rhythm, and form indicates a drive for innovation within a solid framework of tradition.

The piano is the privileged instrument in Ravel's art, not only because he was a pianist and composed at the keyboard, but because virtually all of the fresh trends in his style first appear in the piano music. The sophisticated harmonies and the music of Spain (''Habanera''), the dance rhythms and ar-

---

[5] Ravel observed that Mendelssohn's Violin Concerto contained an outstanding example of the art of masking a classical structure. Pointing to the passage following the cadenza in the first movement, he noted how the arpeggio figuration in the violin continued unabated, lulling the ear, as it were, and before the listener was fully cognizant of what had occurred, the recapitulation was already under way. An analogous melodic deception occurs in the first movement of the Sonatine, while in the Trio, the recapitulation in the first movement is merely intimated. Ravel attached great importance to such details, for no aspect of his craft was too small to be given his fullest attention.

chaic pastiche (*Menuet antique*), the impressionistic techniques (*Jeux d'eau*), the thinner texture of the postwar years (*Ma Mère l'Oye, Le Tombeau de Couperin*), and even some of its harsher outlines (*Valses nobles et sentimentales*), together with the initial adaptation of jazz (*L'Enfant et les sortilèges*), are all announced at the keyboard. The piano music derives largely from the clarity and elegance of Scarlatti, Couperin, and the French *clavecinistes*, Mozart, Chabrier, and Saint-Saëns, as well as the color and virtuosity of Chopin and particularly of Liszt.[6]

Ravel's predilection for remodeling his music was a significant aspect of his artistic creed. It appears that once a composition was perfected, the attempt was made to draw out every ounce of its inherent possibilities. Indeed, almost half of his works were reshaped in one manner or another: a goodly number of piano pieces and vocal accompaniments were orchestrated, and several keyboard works were transcribed and then mounted as ballets.[7] Thus, rather curiously, the composer's only orchestral compositions properly speaking are the overture to *Shéhérazade*, the *Rapsodie espagnole, Daphnis et Chloé, La Valse,* a "Fanfare" for the ballet *L'Eventail de Jeanne, Boléro,* and the piano concerti.[8] The key influences on his orchestral technique were the scores of Rimsky-Korsakov (particularly *Shéhérazade, Mlada,* and the *Capriccio espagnol*), and Richard Strauss (largely *Don Juan* and *Till Eulenspiegel*). The treatises of Berlioz and Rimsky-Korsakov were thoroughly assimilated, and Widor's *Technique de l'orchestre moderne* was frequently consulted for its useful technical data. Ravel's orchestral technique was the fruit of long years of study, incessant questioning of per-

---

[6] With regard to Ravel's keyboard virtuosity, Walter Gieseking noted that in his opinion, "Scarbo" and "Alborada del gracioso" were among the most difficult piano works ever written. "The right expression is so important, because these intricate pianistic acrobatics are never deprived of musical sense, of artistic value. . . . It is always real music, which one may call refined, concentrated, perhaps even, too sophisticated, but it is written primarily to create beautiful, enchanting, expressive piano sonorities, and if this music is technically very complex, it is nevertheless based on musically perfectly logical conceptions."

[7] In the course of a review, Ravel commented upon Fauré's *Dolly,* originally a suite for piano four hands, which had been adapted for the stage by Louis Laloy with orchestration by Henri Rabaud. Some may cry sacrilege, he observed, but their protests are unfounded. Any work may be given a fresh interpretation, "on condition that good taste presides." Ravel's transcriptions range in import from his curious arrangements of the *Boléro* for two pianos and piano four hands, to the brilliant orchestrations of *Ma Mère l'Oye* and Mussorgsky's *Pictures at an Exhibition.*

[8] With the possible exception of the *Boléro,* all of these works were composed at the piano and then orchestrated.

formers, much experimentation, and innumerable rehearsals. He was intrigued by the seemingly limitless resources of the modern orchestra, and his scores indicate a natural extension of each instrument's technical resources and range, careful attention to the linearity of each part, and the seeking out of fresh combinations of timbre. He was particularly sensitive to rhythmic and coloristic subtleties in the percussion section and wrote for the harp with marked skill. The brass family, on the other hand, is generally treated in a relatively traditional fashion. It would appear that within the limit of human capability and efficacy of writing, any instrument may assume any role, and here the Ravelian elements of surprise and even paradox came to the fore.[9] The E♭ saxophone will somehow conjure up an old castle in the *Pictures at an Exhibition,* while in *Ma Mère l'Oye,* a melodic passage is given to the weak bass register of the celesta. In the daybreak episode from *Daphnis et Chloé,* the woodwinds and strings perform extended and agile harplike passages, while in the *Chansons madécasses,* the flute will evoke a trumpet and the piano a gong. In orchestrating the works of others as well as his own music, Ravel stressed the importance of the piano and the string family. When orchestrating, he felt the need to isolate the notes of each family of instruments at the keyboard and observe, for example, what the woodwinds were doing at a particular moment. As will be remarked upon later in detail, most of his tutti are organized by families of instruments, which gives a full yet clear resonance. Ravel considered the strings the soul of the orchestra and generally notated their parts before the other instruments. He insisted that the string family sound perfectly in and of itself, and once this task was accomplished, the final choice of instrumentation would be made. In the course of a lesson, Manuel Rosenthal was shown the original version of the "Pavane" from *Ma Mère l'Oye,* which was notated solely for the string family. Only later was the melody given to the flute, while the violas were kept in the accompaniment, doubled by a muted horn. In this simplest of passages, one may note the subtle balance of the contrasting timbres. Moreover, the melody continues in the flute and is soon heard in the clarinet. When the opening theme reappears, it is given to the flute (with modified ac-

---

[9] Writing in *Le Temps* on March 19, 1907, Pierre Lalo criticized this aspect of Ravel's orchestration as follows: *Une Barque sur l'océan* contains, one might say, "a collection of examples for a treatise on orchestration, with all sorts of examples of how to alter the timbre of an instrument. For in Ravel's orchestra no instrument keeps its natural sound; to him, there are no trumpets but muted ones."

companiment), and the listener knows what to expect—the flute will play the melody until the end of the piece. But not at all. The muted first violins, which have remained silent, will complete the melody, thus creating an unexpected and fresh color. Behind all of these subtleties lies the composer's notion of a sound "bathed in a sonorous fluid." He once observed that there was always more to be learned in the art of orchestration, and his scores indicate marked innovation and mastery.

The diversity of Ravel's instrumental music is matched by the striking variety of his vocal works. From the preciosity of Pierre de Ronsard to the complex symbolism of Mallarmé, from the exoticism of Evariste de Parny to Colette's sensitive portrayal of childhood, Ravel rarely repeated himself, setting Alexandrines and poems in prose from the Renaissance through the twentieth century. Most often, he turned to free verse and poems in prose. He believed that setting a text implied creating a new work of art and that the musician thereby became an equal partner with the author. Thus, a text could be modified, as long as its general sense and poetic beauty were in no way jeopardized. The spiritual sources of Ravel's vocal art range from the composers of the French Renaissance *chanson* to the work of Massenet, Mussorgsky, Chabrier, Satie, Fauré, and Debussy. The peripheral influence of Wagner and Schoenberg may also be observed. Unlike the more adventurous instrumental style, the vocal writing indicates traditional tessitura with practically no attempt at virtuosity. At times one observes a lyrical vocal line which extends over a limited range (*Sainte, Ronsard à son âme*), quasi-parlando writing (*L'Heure espagnole*), or some instrumental-like angularity (*Trois Poèmes de Stéphane Mallarmé*). The accompaniment will occasionally establish a uniform atmosphere, deriving from the general mood of the poem (*Chanson du rouet, Epigrammes de Clément Marot*), while at other times the text may be interpreted quite literally (*Histoires naturelles*). Ineluctably attracted to exoticism, Ravel willingly harmonized folk melodies from many nations. He preferred having the melodies sung in their original language, and performed, if possible, with orchestral accompaniment.[10] Thus, our monolingual composer would require an interpreter to cope with some ten languages. Ravel's innate gifts for the theater led him to the divertissement and the operetta, writing atypical yet compelling excursions into

[10] With regard to his own works, Ravel preferred the orchestra or chamber ensemble to the piano, and it is clear that *Shéhérazade,* the Mallarmé poems, and the *Chansons madécasses* are considerably more effective when performed with full instrumentation.

the domains of Hispanic comedy and the unfettered fantasy of childhood. Behind all of this diversity lies the composer's desire for textual clarity, correct prosody, and his individualistic and sophisticated literary taste.

As a creative artist, Ravel was keenly aware of his weaknesses and strengths. He wisely avoided the symphony and never turned to the theme and variations. He wrote neither for the organ nor for the church. A complete accounting of the elements in his art would run a gamut from Gregorian chant to Gershwin, passing through the Renaissance, Baroque, Classical, and Romantic eras. He managed to keep his personal touch in a style which varied from the striking simplicity of *Ma Mère l'Oye* to the transcendental virtuosity of *Gaspard de la nuit,* from the luxuriant, caressing sonority of *Daphnis et Chloé* to the austere violence of the *Chansons madécasses,* and from Renaissance pastiche to adaptations of jazz. His achievement is neither eclectic, nor can it be summed up in one all-encompassing label. It is thoroughly French in orientation, and is solidly based upon traditional practice. Like Chopin, Ravel found his personal path at an early age, and devoted his years to perfecting a small number of works. In the last analysis, like any other significant artist, he fashioned his own laws and created his own universe (see Plate 17).

Ballade de la Reine morte d'aimer
(voice and piano, c.1893;
see Plate 18)

Although the autograph of this song is untitled and undated, its title and approximate date of composition were communicated to Roland-Manuel (see the "Autobiographical Sketch"). The poem, by the little-known Belgian author and journalist Roland de Marès (1874–1955), first appeared in a collection *Ariettes douloureuses* (1892) and was entitled "Complainte de la Reine de Bohême." Ravel was apparently attracted to the poem's gentle preciosity, its pastiche of courtly love, and to its concluding reference to the "small bells of Thulé, which sang the supreme hosanna for the queen who died of love." The marked influence of Satie may be seen in the archaic simplicity of the setting which exploits the Dorian mode, with a key signature of B♮ used throughout. The spiritual influence of the defective modes heard at the

1889 exposition is also apparent. The musical and poetic elements in this youthful work—pastiche, preciosity, modality, and the chiming of bells—indicate the path Ravel will soon follow with increasing maturity.

Sérénade grotesque (piano, c.1893; see Plate 19)

The autograph of this piece is entitled *Sérénade,* but its full title and approximate date of composition were communicated to Roland-Manuel (see the "Autobiographical Sketch"). The opening measures, marked "pizzicatissimo," foreshadow the guitar-like beginning of "Alborada del gracioso," and the alternation of triads between the hands is common to both pieces. The general mood of the serenade is that of grotesque irony, which is realized by rapid, leaping staccato passages in the left hand, accompanied by punctuated dissonances in the right. The tonic triad of F♯ minor is delayed until m. 15, and at m. 57, a slower lyrical melody appears, marked "très sentimental," a rare indication in the composer's scores. The overall structure of the piece (A,B,C,B′,C′,A′), may be analyzed as follows:

(A) opening theme ($\frac{2}{4}$, "très rude," mm. 1–14)
(B) presto ($\frac{6}{8}$, mm. 15–74), numerous changes of tempo, lyrical theme beginning at m. 57
(C) bridge passage (mm. 75–82), derived from sections A and B
(B′) presto (mm. 83–142), largely derived from mm. 15–74; lyrical theme reappears at m. 125
(C′) bridge passage (mm. 143–150), similar to mm. 75–82
(A′) coda ($\frac{2}{4}$, mm. 151–158), concluding statement of the opening theme, and final cadence in F♯ major

The various sections are clear-cut, unlike the composer's more mature achievements. He noted the influence of Chabrier on the *Sérénade grotesque,* and probably had in mind the *Bourrée fantasque* (1891). Both works begin in duple meter with marked, staccato passages, but soon diverge in structure and technique. Nevertheless, as their titles indicate, the pieces evoke grotesque moods. The nascent fantastic irony found in the *Sérénade grotesque* will appear later, more perfectly realized, in "Scarbo."

Un Grand Sommeil noir (voice and piano, 1895)

In an article written in 1922, Ravel acknowledged Fauré's unique empathy for Verlaine's art: "Many musicians have been tempted by the celebrated poetry of Verlaine. Fauré alone knew how to grant him his music." Ravel's settings of Verlaine's poetry are workmanlike, but below his best level. The heavy, somber mood of *Un Grand Sommeil noir,* from the collection *Sagesse,* is captured by means of low, slow-moving repeated notes in the vocal line, followed by a rapid lyrical ascent, which suggest the spiritual influence of Massenet. The vocal line and the chromatic harmonies are not unrelated to Debussy's "De Fleurs" from the *Proses lyriques,* and the peripheral influence of *Tristan und Isolde* may also be observed. Other settings of Verlaine's poem include those by Stravinsky (1910) and Honegger (1944).[11]

Menuet antique (piano, 1895)

The *Menuet antique* is a spiritual descendant of Chabrier's *Menuet pompeux* (1881), which Ravel later orchestrated. Both pieces are in the traditional A–B–A form, contrasting the tonic minor (A) with the tonic major (B), and alternating moods of brusque accentuation (A) with gentle lyricism (B). The use of the natural minor scale with its lowered leading tone gives a pseudo-antique touch, as do the many sequential phrases. Shortly before the recapitulation (Enoch edition, 5/3/2),[12] the themes of the minuet and trio are joined, a technique which will be encountered in an analogous position in the "Menuet" from *Le Tombeau de Couperin.*

[11] With its slow, chordal texture, Stravinsky's setting is somewhat similar to Ravel's. (*Un Grand Sommeil noir,* Op. 9, No. 1, P. Jurgenson and R. Forberg.) Utilizing a running sixteenth-note pattern throughout, Honegger interpreted the poem in a completely different manner. (*Quatre Chansons pour voix grave,* Salabert, 1947.)

[12] The first number stands for the page, the second for the system, and the third for the measure number. When only two numbers appear, the second stands for the measure number.

Sites auriculaires (two pianos, 1895–97)
1) "Habanera"
2) "Entre cloches"

Three autographs of the "Habanera" bear a quotation from Baudelaire's celebrated collection *Les Fleurs du mal:* "Au pays parfumé que le soleil caresse" (In the perfumed land which the sun caresses), the opening verse of *A une Dame créole.* The twenty-year-old composer was probably attracted to the poem's exoticism and youthful sensuality, and many years after completing the "Habanera," he commented on it as follows: "I believe that this work, with its ostinato pedal point and its chords with multiple appoggiaturas, contains the germ of several elements which were to predominate in my later compositions." [13] Ravel undoubtedly had in mind the nascent appearance of Spanish dance rhythms, as well as the element of exoticism. Furthermore, his comment about an ostinato pedal point with chords containing multiple appoggiaturas would accurately describe "Le Gibet." Part of the subtlety of the opening passage, which may be interpreted as a D_7 to a G_7 progression over a pedal point on $C\sharp$, is seen in the fact that the tonic appears to be $C\sharp$, but it turns out to be $F\sharp$. The "Habanera" was later transcribed for orchestra and inserted as the third movement of the *Rapsodie espagnole.* Although the orchestral version is a faithful transcription, containing only minuscule deviations from the two-piano score, Ravel told Francis Poulenc that the transcription was unsuccessful, because it contained "too much orchestration for the number of measures." [14] Little attention has been paid to this overly critical opinion, and it is now apparent that the original version of the "Habanera" marks a significant turning point in the composer's style.

Unlike the "Habanera," which has been frequently performed in its orchestral transcription, "Entre cloches" has remained virtually unknown. [15] Much speculation has been raised over the relationship, or lack thereof, between "Entre cloches" ("Among Bells") and "La Vallée des cloches"

[13] "Autobiographical Sketch," p. 20. See p. 51, footnote 10.

[14] Poulenc, *Moi et mes amis,* p. 184. The original version consists of 68 measures, while the orchestral transcription contains only 61, because several measures were condensed. For example, in the two-piano score, an accompaniment figure which is repeated three times (mm. 14, 15, and 16), is found only twice in the transcription (mm. 14 and 15).

[15] Using the manuscript of *Sites auriculaires* belonging to Manuel Rosenthal, pianists Jacques Février and Gabriel Tacchino recorded the work in 1972 (Adès label, record 7044).

("The Valley of the Bells"), the concluding piece of *Miroirs* (1905).[16] A comparison of the scores shows many important points of contact: both works contain many successions of fourths and accented repeated notes, which suggest the chiming of bells. Moreover, both pieces exploit the interval of the fourth to a striking degree, melodically as well as harmonically. Finally, both compositions begin with rapid motion in fourths, followed by a much slower lyrical section, and after diverging somewhat in structure, they conclude with references to their opening themes.[17] "La Vallée des cloches" was completed almost a decade after "Entre cloches," and is a more successful work, owing to its greater harmonic and rhythmic subtlety. Nevertheless, "Entre cloches," with its bold, driving sonorities and its modally inflected lyricism, is an achievement of considerable merit. *Sites auriculaires* proved to be the composer's only work for two pianos.[18]

Sainte (voice and piano, 1896)

In December, 1865, Mallarmé wrote to the poet Théodore Aubanel, describing *Sainte* as "a short melodic poem." The poem's original title was "Sainte Cécile jouant sur l'aile d'un chérubin" ("Saint Cecilia Playing on the Wing of a Cherub"), and the composer's setting captures the contemplative mood by means of a quasi-liturgical vocal line accompanied by slow-moving chords. The many unresolved chords of the seventh and ninth point to the influence of Satie's *Sarabandes* or *Prélude de la porte héroïque du ciel*.

---

[16] Alfred Cortot, who was present at the première of *Sites auriculaires,* believed "La Vallée des cloches" to be a spiritual descendant of "Entre cloches" (*La Musique française de piano*, II, 36), while Roland-Manuel discounted his statement (*Ravel*, p. 32).

[17] The compositions may be summarized as follows:

"Entre cloches":

    (A) opening section-allègrement, $\frac{10}{8}$, A♭ major, mm. 1–12;

    (B) second section-lent, $\frac{3}{4}$, F major, mm. 13–28;

    (A') modified statement of the opening section, $\frac{10}{8}$, A♭ major, mm. 29–38;

    (A'') lent-concluding reference to the opening theme, mm. 39–43.

"La Vallée des cloches":

    (A) opening section (très lent), mm. 1–11;

    (B) second section (très calme), mm. 12–48;

    (A') concluding reference to the opening section, mm. 49–54.

[18] Although the little-known *Frontispice* is technically written for two pianos, it requires a fifth hand for performance (see p. 188).

Aside from one brief crescendo, the dynamics do not exceed p, and the song ends quietly and somewhat mysteriously on an unresolved chord of the ninth. The purity and challenge of Mallarmé's art will be re-encountered with greater maturity in the *Trois Poèmes de Stéphane Mallarmé*.

Sonata for Violin and Piano (in one movement, 1897)

The autograph of this work, which is dated April, 1897, is entitled "Sonate pour piano et violon." The Sonata conforms to the classical scheme of exposition, development, and recapitulation. The tonic key of A minor is established at the outset, and the opening theme adumbrates the beginning of the Trio, both in melodic contour and in mood (see Example 5). Moreover, on occasion, the theme is treated similarly in both pieces (see Example 6).

Example 5

Example 6

Thus, if the opening theme of the Trio is "Basque in color," as the composer asserted, it would appear that the same observation applies to the opening of the Sonata. A modified statement of the opening theme (mm. 28–39), contains a series of chords with parallel fifths in the bass. This "illegal" progression became acceptable in the late nineteenth century, and parallel fifths will reappear frequently in the composer's œuvre. A secondary lyrical theme (mm. 40–63), leads to the conclusion of the exposition (mm. 64–80), and a triplet figure (m. 74) will play an important role in the development section. This section (mm. 81–200) is predominantly lyrical, largely exploiting the opening theme, which is easily recognizable in its various transformations. A gradual increase in rhythmic motion, from triplets to sixteenth notes to trills, leads to the recapitulation, which is partially masked. In the exposition, the opening theme appears unaccompanied in single notes, but it is now presented in octaves, in a slower tempo, with a full texture in the piano (m. 201). The material in the recapitulation is considerably condensed in relation to the exposition, and the brief coda (mm. 244–51) contains a characteristic progression which recalls the chromaticism of Franck or d'Indy.

In evaluating this composition, it should be recalled that it was Ravel's first chamber work, as well as his first essay in the complex area of sonata form. By 1897 he was undoubtedly acquainted with the standard masterworks of the violin-piano repertory, and he also must have known the recently written sonatas of Fauré (1876) and Franck (1886). Although their influence is perceptible in the Sonata, the composer's distinctive lyricism and harmonic subtlety are in evidence. The melodic material, however, is overly repetitious, and the violin part, although reasonably well written, is not particularly idiomatic. It may be assumed that the composition was ultimately judged too imperfect to warrant publication. As it turns out, the Sonata is not a forerunner of the well-known Sonata for Violin and Piano, but is rather an independent work, whose opening theme foreshadows the beginning of the Trio.

Chanson du rouet (voice and piano, 1898; see Plate 20)

The autograph of *Chanson du rouet* (Song of the Spinning Wheel) is signed by the composer and dated June 2, 1898. The text, by Leconte de

Lisle (1818–94), is taken from a collection of six poems entitled *Chansons écossaises* (Scottish Songs), which appeared in 1852. Other important adaptations from this collection include Fauré's *Nell* and Debussy's *La Fille aux cheveux de lin*. The first two stanzas of the poem are joyful and carefree: the poet sings of his love for the spinning wheel, which provides him with all his needs. But in the final stanza, a foreboding mood appears, as the poet contemplates that the whirring spinning wheel will weave his shroud when he approaches death. As in Schubert's *Gretchen am Spinnrade,* an undulating accompaniment appears throughout the song, suggesting the continual motion of the spinning wheel. The highly chromatic accompaniment suggests the spiritual influence of Chopin, and in the course of setting the final stanza, the requiem sequence *Dies Irae* is quoted in the piano. In addition to this adaptation of Gregorian chant, which is unique in Ravel's œuvre, the words "je ferai mon lit éternel et froid" are set in a quasi-Gregorian manner, the melody being restricted to two notes. In the course of an interview, Roland-Manuel recalled Ravel's somewhat paradoxical opinion of Gregorian chant: although not particularly attracted to it, he found it arresting when harmonized by chords of the seventh and ninth! Of course, the composer's unorthodox use of the *Dies Irae* chant is justified solely on aesthetic grounds. *Chanson du rouet* proved to be a unique encounter with the Parnassian art of Leconte de Lisle, and the motif of a spinning wheel will reappear in the "Danse du rouet" from *Ma Mère l'Oye*.

Si morne! (voice and piano, 1898)

Shortly after completing *Chanson du rouet,* Ravel turned to the Belgian symbolist poet Emile Verhaeren (1855–1916), setting *Si morne!* (So Mournful!), from a group of poems entitled *Les Débâcles* (The Debacles, 1888). The composer's autograph is signed and dated November, 1898. Verhaeren's poem consists of nine stanzas of two verses each (aa, bb . . .), set in the traditional Alexandrine. The pervading mood, that of gloom and foreboding, has been encountered in *Un Grand Sommeil noir,* and the melodic line of both songs is quite similar, pointing to the spiritual influence of Massenet. A whole-tone scale appears in the vocal line at one point, and this mode will soon be exploited extensively in the overture to *Shéhérazade*. The chromatic harmony exhibits considerable sophistication, and the piano accompaniment is an important precursor of "Le Martin-Pêcheur." Together with *Chanson du rouet, Si morne!* constitutes a significant addition to the composer's catalogue of works.

Ouverture de Shéhérazade (orchestra, 1898; see Plate 21)

Much speculation has centered on the overture to *Shéhérazade,* and one author has even claimed that it was destroyed. In reality, there are three autographs of the work, an earlier version for piano four hands, and two complete orchestral holographs. The orchestral versions are signed by the composer and dated November, 1898.[19] As far as is known, Ravel's projected opera based on the *Thousand and One Nights* was never even partially sketched. It is possible, of course, that his original concept was later modified, resulting in the well-known song cycle, *Shéhérazade.* We may refer to the composer's program note found on page 24, and make some additional observations. Pierre Lalo's critique notwithstanding, the overture is classically oriented, as follows: (1) Introduction (mm. 1–24); (2) Exposition (mm. 25–88); (3) Development section (mm. 89–179); (4) Modified restatement (mm. 180–217); (5) Return of the introduction, which serves as the coda (mm. 218–34).

The whole-tone scale is used extensively throughout the work, not to suggest a nebulous mist as in Debussy's *Voiles,* but rather to evoke oriental exoticism. Thus, in the overture, the scale is always presented in a pointed manner. There are five basic elements in the development section: four themes [the oboe solo (m. 1), the initial theme (m. 25), the episodic theme (m. 71), the Persian melody (m. 75)], and a sixteenth-note pattern derived from the initial theme, first presented in the clarinet (mm. 41–43). The various elements are easily recognizable, and are juxtaposed and combined,

---

[19] The piano version contains several omissions and numerous minor errors. One of the orchestral holographs served as a conductor's score, and it contains many cues as well as some minor slips. Although the second orchestral holograph is a cleaner copy, it too contains errors. At measure 85, a significant difference between the two holographs may be observed. The "clean copy" has the Persian melody played by the basses, while the "conductor's score" has the melody for the basses doubled by one bassoon. It is evident that the conductor's score is the correct version.

rather than treated in motivic fashion. At measure 113, we come to the section which was described as "a pedal point based on the expanded initial theme." The term "pedal point" is apparently used to suggest a repeated melody which is not restricted to the bass. As this repeated melody unfolds (derived from mm. 41–43), it is combined with material which has been previously presented (mm. 113–38). Soon after, utilizing the whole-tone scale, the orchestra crescendos to the most climactic point of the overture, which is followed by a brief pause (mm. 177–79). The return of the initial theme, which is soon combined with the introductory theme (m. 187), leads to a full orchestral presentation of the Persian melody. This brief and modified restatement is followed by the coda, which is subdued and retrospective. Ravel later found the overture "poorly constructed;" he probably meant that its structure lacked subtlety. Thus, for Pierre Lalo, the structure was chaotic, but for the composer, it was apparently too obvious. Is it any wonder, then, that the views of the critic and the composer were to remain so divergent?

Much speculation has arisen as to the relationship, or lack thereof, between the overture to *Shéhérazade* and its homonymous song cycle.[20] As perhaps might be expected, there are many similarities, and in particular, the opening theme of "Asie" appears to have been derived to some extent from part of the initial theme of the overture (see Example 7). The similarity between these melodies should not be overemphasized, as they are both based upon a modally inflected scale which evokes "oriental" music to western ears. Strictly speaking, neither the overture to *Shéhérazade* nor its homonymous song cycle bears any relationship to authentic oriental music. As Jules Van Ackere has pointed out, "it is the Orient as a western artist sees it and understands it through illusion, evoked by imagination and by entirely personal means."[21] The most important spiritual influence on the overture was Rimsky-Korsakov's orchestral suite *Shéhérazade* (1888). In both scores, one observes the active participation of the percussion family, and in one passage for the full orchestra, Ravel calls for a tympani roll, coupled with the gong, the celesta, a roll of the cymbals rubbed against each other, and harp glissandi (mm. 135–37). This may well have been one of the "piquant ef-

---

[20] René Dumesnil incorrectly claimed that the two *Shéhérazades* were similar in name only (*Portraits de musiciens français,* p. 228), while Roland-Manuel noted their spiritual kinship (*Ravel,* p. 34).

[21] Van Ackere, *Maurice Ravel,* p. 46.

Oboe solo   2 oboes

(m. 2)   (m.27)

"Asie" (très lent)   Overture to *Shêhêrazade*
             (mouvement modéré de marche)

Example 7

fects of timbre'' which Lalo commented upon. The strings, woodwinds, and brass are generally used in traditional fashion, while an ad libitum accompaniment in the cellos (mm. 132–35), suggests the direct influence of Rimsky-Korsakov's orchestral technique. The overture to *Shéhérazade* is thus a Janus-faced work, looking back in workmanship to the Russian school, while looking ahead to its homonymous song cycle. The relationship between Ravel's overture and song cycle is analogous to that of "Entre cloches" and "La Vallée des cloches": although the earlier composition indicates marked ability, the complete fulfillment of the composer's vision is found only in the latter work.

Epigrammes de Clément Marot (voice and piano, 1896–99)
 1) "D'Anne qui me jecta de la neige" (1899)
 2) "D'Anne jouant de l'espinette" (1896)

The art of Clément Marot (1496–1544) has qualities that appeal to most Frenchmen: delicate charm, polish, clarity, and wit. Ravel was particularly attracted to the orthographical curiosities of Renaissance French, and the poet's original titles, "D'Anne qui luy jecta de la neige," and "D'Anne," appear to have been modified by the composer. The songs continue in the directions of refinement and preciosity coupled with archaic pastiche.

 1) "D'Anne qui me jecta de la neige" (très lent). The accompaniment of this gentle love poem exhibits a deliberately archaic use of parallel fifths and octaves. The supple vocal line is occasionally underpinned by chords of the seventh and ninth with parallel fifths in the bass, which recall those found in the *Pavane pour une Infante défunte*.

 2) "D'Anne jouant de l'espinette" (très léger et d'un rythme précis).

A dance-like and crisp accompaniment for the harpsichord or piano with the soft pedal underscores the poet's dainty portrait of Anne singing and playing the spinet. The setting exhibits a recurring interplay of tonic minor and modal dominant, and the song concludes rather unexpectedly on the modal dominant.

Pavane pour une Infante défunte (piano, 1899)

The composition of a pavane reaffirms Ravel's interest in stylized dance rhythms, while the remainder of the title, "pour une Infante défunte," apparently signifies nothing more than the composer's enjoyment of its alliteration. In criticizing its "rather poor form," (A,B,B',A',C,C',A″), the composer implied that the subdivisions of the *Pavane* are overly obvious, and the "excessive influence of Chabrier" may be seen in comparing the *Pavane* with the "Idylle" from the *Dix Pièces pittoresques* (1881). One observes a similar gentle lyricism, and the opening disposition of the hands is identical in both pieces. The orchestral transcription of the *Pavane,* like that of the *Menuet antique,* is efficacious, calling for no special commentary.

Music for the Prix de Rome (1900–1905)

Ravel's official essays for the Prix de Rome are dated 1900, 1901, 1902, 1903, and 1905. Rather than discuss these works separately, it will be more useful to comment upon them with regard to their respective genres: fugues, choral pieces, and cantatas. The following table lists the composer's essays:

PRELIMINARY ROUND			FINAL ROUND
Year	*Fugue*	*Choral piece*	*Cantata*
1900	D major,$\frac{3}{4}$, 4 pp.	*Les Bayadères* (The Bayadères)$\frac{6}{8}$, G minor, soprano soloist, mixed chorus, and orchestra. 23 pp.	No cantata, as Ravel was eliminated in the preliminary round.

1901	F major,$\frac{4}{4}$, 6 pp.	*Tout est lumière* (All Is Light), $\frac{6}{8}$, A major, soprano soloist, mixed chorus, and orchestra. 26 pp.	*Myrrha,* text by Fernand Beissier, based on the drama *Sardanapalus,* by Lord Byron. For three solo voices and orchestra. 102 pp.
1902	B♭ major,$\frac{4}{4}$, 6 pp.	*La Nuit* (Evening),$\frac{12}{8}$, E♭ major, soprano soloist, mixed chorus, and orchestra. 17 pp.	*Alcyone,* text by Eugène and Edouard Adénis, based on Ovid's *Metamorphoses.* For three solo voices and orchestra. 106 pp.
1903	E minor,$\frac{3}{2}$, 4 pp.	*Matinée de Provence* (Morning in Provence), $\frac{4}{4}$, A major, soprano soloist, mixed chorus, and orchestra. 21 pp.	*Alyssa,* text by Marguerite Coiffier, based on an Irish legend. For three solo voices and orchestra. 111 pp. (In the autograph the concluding passage is missing.)
1905	C major,$\frac{2}{4}$, 4 pp.	*L'Aurore* (Dawn), mostly in $\frac{3}{4}$, E♭ major, tenor soloist, mixed chorus, and orchestra. 28 pp.	No cantata, as Ravel was eliminated in the preliminary round.

These competition essays, which are virtually unknown, date from the very same years which saw the creation of *Jeux d'eau,* the String Quartet, and the song cycle *Shéhérazade.* They are easily the most unimaginative works to come from Ravel's pen, principally because he deliberately curtailed his creativeness in a vain attempt to satisfy the highly conservative judges. Coupled with uninspired choral and cantata texts, which were set in haste, the net result is a large body of music whose interest is purely historical and academic.

1) *Fugues.* The fugues are based upon given subjects, and each part is notated in a different clef (soprano, alto, tenor, and bass). The various technicalities of fugal discipline (subject, countersubject, stretto, and so on), are marked in the autographs.[22] From the Middle Ages until the generation of Johann Sebastian Bach, strict contrapuntal technique was a natural form of aesthetic expression, but for the generation of Haydn and Mozart, it had already become a conscious turning back toward a previous style. The nineteenth century had relatively little use for strict counterpoint, and for Ravel's generation it was a discipline to be mastered as a musical gymnastic. His views of the Conservatoire's rigorous fugal discipline were probably summed up by Debussy, in the course of a conversation with Ernest Guiraud.

[22] The opening page of Ravel's fugue for the 1905 Prix de Rome is printed in *The Music Forum,* 3 (1973), 302.

GUIRAUD: I am not saying that what you do isn't beautiful, but it's theoretically absurd.

DEBUSSY: There is no theory. You have merely to listen. Pleasure is the law. . . .

GUIRAUD: Come now, you are forgetting that you yourself were ten years at the Conservatoire. . . .

DEBUSSY: I can't reconcile all this. True enough, I feel free because I have been through the mill, and I don't write in the fugal style because I know it.[23]

Ravel had also "been through the mill" with regard to academic discipline, and his fugues as well as his harmony exercises were notated in open score, utilizing four different clefs. He believed this type of rigorous academic training to be indispensable, for it assisted the composer in mastering his craft. Although elements of contrapuntal discipline will appear in the Sonatine, the "Fugue" from Le Tombeau de Couperin, and the concluding chorus of L'Enfant et les sortilèges, all of these exhibit considerably more harmonic orientation than the Prix de Rome fugues. Furthermore, the fugue from Le Tombeau de Couperin is at once distinguished from its predecessors by its triadic subject, its three-part texture, making it the only such fugue that Ravel ever wrote, and, above all, by its sensibility.

2) *Choral pieces.* The harmony in these compositions is strikingly simple, not exceeding the diatonicism found in Schubert's earliest symphonies. The texts are commonplace, calling for no special commentary, and the autographs have several obvious errors, because of the short span of time within which both the fugue and the choral piece had to be completed. The first choral work, *Les Bayadères* (1900), is poor in musical substance and is carelessly notated. The next three compositions, *Tout est lumière* (1901), *La Nuit* (1902), and *Matinée de Provence* (1903), are better, and are on the whole more carefully worked out. As we have observed, the composer's final choral entry, *L'Aurore* (1905), was not academically acceptable. Following these Prix de Rome essays, Ravel wrote for mixed chorus on three other occasions: in *Daphnis et Chloé,* the Three Songs for Unaccompanied Mixed Chorus, and the brief choral section which concludes *L'Enfant et les sortilèges.*

3) *Cantatas.* The cantatas, which were composed at the piano and then orchestrated, offer a kaleidoscopic pastiche of nineteenth-century practice, ranging from Schubert through Wagner, passing by Gounod, Massenet, Liszt, Schumann, Weber, Bellini, and Donizetti. One observes string trem-

[23] Lockspeiser, *Debussy: His Life and Mind,* I, 206–07.

olos on diminished chords, passionate Italianate love duets, swelling chromatic scales which evoke storm scenes, and, in general, a romantic style of lyricism and brooding which would be worthy of any second-rate contemporary of Meyerbeer. Nevertheless, the music is of some historical interest as it does reveal what the Conservatoire was teaching its pupils, and a comparison of Ravel's cantatas with those of the prize winners indicates that he fulfilled his assignments in traditional fashion.[24] It has been claimed that Ravel's cantatas were actually parodies of academically correct work, but I believe they should be accepted at face value, keeping in mind the composer's observation about writing "dull" and "accessible" music for the "gentlemen of the Institute." In *Myrrha* (p. 75 of the autograph), one passage exhibits the harmonic minor scale, which is found nowhere else in Ravel's œuvre. Two excerpts may be taken as representative:

1) In Alcyone's dream, as King Céyx's ship is struck by the waves, one observes Wagnerian orchestration: the melody is played by three trombones and tuba, accompanied by diminished chords, string tremolos, and chromatic scales (see Plate 22).

2) In Alyssa and Braïzyl's love duet, the melody soars up to a high A$\sharp$, in the tradition of nineteenth-century Italian opera, accompanied by string tremolos and a full orchestral texture (see Plate 23).

On the basis of the autographs, it seems to me that the prizes awarded to André Caplet and Aymé Kunc might just as well have been given to Ravel. All of the cantatas appear equally acceptable, and all of the autographs contain about the same number of errors and corrections. In 1903, the Grand Prix was awarded to Raoul Laparra, whose cantata is carefully notated and, I believe, superior to Ravel's. It is perhaps idle to speculate upon what changes would have come about in the composer's career had he won the Grand Prix. What is known is that without the benefit of any official recompense, he promptly embarked upon a period of important creative activity.

---

[24] The prize-winning essays for the Prix de Rome are found in the Music Division of the Bibliothèque Nationale:

1901	André Caplet	MS. 3866–3868
1902	Aymé Kunc	MS. 7027 (1–3)
1903	Raoul Laparra	MS. 7096 (1–3)

Jeux d'eau (piano, 1901)

The score of *Jeux d'eau* (Fountains) bears a quotation from "Fête d'eau," a poem in Henri de Régnier's collection *La Cité des eaux:* "Dieu fluvial riant de l'eau qui le chatouille" (A river god laughing at the water which titillates him). From the first poem in his collection, "Salut à Versailles," until the last, "La Louange des Eaux, des Arbres et des Dieux," Henri de Régnier conjured up a remarkable variety of undulating images, and Ravel's epigraph aptly focuses upon a suggestion of joyful sensuality which is omnipresent in the music.

The title apparently derives from Liszt's *Les Jeux d'eau à la Villa d'Este* (1883). Both compositions make many technical demands upon the performer, and both exploit the upper register of the keyboard. The opening and closing sonorities of *Jeux d'eau* are the chord of the major seventh, which enjoys a privileged position throughout. The composition is based upon two themes (1/1/1 and 3/1/1, Eschig edition), the second pentatonic, which are treated quite freely. Following an extensive development, the two themes return (10/1/1, and 12/2), and the work ends in a sweeping cascade of sixty-fourth notes. The development builds to a climactic trill and descending glissando on the black notes (7/4), which is then underpinned by a nonharmonic low A (7/5/1). It is possible that Ravel would have wanted a low G♯ (which of course does not exist on the piano), as the following two pages and the recapitulation are underpinned by a pedal point on G♯.[25] The unmeasured cadenza just after the recapitulation is of particular significance (11/2), pitting F♯ major against C major triads, in an early example of bitonality. With its unique melding of Lisztian virtuosity, bitonality, pentatonicism, and impressionism, *Jeux d'eau* marks a distinguished achievement of far-reaching importance.

[25] In the piano version of the overture to *Shéhérazade,* (Autograph, p. 24), a low A appears in the bass, with the following note by the composer: "The A replaces G, which is nonexistent on the modern piano."

Quatuor (String Quartet, 1902–03) [26]

1) Allegro moderato—très doux (F major)
2) Assez vif—très rythmé (A minor)
3) Très lent (Gb major)
4) Vif et agité (F major)

The String Quartet marks the composer's first important chamber work, and the advance from the early Sonata for Violin and Piano is indeed striking. Although modeled on Debussy's Quartet (1893), Ravel's achievement is both mature and personal. The composer's fascination with instrumental color and virtuosity is apparent, and the overall modus operandi is that of thematic transformation, which occurs within individual movements as well as between the movements.

1) Allegro moderato—très doux. The prevailing mood is lyrical, with an underlying optimism and classical restraint. The sonata form is clear, with themes one and two joined in various transformations in the development section (cf. 5/2/3). As in the early Sonata for Violin and Piano, the development section is predominantly lyrical, building to its most climactic point shortly before the recapitulation (8/2/3). In the recapitulation, the return of the second theme is clear yet subtle, as the upper three parts are identical to the exposition, but the cello is raised a minor third, altering the passage from D minor to F major (12/2/1). The thematic transformations found in this movement will recur in the third and fourth movements, producing a tightly knit structure which will soon reappear in the Sonatine.

2) Assez vif—très rythmé. Like the second movement of Debussy's Quartet, the opening of this virtuoso scherzo may be said to bear the spiritual imprint of the Javanese gamelan. The scherzo is largely based upon two themes, the first pizzicato in the aeolian mode, and the second lyrical (14/3/3). Two rhythmic variants of the opening theme may be pointed out (20/3/1 and 21/1), the second of which is marked "quasi arpa."

3) Très lent. This lyrical and rhapsodic movement contains numerous changes in tempo, many references to the first movement (cf. 26/4/4 and 4/1/2, with regard to the melody and the use of parallel fifths), and material from the first and third movements skillfully woven together (31/4/3). Ex-

---

[26] The first edition of the String Quartet was published by Gabriel Astruc in 1904. Six years later, at Ravel's request, the rights were ceded to Durand, and a "new edition reviewed by the author" was published. Aside from two minor corrections, both scores are identical.

amples of instrumental color include the four soloists playing on the finger-board (30/3/1), or entirely in the treble clef (33/4/5).

4) Vif et agité. The finale alternates driving tremolo passages, mostly in quintuple meter, with lyric material derived from the first movement, chiefly in triple meter (cf. 37/3/6 and 4/2/4). The agitato passages are spiritually akin to Schubertian drama rather than Beethovenian struggle, and the movement concludes brilliantly, with a brief reprise of the opening of the finale, followed by an ascending series of major triads. Although Ravel later criticized the Quartet's "imperfectly realized" structure, it now appears to be a fresh and felicitous achievement, marking a distinctive addition to the chamber music repertoire.

Manteau de fleurs (voice and piano, 1903)

With its numerous measured thirty-second notes, the piano accompaniment of *Manteau de fleurs* is unidiomatic, suggesting orchestral sonorities. Although the orchestral version is somewhat better, the poem is commonplace and the accompaniment is rather repetitious. It may be added that Debussy (*Dans le jardin*) and d'Indy (*Mirage*) were equally unable to overcome the banality of Gravollet's texts. Ravel later returned to the motif of flowers in his ballet libretto *Adélaïde, ou le langage des fleurs*.

Shéhérazade (voice and orchestra or piano, 1903)
1) "Asie"
2) "La Flûte enchantée"
3) "L'Indifférent"

Tristan Klingsor sent his earliest verses to Leconte de Lisle, who encouraged him. In his poems Klingsor strove for clarity, balance, and, above all, communication with the reader: "My poems are like sketches. . . . A poem should be that already; a point of departure for a song, or a melody. . . . Perhaps that is why I have had the good fortune to please musicians. You see, I attempted not to be merely a rhymer. I attempted to be a rhythmist. Rhythm, in poetry, music and in painting, is the artist's foremost resource." [27]

Ravel was attracted not only to the oriental lure of Klingsor's collection, but also to its subtle free verse, and its vivid pictorial imagery. The text is set syllabically, often in a quasi-recitative fashion, underpinned by orchestral motifs, and this apparently accounts for the composer's acknowledgment of Debussy's "spiritual influence" on the song cycle. The vocal line in *Pelléas et Mélisande,* however, is generally closer to recitative. In adapting Klingsor's poems, Ravel was primarily concerned with transforming the rhythmic subtleties of free verse into melody, a direction he would pursue in the *Histoires naturelles* and *L'Heure espagnole*. The first poem, "Asie," is long, offering a sweeping panorama of oriental fantasy. It is built upon two orchestral themes (1/2, oboe solo, and 4/1/2, clarinets, Durand miniature score for voice and orchestra), which will reappear in various transformations (cf. 36/2 and 31/1). The text is subdivided into various sections separated by brief interludes. The imaginary visit to China, for example, is distinguished by a rapid tempo in a strict beat, coupled with parallel fifths in the horns and parallel seconds in the celesta (20/2), which evoke a dainty "oriental" scene. "La Flûte enchantée" and "L'Indifférent" are considerably shorter, and each song concludes with a brief yet subtly modified reference to its opening theme. The cycle gradually decreases in intensity, from the rich voluptuousness of "Asie" through the gentle lyricism of "La Flûte enchantée" to the languid sensuousness of "L'Indifférent." One particular motif, a simple alternation of neighboring notes, may be found not only in each of the three songs (cf. 16/2/1, horn; the opening theme of "La Flûte enchantée," and 52/1, oboe), but in the String Quartet (opening of the third movement), the Sonatine (second theme of the first movement), and the *Introduction et Allegro*. In the course of an interview, Manuel Rosenthal recalled the following conversation, which took place during a lesson. "Your earliest works," Ravel explained, "although containing technical imperfections, have one vital quality—the freshness of youth. Later on, you will acquire greater technical mastery, but one

---

[27] L. J. Pronger, *La Poésie de Tristan Klingsor* (Paris: M. J. Minard, 1965), p. 95. Among Klingsor's most important collections of poems are *Filles-Fleurs* (1895), *Humoresques* (1921), and *Cinquante Sonnets du dormeur éveillé* (1949). In 1959, he was awarded a Grand Prix in poetry by the Académie Française, and three years later he won the Prix Ronsard for his collected works.

does not have both freshness of youth and full technical mastery, for the latter replaces the former." When asked which of his own works had best captured this freshness of youth, the composer immediately replied *"Shéhérazade,"* and candidly admitted that, in his opinion, the song cycle contained technical imperfections. From our vantage point, *Jeux d'eau,* the String Quartet, and *Shéhérazade* indicate both freshness of youth and mastery.

Sonatine (piano, 1903–05)

1) Modéré (doux et expressif)
2) Mouvement de menuet
3) Animé

The title of this work indicates a willing return to late eighteenth-century elegance and structural clarity. The opening movement is set in a closely knit sonata form, beginning with a descending fourth (F♯–C♯), which will be prominent throughout the work. The accompaniment of the second theme, with its parallel fifths in the bass and the tenth above, is commonly found in the composer's earlier works (*Pavane pour une Infante défunte,* or *Manteau de fleurs*). The texture is lucid throughout, even at the most climactic point in the development section, and the concluding measures of the movement appear to foreshadow the opening of the minuet (cf. the melody, 5/6/4–5/6/6 and 6/1/1–6/1/2).

The embellishments and modal inflections in the minuet carry on in the tradition of the *Menuet antique.* A slower, secondary theme, deriving from the opening of the first movement, is presented in augmentation with itself (7/1/1), and leads to a modified reprise of the minuet.

The finale is virtually a perpetual motion, whose agitato passages are spiritually related to those of the String Quartet. The descending fourth, recalling the first movement, appears frequently (cf. 9/4/1 and 15/2/1), while an accompaniment figure, outlining the fourth, derives from the minuet (cf. 10/5/2 and 7/2/3). Several sequential patterns based on the chord of the minor ninth are characteristic (12/1/1–12/2/3), and the coda, in F♯ major, brings the work to a brilliant conclusion. Although well written and attractive, the Sonatine does not match the composer's next achievement for the keyboard, the *Miroirs*.

Miroirs (Mirrors, piano, 1904–05)

1) "Noctuelles" ("Night Moths")
2) "Oiseaux tristes" ("Sorrowful Birds")
3) "Une Barque sur l'océan" ("A Boat on the Ocean")
4) "Alborada del gracioso" ("Aubade of the Jester")
5) "La Vallée des cloches" ("The Valley of the Bells")

The title *Miroirs* implies an objective, though personal, reflection of reality, and each composition is pictorial to some extent. Ravel observed that the *Miroirs* "marked a rather considerable change in my harmonic evolution, which disconcerted even those musicians who had been accustomed to my style . . . The most characteristic piece, in my opinion, is 'Oiseaux tristes.' In this work, I evoke birds lost in the torpor of a somber forest, during the most torrid hours of summertime" ("Autobiographical Sketch"). The "disconcerting" harmonies may refer to the avoidance of tonic triads over extended periods or to the many unresolved chords over pedal points. The structures found in *Miroirs* are freer than in any of Ravel's previous works, and in this regard, the spiritual influence of Debussy's *D'un cahier d'esquisses* (1903) is significant. Debussy told Ricardo Viñes that he wished to write music whose form would be so free as to appear improvised. When Viñes related this to his *Apaches* friends, Ravel was enthusiastic, and it was not long after that he performed "Oiseaux tristes" for his colleagues.

1) "Noctuelles" (très léger). With its many changes of meter and brief unmeasured runs, the rhythm is quite free in this impressionistic étude. A contrasting section, built over a pedal point (5/1/1, Eschig edition), recalls the Sonatine, with its repeated descending fourth (5/3/3). Following a return to the original tempo, there is a free reprise of the opening section, a brief evocation of the contrasting section (10/3/1), and a quiet, rapid codetta. As in the conclusion of the Sonatine, the final passage opposes the lowered and raised third.

2) "Oiseaux tristes" (très lent). This second portrait of nature is based

upon a number of bird calls, the most important of which appears at the beginning of the piece. A repetition of the opening theme (11/3/2) leads to fresh material by means of an enharmonic change from E♭ to D♯ (12/1/1). An evocative nonmeasured cadenza is followed by an insistent D♯ (14/4/1–3), which finally resolves enharmonically to the tonic, which, as in "Noctuelles," has been avoided virtually throughout the piece.

3) "Une Barque sur l'océan" (d'un rythme souple—très enveloppé de pédales). This piece, the longest of the set, is technically even more difficult than *Jeux d'eau,* to which it is spiritually akin. Despite the sweeping arpeggios up and down the breadth of the keyboard, the melodic thread is clear, and the work ends with a characteristic reference to the opening theme. The orchestral transcription, which is not particularly successful, was disavowed by Ravel and was first published posthumously.

4) "Alborada del gracioso" (assez vif). The title of this composition focuses upon Hispanic lyricism coupled with humor, which will soon reappear in *L'Heure espagnole.* In this brilliant panorama, the piano acts as a guitar, a languid voice, or a full orchestra. The pointed opening, with its triplet figures, is contrasted with an extended lyrical section (36/1/5), which features many chords over pedal points and much rhythmic variety. A reprise of the opening mood (40/4/3) has rapid repeated notes and glissandi in double notes, together with stretto-like condensation of material previously presented (cf. 43/1/3–43/2/2 and 37/3/1–37/5/2). The piece ends orchestrally, with a parting reference to the opening theme. The transcription of "Alborada del gracioso" has been exhaustively analyzed by Van Ackere (*Maurice Ravel,* pp. 164–68). Attention may be called to the active percussion section, the lyrical exploitation of the bassoon, the subtle string divisi, and four additional measures of dental tremolos in the woodwinds, which do not exist in the piano version (cf. 31/3–6, Eschig miniature score). Trombone glissandi highlight the humor and brilliance of the concluding measures.

5) "La Vallée des cloches" (très lent). (See the commentary on "Entre cloches," p. 143.) Ravel told Robert Casadesus that "La Vallée des cloches" was inspired by the many Parisian church bells which toll at noon, and the composer soon returned to the sound of bells in *La Cloche engloutie, L'Heure espagnole,* and *Gaspard de la nuit.* With their sensitive portrayals of animal life, the nostalgia of water, Hispanic fantasy, and the tin-

tinnabulation of bells, the *Miroirs* constitute a varied landscape, and mark a distinguished contribution to the literature of the piano.

Cinq Mélodies populaires grecques
(Five Greek Folk Songs,
voice and piano, 1904–06)

1) "Chanson de la mariée" ("Song for the Bride")
2) "Là-bas, vers l'église" ("Yonder, by the Church")
3) "Quel galant m'est comparable" ("What Suitor Can Compare with Me?")
4) "Chanson des cueilleuses de lentisques" ("Song of the Girls Gathering Mastic")
5) "Tout gai!" ("Be Gay!")

A comparison of the Durand edition with Hubert Pernot's collection of folk songs shows that several minor rhythmic adjustments were made in the melodies. The accompaniments, which apparently were composed with little difficulty, blend perfectly with their respective melodies, skillfully capturing the various folk expressions of love, faith, and joy.

Noël des jouets (The Toys' Christmas, voice and piano
or orchestra, 1905)

The depiction of a Christmas manger, with toy animals, flocks, and angels, affirms Ravel's fascination with the pristine world of childhood. The clarity and tenderness of the composer's poem are not unrelated to some of Jules Renard's *Histoires naturelles,* and passages in the piano recall the second movement of the Sonatine. Ravel commented that the music is "clear and plain, like the mechanical toys of the poem," and the parallel seconds and concluding fanfare in the accompaniment will reappear with increased effect in *Ma Mère l'Oye.*

Introduction et Allegro (for harp, accompanied by string quartet, flute, and clarinet, 1905)

Although the full title of this work is rather cumbersome, Ravel apparently wished to stress the privileged position of the harp, and the composition should thus be considered a miniature harp concerto rather than a septet. The *Introduction et Allegro* is spiritually akin to the refinement of the Marot epigrams and the languid sensuality of "L'Indifférent." The score is replete with brilliant passages for the harp, and as in Mendelssohn's Violin Concerto, the cadenza appears just before the recapitulation. The introduction presents three themes (1/1/1, woodwinds; 2/1/2, woodwinds; and 2/2/3, cello, Durand miniature score), which reappear in the allegro, which is set in the traditional sonata form. A fourth theme, in $\frac{3}{4}$, exploits hemiola rhythm (11/2/2). If the structure of the *Introduction et Allegro* is straightforward, the score indicates an innovative approach with regard to instrumental color, coupled with many subtleties in rhythm and phrasing. The pleasure-loving sensuousness found in this composition will recur with greater maturity in the *Valses nobles et sentimentales*.

Histoires naturelles (voice and piano, 1906)
1) "Le Paon" ("The Peacock")
2) "Le Grillon" ("The Cricket")
3) "Le Cygne" ("The Swan")
4) "Le Martin-Pêcheur" ("The Kingfisher")
5) "La Pintade" ("The Guinea Fowl")

In September, 1895, shortly before the publication of the *Histoires naturelles,* Jules Renard (1864–1910) wrote in his *Journal: "Histoires naturelles*—Buffon [28] described animals in order to give pleasure to men. As for me, I would wish to be pleasing to the animals themselves. If they were

---

[28] Renard's title is indebted to the distinguished eighteenth-century French naturalist Georges-Louis Leclerc, Comte de Buffon, whose monumental *Histoire naturelle* was published in forty-four volumes between 1749 and 1804. It appears that Renard also borrowed some of Buffon's phraseology. See Léon Guichard, *L'Œuvre et l'âme de Jules Renard* (Paris: Nizet et Bastard, 1935), pp. 200–05.

able to read my miniature *Histoires naturelles,* I should wish that it would make them smile." The subtlety of Renard's technique has been perceptively analyzed as follows:

> Intimately bound with the overall sentence structure is the skillful interlocking of linguistic levels. Rhetoric and colloquialism are juxtaposed; the polished literary phrase is preceded or followed by a matter-of-fact aside. This variation enables Renard to change his point of view, moving into and out of the mind of his subject at will (and in this respect at least he is indebted to La Fontaine). In this way he is able to achieve changes of tempo and subtle effects of irony.[29]

Two important spiritual ancestors of Ravel's song cycle were Chabrier's charming and humorous animal songs and Mussorgsky's incomplete opera *The Marriage.* In setting Gogol's play, Mussorgsky observed that he was "crossing the Rubicon. This is living prose in music . . . this is reverence toward the language of humanity, this is a reproduction of simple human speech." [30] Mussorgsky's goal was adopted by Ravel, who observed that in the *Histoires naturelles,* "the diction must lead the music." In order to approximate the tone of conversation, the meter is frequently changed, and the melody often moves within a limited range. In this regard, Emile Vuillermoz made the following personal observation:

> When Ravel made one of those razor-edged remarks of which he alone possessed the secret, he used to make a characteristic gesture: he put his right hand quickly behind his back, described a sort of ironical pirouette, cast down his mischievously sparkling eyes and let his voice suddenly drop a fourth or a fifth. In the *Histoires naturelles* and *L'Heure espagnole* one finds this characteristic intonation in all sorts of places. It is Ravel's own voice, his pronunciation, his well-known mannerisms, that have produced this *quasi parlando* melody.[31]

The accompaniment frequently underscores the humor of the poems. Thus, one encounters rapid glissandi as the peacock spreads his tail, or when the impetuous guinea fowl bumps into a turkey. Above all, the *Histoires naturelles* reaffirm the marked sensitivity of author and composer in depicting the magical world of animal life.

1) "Le Paon" (sans hâte et noblement). The recurring dotted pattern in

---

[29] Basil Deane, "Renard, Ravel, and the 'Histoires naturelles,' " *Australian Journal of French Studies,* 1 (1964), 179.

[30] J. Leyda and S. Bertensson, *The Mussorgsky Reader* (New York: W. W. Norton, 1947), p. 112.

[31] Vuillermoz et al., *Maurice Ravel par quelques-uns de ses familiers,* p. 60.

the accompaniment, which humorously recalls the splendor of the French Baroque overture, introduces the vain peacock, who is jilted on his wedding day. The phrase "La fiancée n'arrive pas," is set to six notes: La fian-cée n'a-rrive pas (instead of the traditional nine: La fi-an-cé-e n'a-rriv-e pas), which apparently was an important factor in the scandalous reception of the song.

2) "Le Grillon" (placide). Running sixteenth notes evoke the household activities of this industrious cricket, and the dynamic range lies between pppp and p. As in Haydn's oratorio *The Seasons,* the cricket's chirps are suggested by the interval of the second. Although beginning in A minor, the song ends in D♭ major, as the A moves to G♯ (7/4/4), which enharmonically resolves to D♭ (8/1/1 and 10/1/4). In contrast to the playful simplicity throughout, the concluding verse is set solemnly, with a full texture.

3) "Le Cygne" (lent). The opening accompaniment figure recalls the undulations of *Jeux d'eau,* as the graceful swan glides over the water. The bold irony of the poem appears only at the conclusion. With the accompaniment marked "très sec et bien rythmé," the graceful swan is compared to a fat goose.

4) "Le Martin-Pêcheur" (on ne peut plus lent). The dynamic range is between ppp and mf in this hushed evocation of a kingfisher alighting on a fisherman's rod. The vocal line is supple, underpinned by some of Ravel's most intricate and sensuous harmonies. The concluding measures (17/4/1), with their characteristic parallel fifths in the bass, proceed from the subdominant minor ninth to a tonic chord, with added sixth and second. "Le Martin-Pêcheur" is perhaps the outstanding achievement of the cycle.

5) "La Pintade" (assez vite). Following the hushed portrait of the kingfisher, the raucous guinea fowl bursts upon the scene. The introduction, "ff rageusement," depicts the discordant cry of this combative, hunchbacked creature. In essence an E major chord, it pits G♮ against G♯, and F♮ against E. Following the guinea fowl's amusing antics, his piercing cry is heard at the end of the song, bringing the cycle to a spirited conclusion.

The *Histoires naturelles* were illustrated by Vallotton (1896), Toulouse-Lautrec (1899), and Bonnard (1904), and were declaimed in public by Lucien Guitry and other leading actors of the day. Although viewed with much suspicion and hostility in 1907, time has vindicated Ravel's interpretation of the *Histoires naturelles,* and the cycle now appears to be an important and original contribution to French song.

Vocalise-Etude en forme de Habanera (voice and piano, 1907)

This song was commissioned by A. L. Hettich, a professor of voice at the Conservatoire, to introduce the students to contemporary vocal études. Many composers responded to Hettich's request, among them Fauré, Honegger, Ibert, and Roussel. Ravel's vocalization, which is underpinned by the habanera rhythm, gives the performer ample opportunity for display within a limited range of virtuosity. The composition later achieved considerable popularity in a violin transcription entitled *Pièce en forme de Habanera,* and thus for once the tables were turned on the master adapter of the art of others.

Les Grands Vents venus d'outremer (voice and piano, 1907)

This symbolist poem by Henri de Régnier (1864–1936) first appeared in a collection *Tel qu'en songe* (1892). The pathos and violence of the poem are reasonably well matched by a turbulent, highly chromatic, and somewhat overcharged accompaniment, which is frequently quite independent of the vocal line. Although the chromaticism partially recalls *Si morne!,* the setting is somewhat atypical, and the song occupies a relatively isolated position in the composer's catalogue.

Sur l'herbe (voice and piano, 1907)

In a letter to Jean-Aubry, written in September, 1907, Ravel commented on *Sur l'herbe:* "In this piece, as in the *Histoires naturelles,* the im-

165

pression must be given that one is almost not singing. A bit of preciosity is found there which is indicated moreover by the text and the music.'' [32] The abbé's charming and incoherent comments, which include two allusions to music, are underscored by a graceful accompaniment, which evokes an eighteenth-century dance. The autograph of *Sur l'herbe* suggests that Ravel contemplated setting a series of poems from *Fêtes galantes,* but as it turned out, the song proved to be his final adaptation of Verlaine's poetry. Another creditable setting of *Sur l'herbe* was composed by Raoul Laparra (Emile Gallet et Fils, 1927).

Rapsodie espagnole (orchestra 1907–08)

1) "Prélude à la nuit" ($\frac{3}{4}$, A major)
2) "Malagueña" ($\frac{3}{4}$, A major)
3) "Habanera" ($\frac{2}{4}$, F♯ minor-major)
4) "Feria" ($\frac{6}{8}$, C major)

The *Rapsodie espagnole* marks Ravel's first important orchestral work. Two significant spiritual ancestors of the rhapsody are Chabrier's *España* (1883), with its pleasure-loving ebullience, and Rimsky-Korsakov's *Capriccio espagnol* (1888), with its brilliant orchestral technique. Although actual folk melodies are not quoted in the rhapsody, the colorful rhythms, modality, and the ornamental traits of Spanish music are utilized as a point of departure. The violent contrasts in mood found in the "Malagueña" and "Feria" are also characteristic of the Spanish idiom, while the tightly knit structure and adventurous orchestral technique bespeak the composer's personal stamp.

1) "Prélude à la nuit" (très modéré). The dynamic range does not exceed mf in this hushed, nostalgic evocation. The opening motif (F, E, D, C♯) is virtually omnipresent, and will reappear in the second and fourth movements, recalling the structure of the String Quartet. Furthermore, a melody which is heard above the opening motif (3/2, clarinets, miniature score), will also reappear in the fourth movement (cf. 64/2, first violins).

---

[32] Unpublished letter dated Sept. 4, 1907, in the private collection of Mme G. Jean-Aubry.

The orchestral texture is transparent, and the sonority veiled and sensuous. A characteristic passage (9/1), calls for muted divisi strings playing on the fingerboard, offset by pizzicati in the cellos and basses, coupled with the harps and the celesta. The brief solo cadenzas clearly derive from Rimsky-Korsakov's orchestral technique, but their accompaniment and sonority are thoroughly personal.

2) "Malagueña" (assez vif). The first orchestral tutti in the rhapsody merits careful attention, as many of its details are characteristic (22/1). The four horns are grouped traditionally in interlocking fashion, the three trumpets are closely spaced, and the large percussion section is active, yet clearly subdivided. The tutti is organized by families of instruments: the strings, woodwinds, and brass double one another with regard to the bass note, the harmony, and the melody. In this particular passage, even the tympani share in doubling the bass. This procedure is not a formula, of course, but is rather one important method of organization which will be found later on in the rhapsody (pp. 79 and 88) and in the composer's subsequent works. Following the tutti, a languid recitative for the English horn, underpinned by glissandi in the harp and strings, recalls its counterpart in "Alborada del gracioso."

3) "Habanera" (assez lent et d'un rythme las; see the commentary on *Sites auriculaires,* p. 142). Composed in 1895, the "Habanera" stands apart to some extent from the other movements. Nevertheless, it shares the element of ostinato with the opening movement, and its brevity, languid dance rhythm, and subtle orchestration make it a logical component of the rhapsody. As perhaps might be expected, the pedal point will pass from the woodwinds to the brass, and from the strings to the percussion family.

4) "Feria" (assez animé). The "Feria" is considerably more extended than the preceding movements, and it brings the rhapsody to a brilliant conclusion. The opening section contains three principal themes (39/4, flute; 45/3, muted trumpets; 52/3, flute), and is followed by a languid recitative similar to that found in the "Malagueña." A return of the opening motif, combined with glissandi in diminished chords for four muted violins (64/5), leads to a resumption of the original tempo, and in a free restatement, material from the "Feria" is combined with the opening motif (cf. 82/1, English horn and violins). The rhapsody concludes in a joyous burst of color, as the entire orchestra swells in glissandi, whole-tone scales, and augmented triads, which resolve to C major. With its innovative orchestration and dis-

167

tinctive dancelike and voluptuous moods, the *Rapsodie espagnole* is an important link in the chain of Hispanic exoticism extending from Liszt, Edouard Lalo, and Bizet, through Chabrier, Rimsky-Korsakov, and Debussy.

L'Heure espagnole (The Spanish Hour, opera, 1907–09; see Plate 24 and the composer's comments, pp. 55–56)

The vocal writing and ironic humor of *L'Heure espagnole* have been observed in the *Histoires naturelles,* and the opera's scintillating orchestration and Hispanic fantasy are equally evident in the *Rapsodie espagnole.* In his writings, Franc-Nohain particularly relished odd turns of phrases, curious comic situations, and verbal buffoonery, all of which abound in *L'Heure espagnole.* The opera consists of an orchestral introduction and twenty-one brief scenes, followed by a habanera for the five soloists. Aside from the concluding quintet, much of Gonzalve's role, and Concepcion's scene "Oh! la pitoyable aventure!," the vocal line is set in the *quasi parlando* style of the *Histoires naturelles,* and *L'Heure espagnole* marks the composer's final adaptation of this technique. As in the *Histoires naturelles,* the accompaniment contains most of the thematic material, properly speaking, and the orchestra frequently comments upon the text humorously. In a free adaptation of the Wagnerian leitmotif, most of the roles have their own rhythmic and melodic characteristics. The introduction is an unusually evocative depiction of ticking clocks and dancing automatons, with its pendulums, bells, muted strings, celesta, piccolo, and even one passage played by the detached mouthpiece of the sarrusophone. It will be recalled that *L'Heure espagnole* was written for Joseph Ravel, and the introduction might be summed up as a highly poetic example of Swiss precision engineering. The opening theme of the introduction will evoke the shop as well as its owner Torquemada, who is presented with Ramiro the muleteer in the opening scene. A brief melody (11/2, miniature orchestral score), will be used throughout to identify the robust muleteer, while Concepcion sings mostly in recitative, without any distinguishing characteristics. Unaware of the time, Torquemada is late for his weekly appointment to regulate the municipal clocks. In order to keep the muleteer occupied during her husband's absence, Concepcion asks him to transport a large clock into her bedroom. Her foppish lover Gonzalve soon appears, singing his modally inflected vocalizations (36/1) and absurd rhapsodical poetry, but he is followed unexpectedly by the rich banker Don Inigo Gomez, whose dotted theme promptly depicts him as a vain, human peacock (63/2). In a burlesque scene, he manages to squeeze his corpulent frame into a clock, accompanied by a graceful waltz (79/1/1). Following two off-stage fiascos with Gonzalve and Don Inigo Gomez, who have been transported by Ramiro to her bedroom hidden inside clocks, Concepcion begins to notice the muleteer and invites him to accompany her, this time "without a clock." Torquemada soon returns to find Gonzalve and Don Inigo Gomez still inside their respective clocks, which, of course, they are planning to purchase. All of the players reassemble to join in the final quintet, in which they satirize one another, and conclude with a quotation from Boccaccio: "There comes a moment in the pursuit of love when the muleteer has his turn!"

One of the most arresting features of the score is the seemingly inexhaustible color and variety of the orchestral timbres. Among the solo instruments one finds the trombone, the sarrusophone, the tuba, and the celesta. The writing for the woodwinds calls for considerable agility, and at one point, the xylophone and bells depict the small steps of Ramiro's mules (11/2), while Concepcion's anxiety at Torquemada's lateness is suggested by a series of brief trills in the bassoon, muted trumpet, horn, and trombone (18/1/3). In addition to the concluding habanera, which effectively combines $\frac{6}{8}$ and $\frac{2}{4}$, the composer indulges freely in his penchant for Spanish rhythms and modally inflected passages (cf. 13/2, 40/3, or 157/2/2). Besides the effective addition of Gonzalve's vocalizations, Ravel made several brief cuts in Franc-Nohain's play, the most important of which occurs in Don Inigo Gomez's soliloquy (Scene Nine). Furthermore, the play is situated in "a Spanish clockmaker's shop," which the composer specified as "Toledo, in the eighteenth century." These modifications are less significant than his attitude toward the text, which has been perceptively analyzed by Roland-Manuel:

> He leaves to Franc-Nohain the tone of apparent artlessness which makes the spectator blame himself for giving double meanings to certain conversations which their author did not intend to be perfectly innocent. Ravel did even more than refuse to connive: instead of humanizing the characters, and softening the passions which inflamed them, he ruthlessly lays bare the elementary mechanisms of their

instincts. . . . But by a weird substitution, the hearts he tore from them come to beat tenderly in the breasts of clocks and automatons, lending to these little steel bodies the semblance of a soul and the sweet warmth of life.[33]

Ravel thus eschews traditional operatic passion, and focuses upon mock libertinage and ironic comedy. One present-day author has called *L'Heure espagnole* "a tour de force of rhythm and orchestration, varied and witty in declamation, with a libretto in which the art of the double entendre is carried to a height worthy of Favart." [34] Above all, the opera is a divertissement, and it should be heard and judged in that light.

Following the creation of *L'Heure espagnole,* Franc-Nohain sent his colleague two volumes of his works with the following dedications: "For Maurice Ravel, with the hope that *La Marche indienne* will sing to him like *L'Heure espagnole.*" The inscription in *L'Orphéon* reads: "For Maurice Ravel, hoping for other music by him." It turned out that *L'Heure espagnole* remained the composer's sole adaptation of Franc-Nohain's writings.

Gaspard de la nuit (piano, 1908)
1) "Ondine"
2) "Le Gibet" ("The Gibbet")
3) "Scarbo"

The reputation of Aloysius Bertrand rests entirely upon *Gaspard de la nuit,* which was written about 1830 and first published posthumously in 1842. This collection of poems in prose conjures up mystery, bewitchment, lakes, castles, bells, and strange nocturnal visions. Subtitled "Three Poems for Piano," the complete texts of "Ondine," "Le Gibet," and "Scarbo" appear in the Durand edition, emphasizing the interpretive nature of the music. The influence of Balakirev's *Islamey* and Liszt's *Transcendental Etudes* may be observed in "Ondine" and "Scarbo," while the spiritual imprint of Poe is evident in "Le Gibet." The hauntingly evocative Romanticism of Bertrand's visions are remarkably interpreted in these descriptive tone poems.

[33] Roland-Manuel, *Ravel,* p. 62.

[34] Donald Jay Grout, *A Short History of Opera* (New York: Columbia Univ. Press, 1947), p. 432.

1) "Ondine" (lent). This piece continues in the path outlined by *Jeux d'eau* and "Une Barque sur l'océan," but with even greater virtuosity and opulent iridescence. The introductory figure outlines a major triad with the added minor sixth, which will enjoy a privileged position throughout the piece. The structure is free, deriving largely from the extended opening theme, which recalls a "tender and sad voice." The theme is soon heard in octaves and reappears with various modifications (6/2/1, 7/3/1, and 13/2/1). The most climactic point in the piece (11/2/1), features a series of accented appoggiaturas which descend stepwise, and the rich, sweeping sonority is achieved by nothing more than single notes in both hands. The conclusion of the text is paralleled rather closely in the music. "Her murmured song completed" (13/2/1, the final presentation of the opening theme), she asked me "to accompany her to her palace, in order to be the king of the lakes. And when I told her that I loved a mortal woman, sulky and vexed, she shed several tears" (13/4/2, très lent), "then burst out in laughter" (14/1, rapide et brilliant), "and vanished in a sudden shower which streamed down the length of my blue stained-glass windows" (14/4). "Ondine" concludes with an arpeggiation of the tonic chord with the added minor sixth.

2) "Le Gibet" (très lent—sans presser ni ralentir jusqu'à la fin). "Le Gibet" marks the culmination of the path from the *Ballade de la Reine morte d'aimer* and "Entre cloches," through "La Vallée des cloches," evoking a macabre landscape engulfed in bells. "It is the bell which tolls from the walls of a city beyond the horizon, and the corpse of a hanged man reddened by the setting sun." Within the short space of four pages, Ravel has created a highly poetic tour de force, with an obsessive tolling pedal point which conjures up the tension and terror found in the work of Edgar Allan Poe. The writing frequently calls for three staves, with the pedal point presented in the melody, the bass, and the inner voices as well, suffused in a web of intricate chordal progressions. The soft pedal is held throughout the piece, and the dynamic range lies between ppp and mf. The indication "sans expression" (19/1/1), apparently refers to the throbbing yet steady mute terror found throughout this extraordinary composition.

3) "Scarbo" (modéré). The setting of "Scarbo," the wily dwarf, is replete with nervous agility and unusual technical demands. Indeed, Reynaldo Hahn's comment about the orchestral writing in *L'Heure espagnole*— "transcendental jiujitsu"—is perfectly apt. The structure is quite free, deriving principally from three thematic cells: the introduction (23/1/1), a re-

peated figure (24/4/1), and a rhythmic pattern (26/2/7). Henri Gil-Marchex has recalled the composer's indication "quelle horreur!," in describing the opening theme (24/1/1), which is a variant of the introduction. A free reprise of the introduction (34/4/4) leads to further manipulation of the thematic cells, with an unusual passage in seconds (37/2/1), which derives in part from Ravel's extremely agile thumb which could comfortably strike three notes. As in "Ondine," the climactic point in "Scarbo" is dramatic, with a rich sonority (p. 41). A concluding appearance of the repeated figure in augmentation (42/1/2), and the rhythmic pattern (42/2/3), leads to the final cadence, which vanishes as mysteriously as the conclusion of the poem.

In the course of an interview, Beveridge Webster recalled a performance of *Gaspard de la nuit,* given in the 1920s by Robert Casadesus. Many musicians in the audience were incredulous. "What is Ravel trying to do in 'Le Gibet,' " they asked. "How can one be sure all the right notes are being played in 'Scarbo' "? These reactions have given way to a very different appraisal of *Gaspard de la nuit,* which now appears to be one of Ravel's most impressive achievements.

Ma Mère l'Oye (Five Children's Pieces for Piano 4 Hands, 1908–10, orchestral transcription and ballet, 1911)

1) "Pavane de la Belle au bois dormant" (lent, A minor)
2) "Petit Poucet" (très modéré, C minor)
3) "Laideronnette, Impératrice des pagodes" (mouvement de marche, F♯ major)
4) "Les Entretiens de la Belle et de la Bête" (mouvement de valse très modéré, F major)
5) "Le Jardin féerique" (lent et grave, C major)

Ma Mère l'Oye is a charming evocation of childhood's pristine enchantment. In arranging the suite, Ravel turned to the children's stories of Charles Perrault (1628–1703), Marie-Catherine, Comtesse d'Aulnoy (ca. 1650–1705), and Marie Leprince de Beaumont (1711–80). Of the three authors, Perrault proved to be the most important, in that his delightful collection *Contes de ma Mère l'Oye* (Mother Goose Tales, 1697) furnished the composer with his title. Furthermore, the author's opening tale, "La Belle au bois dormant,'' was adapted for the first composition, and "Le Petit Poucet'' furnished the title of the second piece, which bears a quotation from the well-known passage in which Tom Thumb is surprised that the birds have eaten all his crumbs. "Laideronnette, Impératrice des pagodes'' is taken from Madame d'Aulnoy's *Serpentin Vert*. The scene describes an oriental empress taking her bath, accompanied by singing and the playing of viols and lutes. Madame Leprince de Beaumont wrote stories of a moralizing, didactic nature, and an example of her professorial bent is found in the story of Beauty and the Beast, from the *Magasin des Enfants, Contes Moraux* (1757). In "Les Entretiens de la Belle et de la Bête,'' Beauty finally agrees to marry the Beast, who is then magically transformed to his former state as a handsome prince.

Ma Mère l'Oye exists in three versions: the original suite for piano four hands, an orchestral transcription of the suite, and a ballet adaptation, for which Ravel added a "Prélude,'' the "Danse du rouet,'' and various interludes. The scenario generally follows the argument found in the piano suite, and it concludes as the Good Fairy blesses the Princess and Prince Charming, followed by an apotheosis. In commenting upon the piano suite, the composer observed that he wished to evoke "the poetry of childhood,'' which led him to simplify his style and writing. The exploitation of the Aeolian mode and the striking simplicity of the "Pavane,'' the bird cheeps and sudden changes in direction of the parallel thirds, evoking the wanderings of Tom Thumb, the straightforward A–B–A forms with the characteristic joining of the themes at the reprise ("Laideronnette,'' "Beauty and the Beast''), the exploitation of the pentatonic mode ("Laideronnette''), the gentle homage to the composer of the *Gymnopédies* ("Beauty and the Beast''), and the brilliant fanfare at the conclusion of "Le Jardin féerique''—with the simplest of means, Ravel has fashioned a most distinguished achievement. The orchestral transcription of *Ma Mère l'Oye* has been commented upon previously. Mention may be made of the additional bird cheeps in "Petit Poucet'' (see miniature orchestral score, 7/2/2) and the resplendent conclusion of "Le Jardin féerique,'' which fully realizes the inherent possibilities of the original version. The innocence and sophistication of *Ma Mère l'Oye* make it a delightful spiritual companion of Schumann's *Kinderszenen,* Mussorgsky's *Nursery,* and Debussy's *Children's Corner*.

Menuet sur le nom d'Haydn (piano, 1909)

In a free adaptation of the Renaissance "soggetto cavato" (a "carved-out subject"), the name H–A–Y–D–N turns out to be B–A–D–D–G. H stands for B♮ in German, and the remaining letters derive from the alphabet as below:

A	B	C	D	E	F	G	H	I	J	K	L	M	N	O	P	Q	R	S	T	U	V	W	X	Y	Z
A	B	C	D	E	F	G	A	B	C	D	E	F	G	A	B	C	D	E	F	G	A	B	C	D	E

In the score, each appearance of the Haydn motif is indicated (forward, backward, and upside down = D–G–G–C–B), with the exception of three backward presentations in the middle voice (3/2/1–3/1/1). The minuet is an agreeable eighteenth-century pastiche, with its underlying motif skillfully concealed.

Tripatos (voice and piano, 1909)

Hubert Pernot has explained that the melody of *Tripatos* is linked to the dance: "one takes three steps forward, three steps backward (whence comes the name of the dance), then one turns around in place." [35] For whatever reason, the harmonization of *Tripatos* remained unpublished during Ravel's lifetime, and with its straightforward accompaniment, it is a natural pendant to the *Cinq Mélodies populaires grecques*.

Chants populaires (voice and piano, 1910)

1) "Chanson espagnole"
2) "Chanson française" (gathered by L. Branchet and J. Plantadis, this song was published by the Schola Cantorum in 1904)
3) "Chanson italienne"
4) "Chanson hébraïque" (gathered by J. Engel in Vilna, Russia, in 1909)

The accompaniments to these folk melodies are indicative of Ravel's broad empathies. The guitarlike accompaniment of the Spanish song effec-

[35] Pernot, *Rapport sur une mission scientifique en Turquie,* p. 30.

tively captures its bitter irony, while the French song is elegant and charming. The Italian song, dealing with the pangs of unrequited love, is the shortest and perhaps least successful of the group, and the Hebraic song, a dialogue between father and son, is in Yiddish, Hebrew, and Aramaic. It alternates a dancelike section (the father's questions), with recitative (the son's replies), in a simple, tasteful manner. The Scottish song, based upon a wistful love poem by Robert Burns ("The Banks o' Doon," 1791), is an important addition to the collection.

Valses nobles et sentimentales (piano, 1911, orchestral transcription and ballet, *Adélaïde, ou le langage des fleurs,* 1912)

Valses nobles et sentimentales, like *Ma Mère l'Oye,* consists of an original version for piano, an orchestral transcription, and a ballet argument based upon the transcription. "The title *Valses nobles et sentimentales* sufficiently indicates my intention of writing a series of waltzes in imitation of Schubert. . . . The seventh waltz seems to me to be the most characteristic" ("Autobiographical Sketch"). The model then is the Schubertian waltz, with its lilting rhythm, rubato, balanced phrases, straightforward form, and unexpected harmonic subtleties. The score contains a quotation from Henri de Régnier's novel *Les Rencontres de Monsieur de Bréot* (1904): "The delightful and always novel pleasure of a useless occupation." In the preface, the author states his point of departure:

> I would not have wished to publish my *Rencontres de Monsieur de Bréot* without a word of introduction. One might have replied, it is true, that the way to eliminate the explanation would have been to suppress the book. I might have done so, were I not convinced that it is one of mine which best illustrates what I have sought in writing, which is nothing but the delightful and always novel pleasure of a useless occupation.

The author's high spirits and pleasure-loving sophistication are well matched in the *Valses nobles et sentimentales.*

Although much ink has been spilled over the opening of the first waltz, the simplest and best explanation, I believe, was given by the composer in the course of a lesson with Roland-Manuel. The opening two measures,

Ravel stated, consist of a linear progression, E♯ (beats one and two), to F♯ (beat three), to G (prolonged through measure two). The vigorous acidity of the unresolved appoggiaturas sets the tone of this incisive waltz. For all of its harsh gaiety, the reprise of the opening theme is preceded by the bass moving in the traditional cycle of fifths (cf. 3/3/2–3/3/5, piano edition). In marked contrast, the second waltz is "sentimental" and somewhat nostalgic, and the indication "rubato" appears rarely in the composer's scores. The opening section of the third waltz is in E minor, with several rhythmic displacements over the bar line, and the second section (8/3/1–9/2/4), unfolds over two pedal points on F♯ and B. One expects the B to resolve to E at the reprise (9/2/5), but the opening theme is unexpectedly set in G major, an elegant "Schubertian" touch, in an abridged statement. The fourth waltz frequently suggests duple meter, while the fifth is sensuous and dreamlike, with a full texture, in contrast to its nimble successor. The seventh waltz is the longest, set in the traditional A–B–A form. Ravel found it the "most characteristic" of the series, perhaps because it encompasses languid and brilliant moments, coupled with the rhythmic hesitation of the Viennese waltz. The epilogue recalls all of the preceding waltzes (except for the fifth), which are skillfully juxtaposed. The concluding passages, for example, recall the opening of the eighth waltz, a series of triads over a pedal point (25/2/2), and the theme of the second waltz (25/3/3), now presented over a tonic pedal point, which concludes the work quietly in G major.

Adélaïde, ou le langage des fleurs is set in Paris about 1820, at the home of the courtesan Adélaïde. On each side of the stage, vases are filled with flowers, and as the curtain rises, couples are dancing or conversing quietly. The story centers about the fickle Adélaïde and her rival suitors, Lorédan and the duke. The various emotions of love, hope, and rejection, are symbolized by the flowers which the dancers exchange. In the concluding scene, Adélaïde offers the duke a branch of acacia (platonic love), while Lorédan at first receives a corn poppy (forgetfulness), but after threatening suicide, he is given a red rose, as Adélaïde falls into his arms. The orchestral transcription has a good deal of solo work for the woodwinds and many tutti organized by families of instruments. Several orchestral adjustments may be noted, among them measured tremolos, harmonics, and triplets in the strings (miniature orchestral score, 7/1, 8/5), double notes in the woodwinds originally written as single notes (29/2–3), together with several changes in pitch (cf. 30/5–6, flutes, harps, and violins). In the epilogue, the strings are divided into eighteen parts at one point (70/1), playing trills and glissandi on the fingerboard. The piano and orchestral versions of *Valses nobles et sentimentales* are equally effective, and the waltzes are significant both in their own right and as an important gateway to *La Valse*.

Daphnis et Chloé (ballet, 1909–12; two orchestral suites derived from the ballet score; see Plate 24)

Daphnis et Chloé is Ravel's most extended composition and is generally considered to be his most impressive achievement. Stravinsky has called it "one of the most beautiful products in all of French music," and many critics have commented on its rhythmic diversity, its supreme lyricism, and its magical evocations of nature. The ballet forms a natural culmination of several elements previously observed: the composer's marked interest in the dance, which was of course stimulated by his contact with the members of the Ballets Russes, his keen observations of nature, and his innovative orchestral technique. The score calls for a relatively large orchestra, including fifteen distinct members of the percussion family, and a mixed chorus, heard both offstage and onstage. The spiritual influence of Richard Strauss and particularly the Russian school may be observed in the orchestration. The structure of the ballet, like that of *L'Heure espagnole*, derives largely from a free adaptation of the leitmotif. The introduction establishes the tonality of A major, and several of the important motifs appear in rapid succession (miniature orchestral score, 1/6, horns, a series of parallel fourths, whose rhythmic pattern will frequently be sung by the chorus; 1/7, flute, with its distinctive triplet figure). The initial interval of the fifth (1/3–1/6), will be prominent in the first of two motifs representing Daphnis and Chloé (2/5, horn), and following the Religious Dance, the scene concludes as two of the opening motifs are joined (23/3). The General Dance in $\frac{7}{4}$ is followed by the second motif of Daphnis and Chloé (41/4, violin solo), and Dorcon and Daphnis now compete for Chloé's kiss, with Dorcon's grotesque movements followed by Daphnis's graceful dance. One plodding phrase will depict Dorcon in the finale (cf. 45/6 and 274/2), and humorous glissandi in the trombones recall an analogous passage in the first scene of *L'Heure espagnole*. Shortly after the abduction of Chloé (cf. 79/1, trumpets, the pirates' motif),

177

the scene is enveloped in an "unreal light," as several quasi-cadenza passages are accompanied by muted strings playing measured tremolos on the fingerboard, together with a wind machine (pp. 84–86). This arresting example of orchestral color soon leads to the second tableau, which takes place in the camp of the pirates. The warlike dance (animé et très rude), contains two principal elements, a leaping staccato figure which outlines the diminished fifth (99/3), and a rapid, modally inflected melody (117/2/3), which are later modified and combined with the pirates' motif in a dramatic climax (cf. 148/1, trumpets, cellos and basses, piccolos and flute). This episode highlights the spiritual influence of the Russian school, as the leaping staccato figure passes from the strings to the woodwinds and brass, and the modus operandi is essentially that of repetition with changes in the instrumentation (cf. 117/2/3, 122/5, 127/2/5). Chloé's Suppliant Dance effectively alternates one measure in a moderate tempo followed by one in a markedly slower tempo (153/1), a rare occurrence in Ravel's scores. Following several motivic reminiscences of Daphnis, the menacing shadow of Pan appears, and the pirates flee in disarray. The third tableau begins with the well-known daybreak episode. For all the complexity of the innovative writing for the woodwinds, the meter is essentially a straightforward $\frac{3}{4}$. Various bird calls are evoked by the violins and the piccolo, which at one point appears onstage (cf. 188/2, 196/2), and an expansive theme in the violas and clarinet (193/2) is soon repeated with modified orchestration and fresh harmony (202/2). The undulating accompaniment melds with the motif of Daphnis and Chloé as they are reunited (211/1), after which the daybreak motif rises pictorially through the strings, with the other instruments imperceptibly joining forces, leading to an exhilarating climax for the full orchestra and chorus. In the course of a lesson with Roland-Manuel, Ravel observed that the daybreak episode was nothing more than a D major chord with an added sixth, an analysis which is of course technically correct. It need only be added that the passage is also one of the composer's most poetic achievements. The old shepherd Lammon explains that Pan saved Chloé in remembrance of the nymph Syrinx whom he once loved, and in an episode containing brilliant passage work for the flute, Daphnis and Chloé mime the story of Pan and Syrinx. The concluding General Dance was completely reworked and will be examined later in closer detail (see pp. 215–16). Its throbbing rhythm and instrumentation recall the Polovetsian

Dances from *Prince Igor,* and, with brief reminiscences of Daphnis, Chloé, and Dorcon, it brings the ballet to a joyful and tumultuous conclusion.

Trois Poèmes de Stéphane Mallarmé (voice, accompanied by piccolo, flute, clarinet, bass clarinet, string quartet, and piano; also voice and piano, 1913)

1) "Soupir" ("Sigh")
2) "Placet futile" ("Futile Petition")
3) "Surgi de la croupe et du bond"
   ("Risen from the Crupper and Leap")

In his *Journal* entry dated March 1, 1898, Jules Renard noted, "Mallarmé, untranslatable, even into French." Although Mallarmé's art no longer appears "untranslatable," it does pose considerable intellectual challenge. Ravel once commented upon the poet's "unbounded visions, yet precise in design, enclosed in a mystery of sombre abstractions—an art where all the elements are so intimately bound up together that one cannot analyze, but only sense, its effect" ("Contemporary Music"). On another occasion, the composer made the following observation: "I wished to transcribe Mallarmé's poetry into music, especially that preciosity so full of meaning and so characteristic of him. 'Surgi de la croupe et du bond' is the strangest, if not the most hermetic of his sonnets" ("Autobiographical Sketch"). Although the instrumentation of *Pierrot Lunaire* was adapted for these poems, the music bears only the slightest similarity to Schoenberg's score. If on occasion the vocal line is unusually angular and tonality is suspended in "Surgi de la croupe et du bond," the harmonic sensuousness, the interpretation of the text, and the masterful exploitation of the chamber ensemble are thoroughly characteristic.

1) "Soupir" (lent). Mallarmé described this poem as "an autumnal reverie." The poem is divided into two parts by the composer, the first of which focuses upon the "white fountain" which "sighs toward the azure." The melody is slow and sustained, with rapid string passages in harmonics and glissandi evoking water images. Several chords of the minor ninth lead to the second section, which is considerably more static (9/2/1, full score).

179

The poem's somber autumnal associations are realized by complex harmonic progressions, one of which (10/2/1) distinctly recalls a passage in *Daphnis et Chloé* (cf. piano edition, 39/1/3). Both passages might be interpreted as chords with multiple appoggiaturas over pedal points. The concluding measures of ''Soupir'' contain a characteristic reminiscence of the opening section. Debussy's setting of the same poem is more uniform, and in neither piece does the dynamic range exceed p. Both interpretations are effective, although very different, and it is perhaps symbolic that at the point where Ravel calls for slower motion (9/2/1), Debussy indicates ''En animant un peu.''

2) ''Placet futile'' (très modéré; see Ravel's comments, pp. 128–29). This gentle love poem, which is not unrelated to the preciosity of *Sur l'herbe,* has been described by Mallarmé as an evocation of a painting by Boucher or Watteau. Although the opening measure does not suggest a tonal center, there is a tonal orientation throughout most of the song. The vocal line is unusually angular, underpinned by some of the composer's most intricate chromaticism, together with several evocative arabesques in the piano. The tempo is altered frequently, as a lyrical effusion (16/2/2), for example, is followed by a gentle dancelike interpretation of the text (17/2/1). The poet's reference to the flute will evoke a dialogue with that instrument, and the concluding phrase contains a ''Schoenbergian'' progression in the melody (19/1/2), which is however underpinned by the dominant, which will resolve to the tonic chord with added sixth and seventh. Once again, Debussy's interpretation of the same poem is efficacious, but considerably more straightforward, set ''in the tempo of a slow minuet.''

3) ''Surgi de la croupe et du bond'' (lent). This difficult evocation of an empty vase has been interpreted by Wallace Fowlie as follows:

> The poet is alone and looking down at the empty vase as if he were a sylph painted on the ceiling. . . . No water is in the vase. It seems to be dying because of its emptiness. . . . The waiting of the vase for water is comparable to the waiting of the poet throughout the darkness of the night. A rose, placed in the opening of the vase, would have fulfilled the vase in its reason for being, as a poem or some act of creation would have justified the poet's vigil.[36]

Ravel's setting of the poem manages to match its verbal wizardry, primarily by exploiting a harmonic scheme which is not tonally oriented. The accom-

---

[36] Fowlie, *Mallarmé* (Chicago: Univ. of Chicago Press, 1953), p. 51.

paniment might be interpreted as a free A-B-A, in which A (20/1–22/1/1; 24/1/1–24/2/3), is based upon a repeated melody, and B (22/1/2–23/2/3), is a complex harmonic progression, pitting a root of E♭ against D major (22/1/2), or B♭ against A major (22/1/3), with a resulting tonal ambiguity. Although there is no key signature and the concluding bass note is C, the complex final cadence is also not tonally oriented. The songs thus progress from traditional tonality ("Soupir"), to a suggestion of atonality within a tonal framework ("Placet futile"), to genuine atonality ("Surgi de la croupe et du bond"). Ravel never returned to the atonality of his concluding song, and it is a work of extraordinary interest. The Mallarmé poems occupy a rather isolated position in the composer's catalogue, and although relatively unknown, they constitute a superb achievement.

Prélude (piano, 1913)

Like the *Vocalise–Etude en forme de habanera*, this piece was written for students at the Conservatoire. The prelude's twenty-seven measures contain many accidentals and one passage in octaves, which are, however, relatively easy to sight-read because of the slow tempo. The gentle lyricism of the prelude is not unrelated to the *Pavane pour une Infante défunte*.

A la manière de . . . (piano, 1913)
   1) "Borodine"
   2) "Chabrier"

These pastiches reiterate the composer's ability to assimilate and reproduce the style of others. The tribute to Borodin is a rapid waltz in D♭ major, whereas the Chabrier piece is actually a pastiche of a pastiche—that is, it is Ravel's interpretation of how Chabrier would have paraphrased Siebel's flower song from Gounod's *Faust*. In the first edition published by A. Z. Mathot, Ravel's pieces appeared with two compositions by Alfredo Casella, the second of which is a pastiche of the suave elegance found in the *Valses nobles et sentimentales*.

Deux Mélodies hébraïques (voice and piano, 1914, orchestrated)

1) "Kaddisch"
2) "L'Enigme éternelle" (text and melody first published by the Society for Jewish Folk Music, Russia, 1911)

The Hebraic melodies form an interesting contrast, with the rhapsodic cantorial melismas of the "Kaddisch" offset by the folklike simplicity of "L'Enigme éternelle." Although the latter text is of no particular import, the Aramaic text of the "Kaddisch" is one of the masterpieces of the Jewish liturgy. Abraham Idelsohn has criticized Ravel's setting of "L'Enigme éternelle" as "ultramodern . . . without regard for its scale and the nature of the mode." [37] This observation was made in 1929, and today, of course, the accompaniment no longer appears "ultramodern." It should be pointed out that in all of his harmonizations, Ravel's sole concern was to write a tasteful accompaniment, and thus any restrictions imposed upon his choice of harmony would have been totally unacceptable. The French texts of the Hebraic melodies were arranged by the composer, after being supplied with a literal translation.

Trio (piano, violin, and cello, 1914)

1) Modéré ($\frac{8}{8}$)
2) Pantoum (assez vif, $\frac{3}{4}$)
3) Passacaille (très large, $\frac{3}{4}$)
4) Final (animé, $\frac{5}{4}$)

Following the youthful mastery of the String Quartet, the Trio bespeaks a more mature and dramatic expression which will be re-encountered in the Sonata for Violin and Cello. The texture throughout the Trio is full, and as one would expect, a maximum of virtuosity and instrumental color is expected from each of the soloists.

1) Modéré (cf. the commentary on the Sonata for Violin and Piano, pp. 144–45). This movement, which is in sonata form, contains many pedal

---

[37] Idelsohn, *Jewish Music in its Historical Development* (New York: Henry Holt, 1929), p. 486. See also p. 490, example 5, for a "correct" harmonization of another version of the melody.

points, which will also be found in each of the subsequent movements. The opening theme, constructed over a pedal point on the dominant, is balanced in phrasing, although easily subdivided into units of one measure. Another pedal point on E (3/3/2, miniature score), underpins the measures preceding the lyrical second theme (4/1/1), whose unbalanced phrasing may also be subdivided into one-measure units. The development section is largely based upon theme one, beginning with consistent alternations of tempo (5/2/4) which spiritually derive from Chloé's Suppliant Dance. Although the recapitulation is intimated, it is in fact bypassed. A characteristic detail in workmanship is found at this point (7/3/2): as the piano performs a modified statement of the opening theme, the tremolos in the strings outline the second theme in thirty-second notes, then in sixteenth notes, and finally the second theme is presented in eighth notes (8/1/1). The coda recalls the beginning of the development section (cf. 8/4/2 and 4/4/4), leading to a pedal point on C, over which the opening theme is heard, concluding the movement in C major.

2) Pantoum. In selecting this unusual title, Ravel apparently wished to associate the movement's rhythmic subtleties with those found in the Malayan pantun. Thus, as in the second movement of the String Quartet, one may note the spiritual imprint of the exotic rhythms heard at the 1889 International Exposition. The structure of this virtuoso scherzo is rather free, based upon three elements: the opening staccato theme in A minor, a lyrical modal theme in F♯ major (10/3/1), and a spacious choralelike melody in F major (15/2/1). The latter theme is set in $\frac{4}{2}$ against references to the opening two themes in $\frac{3}{4}$, in an interplay of meters whose complexity is unique in Ravel's scores (cf. 15/2/1 and 16/4/1). The opening themes are joined in the coda (20/1/1), which brings the movement to a brilliant conclusion.

3) Passacaille. The spacious melody of this passacaglia is virtually omnipresent, passing freely between the soloists, and the movement's hymnlike serenity might be considered a Latin counterpart of the adagio cantabile in Beethoven's Sonata Opus 13, or of Schumann's *Romanze,* Opus 28, No. 2. The theme is first presented in the lowest register of the keyboard and is then taken up by the other soloists with a continually increasing texture. Eventually, three staves are required for the piano, and, following a presentation of the theme underpinned by a pedal point, the texture is reduced, and the theme, which wavers between the tonal centers of F♯ and C♯, finally resolves to C♯.

4) Final. The finale calls for much brilliant technical display and a rich texture, which at times is virtually orchestral. Set in $\frac{5}{4}$ and $\frac{7}{4}$ meter, often found in Basque music, the exposition has a lyrical first theme (25/1/2) and an expansive second theme (28/1/2), which is largely a series of massive triads accompanied by extended trills in the strings. At one point in the development section the piano is given a trumpetlike fanfare (30/2/2–30/3/1; cf. 28/3/3 and 35/3/2) which distinctly recalls the concluding passage of *Daphnis et Chloé* (cf. miniature orchestral score, 307/2, trumpets). The recapitulation is well disguised (31/4/1), but generally parallels the exposition, coupled with the composer's penchant for modifying his original statement (cf. 32/2/3 and 26/1/1). Themes one and two are re-exposed in the coda, both in a marked, dramatic fashion, leading to a sweeping conclusion in A major. In both depth of emotion and breadth of vision, the Trio marks an important advance in Ravel's catalogue of chamber works.

Trois Chansons pour chœur mixte sans accompagnement (Three Songs for Unaccompanied Mixed Chorus, 1914–15)

1) "Nicolette"
2) "Trois Beaux Oiseaux du Paradis"
3) "Ronde"

Like Debussy's *Trois Chansons de Charles d'Orléans* (1908), these songs recall the French Renaissance *chanson*. "Trois Beaux Oiseaux du Paradis" revives the traditional *chanson,* while "Nicolette" and "Ronde" recall the programmatic *chansons* of Jannequin. The texts, set in free verse, reaffirm the composer's modest poetic gifts, as well as his predilections for ironic humor ("Nicolette") and verbal virtuosity ("Ronde").

1) "Nicolette" (allegro moderato). This folklike text is somewhat related to the story of Little Red Riding Hood. The choral writing contains several modal inflections and effectively underscores the amusing situations in the story.

2) "Trois Beaux Oiseaux du Paradis" (moderato). The colors of the three lovely birds from Paradise are those of the French flag, and the poem's colloquial refrain refers to the burden of war. The text is performed by a

series of soloists, underpinned by choral vocalizations, and the opening phrase, repeated virtually throughout the song, outlines the tonic minor triad with the lowered seventh step, evoking a subdued, plaintive mood.

3) "Ronde" (allegro). Ravel asked Jean-Aubry and Roland-Manuel for their assistance in assembling a large number of unusual sylvan nouns, and soon after, with a generous supply of words at his disposal, he apparently encountered greater difficulty in arranging his text than in composing the music.[38] The title of the piece, "Roundelay," describes its setting, as the opening verses sung by the old women are later taken up by the old men and the young boys and girls. The song's folklike simplicity and rapid tempo afford an attractive and virtuoso conclusion to the set.

Le Tombeau de Couperin (piano, 1914–17; transcription for orchestra, 1919, and ballet)

1) "Prélude"   4) "Rigaudon"
2) "Fugue"   5) "Menuet"
3) "Forlane"   6) "Toccata"

Le Tombeau de Couperin follows a pattern previously observed with regard to Ma Mère l'Oye and Valses nobles et sentimentales: after the original version for piano, the work was transcribed for orchestra and mounted as a ballet. The suite consists of a prelude and fugue in E minor, three dances, a forlane (E minor), rigaudon (C major), and minuet (G major), and a concluding toccata (E minor, ending in E major). Ravel explained that his composition was a homage to eighteenth-century French music, rather than a personal tribute to François Couperin (1668–1733). Nevertheless, he prepared for the task at hand by transcribing a suitable model: a forlane from Couperin's chamber works entitled Concerts royaux.[39] The piano edition of

[38] For example, the original version, "Oui, des satyres, des faunes, des ogres, des diables, des gnomes, des elfes, des lamies, loups-garons, myrmidons, chèvre-pieds, farfadets," was later altered to "Des enchanteurs et des mages, des stryges, des sylphes, des moines-bourrus, cyclopes, des djinns, gobelins, korrigans, nécromans, kobolds." Another notation, "Oui, des satyresses, des centauresses, des fées et des goules, des nymphes, des dryads, ogresses, bacchantes, faunesses, diablesses," finally became "Hamadryades, dryades, naïades, ménades, thyades, follettes, lémures, gnomides, succubes, gorgones, gobelines."

[39] The complete works of François Couperin, Editions de l'Oiseau Lyre, VII, 98–105. Ravel's transcription has been printed in The Music Forum, 3 (1973), 330–31.

Le Tombeau de Couperin contains the composer's drawing of a funerary urn. Although each piece is dedicated to the memory of a fallen comrade in arms, it may be recalled that most of the music was written before the outbreak of World War I. Thus, despite the elegiac mood of the fugue and the forlane, the suite is essentially a return to eighteenth-century clarity and elegance.

1) "Prélude" (vif, $\frac{12}{16}$). With its spare texture, rapid ornaments, and perpetual motion, the prelude recalls the harpsichord works of Rameau, Couperin, or Scarlatti. The harmonies are contemporary, as are two sweeping passages (6/2/2–6/3/3, and 6/6/1–6/6/5) which are purely pianistic.

2) "Fugue" (allegro moderato, $\frac{4}{4}$; see the commentary on p. 152). The fugal subject is somewhat related to the opening of the prelude, as both themes proceed from A to G and then outline the tonic triad. The fugue is closely knit in texture with many examples of inversion and stretto. The concluding passage (9/5/1) contains a stretto for the three voices.

3) "Forlane" (allegretto, $\frac{6}{8}$). It was Renoir who observed that his model served only to stimulate him—a notion which is particularly apt in describing the relationship between this piece and Couperin's forlane. The compositions are related in texture, rhythm, ornamentation, and structure (the opening passage serving as a refrain), and it is the melody and harmony which place Ravel's forlane in the twentieth century. The concluding measures juxtapose old and new elements: two subtly altered chords based on the subdominant resolve to the tonic, followed by several tonic chords with the added major seventh. A mordent on the tonic chord without the third gives a parting antique touch. The forlane is perhaps the outstanding achievement of the suite.

4) "Rigaudon" (assez vif, $\frac{2}{4}$). This dance contrasts an exuberant opening section in C major with a slower pastoral-like section beginning in C minor. In the opening measures, the rapid crossing of the hands recalls the technique of the *clavecinistes*. The reprise is relatively literal, and in traditional fashion it omits the repetitions found in the opening section.

5) "Menuet" (allegro moderato, $\frac{3}{4}$). A comparison of this minuet with the *Menuet antique* or the second movement of the Sonatine indicates broad similarities in structure, procedure, modal harmony, and classically balanced phrases. The comparison will also highlight the path from youthful skill to mature mastery. The musette is folklike, recalling its counterpart in the rigaudon, and a series of triadic chords underpinned by a pedal point leads

to the reprise, at which point the themes of the minuet and the musette are joined (22/1/1). Following the B major chord (22/2/2), a D♯ minor chord unexpectedly replaces B minor (cf. 20/2/2–3), and a fresh path is pursued to the tonic key. The extended coda basically derives from the opening measures of the minuet.

6) "Toccata" (vif, $\frac{2}{4}$). Despite all the technical difficulties in the toccata, the melodic thread is always clear. The texture, like that of the prelude, is spare, and the structure appears to be sonata form, as the punctuated opening theme leads to a lyrical theme at the dominant (26/1/1).[40] In place of a development section, a sustained melody (27/3/2) will frequently be juxtaposed with the opening theme. Themes two (31/4/5) and one (32/2/3) reappear in fortissimo interlocking passages, which momentarily recall Liszt rather than Couperin, and bring the suite to a brilliant conclusion in E major.

The orchestral suite derived from *Le Tombeau de Couperin* consists of the prélude, forlane, menuet, and rigaudon. The instrumentation calls for a small number of woodwinds, two horns, trumpet, harp, and the usual strings. The texture is limpid, in keeping with the clarity and restraint of the music. The melodic material is largely divided between the woodwinds and the strings, with fresh color occasionally contributed by the trumpet or horn. Among the orchestral adjustments are many mordents which are not found in the piano suite, changes in harmony (cf. miniature orchestral score, 8/1, or 18/3), and the addition of harmonics (cf. 24/2/4). In the orchestral version, the minuet precedes the rigaudon, which brings the suite to a spirited conclusion.

At the suggestion of Désiré-Emile Inghelbrecht, Jean Borlin and Rolf de Maré worked out a choreographic interpretation of the forlane, minuet, and rigaudon. The dances evoked the eighteenth-century style of the music, and within a period of several years the Swedish Ballet presented some 165 performances of the work.

---

[40] A comparison of this melody with a passage in the finale of the Sonatine (cf. 12/1/1–12/2/2) shows a similar treatment of the chord of the minor ninth together with unbalanced phrases.

Frontispice (two pianos, five hands, 1918)

This little-known composition consists of but fifteen measures. Written as a frontispiece for Ricciotto Canudo's *S.P. 503 Le Poème du Vardar,*[41] it was first printed in *Les Feuillets d'Art* (No. 2, 1919). Canudo's poems are essentially a series of philosophical reflections based upon his combat experiences in World War I, and the *Frontispice* evokes some of the mystery, exoticism, and water images found in the poetry. Rather curiously, this minor and somewhat atypical achievement requires a fifth hand for performance.

La Valse (poème chorégraphique pour orchestre, 1919–20)

La Valse gestated in Ravel's mind over a period of some fourteen years. Its genesis may be seen in a letter to Jean Marnold, written in February, 1906, in which the composer observed that he was planning to write a waltz which would be a sort of homage to Johann Strauss. By 1914 the work was entitled *Wien* and was conceived of as a "symphonic poem." In addition to the definitive change in title, the "symphonic poem" ultimately became a "choreographic poem." Ravel described the work as "a sort of apotheosis of the Viennese waltz," intermingled with "the impression of a fantastic and fatal whirling." The composer's argument further clarifies his intentions:

> Through whirling clouds, waltzing couples may be faintly distinguished. The clouds gradually scatter: one sees at letter "A" [11/5, miniature orchestral score], an immense hall peopled with a whirling crowd. The scene is gradually illuminated. The light of the chandeliers bursts forth at the fortissimo at letter "B" [25/3]. An imperial court, about 1855.

Although *La Valse* consists of an uninterrupted series of waltzes, its structure may be divided into two large sections, the first of which encom-

[41] Canudo, *S.P. 503 Le Poème du Vardar suivi de la sonate à salonique* (Paris: Les Poètes de la Renaissance du Livre, 1923). In addition to Ravel's frontispiece, the book contains a portrait of the author by Picasso. S.P. 503 refers to the postal sector of the author's combat division.

passes the material up to the recapitulation (75/2). This section contains the material referred to in the argument plus a series of refined and exuberant waltzes. The second section is essentially a free restatement, with virtually no new material presented as the "fatal whirling" begins to impose itself upon the elegant waltzes. One particular theme undergoes a thorough transformation, not unlike the manner of Liszt's symphonic poems (cf. 63/1 and 111/4). Among the many arresting details in the orchestration, one may note the plentiful and efficacious writing for the harps and a brief passage which focuses upon the percussion family (100/2). The strings perform in all but a handful of measures and are given a wide variety of tasks, including glissandi which extend over several measures. A number of tutti are organized by families of instruments (see pp. 26, 51, or 123), and even in those which are not (p. 24 or 42), it is clear that the string family still contains the essence of the material presented. The unusually dark color of the opening passage will recur at the beginning of the Piano Concerto for the Left Hand. The woodwinds are active, with several flute tremolos, harplike passages (cf. 63/1–2, clarinet and harp), and many solos, while one waltz features the brass family (38/3). In addition to many traditional doublings, one pedal point is shared by the glockenspiel and the violins in harmonics (69/1). The writing ebbs and flows, with imposing tuttis often followed by chamberlike passages, and the orchestral resources are deftly husbanded until the turbulent climax, which features sudden swells (123/1) and a series of clashing triads (cf. 127/1, trumpets and the violins and woodwinds). Following an extended pedal point on A$\sharp$ (pp. 129–32), the resolution to the tonic is delayed until the very last note.

Although *La Valse* carries on in the tradition of the *Valses nobles et sentimentales,* the concluding passages open up a fresh dimension in Ravel's art, that of tension bordering on the breaking point. It is apparent that the disorientation of World War I and the composer's personal grief following his mother's death have been sublimated in this "fantastic and fatal whirling." This unprecedented tension will achieve its culmination in the Piano Concerto for the Left Hand.

Sonate pour violon et violoncelle (1920–22)

1) Allegro   3) Lent
2) Très vif   4) Vif, avec entrain

The Sonata for Violin and Cello marks an important turning point in Ravel's style, as the composer himself acknowledged. The harmonic austerity and increasing interest in linear motion will recur periodically, as will the exploitation of bitonality. Although dedicated to Debussy's memory, the composition is not elegiac but rather an outstanding example of the thin, decongested texture that Debussy had called for and that was taken up by the postwar generation. At the première of the Sonata, it was still called Duo for Violin and Cello, which is the title of Kodály's chamber work Opus 7 (1914). Ravel was apparently acquainted with Kodály's score, as the Sonata occasionally indicates a Hungarian folk flavor, as well as some of the driving and harsh dissonances found in the work of Kodály and Bartók. In addition, the peripheral imprint of Schoenberg may be observed. If the orientation and spiritual influences on the Sonata are fresh, the overall structure recalls the String Quartet, with material in the first movement reappearing in the subsequent movements.

1) Allegro. This movement is set in a straightforward sonata form, and the initial figuration in the violin, as well as a secondary theme in the cello (2/4/11),[42] will reappear in later movements. The opening theme is modal and lyrical, with a harmonic underpinning, in contrast to the wide leaps of the quasi-Schoenbergian secondary theme (2/4/11), at which point the distinctive linear motion of each instrument is evident. A lyrical second theme (2/6/9) leads to the development section, which is set in a quicker tempo. Here, a fresh dancelike theme is exploited (3/3/4), together with theme two (3/5/7), and the initial violin figuration. While generally following the outline of the exposition, the recapitulation has a large number of modifications, achieved largely by fresh accompaniment figures or by reversing the roles of the soloists. The concluding measures in harmonics (A minor, G major, D minor, and A major), reaffirm the interplay of minor and major seen in the initial violin figuration.

2) Très vif. This brilliant scherzo alternates $\frac{3}{8}$ and $\frac{2}{8}$, occasionally pitting one meter against the other. The opening theme, a series of major and minor triads divided between the soloists, derives from the initial figuration

---

[42] The references in this score are to the violin part.

of the first movement. A second theme (5/5/8) will reappear in an extended bitonal passage (8/1/1), as will a folklike theme in Hungarian style (cf. 6/1/1 and 9/5/7). One clashing bitonal passage will pit B major against C minor (6/4/2), and so on. The concluding four measures once again suggest the interplay of A major and A minor, but the final note is C, an unexpected humorous touch. Extended trills and rapid harmonics are frequent in this pyrotechnic movement.

3) Lent. The expansive opening theme is a spiritual descendant of its counterpart in the Trio. A secondary lyrical theme (10/4/2) leads to a markedly dissonant fortissimo passage (11/1/1), which partially derives from the secondary theme of the first movement. A return of the opening theme with fresh accompaniment restores the initial contemplative mood (11/3/4), and the concluding parallel fifths highlight the austerity of the texture.

4) Vif, avec entrain. This spirited finale contains a generous number of themes juxtaposed and joined with material from the first movement (cf. 13/3/7–12 and 13/6/7–12). The opening theme is nimble, with several changes in meter, while a secondary theme is soon presented in imitation (cf. 12/3/9 and 12/4/6). Following a decisive cadence in C major, a folklike melody in Hungarian style is presented in F♯ minor (14/2/6), which leads to a modified recapitulation (15/1/9). The spirit of the Hungarian school may be seen in the fact that the melody (14/6/5) evolves around the tonal center of A and contains the characteristic interval of the augmented fourth, while the accompaniment outlines boldly contrasting triads. In the recapitulation the secondary theme of the first movement reappears (15/7/7), is presented in stretto in inversion (16/1/7), and is then joined with the opening theme (16/1/12). Similarly, the folklike theme reappears in F♯ minor, is coupled with the opening theme (16/2/13), and then with the secondary theme of the first movement (16/3/3). Further manipulations of the themes lead to an insistent F♯ (16/8/7), which abruptly resolves to C major, once again suggesting the spiritual influence of the Hungarian school.

If *Jeux d'eau* may be said to mark the point of departure for much of Ravel's keyboard writing, the Sonata for Violin and Cello analogously opens up the path toward the postwar compositions. Although relatively unknown, the Sonata is a brilliant achievement.

Berceuse sur le nom de Gabriel Fauré
(violin and piano, 1922)

The opening melody of this simple lullaby derives from Fauré's name, as below [43] (cf. p. 174):

G	A	B	R	I	E	L		F	A	U	R	E
G	A	B	D	B	E	E		F	A	G	D	E

The melody is easily recognizable, appearing in the violin with piano accompaniment, and vice versa. The violin is muted throughout, and the concluding parallel seconds recall "Jimbo's Lullaby" from Debussy's *Children's Corner*.

Ronsard à son âme (voice and piano, 1924)

In his *Abrégé de l'art poétique français* (1565) Pierre de Ronsard advocated the union of poetry and music, and his poems were frequently set by Renaissance composers. Ravel selected the poet's swan song, whose gentle preciosity is effectively underscored by a strikingly simple accompaniment, which consists of little more than a series of organumlike parallel fifths. Moreover, the final cadence is nothing but an accretion of perfect fifths. The setting of *Ronsard à son âme* recalls the elegance of "D'Anne qui me jecta de la neige," and the song marks the composer's final adaptation of Renaissance poetry.

Tzigane (Gypsy; Concert Rhapsody for violin and piano, 1924, orchestrated)

The spiritual influence of Paganini and Liszt may be observed in this bravura adaptation of the Hungarian rhapsody. The writing for the violin is

---

[43] In the original version printed in *La Revue Musicale*, the fourth and fifth notes of the melody are G and D. The final version constitutes an improvement in the melody, in addition to following the soggetto cavato literally.

replete with challenges, among them rapid harmonics and pizzicati, quadruple stops, and brilliant passages in perpetual motion. The many subtle changes in tempo, the rhythmic figures, the straightforward harmony, and the frequent use of the "gypsy" mode (E, F, G♯, A, cf. 1/2/5, violin and piano edition) give an "authentic" flavor to this work, while the clarity of the workmanship points to the composer's hand.

The introduction for unaccompanied violin (lento, quasi cadenza) presents several themes, one of which (1/4/2) will reappear in a number of transformations (cf. 5/2/1 and 10/4/1). Two other themes, one dancelike (9/2/1) and the other marked "grandioso" (12/1/1), lead to the concluding section in D major (13/1/1), whose perpetual motion includes references to previous material (cf. 16/3/3 and 17/1/1). *Tzigane* exists in a version for violin and "luthéal," a short-lived attachment to the keyboard which produces the approximate timbre of a Hungarian cimbalom or a harpsichord. The orchestral accompaniment is chamberlike, calling for no special commentary.

L'Enfant et les sortilèges (The Child and the Sorceries, opera, 1920–25; see Plate 25 and the commentary on *La Cloche engloutie,* p. 210)

Sidonie-Gabrielle Colette (1873–1954) frequently wrote about life as she had experienced it, from her childhood in Burgundy to her career as a mime dancer in the music halls of Paris. The enchanting world of animals, particularly cats, is another important motif in her work, and herein lies the link between the author of *Dialogues de bêtes* and the composer of the *Histoires naturelles*. Although all of the modifications in Colette's libretto cannot be fully determined, it is clear that Ravel was responsible for the ragtime between the black Wedgwood teapot and the Chinese cup,[44] the squirrel's aria, and many of the dances. From the outset, he planned to highlight the fantasy of the libretto by juxtaposing a wide variety of styles, ranging from traditional opera through operetta and the music hall. Thus, as in *L'Heure espagnole,* the composer avoids traditional operatic drama, this time by entering a make-believe world of childhood fantasy, in which a love aria is in-

[44] Colette's original draft of this scene, which differs markedly from the final version, has been printed in Jordan-Morhange, *Ravel et nous,* Plate IX, opposite p. 112.

toned by two meowing cats, trees sing of anguish and pain, armchairs and animals dance, and, of course, four and four equal eighteen. Ravel explained that *L'Enfant et les sortilèges* was composed "in the spirit of an American operetta. . . ."[45] The vocal line should dominate. The orchestra, though not renouncing virtuosity, is nevertheless of secondary importance." In comparison with *L'Heure espagnole,* the vocal line is generally lyrical and expansive, rather than conversational, and although the orchestra is quite large, the writing is frequently chamberlike. The opera is organized by a simple accretion of brief episodes, each of which is self-contained with regard to content and style. The libretto centers about a naughty child who is taught the meaning of compassion by the various animals, trees, and fairy-tale figures he has mistreated. As in the eighteenth-century *opéra-ballet,* dancing accompanies much of the action, ranging from a minuet, polka, and round, to an American waltz and a fox trot. The many novel combinations of timbre found in the opera may be observed in the very opening passage for the oboes and a solo double bass playing harmonics in the treble clef. In addition to the use of the piano with its luthéal attachment (for which a substitute version exists), several special effects are obtained by a wind machine, a slide whistle, and a cheese grater. The child's tantrum is effectively underscored by the woodwinds, brass, and percussion, together with a series of passages for the piano which offset the black and white keys (cf. miniature orchestral score, 8/1/1, 10/1/2, and 12/1). The sympathetic clock's aria leads to one of the most curious dialogues in the operatic repertoire, as the black Wedgwood teapot and the Chinese cup converse and sing in a combination of French, English, and pseudo-Chinese. The teapot's ragtime (originally planned as a bourrée) is a pastiche of tin-pan alley, complete with piano, sliding trombone, xylophone, wood block, and cheese grater, marking an initial adaptation of jazz which will soon reappear in the Sonata for Violin and Piano. Following the cup's aria, with its exploitation of the pentatonic mode and its parallel fourths in the celesta, the disparate melodies of the teapot and the cup are joined, in an amusing example of learned counterpoint (43/3). The vocal virtuosity found in the fire's aria is unprecedented in Ravel's scores, although, of course, it is modest in comparison with the nineteenth-century Italian school. The scene of the shepherds and shepherd-

---

[45] The composer was particularly attracted to Vincent Youmans' *Tea for Two,* the harmonies of which are quite Ravelian, and the library at Montfort l'Amaury contains a sizeable collection of French operettas written in the early 1920s. See "Autobiographical Sketch," pp. 22–23.

esses recalls the folklike simplicity of "Nicolette," while the sentimentality of the child's aria "Toi, le cœur de la rose," recalls the *Pavane pour une Infante défunte,* with perhaps even a touch of Puccini. This gentle episode is abruptly interrupted by the scintillating arithmetic scene, with its children's chorus, spinning dances, and orchestral pyrotechnics. Two bitonal passages in the clarinets introduce the cats' aria. Rather than notate his own Siamese cats, Ravel asked Hélène Jourdan-Morhange to imitate their meows, and this marked the duet's point of departure. The portamenti for the voices and the divisi strings (126/1) continue in the best tradition of the *Histoires naturelles.* The second scene, in the child's garden, contains a wealth of imitative writing. The off-stage chorus of the frogs is particularly evocative (cf. 134/1 and 150/1), while the waltzes of the dragon-flies and hawk-moths (145/1) and the frogs (166/2) recall the *Valses nobles et sentimentales* and *La Valse.* A brief scene whose declamation is spoken rather than sung (201/1/3) leads to a gentle chorus in praise of the child, which concludes with a reference to the opera's initial passage for the oboes (212/1/1). The concluding chord of the major seventh and the descending interval of the fourth are characteristic elements in the composer's style.

L'Enfant et les sortilèges is a virtuoso potpourri of styles, many of them recalling Ravel's own works. It reaffirms the composer's gifts as an expert miniaturist and his sympathetic understanding of the magical worlds of children, animals, and make-believe.

Chansons madécasses (voice, flute, cello, and piano, also voice and piano, 1925–26)

1) "Nahandove"
2) "Aoua!"
3) "Il est doux . . ."

The poetry of Evariste-Désiré de Parny (1753–1814) is simple and voluptuous, with a penchant for exoticism. The *Chansons madécasses, traduites en françois, suivies de poésies fugitives* appeared in 1787, and the preface explains the author's point of departure:

The isle of Madagascar is divided into an endless number of small territories which belong to as many princes. These princes are always battling one another, the purpose of these wars being to take prisoners in order to sell them to Europeans. Thus, without us, these people would be peaceful and happy. They are skillful, intelligent, kind, and hospitable. Those who live on the coasts justifiably distrust strangers, and in their treaties, they take all the precautions dictated by prudence and even shrewdness. The Madagascans are happy by nature. The men live in idleness and the women work. They are passionately fond of music and dance. I have collected and translated several songs, which may give an idea of their customs and habits. They possess no verse; their poetry is nothing but an elaborate prose. Their music is simple, gentle, and always melancholy.[46]

Ravel commented on his setting of the poems: "I believe the *Chansons madécasses* introduce a new element, dramatic—indeed erotic, resulting from the subject matter of Parny's poems. The songs form a sort of quartet in which the voice plays the role of the principal instrument. Simplicity is all-important" ("Autobiographical Sketch").

The linear orientation of the *Chansons madécasses* is coupled with the element of primitivism, which may be observed in the local color of the poems as well as in the extensive use of repetition in the accompaniments. Several brief suspensions of tonality, together with the treatment of the voice as an instrument, suggest the peripheral imprint of *Pierrot Lunaire*. The songs are unified to some extent by the use of common material in "Nahandove" and "Il est doux," whose voluptuous moods are not unrelated, and a number of novel timbres are elicited from the instruments.

1) "Nahandove" (andante quasi allegretto). The initial figure in the cello will evoke the young Nahandove (cf. full score, 1/1 cello, and 4/2/1, voice), as will the opening rhythmic pattern in the vocal line which reappears periodically. Another motif in the cello (2/2/3) is taken up by the piccolo (5/3/1) and will be played by that instrument in "Il est doux" (cf. 19/2/1). Ravel was apparently bothered by the word "naissante" (2/1/3), and in the autographs of "Nahandove" the adjective is altered each time. The versions read "la rosée nocturne" and "la rosée du soir." Although preferring the latter version, the composer left his author's text unaltered in the score. He did, however, repeat the phrase "c'est elle" (which appears once in the poem) three times, with a rising pattern which effectively high-

[46] Modern scholarship has established that Parny neither set foot in Madagascar nor was acquainted with the Madagascan language. The *Chansons madécasses* were written in India in 1784–85, and it appears that the *hain-tenys,* which are popular Madagascan poems, served as the author's model. In the collection, "Nahandove" is the twelfth and final poem, "Aoua!" is the fifth, and "Il est doux," the eighth. The interpretive lithographs printed in the Durand edition were drawn by Luc-Albert Moreau.

lights the anticipated appearance of Nahandove (3/3/2).[47] The full texture at this point (4/1/1) will not recur, and the remainder of the song is derived almost exclusively from the opening measures.

2) "Aoua!" (andante). This poem begins with a relatively mild phrase, "Méfiez-vous des blancs habitans du rivage," but the composer's addition of the war cry "Aoua!" is an effective emendation which highlights the savage mood. The unusually harsh introduction is followed by an extended bitonal dirgelike passage, in which the piano evokes a gong (10/1/3). A long accelerando leads to the "Allegro feroce," in which the flute will evoke a trumpet call and the piano ostinato, with its bare major sevenths, will suggest the beating of a primitive drum. The vocal line here is largely a rhythmic variant of the dirgelike section (cf. 13/3/1 and 10/2/1). The concluding passages reaffirm the equality of the voice with the instruments (cf. voice, 15/2/3–4, and flute, 15/3/2–5, cello, 15/3/2–5, and voice, 10/2/1–3), and the final cadence is bitonal, pitting D$\sharp$ against G. The violent tension found in this song is a direct outgrowth of *La Valse,* and the distance from the composer's youthful preciosity is indeed striking.

3) "Il est doux . . ." (lento). This song exploits the interval of the major seventh (or the diminished octave), resulting in several brief suspensions of tonality (cf. 17/1/2, 17/3/3). The opening flute solo, which recalls the poet's observation about the simple, gentle, and melancholy nature of Madagascan music, emphasizes the intervals of the second, fourth, and seventh, as does the beginning of "Nahandove." In one ostinato passage, the cello's pizzicati in harmonics suggest a primitive drum (19/2/1), and as if symbolic of the strikingly spare texture found throughout this song, the final passage in D♭ major is sung without accompaniment.

A concluding comment on the *Chansons madécasses* may be granted to their composer, who believed the cycle to be one of his most important works: it achieved a maximum of expression while utilizing a marked economy of means. This perceptive judgment has withstood the test of time, and today the *Chansons madécasses* appear to be at the summit of Ravel's vocal art.

Rêves (voice and piano, 1927)

The poetry of Léon-Paul Fargue has been described as reflecting "a somber and chilly world, a world not yet liberated from sleep, not yet risen again to life's surface, situated at the confluence of dream and memory.[48] This observation is apt with regard to *Rêves,* which first appeared in a collection of poems entitled *Pour la musique* (1898). Ravel's setting underscores the poem's gentle lyricism, utilizing a minimum of notes. An extended ostinato evokes a train whistle (2/4/5), and the postlude restates the melody of the introduction with fresh accompaniment, concluding with a bitonal passage (cf. 3/4/6 and 2/1/1).

Sonate pour violon et piano (1923–27)

1) Allegretto
2) Blues
3) Perpetuum mobile

The Sonata for Violin and Piano marks Ravel's final chamber work. He believed the violin and the piano to be essentially incompatible instruments and observed that the Sonata highlights their incompatibility. The writing continues in the tradition of the Sonata for Violin and Cello, with considerable independence of the parts, a spare texture, and some bitonal passages. The blues movement marks the composer's second adaptation of jazz, and the virtuoso perpetuum mobile continues in the tradition of *Tzigane.* As customary, the work is tightly organized, with material from the first and second movements recurring in the finale. Composed over a period of four years, the Sonata was interrupted by several compositions, whose imprint will be evident in the course of the work.

1) Allegretto (⁶⁄₈, G major). This movement is predominantly lyrical, with four distinct themes in the exposition (1/1/1, 1/3/2, 3/1/4, and 4/1/1). Themes three and four recall some of the angularity and the many diminished octaves found in the *Chansons madécasses.* The independence of the part writing may be seen in the combination of lyrical and dancelike material (cf. 1/3/2 and 3/2/3), while the concluding passage of the exposition recalls

---

[48] Marcel Raval, "Identité de Fargue," *Les Feuilles Libres* (June, 1927), p. 55.

the extensive use of parallel fifths found in *Ronsard à son âme* (4/3/1). The development section is relatively straightforward, lyrical rather than motivic in workmanship, and the most climactic point (8/2/3) characteristically occurs shortly before the recapitulation, which is both disguised and abbreviated. An extended cantabile passage for the violin is superimposed over themes one and two, leading to the concluding three-voice fugato (12/3/3).

2) Blues (moderato $\frac{4}{4}$, A♭ major). In the course of his visit to the United States, Ravel commented upon this movement as follows:

> To my mind, the "blues" is one of your greatest musical assets, truly American despite earlier contributory influences from Africa and Spain. Musicians have asked me how I came to write "blues" as the second movement of my recently completed sonata for violin and piano. Here again the same process, to which I have already alluded, is in evidence, for, while I adopted this popular form of your music, I venture to say that nevertheless it is French music, Ravel's music, that I have written. Indeed, these popular forms are but the materials of construction, and the work of art appears only on mature conception where no detail has been left to chance. Moreover, minute stylization in the manipulation of these materials is altogether essential. To understand more fully what I mean by the process to which I refer, it would be sufficient to have these same "blues" treated by some of your own musicians and by musicians of European countries other than France, when you would certainly find the resulting compositions to be widely divergent, most of them bearing the national characteristics of their respective composers, despite the unique nationality of their initial material, the American "blues." Think of the striking and essential differences to be noted in the "jazz" and "rags" of Milhaud, Stravinsky, Casella, Hindemith, and so on. The individualities of these composers are stronger than the materials appropriated. They mould popular forms to meet the requirements of their own individual art. Again—nothing left to chance; again—minute stylization of the materials employed, while the styles become as numerous as the composers themselves.[49]

Together with traditional elements such as the flattened seventh and much syncopation, one observes Ravel's personal stylization of the blues material, encompassing the use of bitonality and the natural extension of each instrument's timbre, as the violin and the piano suggest a plucked banjo or a sliding saxophone. In addition to the use of imitation (17/1/2), two of the blues melodies will be joined (cf. 19/3/1) and some of the material in this movement will reappear in the finale.

3) Perpetuum mobile (allegro, $\frac{3}{4}$, G major). In this movement, the brilliance of the violin writing is contrasted with the relative simplicity of

---

[49] "Contemporary Music," p. 140.

the accompaniment. Several references to the opening movement are clear (cf. 22/1/1 and 1/3/2; 31/4/3 and 1/1/1), while a number of thematic transformations from the first and second movements are less obvious (24/3/3 and 16/3/3; 26/4/3 and 3/1/4). In addition, an abbreviated reprise of the opening material of the finale is underpinned with a theme from the second movement (cf. 29/3/1 and 23/3/1 with 17/3/1). As the second movement pits the keys of A♭ and G, the conclusion of the finale offsets F♯ and G (32/3/1).

Although solidly crafted, the Sonata for Violin and Piano does not appear to match the consistently high level of its counterpart for violin and cello. The first movement is perhaps the strongest, while the jazz idiom will be integrated more successfully in the piano concerti. The finale, like *Tzigane,* is brilliant, but both pieces lack the distinctive poetry found in *Gaspard de la nuit,* which makes the latter work far more than a study in transcendental virtuosity.

"Fanfare" (orchestra, for a ballet in one act, *L'Eventail de Jeanne,* 1927)

This Lilliputian fanfare contains several clear examples of bitonality. As Debussy's "Golliwogg's Cake Walk" parodies *Tristan und Isolde,* the notation "Wagneramente" suggests a good-natured poke at the composer of *Götterdämmerung,* who apparently could be ridiculed, but not ignored.

Boléro (ballet for orchestra, 1928)

Ravel communicated the following statement to Calvocoressi, which was published in the *Daily Telegraph* on July 11, 1931:

I am particularly desirous that there should be no misunderstanding as to my *Boléro.* It is an experiment in a very special and limited direction, and should not be suspected of aiming at achieving anything different from, or anything more than, it actually does achieve. Before the first performance, I issued a warning to the effect that what I had written was a piece lasting seventeen minutes and consisting wholly of orchestral tissue without music—of one long, very gradual *crescendo.* There are no contrasts, and there is practically no invention except in the plan and the manner of the execution. The themes are impersonal—folk tunes of the usual Spanish-Arabian kind. Whatever may have been said to the contrary, the orchestral treatment is simple and straightforward throughout, without the slightest attempt at virtuosity. In this respect, no greater contrast could be imagined than that between the *Boléro* and *L'Enfant et les sortilèges,* in which I freely resort to all manners of orchestral virtuosity.[50]

The *Boléro* reaffirms Ravel's longstanding interest in the dance and his continuing preoccupation with Spanish music and orchestral color. The obsessive repetition found in "Le Gibet" is carried even further, as the snare drum ceaselessly repeats a simple rhythmic pattern until the penultimate measure, and the harmonic underpinning of C to G is heard for no less than 326 measures. Madame Rubinstein's interpretation of the *Boléro* called for a dimly lit Spanish café. A young woman begins to dance a languid bolero on a platform as the other performers gradually take notice. The dancers become increasingly obsessed by the bolero rhythm, ending in an apotheosis. In addition to the customary instruments, the score calls for three saxophones, which superimpose an element of jazz on the Hispanic setting. Although the melody is most frequently harmonized with chords in parallel motion, one presentation is bitonal (see miniature orchestral score, 23/3, the oboe d'amore), while another is tritonal, a unique occurrence in the composer's scores. This passage (19/1) epitomizes several aspects of Ravel's orchestral technique. The rhythmic pattern is heard in the snare drum, a flute, and a horn—one may note the balance of contrasting families of instruments, as well as the paradoxical aspect of having a flute and a horn performing a role traditionally given to the percussion family. (Together with the woodwinds and strings, the horns will frequently double the rhythmic pattern in the snare drum.) The melody is played in C major by the celesta and a horn, a somewhat unexpected coupling, in E major by one piccolo and in G major by the other piccolo. Thus, the famous modulation to E major has in a sense been prepared by a full rendition of the melody in that key. Although a tour de force of orchestral timbre and rhythm, the significance of the *Boléro* should not be overestimated. It is skillfully crafted, as one would expect, but in the last analysis, it is, as the composer acknowledged, "an experiment in a very special and limited direction."

[50] See Calvocoressi, "Ravel's Letters to Calvocoressi," *Musical Quarterly,* 27 (1941), 17–18. (Calvocoressi inadvertently misdated the interview as July 16, 1931.)

Concerto pour la main gauche (piano and orchestra, 1929–30)

The Piano Concerto for the Left Hand is Ravel's most dramatic work, combining expansive lyricism, tormented jazz effects, a playful scherzo, and driving march rhythms, all of which are scaffolded into one movement of modest dimensions. One autograph of the Concerto has a comment by the composer, "musae mixtatiae" (mixed muses), thus suggesting a deliberate juxtaposition of differing styles, evident in *L'Enfant et les sortilèges* and found in both piano concerti. The writing for the keyboard is immensely difficult, deriving ultimately from Liszt and the transcendental virtuosity found in *Gaspard de la nuit.*[51] The unusually somber introduction presents two themes, one dotted (1/2, contrabassoon, miniature orchestral score) and the other derived from jazz, with "blue" notes and syncopation (2/2/2, horns). The entire introduction is built upon a pedal point on E, which functions as an applied dominant, resolving to A at the entrance of the soloist (10/2), and finally to the tonic of D major (11/3/1–2). The introductory statement for the piano is remarkably full in texture and unusually heroic and grandiose in breadth. An orchestral tutti organized by families of instruments (cf. pp. 13–19), leads to a contrasting lyrical theme (21/5–22/1/1), soon followed by a rapid marchlike section, whose opening theme, a series of triads (31/2), recalls analogous passages in the first movement of the Sonata for Violin and Piano. Within this section is found a dancelike, spiccato melody for the soloist, together with many chords with raised and lowered thirds typical of the jazz idiom. The playful scherzo which follows brings to mind Poulenc's observation that French composers are capable of writing profound music, but when they do, "it is leavened with that lightness of spirit without which life would be unendurable." The melody in this brief section is shared by the piccolo and the harp (49/1/1), with the piano performing harplike passages. The development section begins with the opening jazz theme in C minor, at first underpinned tonally (with many chords containing raised and lowered thirds, 52/2/4), but soon presented in bitonal settings (cf. 57/3 and

[51] In preparing for the special demands of the concerto, Ravel studied the *Six Etudes pour la main gauche* by Saint-Saëns, Godowsky's transcriptions for the left hand of Chopin's Etudes, and works by Czerny (*Ecole de la main gauche,* Opus 399, and *24 Etudes pour la main gauche,* Opus 718), Alkan (Etude, Opus 76, No. 1), and Scriabin (Prelude and Nocturne, Opus 9). Similarly, while writing the G major concerto, the composer asked his editor for scores of all the piano concerti by Mozart and Saint-Saëns.

61/3). Two further statements of the theme appear in diminished octaves (cf. 64/1/1–2, and 66/4). This strikingly relentless episode exploits the snare drum and the wood block, coupled with references to other material which is joined with the jazz theme (cf. 59/1, trombone and piano; 62/2/5, muted trumpets and piccolo; 64/1/2, violins and piano; 66/4, violins and trumpets). A free reprise of the marchlike theme and the scherzo (cf. the modifications in orchestration and harmony, 76/4 and 49/1/1) leads to a partial restatement of the initial passage for the soloist (cf. 81/3 and 11/6/2–12/1/1), followed by the cadenza. In the course of recalling the opening themes, one passage has an upper and lower voice with accompaniment in the middle (90/4), all of which, of course, is played by one hand. A return of the jazz themes in the orchestra leads to a sweeping conclusion in D major.

The Piano Concerto for the Left Hand has given rise to a number of psychological interpretations, among them the composer's premonition of his oncoming mental affliction or a commentary on the tragedy and uselessness of World War I. It seems to me to be rather a culmination of Ravel's longstanding preoccupation, one might say obsession, with the notion of death. From the *Ballade de la Reine morte d'aimer, Chanson du rouet, Les Grands Vents venus d'outremer,* and "Le Gibet," through "Soupir," "Trois Beaux Oiseaux du Paradis," *Ronsard à son âme,* and "Aoua!," the motif of death recurs insistently in the composer's œuvre.[52] The tormented conclusion of *La Valse* and the Concerto for the Left Hand are but additional manifestations of this phenomenon. Whether or not one accepts these psychological interpretations, it is evident that the Concerto marks one of Ravel's crowning achievements. The G Major Concerto returns to the composer's more characteristic bent for sparkling humor and elegant lyricism.

Concerto pour piano et orchestre (1929–31)

1) Allegramente
2) Adagio assai
3) Presto

[52] In this light, one might also consider Ravel's title *Pavane pour une Infante défunte* as well as his settings of *Un Grand Sommeil noir* and *Si morne!*

Although written "in the spirit of Mozart and Saint-Saëns," passages in this concerto recall the work of Stravinsky and Gershwin, together with elements of Basque and Spanish music. Once again, the notion of "mixed muses" is particularly apt. The instrumentation specifies a total of thirty-two strings, and the chamberlike writing bespeaks a classical orientation. The rhythmic verve and jazz effects of the outer movements stand in sharp contrast to the poise and serenity of the second movement.

1) Allegramente ($\frac{2}{2}$, G major). The exposition contains no less than five distinct themes, the first of which suggests a Basque folk melody [53] (1/2, miniature orchestral score) and the second, the influence of Spain (8/5), while the remaining three derive from the idiom of jazz (9/2/3, 10/1/2, and 12/1/4). The opening mood is buoyant, with a brittle pungency achieved by the exploitation of bitonality in the piano, and solos for the piccolo and trumpet. As in the Concerto for the Left Hand, this movement will make effective use of the wood block, sliding and tonguing effects, syncopation, "blue" notes, and chords with raised and lowered thirds (cf. 30/4). The development section is a lively romp (15/5), largely exploiting the opening theme and the jazz material. A brief cadenzalike passage precedes the recapitulation, which, as usual, will contain some uncustomary restatements. Following the opening theme in G major, with modified orchestration (24/3/1), a bridge passage originally in B minor for the full orchestra reappears in B♭ major for the woodwinds and brass (cf. 7/3 and 26/3), leading to the second theme (cf. 27/5 and 8/5). Two exceptional cadenzas precede the traditional one for the soloist, one of which is for the harp (29/1/1 and 30/1), while the other focuses upon the woodwinds performing harplike passages (cf. pp. 32 and 33). The piano cadenza derives from the fifth theme of the exposition, with the melody presented in the left hand accompanied by trills, followed by a long series of trills which contain the melody. An extended coda recalls some of the material in the development section (cf. 37/2/2 and 15/5), and the concluding series of descending major and minor triads appears analogously in the penultimate measure of the *Boléro*.

2) Adagio assai ($\frac{3}{4}$, E major). As in Mozart's Piano Concerto in C Minor (K. 491), this movement features two soloists, the piano, and the woodwind family. The spacious opening theme, a spiritual descendant of its

---

[53] Gustave Samazeuilh, who was well acquainted with *Zaspiak-Bat,* believed that parts of it were utilized in the concerto. See "Maurice Ravel en Pays Basque," in *La Revue Musicale* (Dec., 1938), p. 202.

counterpart in the Trio, returns to the archaic lyricism of the *Pavane pour une Infante défunte* and, ultimately, to Satie's *Gymnopédies*. Another related spiritual source appears to be Chopin's *Berceuse,* with its Baroquelike ostinato in the bass, gradual rhythmic intensification in the melody, and its arabesques. A poetic dialogue between the English horn and the piano presents a partial restatement of the opening theme, and a subtle deceptive cadence (58/2/2) leads to a parting allusion to the theme in the muted strings.

3) Presto ($\frac{2}{4}$, G major). The initial drum roll and fanfare in this lighthearted movement recall the circus atmosphere of Stravinsky's *Petrushka* or Satie's *Parade*. The themes in the exposition are fleeting and motley, the first resembling a piercing train whistle (61/2/5), the second, folklike and syncopated (64/1/1), while the third is a boisterous march (68/3). The development section (76/2/4) is set in perpetual motion, with the strings and bassoons sharing in the nimble passage work. The recapitulation is abbreviated, presenting the opening themes in relatively rapid succession with fresh orchestration (cf. 86/1/4, 87/2/4, and 89/1/5). Further passage work (cf. 91/1/5 and 75/2/1) soon leads to the final resounding fanfare. The outer movements of the Concerto reiterate the composer's proclivity for innovation with the traditional sonata form, and the busy activity of the finale recalls the concerti of Prokofiev and Gershwin, coupled with Gallic clarity and wit.

The piano concerti contain Ravel's most successful adaptations of American jazz, and they reflect the spiritual fruit of the composer's trip to North America. The compositions are widely divergent, and rather curiously the Concerto for the Left Hand shows a fuller texture than its counterpart for two hands. The pieces bear witness to the renewed interest in the piano concerto which came about during the postwar years, and both works mark distinguished additions to the standard repertoire.

Don Quichotte à Dulcinée (voice and orchestra, or piano, 1932–33)
   1) "Chanson romanesque"
   2) "Chanson épique"
   3) "Chanson à boire"

Although the orchestral holographs of *Don Quichotte à Dulcinée* are in Ravel's hand, he was already quite ill when writing them and was assisted in his transcription by Lucien Garban and Manuel Rosenthal. The orchestral texture is chamberlike, and each song is based upon the rhythm of a Basque or Spanish dance. The music is straightforward and occasionally folklike, matching the simplicity of Paul Morand's texts.

1) "Chanson romanesque" (moderato). This song alternates $\frac{6}{8}$ and $\frac{3}{4}$ throughout, which is characteristic of the Spanish *guajira*. The text is rigorously molded by the dance pattern, and the folklike setting recalls the "Chanson espagnole."

2) "Chanson épique" (molto moderato). The most successful of the group, the "Chanson épique" is based upon the rhythm of the *zortzico*, a Basque dance in quintuple meter. The opening parallel $\frac{6}{4}$ chords establish the devotional mood, and the appearance of the vibraphone marks the composer's initial utilization of this instrument.

3) "Chanson à boire" (allegro).[54] Based upon the lively triple meter of the Spanish *jota,* this strophic drinking song contains several amusing portamenti for the soloist. It is perhaps symbolic that Ravel bade farewell to his art with a homage to the Spain of his fantasy, concluding with an exuberant toast to the joy of living.

[54] A statement appearing with the autograph indicates that the onomatopoeias in the text were inserted at Chaliapin's request.

CHAPTER NINE

The Creative Process

I am continuing to work, still rather slowly it is true, but more surely. I am counting on the participation of the weather, which is turning fair again. This morning I resumed my nautical pastimes, which, I hope, will stir up inspiration.

LETTER, RAVEL TO JACQUES DURAND, JULY, 1914

In my own work of composition I find a long period of conscious gestation, in general, necessary. During this interval, I come gradually to see, and with growing precision, the form and evolution which the subsequent work should have as a whole.

MAURICE RAVEL

IN AN ARTICLE written in 1938, Henri Gil-Marchex observed that absolutely no sketches of Ravel's piano concerti were available for study. "One day, of course," he continued, "legends will be created about Ravel's gestations. We, who knew him, will always respect the mystery with which he wished to surround the perplexities of his creative imagination." Indeed, owing to a lack of source material, the mystery surrounding the composer's creative process has been all but impenetrable. Throughout his career, Ravel destroyed hundreds of sketches, which he probably considered to be of little

207

importance to anyone. He apparently enjoyed giving the impression that his music was created effortlessly, magically, as if out of thin air. In reality, nothing could have been further from the truth.

Ravel's autographs and sketches bear witness to his relentless inner drive towards technical perfection. Rather than correct some minuscule details, he would frequently recopy an entire autograph. Thus, there exist five autographs of *Sites auriculaires* and two complete orchestral holographs of the overture to *Shéhérazade*. Following all this labor, both works remained unpublished. Ravel's battles against errors in notation were incessant, and he continued to make corrections in his scores even after they had been published.[1] In his lecture on contemporary music, the composer commented upon his method of working:

> In my own work of composition I find a long period of conscious gestation, in general, necessary. During this interval, I come gradually to see, and with growing precision, the form and evolution which the subsequent work should have as a whole. I may thus be occupied for years without writing a single note of the work—after which the writing goes relatively rapidly; but there is still much time to be spent in eliminating everything that might be regarded as superfluous, in order to realize as completely as possible the longed-for final clarity. Then comes the time when new conceptions have to be formulated for further composition, but these cannot be forced artificially, for they come only of their own free will, and often originate in some very remote perception, without manifesting themselves until long years after.[2]

It should be pointed out that Ravel was capable of writing with considerable speed and facility. The accompaniments for five Greek folk melodies were written in some thirty-six hours, *L'Heure espagnole* was completed in about six months, and the orchestration of *Valses nobles et sentimentales* required but two weeks. However, the vast majority of his works were thought out at a leisurely pace, notated rather quickly, and then painstakingly refined and polished. He noted the highly intricate processes at work in attempting to perfect a composition:

> When the first stroke of a work has been written, and the process of elimination begun, the severe effort toward perfection proceeds by means almost intangible, seemingly directed by currents of inner forces, so intimate and intricate in character as to defy all analysis. Real art, I repeat, is not to be recognized by definitions,

[1] In a letter to Lucien Garban, written in March, 1923, the composer observed that *La Valse* and *Ma Mère l'Oye* had quite a number of errors, and he was taking careful note of them.

[2] "Contemporary Music," p. 141.

or revealed by analysis: we sense its manifestations and we feel its presence: it is apprehended in no other way.[3]

Thus, in the last analysis, the logician and craftsman par excellence candidly acknowledged the ineffable and mysterious nature of art and of musical creation.

Ravel's creative personality has been touched upon in the course of this biography. Although a relatively diligent student who spent many hours on dry-as-dust textbook assignments, once he left the Conservatoire he did not generally work methodically on a daily basis. He might suddenly vanish one day, completely isolating himself in order to compose. He discouraged visitors, did not answer mail, worked day and night, and took a vacation only when the piece was completed. At times, however, the composition did not progress, and since it could not be forced, it was temporarily abandoned. A curious aspect of his creative personality was that he felt practically no need to consult the authors whose texts were set. Thus, there was little collaboration with Tristan Klingsor, Franc-Nohain, or Colette, for Ravel worked out virtually everything by himself. Fresh projects were sketched and composed at the piano and were frequently reflected upon during the composer's innumerable long walks.

Many of Ravel's sketches are similar or even identical to their printed versions. The sketches for *La Cloche engloutie* form a striking contrast, in that they appear to depict the genesis of the composer's creative process. What is particularly striking is that several of these sketches consist of a melody and figured bass. We are not dealing with Baroque harmonies, of course, but it is difficult to imagine a highly polished and sophisticated art emanating from such a bare sketch. Manuel Rosenthal was similarly struck when he saw the initial sketches of *Morgiane;* they consisted of about ten pages of melody and figured bass. We may follow the gradual evolution of Ravel's method of working on the basis of two versions of the opening six measures of *La Cloche engloutie* (see Plate 26). The earlier sketch is written in light pencil and contains one indication for figured bass ($\frac{9}{+}$ in the opening measure). The vocal part appears at times without the text, and one can imagine Ravel with Hérold's translation of Hauptmann's play before him setting the text phrase by phrase, without bothering to copy the complete text. The second sketch, which is more developed, is written in ink. It too is

[3] "Contemporary Music," p. 142.

for voice and piano, but now the suggestions for orchestral instrumentation are noted in the piano part. In addition, the figured bass disappears. Thus, the composer's rigorous academic training seems to have rubbed off to some extent on the initial sketches of his own compositions. While at the Conservatoire, he wrote an analysis of Beethoven's Eighth Symphony; he copied out the melody and bass, analyzed the structure, and interpreted the harmonies in terms of figured bass.[4] Although dealing with differing plots, the libretti of *La Cloche engloutie* and *L'Enfant et les sortilèges* unfold within the realm of sheer fantasy and enchantment, and it is indeed a brief distance from the forest and dancing elves of Hauptmann's play to the garden and dancing animals of Colette's libretto. Moreover, it is clear that the beginning of *L'Enfant et les sortilèges* was adapted from the opening of the second act of *La Cloche engloutie* (see Example 8). Thus, *La Clouche engloutie* was not totally abandoned, and it proved to be one of the most important of the composer's numerous incomplete projects.

Ravel's sketches unequivocally indicate that the path toward technical perfection was fraught with difficulties at all stages. Thus, the apparent simplicity of the Musette in the "Menuet" from *Le Tombeau de Couperin* was

La Cloche engloutie, beginning of Act II

L'Enfant et les sortilèges, p. 1

(Autorisation Durand & Cie, Editeurs-propriétaires, Paris)

Example 8

[4] Printed in *Musical Quarterly* (Oct., 1967), Plate II, following p. 478.

Example 9

by no means easily achieved (see Example 9).[5] Similarly, the opening theme of the Sonata for Violin and Cello achieved its final version well after the accompaniment figure had been decided upon. (One may also note the original key signature of three sharps and the obvious omission of accidentals; see Example 10.)

Example 10

[5] Although sketch B is somewhat weaker, sketch A differs from the final version in one note only.

A primitive jotting from the "Prélude" of *Le Tombeau de Couperin* (probably corresponding to 5/5/3) appears to concretize Ravel's notion of "an implied melodic outline in all vital music." In this particular sketch the composer wrote his melodic outline first and later filled in the remaining notes. Note the figured bass indication (♯) in the first measure (see Example 11). A relatively developed sketch of the opening of the "Forlane" from *Le Tombeau de Couperin* epitomizes several problems (see Example 12). Ravel was apparently undecided whether to begin the piece on the first or the fourth beat, and whether or not to dot various eighth notes. Furthermore, too much material was apparently put in the opening measure, and it was therefore excised and inserted later (cf. 10/1/1 and 10/2/5; the obvious slips in the sketch have not been corrected).

Sketches of the first movement of the Sonatine have been preserved, and they are of particular interest (see Plates 27 and 28). It is apparent that Ravel's failure to repeat his original key signature on each new brace led to innumerable slips in notating accidentals. In addition, he was somewhat careless about clef changes, and, as a result, a great deal of time was spent correcting sketches. The most important difference between the sketches and the printed score was the deletion of eleven measures in the passage leading to the second theme. These measures are uncharacteristic, in that they ramble rather aimlessly, and they were wisely excised in toto (see Plate 27, mm.

Example 11

Example 12

11–21).[6] The recapitulation is of particular significance (see Plate 28). The sketch (see Example 13) indicates that it was originally intended to be identical to the opening measure (note the indication D.C.). Only later was the G♯ added to the melody, a subtle and effective emendation.

Original version   Final version

Example 13

The preceding comments should refute the commonly held notion that Ravel set up a rigid structural frame, arranged his modulations, and lastly composed his themes.[7] In all of his sketches the melody is notated from the very beginning, and most often the composer's initial impulses led him to write too many notes and too many measures.

An important holograph of *Jeux d'eau*, now in the Bibliothèque Nationale, is notated in ink, with many corrections in pencil, and a handful of sketches on several of the verso folios. The numerous modifications are most often refinements of texture and deletions of extraneous material. For example, a chord of three notes in the autograph is later reduced to two in the printed score (see Plate 29, bottom brace, final chord in the right hand), or a sequential pattern is abbreviated, rather than a precise repetition of the original statement (top and bottom braces). On occasion passages will be lengthened, as in the measures immediately following the climactic glissando on the black keys (third brace from the bottom). In these measures we may also observe Ravel's corrections of the 32nd-note pattern in the left hand. The four measures preceding the recapitulation and the recapitulation itself are of particular interest (see Plate 30, braces 2, 3, and 4). The autograph contains an overly complex spelling, which uses numerous flats in a key signature of four sharps. Furthermore, the measure in $\frac{2}{4}$ is rhythmically static, and the recapitulation contains several chords in the left hand which are awkwardly disposed. A sketch on the verso folio of page three (see Example 14) contains several important changes: greater clarity of spelling,

---

[6] Other changes from the printed score involve rhythmic modifications (Plate 27, m. 3), changes in harmony (Plate 27, staves 5 and 6 from the bottom, penultimate measure, and staves 3 and 4 from the bottom, mm. 1 and 2), and the discarding of extraneous repetition (Plate 28, mm. 4 and 5).

[7] Norman Demuth, *Ravel,* p. 202.

Example 14

considerable condensation of material, increased rhythmic interest, and an improvement in the disposition of the left hand.

In the closing measures of the printed score, three staves are used in order to clarify the part-writing, but the autograph contains only two (see Plate 31). This striving for clarity of notation is characteristic, and it should be emphasized that all of Ravel's modifications are an improvement, however minute. Nuances of phrasing, tempo, and related matters were frequently added during rehearsals with interpreters, and it may have been Ricardo Viñes who suggested holding the pedal for the last four measures of the piece, rather than only the last two as in the autograph. In the penultimate measure, four notes are present which were later deleted from the concluding arpeggio, resulting in greater rhythmic propulsion toward the final chord of the major seventh.

Before surrendering the autograph of *La Valse* for publication, Ravel asked Ernest Ansermet to conduct the work in private audition. Two modifications appear to have been made at this time: a passage in chromatic scales for the double basses was altered to glissandi (cf. miniature score, pp. 6 and 7), and the final two measures of the piece were extended to three (see Example 15). Although the piano editions of *La Valse* conform to the original version (as do all the autographs), it is probable that Ravel found the orchestral sonority lacking in clarity. Furthermore, the final version dramatically severs the rhythmic propulsion, thereby highlighting the frenzied conclusion of the piece.

214

Original version   Final version

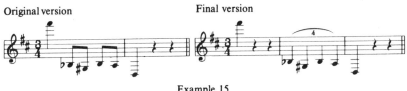

Example 15

With regard to *Daphnis et Chloé,* several points may be made concerning the complete reworking and expansion of the "Danse générale." [8] Not only was this section ultimately doubled in length, but the concluding $\frac{5}{4}$ meter originally appeared entirely in $\frac{3}{4}$ or $\frac{9}{8}$ (see Example 16). (One may also observe the modifications in dynamics resulting from the change in meter.) In the original version, the theme of Daphnis and Chloé (98/3/2)

(94/1/1) Piano edition

Daphnis et Chloé, " Danse générale"

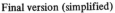

(95/2/1) Piano edition

Daphnis et Chloé," Danse générale"

Example 16

[8] Jacques Chailley, "Une Première Version inconnue de 'Daphnis et Chloé' de Maurice Ravel," in *Mélanges Raymond Lebègue,* pp. 371–75. Apparently a small number of uncorrected proofs were inadvertently sold, and the original version of *Daphnis et Chloé* was thus preserved. Copies of this rare piano score are found in the Music Division of the Bibliothèque Nationale and in the Library of Congress. The score, which has 102 pages (rather than 114), is analyzed in detail by Chailley. In the original version, one finds the names Darion and Lyceia rather than Dorcon and Lyceion, while Bryaxis is referred to as "the chief of the pirates." The "Danse générale" consists of nine pages (93–102), while in the final version it extends over twenty pages (94–114).

does not reappear, and the ballet concludes with the chorus participating in the final six measures only. Furthermore, the driving triplet figure is lacking (see Plate 32). In sum, the reworking of the "Danse générale" constitutes a striking improvement in rhythmic subtlety and offers a peroration of considerably greater sweep and emotional tension.

The foregoing commentary indicates that the perfecting of a composition was most often a long and agonizing task, and this may well account for Ravel's small output. He contemplated and even began to sketch many projects which were ultimately abandoned, largely because of his rigorously self-critical attitude. Ravel's creative process was, in the last analysis, a relentless search for clarity of expression; with his innate artistic conscience he created an art of uncommon integrity, lucidity, and excellence.

Conclusion

On the initial performance of a new musical composition, the first impression of the public is generally one of reaction to the more superficial elements of its music, that is to say, to its external manifestations rather than to its inner content. The listener is impressed by some unimportant peculiarity in the medium of expression, and yet the idiom of expression, even if considered in its completeness, is only the means and not the end in itself, and often it is not until years after, when the means of expression have finally surrendered all their secrets, that the real inner emotion of the music becomes apparent to the listener.

MAURICE RAVEL

IN EVALUATING Ravel's achievement, one might well recall the Biblical maxim that there is nothing new under the sun: a skilled craftsman with a keen awareness of his national consciousness, turning to models for inspiration—this would describe Ravel as well as Bach or Couperin. Moreover, whether it be Bach turning to Vivaldi, or Mozart to Bach, or Chopin to Mozart, or Debussy to Chopin, the fact is that in composition, as in human existence, no man is an island. Of course, one must acknowledge Ravel's unique extensions of piano technique, orchestral timbre, and harmony, all of which were widely influential from the 1920s to the 1950s.[1] At this writing, however, his achievement appears to be self-contained rather than seminal, and his legacy might thus be compared with those of Bartók, Falla, Hindemith, Prokofiev, or Vaughan Williams—composers whose innovative techniques were solidly based upon traditional practice. With atonality, electronic music, and "musique concrète" at the forefront of contemporary developments, the styles of these composers have joined the mainstream of music history, and once again, it may be observed that what appeared revolutionary in one generation was considered evolutionary in the next. If Ravel's art has declined in influence, its reputation has continued to grow, and the composer's eminent position in the annals of twentieth-century music is now established. Above all, his achievement is unthinkable without France. Ravel's art is a direct continuation of the work of Rameau and Couperin, embodying the subtle humor of a La Fontaine, the sensuousness of a Renoir, and the intellectual discipline and rigorous craftsmanship of a Mallarmé. In the last analysis, Ravel's reputation will rest largely upon some thirty-five major achievements, whose beauty and perfection of workmanship constitute a distinguished and unique legacy.

[1] In an article written in 1921, Roland-Manuel commented upon Ravel's marked influence on the younger generation in Austria, England, France, Hungary, Italy, and Spain. The composer's imprint is naturally closest in spirit to the French school and may be seen in the work of Jacques Ibert, Louis Durey, Francis Poulenc, Germaine Tailleferre, and in the generation of French composers whose formative development took place in the 1930s. See Milhaud, "Hommage à Ravel," *La Revue Musicale* (Dec., 1938), p. 40.

Mairie de CIBOURE

Copie intégrale d'Acte de NAISSANCE

Acte n° 27

RAVEL

Joseph

Maurice

L'an Mil-huit-cent-soixante-quinze, le huit
Mars à midi, par devant Nous Maire, Officier de l'Etat-
Civil de la Commune de CIBOURE, Canton de Saint-Jean-de-
Luz, Département des Basses-Pyrénées, est comparue
Gracieuse BILLAC, âgée de cinquante ans, marchande de
poisson, domiciliée dans cette commune, laquelle nous
a déclaré que Marie DELOUART, âgée de vingt-huit ans,
demeurant actuellement à CIBOURE, épouse de Pierre
Joseph RAVEL, est accouchée hier à dix heures du soir,
Rue du Quai N° 12, d'un enfant du sexe masculin, qu'elle
nous présente, et auquel elle a déclaré vouloir donner
les prénoms de JOSEPH MAURICE; Les dites déclarations et
présentation faites en présence de HARAMBOURE Renaud, âgé
de quarante-trois ans, receveur de l'octroi et de HARISPU-
RU Michel, âgé de trente-six ans, instituteur, domiciliés
à CIBOURE et ont les témoins signé avec nous le présent
acte, non la déclarante, pour ne savoir écrire, à ce qu'elle
a déclaré, après que lecture leur en a été faite.

Le Maire,
Signé: Besselère

Signé: Harispuru
Haramboure

Pour copie certifiée conforme au registre.
Fait à CIBOURE, le..11. juillet 1946..........

P Le Maire,

Le secrétaire général *[signature]*

Copy of the birth certificate of Joseph Maurice Ravel

PLATE 1

At the Conservatoire, c.1894. Ravel at the left. Seated at the left of the piano, Professor Charles de Bériot. Fourth from right, Ricardo Viñes; fifth from right, Marcel Chadeigne

PLATE 2

SOCIÉTÉ NATIONALE
DE MUSIQUE

266me CONCERT

SAMEDI 5 MARS 1898, à 9 heures précises.

Ouverture des portes à 8 heures 1/2.

Fondée en 1871

1 **QUINTETTE** pour piano et instruments à cordes (op. 10) **G. M. WITKOWSKI**
   1 *Très lent, assez vif.* 2 *Modéré et soutenu (dans le* "1re Audition"
   style d'un nocturne). 3 *animé (Alla Zingara).*
   Mlle M. DRON, MM. PARENT, LAMMERS, DÉNAYER
   et BARETTI.

2. A **2 CHANSONS POPULAIRES**...... .... **P. DE BRÉVILLE**
   1 *La Tour prends garde.* "1re Audition"
   2 *Sur le Pont* (Emile Cottinet).
   B **LES FÉES** (H. Gauthier Villars).
   Mme J. REMACLE.

3. **3 ÉTUDES** pour piano, à 4 mains. .... **R. DUCASSE**
   1 *Souvenance.* "1re Audition"
   2 *Berceuse.*
   3 *Claironnerie.*
   Mlle M. DRON et M. RICARDO VINES.

4. **2° QUATUOR** pour 2 violons, alto et violoncelle .... **V. D'INDY**
   1 *Lentement, animé.* 2 *Très animé.* 3 *Très lent.* "1re Audition"
   4 *Lentement, très vif.*
   MM. PARENT, LAMMERS, DENAYER et BARETTI.

5. **3 MELODIES**........................... ..... **J. GAY**
   1 *Berceuse.* "1re Audition"
   2 *Jardin-Rondel.*
   3 *Chanson de Guerre.* (Ernest Jaubert).
   Mlle Jenny PASSAMA.

6. **SITES AURICULAIRES** .... ·. **M. RAVEL**
   1 *Habanera.* "1re Audition"
   2 *Entre Cloches.*
   pour deux pianos.
   Mlle M. DRON et M. RICARDO VINES

---

*Les personnes désirant faire partie de la SOCIETE NATIONALE,
sont priées d'envoyer leur adhésion à l'***AGENCE, 50, RUE
St-SAUVEUR***. La cotisation annuelle est de 25 francs, donnant
droit à ***trois entrées réservées*** par Concert.*

ORGANISATION & DIRECTION DE CONCERTS, AGENCE : 50, RUE St-SAUVEUR

Le 267e CONCERT (avec orchestre) aura lieu le Samedi 19 Mars à la Salle du NOUVEAU-THÉATRE, 15, R. Blanche.

SALLE PLEYEL, 22, Rue Rochechouart
SOCIÉTÉ NATIONALE DE MUSIQUE

266me CONCERT

Samedi 5 Mars 1898, à 9 heures précises.

PRIX DES BILLETS : Fauteuils de Parquet : 10 fr. - Entrée, 5 fr.

On trouve des billets à la Salle PLEYEL, 22, Rue Rochechouart.

(Ouverture des portes à 8 h. 1/2.)

Ravel's formal debut as a composer

PLATE 3

SALLE ÉRARD, 13, RUE DU MAIL

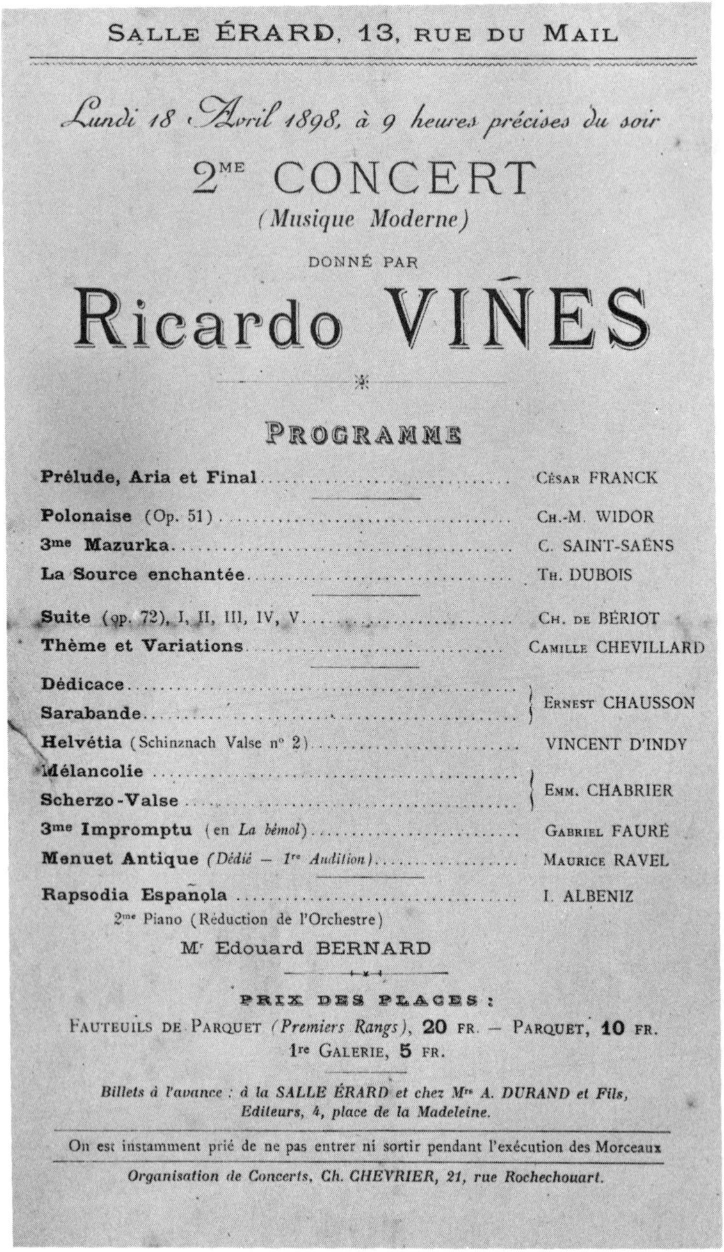

Lundi 18 Avril 1898, à 9 heures précises du soir

2ME CONCERT

(Musique Moderne)

DONNÉ PAR

Ricardo VIÑES

PROGRAMME

Prélude, Aria et Final	CÉSAR FRANCK
Polonaise (Op. 51)	CH.-M. WIDOR
3me Mazurka	C. SAINT-SAËNS
La Source enchantée	TH. DUBOIS
Suite (op. 72), I, II, III, IV, V	CH. DE BÉRIOT
Thème et Variations	CAMILLE CHEVILLARD
Dédicace / **Sarabande**	ERNEST CHAUSSON
Helvétia (Schinznach Valse nº 2)	VINCENT D'INDY
Mélancolie / **Scherzo-Valse**	EMM. CHABRIER
3me Impromptu (en *La bémol*)	GABRIEL FAURÉ
Menuet Antique *(Dédié — 1re Audition)*	MAURICE RAVEL
Rapsodia Españ̃ola	I. ALBENIZ

2me Piano (Réduction de l'Orchestre)

Mr Edouard BERNARD

PRIX DES PLACES :

FAUTEUILS DE PARQUET *(Premiers Rangs)*, **20** FR. — PARQUET, **10** FR.
1re GALERIE, **5** FR.

Billets à l'avance : à la SALLE ÉRARD et chez Mrs A. DURAND et Fils, Editeurs, 4, place de la Madeleine.

On est instamment prié de ne pas entrer ni sortir pendant l'exécution des Morceaux

Organisation de Concerts, Ch. CHEVRIER, 21, rue Rochechouart.

A program of modern music given by Ricardo Viñes

PLATE 4

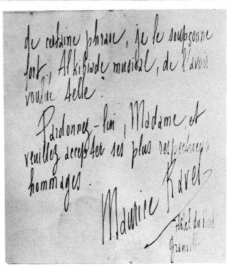

Letter from Ravel to Mme René de Saint-Marceaux, written August 20, 1898

PLATE 5

Ravel's transcription of an opera by Delius, *Margot la Rouge,* p. 1

PLATE 6

Georges d'Espagnat, "Réunion de musiciens chez M. Godebski," 1910. Standing, from left: Florent Schmitt, Déodat de Séverac, M. D. Calvocoressi, Albert Roussel. Seated: Cipa Godebski, his son Jean. Ricardo Viñes at the piano, and Ravel.

PLATE 7

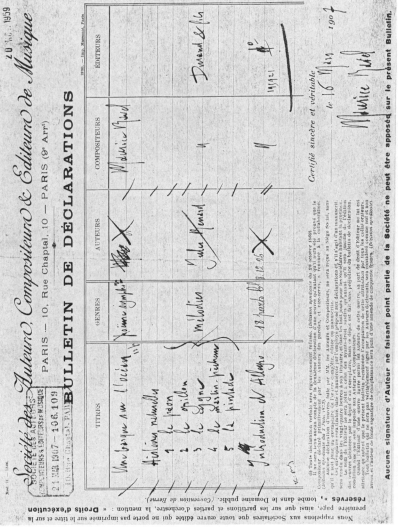

Declaration of copyright of several works by Ravel

PLATE 8

Founding committee of the Société Musicale Indépendante. Standing, left to right: Louis Aubert, A. Z. Mathot, Ravel, André Caplet, Charles Koechlin, Emile Vuillermoz, Jean Huré. Seated: Gabriel Fauré and Roger-Ducasse.

PLATE 9

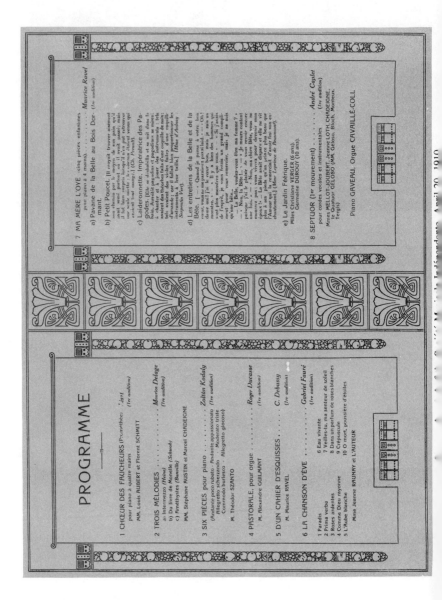

PLATE 10

Le Belvédère

The salon

The composer's desk in the study

The front of the house

A view from the balcony

Plaque on front of the house

The back of the house

PLATE 11

The study at Le Belvédère. The piano and a portrait of Mme Ravel by her brother-in-law
Edouard

PLATE 12

I

Maurice Ravel in Recital *and* Lecture-Recital
Under the Auspices of the Rice Institute
Lectureship in Music
April 6th and 7th, 1928

Assisting Artists:
Esther Dale, *Soprano* :-: Barbara Lull, *Violinist*

PROGRAMME FOR THE RECITAL
April 6th

1. Sonatine
   1. Modéré
   2. Mouvement de Menuet
   3. Animé
      Maurice Ravel

2. *(a)* Sainte
   (b) Nicolette
   (c) Air de l'Enfant
      Esther Dale *and* Maurice Ravel

3. La Vallée des Cloches
   Menuet *(from "Tombeau de Couperin")*
      Maurice Ravel

4. Chansons Hébraiques *(Voice and Piano)*
   (a) Kaddisch
   (b) L'Enigme Eternelle
      Esther Dale *and* Maurice Ravel

5. Sonata for Violin and Piano
   Allegretto
   Blues
   Perpetuum Mobile
      Barbara Lull *and* Maurice Ravel

Recital in Houston, Texas, April 6, 1928

PLATE 13

II

Maurice Ravel in Recital *and* Lecture-Recital
Under the Auspices of the Rice Institute
Lectureship in Music
April 6th and 7th, 1928

Assisting Artists:
Esther Dale, *Soprano* :-: Barbara Lull, *Violinist*

PROGRAMME FOR THE LECTURE-RECITAL
April 7th

1. Lecture

2. (*a*) Habanera
   (*b*) Menuet Antique
   > Maurice Ravel

3. Sheherazade (*Three Poems for Voice and Piano*)
   (*a*) Asie
   (*b*) La Flûte Enchantée
   (*c*) L'Indifférent
   > Esther Dale *and* Maurice Ravel

4. (*a*) Pavane pour une Infante défunte
   (*b*) Rigaudon (*from "Le Tombeau de Couperin"*)
   > Maurice Ravel

5. Chansons Grecques (*for Voice and Piano*)
   (*a*) Le Réveil de la Mariée
   (*b*) Là-bas vers l'Eglise
   (*c*) Quel Galant!
   (*d*) Chanson des meilleuse de lentisques
   (*e*) Tout gai!
   > Esther Dale *and* Maurice Ravel

6. (*a*) Berceuse
   > Barbara Lull *and* Maurice Ravel
   (*b*) Tzigane
   > Barbara Lull *and* Patricio Gutierrez

Lecture-recital in Houston, Texas, April 7, 1928

PLATE 14

Ravel, c.1902

A family portrait, c.1886; Edouard, Mme
Ravel, Maurice, and Joseph Ravel

Ravel, c.1907

Ravel, c.1911

PLATE 15

Fall, 1937. One of the last photographs taken of the composer. With Mme Jacques Meyer and Jacques Février

c.1925: Ravel in the garden at Montfort l'Amaury.

1928: Le Havre. The return from the United States. From the left: Maurice Delage, Marcelle Gerar, Hélène Jourdan-Morhange, Ravel, Nelly Delage and Edouard Ravel

PLATE 16

A graphic interpretation of Ravel's art, by Jacques Devigne. Commissioned by France's Society of Authors, Composers, and Editors of Music, this gold medal was completed in 1965. The artist has depicted some of the important aspects of Ravel's art: irony, humor, animals, Greece, Spain, and water images. A keyboard traverses the entire medal, over which the wily Scarbo and the vain peacock walk, while a Greek muse plays the aulos. Two streams of water join to form a Spanish dancer, with her mantilla, under which a wave arises in the shape of a left hand.

PLATE 17

Ballade de la Reine morte d'aimer, p. 1 of the autograph

PLATE 18

Sérénade grotesque, p. 1 of the autograph

PLATE 19

Chanson du rouet, p. 7 of the autograph. A unique adaptation of Gregorian chant in Ravel's oeuvre

PLATE 20

Overture to *Shéhérazade*, p. 1

PLATE 21

Alcyone (1902), cantata for the Prix de Rome, p. 50

PLATE 22

Alyssa (1903), cantata for the Prix de Rome, p. 78

PLATE 23

Top: L'Heure espagnole, Paris, Opéra-Comique, November 7, 1945. Décor by Mme Suzanne
Roland-Manuel

Bottom: Daphnis et Chloé, Paris, Opéra, 1958. Décor by Marc Chagall

PLATE 24

L'Enfant et les sortilèges, Paris, Opéra, May 17, 1939. Décor and costumes by Paul Colin: (above) First tableau; (below) Scene in the garden

PLATE 25

Two versions of the opening six measures of *La Cloche engloutie:* (above) Initial sketch written in light pencil; (below) A more developed sketch written in ink

PLATE 26

Sonatine, first movement, p. 1. The sketches are written in light pencil.

PLATE 27

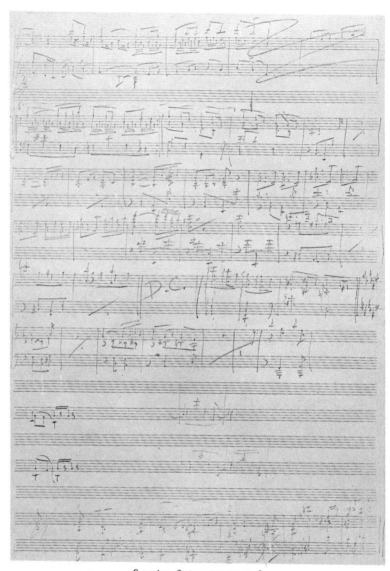

Sonatine, first movement, p. 2

PLATE 28

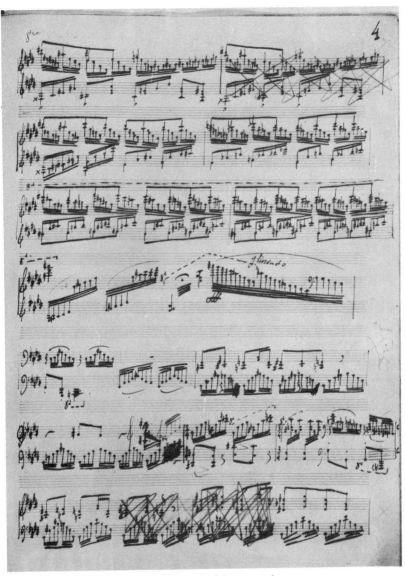

Jeux d'eau, p. 4 of the autograph

PLATE 29

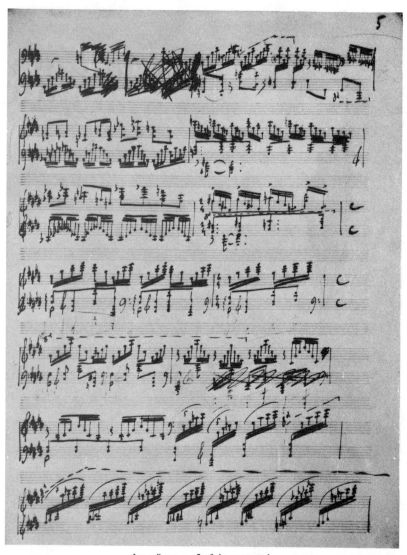

Jeux d'eau, p. 5 of the autograph

PLATE 30

Jeux d'eau, p. 7 of the autograph

PLATE 31

Daphnis et Chloé, p. 102. Original ending of the piano edition (1910)

PLATE 32

Catalogue of Works

I. Completed Works and Transcriptions

Abbreviations used:

HRC	Humanities Research Center, University of Texas at Austin
KOCH	Frederick R. Koch Foundation Collection, on deposit at the Pierpont Morgan Library
MAT	Private collection of Madame Alexandre Taverne
MDBN	Music Division of the Bibliothèque Nationale
ROLC	Robert Owen Lehman Collection, on deposit at the Pierpont Morgan Library
SML	Sibley Music Library at the Eastman School of Music, Rochester, New York

Autog.	Autograph	Perf.	Performance
Comp.	Year or years of composition	Prov.	Provenance
Ded.	Dedication in the printed edition	s. & d.	signed and dated
Dur.	Durand and Company	SMI.	Société Musicale Indépendante
Ed.	Edition	Soc. Nat.	Société Nationale de Musique
MS.	Manuscript	Trans.	Transcription
p., pp.	page, pages		

NOTE: All transcriptions are by Ravel, and all autographs are in pen unless otherwise stated. The *Catalogue de l'Œuvre de Maurice Ravel,* published by the Maurice Ravel Foundation (Paris, 1954), lists transcriptions of Ravel's works carried out by others.

Title: *Ballade de la Reine morte d'aimer* (voice and piano, poem by Roland de Marès). Comp. c.1893
Autog.: MAT, 5 pp., untitled
Ed.: Salabert & A.R.I.M.A., 1975
First Perf.: Sheila Schonbrun, soprano; Arbie Orenstein, piano; February 23, 1975, Charles S. Colden Auditorium, Queens College, Flushing, N.Y.

Title: *Sérénade grotesque* (piano). Comp. c.1893
Autog.: MAT, 5 pp., entitled *Sérénade*
Ed: Salabert & A.R.I.M.A., 1975
First Perf.: Arbie Orenstein, February 23, 1975, Charles S. Colden Auditorium, Queens College, Flushing, N.Y.

Title: *Un Grand Sommeil noir* (voice and piano, poem by Verlaine). Comp. 1895
Autog.: KOCH, 2 pp., s. & d. August 6, 1895. Prov. Mme Lucien Garban
   MAT, 3 pp., s. & d. August 6, 1895
   Private collection, 3 pp., s. & d. August 6, 1895
Ed.: Dur., 1953

Title: *Menuet antique* (piano). Comp. 1895
Autog.: MAT, two copies, 4 pp. and 6 pp., both dated November, 1895. The repetition of the opening section is omitted in one autog.
Ed.: Enoch, 1898
Ded.: Ricardo Viñes
First Perf.: Ricardo Viñes, April 18, 1898, Salle Erard
Trans.: For orchestra, 1929
Autog.: Not traced
Ed.: Enoch, 1930
First Perf.: Maurice Ravel conducting the Lamoureux Orchestra, January 11, 1930

Title: *Sites auriculaires* (two pianos). Comp. 1895–97
 1) "Habanera"
 2) "Entre cloches"
Autog.: MAT, 4 copies, all 12 pp. ("Habanera," pp. 1–6; "Entre cloches," pp. 7–12)
   KOCH, 13 pp. ("Habanera," pp. 1–7; "Entre cloches," pp. 8–13). Prov. Manuel Rosenthal
One MS. of the "Habanera" (MAT) is dated November, 1895, and one MS. of "Entre cloches" (MAT) is dated December, 1897. Two copies (MAT) contain errors and omissions. The three remaining copies are considerably more accurate

and bear an epigraph from Baudelaire's *A une Dame créole:* "Au pays parfumé que le soleil caresse."
Ed.: Salabert & A.R.I.M.A., 1975
First Perf.: Marthe Dron and Ricardo Viñes, March 5, 1898, Soc. Nat., Salle Pleyel
Trans.: The "Habanera" is the third movement of the *Rapsodie espagnole.*

Title: *Sainte* (voice and piano, poem by Mallarmé). Comp. 1896
Autog.: MAT, 4 pp., dated December, 1896
      Private collection, 2 pp., s. & d. December, 1896
Ed.: Dur., 1907
Ded.: Madame Edmond Bonniot, née Mallarmé
First Perf.: Hélène Luquiens and Ravel, June 8, 1907, Cercle de l'art moderne, Paris

Title: Sonate pour piano et violon (Sonata for Violin and Piano). Comp. 1897
Autog.: MAT, 15 pp., dated April, 1897; pp. 1–11, full score; pp. 12–15, violin part
Ed.: Salabert, A.R.I.M.A. & S.E.M.U.P., 1975
First Perf.: Gerald Tarack, violin; Leon Pommers, piano; February 23, 1975, Charles S. Colden Auditorium, Queens College, Flushing, N.Y.

Title: *Chanson du rouet* (voice and piano, poem by Leconte de Lisle). Comp. 1898
Autog.: MAT, 8 pp., s. & d. June 2, 1898
Ed.: Salabert & A.R.I.M.A., 1975
First Perf.: Sheila Schonbrun, soprano; Arbie Orenstein, piano; February 23, 1975, Charles S. Colden Auditorium, Queens College, Flushing, N.Y.

Title: *Si morne!* (voice and piano, poem by Emile Verhaeren). Comp. 1898
Autog.: MAT, 5 pp., s. & d. November, 1898
Ed: Salabert & A.R.I.M.A., 1975
First Perf.: Sheila Schonbrun, soprano; Arbie Orenstein, piano; February 23, 1975, Charles S. Colden Auditorium, Queens College, Flushing, N.Y.

Title: *Ouverture de Shéhérazade* (orchestra). Comp. 1898
Autog.: MAT, 3 copies. The original version for piano, four hands, 29 pp., contains errors and omissions. Two orchestral holographs, each 49 pp., are s. & d. November, 1898. The holographs are similar but not identical.
Ed.: Salabert & A.R.I.M.A., 1975
First Perf.: Maurice Ravel conducting the orchestra of the Soc. Nat., May 27, 1899, Salle du Nouveau Théâtre

Title: *Epigrammes de Clément Marot* (voice and piano). Comp. 1896–99
  A) "D'Anne qui me jecta de la neige"   B) "D'Anne jouant de l'espinette"
Autog.: MAT, 1 copy of A, 3 pp.; 2 copies of B, which are identical, one 2 pp., the
        other 3 pp.
      A) s. & d. December 10, 1899
      B) s. & d. December, 1896
Ed.: E. Demets, 1900; Eschig
Ded.: M. Hardy-Thé
First Perf.: M. Hardy-Thé and Ravel, January 27, 1900, Soc. Nat., Salle Erard

Title: *Pavane pour une Infante défunte* (piano). Comp. 1899
Autog.: Not traced
Ed.: E. Demets, 1900; Eschig
Ded.: Madame la Princesse E. de Polignac
First Perf.: Ricardo Viñes, April 5, 1902, Soc. Nat., Salle Pleyel
Trans.: For small orchestra, 1910
Autog.: Not traced
Ed.: E. Demets, 1910, Eschig
First Perf.: Henry J. Wood, conductor, Gentlemen's Concerts in Manchester,
    England, February 27, 1911

Title: Essay for the Prix de Rome—1900. Unpublished
Autog.: MDBN, 27 pp., MS. 10910 (1–2)
      1) Fugue in D major, 4 pp.
      2) Choral piece, *Les Bayadères,* for soprano soloist, mixed chorus, and
         orchestra, 23 pp.

Title: Essay for the Prix de Rome—1901. Unpublished
Autog.: MDBN, 134 pp., MS. 1050
      1) Fugue in F major, 6 pp.
      2) Choral piece, *Tout est lumière,* for soprano soloist, mixed chorus, and
         orchestra, 26 pp.
      3) *Myrrha,* cantata for three soloists and orchestra, text by Fernand Beis-
         sier, 102 pp.
First Perf.: At the Conservatoire, June 28, 1901 (cantata only)

Title: *Jeux d'eau* (piano). Comp. 1901
Autog.: ROLC, 7 pp., a clean copy. Prov. Alfred Cortot.
      MDBN, 7 pp., contains many corrections. Prov. Georges Jean-Aubry.

Autog. s. & d. November 11, 1901 (MS. 15198). The epigraph "Dieu fluvial riant de l'eau qui le chatouille" is written out by Henri de Régnier.

Ed.: E. Demets, 1902; Eschig

Ded.: à mon cher maître Gabriel Fauré

First Perf.: Ricardo Viñes, April 5, 1902, Soc. Nat., Salle Pleyel

Title: Essay for the Prix de Rome—1902. Unpublished

Autog.: MDBN, 129 pp., MS. 1051

    1) Fugue in B♭ major, 6 pp.

    2) Choral piece, *La Nuit,* for soprano soloist, mixed chorus, and orchestra, 17 pp.

    3) *Alcyone,* cantata for three soloists and orchestra, text by Eugène and Edouard Adénis, 106 pp.

First Perf.: At the Conservatoire, June, 1902 (cantata only)

Title: Quatuor (String Quartet). Comp. 1902–03

    1) Allegro moderato   3) Très lent

    2) Assez vif-très rythmé   4) Vif et agité

Autog.: MAT, 28 pp. At the conclusion of the second movement the autog. is dated December, 1902. Following the fourth movement it is dated April, 1903.

Ed.: G. Astruc, 1904; Dur., 1910

Ded.: à mon cher maître Gabriel Fauré

First Perf.: Heymann Quartet (L. Heymann, De Bruyne, Marchet, De Bruyn), March 5, 1904, Soc. Nat., Salle de la Schola Cantorum

Title: Essay for the Prix de Rome—1903. Unpublished

Autog.: MDBN, 136 pp., MS. 8536 and MS. 8598 (1–2)

    1) Fugue in E minor, 4 pp.

    2) Choral piece, *Matinée de Provence,* for soprano soloist, mixed chorus, and orchestra, 21 pp.

    3) *Alyssa,* cantata for three soloists and orchestra, text by Marguerite Coiffier, 111 pp. (The last page is missing.)

    MAT, *Matinée de Provence,* 13 pp., version for soprano soloist, mixed chorus, and two pianos

First Perf.: At the Conservatoire, June 26, 1903 (cantata only)

Title: *Manteau de fleurs* (voice and piano, poem by Paul Gravollet). Comp. 1903

Autog.: Not traced

Ed.: Hamelle, 1906

Trans.: For voice and orchestra
Autog.: MAT, 9 pp.
Ed.: Unpublished

Title: *Shéhérazade* (voice and orchestra, voice and piano, poems by Tristan Kling-sor). Comp. 1903
1) "Asie"
2) "La Flûte enchantée"
3) "L'Indifférent"
Autog.: HRC, 41 pp., voice and orchestra ("Asie," 27 pp.; "La Flûte enchantée," 7 pp.; "L'Indifférent, 7 pp.).Autog. for voice and piano not traced
Ed.: G. Astruc, 1904 (voice and piano)
    Dur., 1911 (voice and piano)
    Dur., 1914 (voice and orchestra)
Ded.: "Asie": Mademoiselle Jeane [*sic*] Hatto
    "La Flûte enchantée": Madame René de Saint-Marceaux
    "L'Indifférent": Madame Sigismond Bardac
First Perf.: Jane Hatto, soprano; Alfred Cortot, conductor. May 17, 1904, Soc. Nat., Salle du Nouveau Théâtre

Title: Sonatine (piano). Comp. 1903–05
1) Modéré
2) Mouvement de menuet
3) Animé
Autog.: Private collection, first movement only, 3 pp.; second and third move-ments not traced
Ed.: Dur., 1905
Ded.: Ida et Cipa Godebski
First Perf.: Mme Paule de Lestang, Lyon, March 10, 1906. First perf. in Paris: Gabriel Grovlez, March 31, 1906, Soc. Nat., Salle de la Schola Cantorum

Title: *Miroirs* (piano). Comp. 1904–05
1) "Noctuelles"
2) "Oiseaux tristes"
3) "Une Barque sur l'océan"
4) "Alborada del gracioso"
5) "La Vallée des cloches"
Autog.: "Noctuelles," ROLC, 4 pp., dated 10/1905, Prov. Alfred Cortot
    "Oiseaux tristes," Mary Flagler Cary Music Collection, Pierpont Morgan
        Library, 3 pp., MS. signed by Ravel. Prov. Alfred Cortot

"Une Barque sur l'océan," Private collection, 6 pp.; s. & d. May, 1905. A copy with some indications in Ravel's hand is found in MDBN, MS. 13453.

"Alborada del gracioso," MDBN, 8 pp. MS. 14452. Prov. M. D. Calvocoressi

"La Vallée des cloches," Private collection, 3 pp.

Ed.: E. Demets, 1906, Eschig

Ded.: "Noctuelles": Léon-Paul Fargue

"Oiseaux tristes": Ricardo Viñes

"Une Barque sur l'océan": Paul Sordes

"Alborada del gracioso": M. D. Calvocoressi

"La Vallée des cloches": Maurice Delage

First Perf.: Ricardo Viñes, January 6, 1906, Soc. Nat., Salle Erard

Trans.: "Une Barque sur l'océan," for orchestra, 1906

Autog.: Private collection of Henri Dutilleux, last page only (p. 25), s. & d. 10/1906

Ed.: Eschig, 1950

First Perf.: Gabriel Pierné conducting the Colonne Orchestra, February 3, 1907

Trans.: "Alborada del gracioso," for orchestra, 1918

Autog.: Private collection, 32 pp.

Ed.: Eschig, 1923

First Perf.: Rhené-Baton conducting the Pasdeloup Orchestra, May 17, 1919

Title: *Cinq Mélodies populaires grecques* (voice and piano). Comp. 1904–06

1) "Chanson de la mariée" 4) "Chanson des cueilleuses de lentisques"

2) "Là-bas, vers l'église" 5) "Tout gai!"

3) "Quel galant m'est comparable"

Autog.: HRC, 13 pp. The autographs appear to have been hastily written, and the texts of numbers 4 and 5 are missing.

Memorial Library of Music, Stanford University

"Tout gai!", 3 pp. Prov., M. D. Calvocoressi

Ed.: Dur., 1906

First Perf.: Louise Thomasset, February 20, 1904, Ecole des Hautes Etudes Sociales, Paris (Numbers 3 and 4). First Perf. of the five songs given by Marguerite Babaïan at a lecture-recital presented by M. D. Calvocoressi during the 1905–06 season

Trans.: For orchestra, Numbers 1 and 5. The autog. of Number 1 is entitled "Le Réveil de la mariée," Number 5 is signed by Ravel, and Numbers 2, 3, and 4 were transcribed by Manuel Rosenthal. In addition, three other Greek folk melodies were harmonized in 1904, which have not been recovered: 1) A vous, oiseaux des plaines; 2) Chanson de pâtre épirote; 3) Mon Mouchoir, hélas, est perdu.

Title: Essay for the Prix de Rome—1905. Unpublished
Autog.: MDBN, 32 pp., MS. 10911 (1–2)
    1) Fugue in C major, 4 pp.
    2) Choral piece, *L'Aurore,* for tenor soloist, mixed chorus, and orchestra, 28 pp.

Title: *Noël des jouets* (voice and piano, voice and orchestra, poem by Maurice Ravel). Comp. 1905
Autog.: Voice and piano, not traced
    Archives of Salabert & Co., voice and orchestra, 9 pp. The accompaniment was reorchestrated in 1913. At the end of the autog. Ravel wrote: "réorchestré—pour cause de divorce—en Décembre 1913." The autog. contains interpretive suggestions not in Ravel's hand, suggesting that it was used as a conductor's score.
Ed.: Bellon Ponscarme (no date), A. Z. Mathot (1914), Salabert (voice and piano)
    A. Z. Mathot, 1914 (voice and orchestra; unpublished, parts available for rental)
Ded.: Madame Jean Cruppi
First Perf.: Jane Bathori and Ravel (voice and piano), March 24, 1906, Salle Fourcroy
    Jane Bathori and Ravel conducting, April 26, 1906, Soc. Nat., Salle Erard
    First perf. of the reorchestrated version: Lyon, January, 1914

Title: *Introduction et Allegro* (for harp, accompanied by string quartet, flute, and clarinet). Comp. 1905
Autog.: HRC, 20 pp., full score. The part for the harp is also notated separately (14 pp.).
Ed.: Dur., 1906
Ded.: Albert Blondel
First Perf.: Micheline Kahn, harp; Charles Domergue, conductor; Philippe Gaubert, flute; M. Pichard, clarinet; the Firmin Touche Quartet (Firmin Touche, Dorson, Drouet, Baretti). February 22, 1907, Cercle Musical, Hôtel de la Société Française de Photographie
Trans.: 2 pianos, 4 hands
Autog.: MAT, 12 pp.
Ed.: Dur., 1906

Title: *Histoires naturelles* (voice and piano, poems by Jules Renard). Comp. 1906
    1) "Le Paon"   4) "Le Martin-Pêcheur"
    2) "Le Grillon"   5) "La Pintade"
    3) "Le Cygne"

Autog.: HRC, 16 pp., s. & d. "October–December 1906."
    Private collection, "Le Paon" (4 pp.) and "Le Martin-Pêcheur" (2 pp.)
    Private collection, "Le Cygne" (3 pp.)
Ed.: Dur., 1907
Ded.: "Le Paon": Madame Jane Bathori
    "Le Grillon": Mademoiselle Madeleine Picard
    "Le Cygne": Madame Alfred Edwards, née Godebska
    "Le Martin-Pêcheur": Emile Engel
    "La Pintade": Roger-Ducasse
First Perf.: Jane Bathori and Ravel, January 12, 1907, Soc. Nat., Salle Erard

Title: *Vocalise-Etude en forme de Habanera* (voice and piano). Comp. 1907
Autog.: Archives of Editions Alphonse Leduc, 3 pp., s. & d. March, 1907, entitled
    "Vocalise en forme de Havanera"
Ed.: A. Leduc, 1909

Title: *Les Grands Vents venus d'outremer* (voice and piano, poem by Henri de
    Régnier). Comp. 1907
Autog.: MAT, 3 pp., s. & d. April, 1907
Ed.: Dur., 1907
Ded.: Jacques Durand
First Perf.: Hélène Luquiens and Ravel, June 8, 1907, Cercle de L'Art Moderne,
    Paris

Title: *Sur l'herbe* (voice and piano, poem by Verlaine). Comp. 1907
Autog.: HRC, 3 pp., s. & d. June 6, 1907
Ed.: Dur., 1907
First Perf.: In Paris: Jane Bathori and Ravel, December 12, 1907, Salle de la Société
    Française de Photographie

Title: *Rapsodie espagnole* (orchestra). Comp. 1907–08
    1) "Prélude à la nuit"   3) "Habanera"
    2) "Malagueña"   4) "Feria"
Autog.: HRC, 65 pp. ("Prélude à la nuit," 10 pp., "Malagueña," 13 pp., "Habanera," 9 pp., "Feria," 33 pp.). Autog. s. & d. February 1, 1908
Ed.: Dur., 1908
Ded.: à mon cher maître Charles de Bériot
First Perf.: Edouard Colonne, conducting the Colonne Orchestra, March 15, 1908,
    Théâtre du Châtelet
Trans.: Prior version for piano 4 hands

Autog.: MAT, 23 pp., s. & d. "Levallois, October 1907"
Ed.: Dur., 1908

Title: *L'Heure espagnole* (opera, libretto by Franc-Nohain). Comp. 1907–09
Autog.: ROLC, 64 pp., s. & d. "Maurice Ravel—terminé à la Grangette 10/1907."
Note at top of p. 1: "En souvenir de la 'Classe Ravel,' je donne à mon ami Roland-Manuel ce manuscrit de "L'Heure espagnole." (Signed) "Maurice Delage, 14 Mars, 1957." (for voice and piano)
HRC, 212 pp., signed by Ravel (for voice and orchestra)
Ed.: Dur., 1908, voice and piano
Dur., 1911, voice and orchestra
Dur., 1924, voice and piano, *L'Ora spagnola,* Italian translation by Pietro Clausetti
Dur., 1925, voice and piano, *Eine Stunde spanien,* translator not listed
Dur., 1932, voice and piano, *L'Heure espagnole,* French text and English translation by Katherine Wolff
Ded.: Madame Jean Cruppi. Hommage de respectueuse amitié
First Perf.: Opéra-Comique, May 19, 1911. Conductor, François Ruhlmann

Concepcion	GENEVIÈVE VIX
Ramiro	JEAN PÉRIER
Don Inigo Gomez	M. DELVOYE
Gonzalve	M. COULOMB
Torquemada	MAURICE CAZENEUVE

Mise en scène, Albert Carré; décor, M. Bailly; costumes, M. Multzer
Other premières of *L'Heure espagnole:* London, July 7, 1919; New York, January 28, 1920; Paris Opéra, December 5, 1921; Milan, February 19, 1929; Berlin, September 27, 1929; Buenos Aires, September 20, 1932; Bucharest, November, 1932; Amsterdam, November 23, 1933; Cairo, March, 1934; Vienna, February 13, 1935; Copenhagen, January 25, 1940

Title: *Gaspard de la nuit* (3 poèmes pour piano d'après Aloysius Bertrand). Comp. 1908
1) "Ondine"
2) "Le Gibet"
3) "Scarbo"
Autog.: HRC, 18 pp. ("Ondine," 6 pp.; "Le Gibet," 3 pp.; "Scarbo," 9 pp.), s. & d. September 5, 1908. At the beginning of the MS.: "May–September, 1908"
Ed.: Dur., 1909
Ded.: "Ondine": Harold Bauer

"Le Gibet": Jean Marnold
"Scarbo": Rudolph Ganz
First Perf.: Ricardo Viñes, January 9, 1909, Soc. Nat., Salle Erard

Title: *Ma Mère l'Oye* (piano 4 hands). Comp. 1908–10
  1) "Pavane de la Belle au bois dormant"
  2) "Petit Poucet"
  3) "Laideronnette, Impératrice des pagodes"
  4) "Les Entretiens de la Belle et de la Bête"
  5) "Le Jardin féerique"
Autog.: MAT, 18pp., s. & d. April, 1910
    Private collection, "Pavane de la Belle au bois dormant," 2 pp., s. & d.
    20/9/08
Ed.: Dur., 1910
Ded.: Mimie et Jean Godebski
First Perf.: Jeanne Leleu and Geneviève Durony, April 20, 1910, SMI, Salle Ga-
veau
Trans.: For orchestra (1911)
Autog.: HRC, 38 pp. ("Pavane de la Belle au bois dormant," 3 pp., "Petit Poucet,"
  5 pp., "Laideronnette, Impératrice des pagodes," 15 pp., "Les Entretiens de la
  Belle et de la Bête," 8 pp., "Le Jardin féerique," 7 pp.)
Ed.: Dur., 1912
Ded.: Mimie et Jean Godebski
Trans.: Ballet (1911), Argument by Maurice Ravel
    Prélude
    1er Tableau "Danse du rouet et scène"
    2me Tableau "Pavane de la Belle au bois dormant"
    3me Tableau "Les Entretiens de la Belle et de la Bête"
    4me Tableau "Petit Poucet"
    5me Tableau "Laideronnette, Impératrice des pagodes"
    Apothéose "Le Jardin féerique"
Ed.: Dur., 1912
Ded.: Jacques Rouché, en amicale reconnaissance
First Perf.: Théâtre des Arts, Paris, Jacques Rouché, Director, January 29, 1912.
  Conductor, Gabriel Grovlez; décor and costumes, M. Dresa; choreography,
  Jeanne Hugard

	Cast
Florine	MMES ARIANE HUGON
La Belle	HENRIETTE QUINAULT
La Fée	DJAMIL ANIK
Le Prince charmant	GENEVIÈVE DELAUNAY
Le Serpentin vert	CARIYATIS

Laideronnette	Couperant
La Bête	MM. Piere Sandrini
Deux Gentilshommes	Recat
	Terrore
Deux Demoiselles d'honneur	Mmes Renée
	Millet
Deux Dames d'atours	Billitis
	Dhelia

Trois Pagodins, Trois Pagodines, Le Petit Poucet et ses six frères, Trois Oiseaux, Deux Négrillons, L'Amour

Title: *Menuet sur le nom d'Haydn* (piano). Comp. 1909
Autog.: Private collection of Claude Ecorcheville, 2 pp., s. & d. IX/1909. Title in the autog.: "Sur le nom Haydn"
Ed.: *La Revue Musicale de la S.I.M.,* 1909; Dur., 1910
First Perf.: Ennemond Trillat, March 11, 1911, Soc. Nat., Salle Pleyel

Title: *Tripatos* (voice and piano). Comp. 1909
Autog.: Private collection of Vincent Laloy, 2 pp. Prov. Marguerite Babaïan
Ed.: Printed in a special musical supplement of *La Revue Musicale,* December, 1938; Salabert & A.R.I.M.A., 1975
Ded.: Marguerite Babaïan

Title: *Chants populaires* (voice and piano). Comp. 1910
   1) "Chanson espagnole"   3) "Chanson italienne"
   2) "Chanson française"   4) "Chanson hébraïque"
Autog.: Not traced. The opening page of the "Chanson espagnole" has been printed in *Sovyetskaya Muzika,* 26 (December, 1962), 61
Ed.: P. Jurgenson, Moscow, 1911; Dur., 1925
First Perf.: Marie Olénine d'Alheim, Alexander Olénine, piano, December 19, 1910, Salle des Agriculteurs, Paris
Trans.: "Chanson hébraïque," for orchestra, 1923–24
Autog.: ROLC, 3 pp., s. & d. January, 1924
Ed.: Ravel's trans. unpublished. Trans. for orchestra by Maurice Delage, Dur., 1957
"Chanson flamande" and "Chanson russe," not traced. On the basis of a sketch, it has been possible to reconstruct the "Chanson écossaise."
Autog.: MAT, 1 p.
Ed.: Salabert & A.R.I.M.A., 1975

First Perf.: Sheila Schonbrun, soprano; Arbie Orenstein, piano; February 23, 1975, Charles S. Colden Auditorium, Queens College, Flushing, N.Y.

Title: *Valses nobles et sentimentales* (piano). Comp. 1911
Autog.: MAT, 9 pp.
Ed.: Dur., 1911
Ded.: Louis Aubert
First Perf.: Louis Aubert, May 9, 1911, SMI, Salle Gaveau
Trans.: For orchestra (1912) and version for ballet *Adélaïde, ou le langage des fleurs,* Argument by Maurice Ravel
Autog.: HRC, 58 pp. Autog., signed by Ravel, contains indications in crayon not in the composer's hand and was probably used as a conductor's score.
Ed.: Dur., 1912
Ded.: Louis Aubert
First Perf.: Ballet: Troupe of Natasha Trouhanova, Maurice Ravel conducting the Lamoureux Orchestra, April 22, 1912, Théâtre du Châtelet. Décor and costumes, M. Dresa; choreography, Ivan Clustine
Adélaïde: NATASHA TROUHANOVA
Lorédan: M. SEKEFI
The Duke: M. VAN DELEER
For orchestra: Pierre Monteux conducting the Orchestre de Paris, February 15, 1914, Salle du Casino de Paris

Title: *Daphnis et Chloé* (ballet, Argument by Michel Fokine, based upon the pastoral attributed to Longus). Comp. 1909–12
Autog.: MAT, 47 pp., for piano solo, s. & d. May 1, 1910
HRC, 186 pp., s. & d. April 5, 1912. Autog., notated in pen and pencil, served for the edition of the orchestral score
Ed.: Dur., 1910, piano solo
Dur., 1913, orchestra
Two orchestral suites derived from the score:
1) "Nocturne," "Interlude," "Danse guerrière," 1911
2) "Lever du jour," "Pantomime," "Danse générale," 1913
First Perf.: Orchestral Suite No. 1: Gabriel Pierné conducting the Colonne Orchestra, April 2, 1911
Entire Ballet: Ballets Russes, Serge Diaghilev, director. Pierre Monteux, conductor; choreography, Michel Fokine; décor and costumes, Léon Bakst; June 8, 1912, Théâtre du Châtelet

| *Chloé* | MMES THAMARA KARSAVINA | *Daphnis* | MM. VASLAV NIJINSKY |
| *Lyceion* | FROHMAN | *Dorcon* | A. BOLM |

1ʳᵉ Nymphe	PILTZ	*Lammon*	CECCHETTI
2ᵐᵉ Nymphe	TCHERNICHEVA	*Bryaxis*	FEDOROW
3ᵐᵉ Nymphe	KOPATZYNSKA		

Bergers et Bergères, Pirates, Chèvre-Pieds. Chœur: Sopranos, Altos, Ténors, Basses

Trans.: For piano: "Danse gracieuse et légère de Daphnis"; "Nocturne, Interlude et Danse guerrière"; "Scène de Daphnis et de Chloé"

Ed.: Dur., 1912

Title: *Trois Poèmes de Stéphane Mallarmé* (voice and piano; voice and piccolo, flute, clarinet, bass clarinet, string quartet, and piano). Comp. 1913

1) "Soupir"
2) "Placet futile"
3) "Surgi de la croupe et du bond"

Autog.: HRC, 11 pp., voice and piano ("Soupir," 4 pp., signed, undated; "Placet futile," 4 pp., s. & d. Paris, May, 1913; "Surgi de la croupe et du bond," 3 pp., signed, undated)

HRC, 16 pp., voice and instruments ("Soupir," 5 pp., s. & d. Clarens, April 2, 1913; "Placet futile," 7 pp., s. & d. Paris, May, 1913; "Surgi de la croupe et du bond," 4 pp., s. & d. St. Jean de Luz, August, 1913)

Ed.: Dur., voice and piano, 1914
Dur., voice and instruments, 1914

Ded.: "Soupir": Igor Stravinsky
"Placet futile": Florent Schmitt
"Surgi de la croupe et du bond": Erik Satie

First Perf.: Jane Bathori, with a chamber ensemble conducted by Désiré-Emile Inghelbrecht, January 14, 1914, SMI

Title: Prélude (piano). Comp. 1913
Autog.: Not traced
Ed.: Dur., 1913
Ded.: Mademoiselle Jeanne Leleu

Title: *A la manière de* . . . (piano). Comp. 1913
1) *Borodine*
2) *Chabrier*
Autog.: KOCH, each MS. is 2 pp. and each is signed by Ravel
Ed.: A. Z. Mathot, 1914, Salabert
Ded.: Ida et Cipa Godebski
First Perf.: Alfredo Casella, December 10, 1913, SMI, Salle Pleyel

Title: *Deux Mélodies hébraïques* (voice and piano). Comp. 1914
1) "Kaddisch"
2) "L'Enigme éternelle"
Autog.: MAT, 5 pp. ("Kaddisch," 3 pp.; "L'Enigme éternelle," 2 pp.), dated
    May, 1914
Ed.: Dur., 1915
Ded.: Madame Alvina-Alvi
First Perf.: Alvina-Alvi and Ravel, June 3, 1914, SMI, Salle Malakoff
Trans.: For orchestra, 1919
Autog.: ROLC, 13 pp. ("Kaddisch," 8 pp.; "L'Enigme éternelle," 5 pp.)
Ed.: Dur., 1920
First Perf.: Madeleine Grey, with Rhené-Baton conducting the Pasdeloup Orchestra,
    April 17, 1920

Title: Trio (piano, violin, cello). Comp. 1914
1) Modéré   3) Passacaille
2) Pantoum   4) Final
Autog.: HRC, 39 pp. (Modéré, pp. 1–10; Pantoum, pp. 11–22; Passacaille,
    pp. 22–25; Final, pp. 26–39), s. & d. St. Jean de Luz, April 3–August 7, 1914
Ed.: Dur., 1915
Ded.: André Gédalge
First Perf.: Alfredo Casella, piano; Gabriel Willaume, violin; Louis Feuillard, cello;
    January 28, 1915, SMI, Salle Gaveau

Title: *Trois Chansons pour chœur mixte sans accompagnement* (Three Songs for Unaccompanied Mixed Chorus, poems by Maurice Ravel). Comp. 1914–15
1) "Nicolette"
2) "Trois Beaux Oiseaux du Paradis"
3) "Ronde"
Autog.: HRC, 9 pp. ("Nicolette," 2 pp., s. & d. February, 1915; "Trois Beaux
    Oiseaux du Paradis," 3 pp., s. & d. December, 1914; "Ronde," 4 pp.,
    s. & d. February, 1915)
    MAT, "Ronde," 4 pp., s. & d. February, 1915. Autog. has several
    changes in the text
Ed.: Dur., 1916
Ded.: "Nicolette": Tristan Klingsor
    "Trois Beaux Oiseaux du Paradis": Paul Painlevé
    "Ronde": Madame Paul Clémenceau
First Perf.: Louis Aubert conducting the Bathori-Engel Chorus, October 11, 1917,
    Théâtre du Vieux-Colombier
Trans.: Solo voice and piano, 1914–15

Autog.: HRC, 10 pp. ("Nicolette," 3 pp.; "Trois Beaux Oiseaux du Paradis," 2 pp.,
s. & d. December, 1914; "Ronde," 5 pp.)
Ed.: Dur., 1916

Title: *Le Tombeau de Couperin* (piano). Comp. 1914–17
1) "Prélude"   4) "Rigaudon"
2) "Fugue"   5) "Menuet"
3) "Forlane"   6) "Toccata"
Autog.: MAT, 18 pp., s. & d. July, 1914, June–November, 1917
Ed.: Dur., 1918
Ded.: "Prélude": à la mémoire du lieutenant Jacques Charlot
      "Fugue": à la mémoire du sous-lieutenant Jean Cruppi
      "Forlane": à la mémoire du lieutenant Gabriel Deluc
      "Rigaudon": à la mémoire de Pierre et Pascal Gaudin
      "Menuet": à la mémoire de Jean Dreyfus
      "Toccata": à la mémoire du capitaine Joseph de Marliave
First Perf.: Marguerite Long, April 11, 1919, SMI, Salle Gaveau
Trans.: For orchestra, 1919
        1) "Prélude"   3) "Menuet"
        2) "Forlane"   4) "Rigaudon"
Autog.: ROLC, 26 pp., s. & d. June, 1919 ("Prélude," pp. 1–6; "Forlane," pp. 7–14;
"Menuet," pp. 14–20; "Rigaudon," pp. 21–26)
Ed.: Dur., 1919
First Perf.: Rhené-Baton conducting the Pasdeloup Orchestra, February 28, 1920
Trans.: Ballet ("Forlane," "Menuet," and "Rigaudon")
First Perf.: Swedish Ballet, Rolf de Maré, director. Choreography by Jean Borlin
    and Rolf de Maré; Désiré-Emile Inghelbrecht, conductor; November 8, 1920,
    Théâtre des Champs-Elysées

Title: *Frontispice* (two pianos, five hands). Comp. 1918
Autog.: Private collection, 1 p., s. & d. June, 1918
Ed.: *Les Feuillets d'Art* (1919, No. 2); also printed in Canudo, *S.P. 503 Le Poème
    du Vardar* (Paris: Les Poètes de la Renaissance du Livre, 1923); Salabert &
    A.R.I.M.A., 1975

Title: *La Valse* (poème chorégraphique pour orchestre). Comp. 1919–20
Autog.: MDBN, 70 pp., MS. 17140, notated in pencil. Prov. Roger Désormière
        ROLC, 75 pp., s. & d. Lapras, December 1919–March 1920
Ed.: Dur., 1921
Ded.: Misia Sert
First Perf.: Camille Chevillard conducting the Lamoureux Orchestra, December 12,
        1920
            First Perf. as a ballet in Paris at the Opéra, May 23, 1929, troupe of Ida
            Rubinstein. Argument by Maurice Ravel; conductor, Gustave Cloez;

décor, Alexandre Benois; choreography, Bronislava Nijinska

Trans.: Two prior versions, for piano solo, and for two pianos

Autog.: Mary Flagler Cary Music Collection, Pierpont Morgan Library, 15 pp.,
for piano solo, s. & d. 12/1919–2/1920, Lapras. Prov. Robert Owen Lehman

Ed.: Dur., 1920

Autog.: ROLC, 22 pp., for two pianos. Autog. has many corrections in pencil
Private collection, 25 pp., for two pianos, signed by Ravel

Ed.: Dur., 1920

First Perf.: Alfredo Casella and Ravel, October 23, 1920, Vienna, Kleiner Kon-
zerthaussaal (*Neue Freie Presse*, October 23, 1920)

Title: Sonate pour violon et violoncelle. Comp. 1920–22

1) Allegro   3) Lent
2) Très vif   4) Vif, avec entrain

Autog.: HRC, 16 pp., s. & d. April 1920–February 1922 (The first movement is
missing; Très vif, pp. 1–6; Lent, pp. 6–8; Vif, avec entrain, pp. 8–16.)
Private collection, 16 pp. (The first movement is missing, the other
movements, as above.) Autog. dedicated "à Maurice Maréchal, en
souvenir de la belle 1re exécution du 6 avril 1922, son reconnaissant
Maurice Ravel"
SML, 19 pp. (The first movement is missing; Très vif, pp. 1–8 [this MS. has
two different versions of the opening page]; Lent, 2 pp.; Vif, avec
entrain, pp. 1–9.) Prov. Hélène Jourdan-Morhange

Ed.: First movement printed in a special musical supplement, *Le Tombeau de
Claude Debussy* in *La Revue Musicale,* December 1, 1920
Dur., 1922

Ded.: à la mémoire de Claude Debussy

First Perf.: Hélène Jourdan-Morhange, violin; Maurice Maréchal, cello; April 6,
1922, SMI, Salle Pleyel

Title: *Berceuse sur le nom de Gabriel Fauré* (violin and piano). Comp. 1922

Autog.: KOCH, 3 pp. s. & d. Lyons la Forêt, September, 1922. Prov. Claude
Roland-Manuel

Ed.: Printed in a special musical supplement of *La Revue Musicale,* October 1, 1922
Dur., 1922

Ded.: Claude Roland-Manuel

First Perf.: Hélène Jourdan-Morhange, violin; Mme Raymond Charpentier, piano,
December 13, 1922, SMI

Title: *Ronsard à son âme* (voice and piano, poem by Ronsard). Comp. 1923–24

Autog.: Private collection of Marielle and Véronique Temporal, 2 pp., s. & d.
Montfort, January, 1924. Prov. Marcelle Gerar

Ed.: Printed in a special musical supplement of *La Revue Musicale,* May, 1924
Dur., 1924

Ded.: Marcelle Gerar

First Perf.: Marcelle Gerar and Ravel, April 26, 1924, London, Aeolian Hall

Trans.: For orchestra, 1935; dictated by Ravel to Manuel Rosenthal and Lucien Garban

First Perf.: Martial Singher, with Piero Coppola conducting the Pasdeloup Orchestra, February 17, 1935, Opéra-Comique

Title: *Tzigane—Rapsodie de Concert* (violin and piano, also violin and piano with luthéal). Comp. 1924

Autog.: MAT, 15 pp., violin and piano

    MAT, 15 pp., violin and piano, s. & d. Paris–London, April–May, 1924

Ed.: Dur., 1924

Ded.: Jelly d'Aranyi

First Perf.: Jelly d'Aranyi and Henri Gil-Marchex (piano), April 26, 1924, London, Aeolian Hall. Samuel Dushkin and Beveridge Webster (piano with luthéal) October 15, 1924, Salle Gaveau

Trans.: Violin and orchestra, 1924

Autog.: ROLC, 19 pp., s. & d. July, 1924. The opening 58 measures (violin solo) are missing.

Ed.: Dur., 1924

First Perf.: Jelly d'Aranyi, with Gabriel Pierné conducting the Colonne Orchestra, November 30, 1924

Title: *L'Enfant et les sortilèges: Fantaisie Lyrique en deux parties* (opera, libretto by Colette). Comp. 1920–25

Autog.: ROLC, 75 pp., s. & d. "Divers lieux, 1920–25" (for voice and piano)

    HRC, 164 pp. (for voice and orchestra)

Ed.: Dur., 1925, voice and piano

    Dur., 1925, voice and orchestra

    Dur., 1926, voice and piano, *Il bambino e i sortilegi,* Italian translation by Pietro Clausetti

    Dur., 1926, voice and piano, *Das Zauberwort,* German translation by Egon Bloch

    Dur., 1932, voice and piano, *L'Enfant et les sortilèges,* French text and English translation by Katherine Wolff

First Perf.: Monte Carlo Opera, March 21, 1925. Conductor, Vittorio De Sabata

L'Enfant	Marie-Thérèse Gauley
La Chatte	Mmes Dubois-Lauger
La Bergère de salon	Narsay
La Princesse	Bilhon
La Maman	Orsoni
Le Rossignol	Foliguet
Le Feu	Mathilde

La Tasse chinoise	LUCY
La Libellule	VIARDOT
La Chauve-Souris	LACROIX
L'Ecureuil	LECOURT
Une Pastourelle	CHORINA
Une Bête	GIRAND
Un Pastour	GINEL
Une Chouette	TRABUCCHI
Le Petit Vieillard Arithmétique	MM. FABERT
Le Chat, l'Horloge	WARNERY
Le Fauteuil	LAFONT
La Théière	DUBOIS
L'Arbre	BAIDAROFF
La Rainette	SOLLIÈRES
Un Pastour	DAUNIAC
Une Bête	STÉPHANE

Les Chiffres: MMES BARBIERI, BARLA, MOLINARI, TESTA, CHRISTINI, PHILIPPON, BERTRANDO, RINA, FRESLON, ALEXEIEFF, ET LES ARTISTES DES BALLETS RUSSES

Maître de Ballet, George Balanchine; mise en scène, Raoul Gunsbourg; décor, M. Visconti

Other premières of *L'Enfant et les sortilèges:* Paris, Opéra-Comique, February 1, 1926; Brussels, February 11, 1926; Prague, February 17, 1927; Leipzig, May 6, 1927; Vienna, March 14, 1929; Florence, May 2, 1939; Paris Opéra, May 17, 1939

Title: *Chansons madécasses* (voice, flute, cello, and piano, poems by Evariste-Désiré de Parny). Comp. 1925–26
1) "Nahandove"
2) "Aoua!"
3) "Il est doux . . ."

Autog.: HRC, 11 pp., s. & d. April 1925, April 1926. ("Nahandove," pp. 1–5; "Aoua!," pp. 5–8; "Il est doux," pp. 9–11)

Music Division, Library of Congress, 15 pp. ("Nahandove," pp. 1–5; "Aoua!," pp. 1–7, s. & d. May, 1925; "Il est doux," pp. 1–3). In addition to the full score, each part is written out separately.

Prov. Mrs. Elizabeth Sprague Coolidge

Ed.: Dur., 1926

Ded.: Mrs. Elizabeth S. Coolidge, en très respectueux hommage

First Perf.: Jane Bathori; Alfredo Casella, piano; Louis Fleury, flute; Hans Kindler, cello. Recital sponsored by Elizabeth S. Coolidge, May 8, 1926, American Academy in Rome

Trans.: Voice and piano, 1926

Autog.: HRC, 13 pp., s. & d. July, 1926 ("Nahandove," pp. 1–5; "Aoua!," pp. 6–9; "Il est doux," pp. 10–13)
Ed.: Dur., 1926

Title: *Rêves* (voice and piano, poem by Léon-Paul Fargue). Comp. 1927
Autog.: MAT, 2 pp., s. & d. February, 1927
　　　Les Feuilles Libres, June, 1927, pp. 75–77, has a reproduction of a second autog. dedicated "pour Fargue," s. & d. February, 1927.
Ed.: Dur., 1927
Ded.: No ded. in printed edition
First Perf.: Jane Bathori and Ravel, March 19, 1927, Théâtre du Vieux-Colombier

Title: Sonate pour violon et piano. Comp. 1923–27
　1) Allegretto
　2) Blues
　3) Perpetuum mobile
Autog.: Private collection, Paris, 13 pp. violin part only
　　　KOCH, 1 p., s. & d. May, 1927. The first 20 measures of the first movement, notated in pencil
　　　SML, 21 pp., s. & d. 1923–27 (Allegretto, pp. 1–9; Blues, pp. 9–15; Perpetuum mobile, pp. 15–21.) Prov. Hélène Jourdan-Morhange. The opening page of this autog. has been printed in Vuillermoz et al., *Maurice Ravel par quelques-uns de ses familiers,* plate opposite p. 64.
Ed.: Dur., 1927
Ded.: Hélène Jourdan-Morhange
First Perf.: Georges Enesco and Ravel, Concerts Durand, May 30, 1927, Salle Erard

Title: "Fanfare" (orchestra), for a ballet in one act, *L'Eventail de Jeanne.* Comp. 1927
Autog.: Bibliothèque de l'Opéra, 3 pp., MS. Opé. Rés. A 775 (11), notated in pencil and signed by Ravel
Ed.: Heugel, 1929
Ded.: The ballet is dedicated to Madame Jeanne Dubost
First Perf.: Roger Désormière conducting a small orchestra at the home of Jeanne Dubost, June 16, 1927. Official première at the Paris Opéra, March 4, 1929, Jacques Rouché, director. J. E. Szyfer, conductor; choreography, Alice Bourgat and Yvonne Franck; costumes, Marie Laurencin; décor, Pierre Legrain and René Moulaert
　　　L'Eventail de Jeanne consists of the following pieces:
　　　1) "Fanfare" Maurice Ravel
　　　2) "Marche" Pierre-Octave Ferroud
　　　3) "Valse" Jacques Ibert

4) "Canarie" Roland-Manuel
5) "Bourrée" Marcel Delannoy
6) "Sarabande" Albert Roussel
7) "Polka" Darius Milhaud
8) "Pastourelle" Francis Poulenc
9) "Rondeau" Georges Auric
10) "Kermesse-Valse" Florent Schmitt

Trans.: Piano, 4 hands
Autog.: Archives of Heugel & Co., 2 pp., signed by Ravel
Ed.: Heugel, 1929

Title: *Boléro* (Ballet for orchestra). Comp. 1928
Autog.: ROLC, 37 pp., s. & d. July–October, 1928
      Private collection, 31 pp., a first draft notated in pencil
Ed.: Dur., 1929
Ded.: Ida Rubinstein
First Perf.: Troupe of Ida Rubinstein, Paris Opéra, November 22, 1928. Walther
      Straram, conductor; décor and costumes, Alexandre Benois; chore-
      ography, Bronislava Nijinska

    La Danseuse   MME IDA RUBINSTEIN
    Les Hommes   MM VILTZAK, DOLINOFF, LAPITZKY, UNGERER
    First concert perf. in Paris, Maurice Ravel conducting the Lamoureux
      Orchestra, January 11, 1930

Trans.: Piano 4 hands, 1929
Autog.: The British Library, London, Zweig MS. 74, 15 pp.
Ed.: Dur., 1929
Trans.: Two pianos 4 hands
Autog.: Not traced
Ed.: Dur., 1929

Title: Concerto pour la main gauche (piano and orchestra). Comp. 1929–30
Autog.: ROLC, 53 pp., s. & d. 1930. The cadenza is not fully notated.
      Private collection, 53 pp., s. & d. 1930. The cadenza is not fully notated.
Ed.: Dur., 1931
Ded.: Paul Wittgenstein
First Perf.: Paul Wittgenstein, with Robert Heger conducting the Vienna Symphony
    Orchestra, January 5, 1932, Vienna, Grosser Musikvereinssaal (*Neue Freie
    Presse,* January 1 and 5, 1932)
Trans.: Piano reduction of the orchestral part, 1930
Autog.: MAT, 21 pp., s. & d. 1930. On the cover page of this autog. the composer
    wrote "musae mixtatiae."
Ed.: Dur., 1937

Title: Concerto pour piano et orchestre. Comp. 1929–31
1) Allegramente
2) Adagio assai
3) Presto

Autog.: Private collection, 110 pp. (Allegramente, pp. 1–55; Adagio assai, pp. 1–16; Presto, pp. 1–39), signed by Ravel

Ed.: Dur., 1932

Ded.: Marguerite Long

First Perf.: Marguerite Long, with Ravel conducting the Lamoureux Orchestra, January 14, 1932, Salle Pleyel

Title: *Don Quichotte à Dulcinée* (voice and piano, voice and orchestra, poems by Paul Morand). Comp. 1932–33
1) "Chanson romanesque"
2) "Chanson épique"
3) "Chanson à boire"

Autog.: HRC, 7 pp., voice and piano. ("Chanson romanesque," 2 pp.; "Chanson épique," 2 pp.; "Chanson à boire," 3 pp.)

HRC, 18 pp., voice and orchestra. ("Chanson romanesque," 8 pp., "Chanson épique," 5 pp.; "Chanson à boire," 5 pp.)

Ed.: Dur., 1934, voice and piano
Dur., 1934, voice and orchestra

Ded.: "Chanson romanesque": Robert Couzinou
"Chanson épique": Martial Singher
"Chanson à boire": Roger Bourdin

First Perf.: Martial Singher, with Paul Paray conducting the Colonne Orchestra, December 1, 1934, Théâtre du Châtelet

Transcriptions by Maurice Ravel of Works by Other Composers [1]

Delius, *Margot la Rouge* (opera in one act, libretto by Rosenval). Score for voice and piano transcribed from the original orchestral version in 1902.

Autog.: The Frederick Delius Trust, London, Volume 20, 48 pp. The French text is in Ravel's hand, together with an Italian translation in another hand.

Ed.: Lévy-Lulx, Paris, c. 1905; a copy of this rare edition may be found in The British Library.

[1] See Catalogue of Works-II, pp. 242–45.

Debussy, *Nocturnes,* transcribed for two pianos, four hands, in 1909
1) "Nuages"
2) "Fêtes"
3) "Sirènes"
Autog.: KOCH, "Nuages," 5 pp.; "Fêtes," 13 pp.; "Sirènes," not traced. Prov.
Mme D. Jobert-Georges
Ed.: E. Fromont, 1909; Jobert
First Perf.: Louis Aubert and Ravel, April 24, 1911, SMI, Salle Gaveau

Debussy, *Prélude à l'Après-midi d'un faune,* transcribed for piano, four hands, in 1910
Autog.: KOCH, 10 pp., signed by Ravel. Prov. Mme D. Jobert-Georges
Ed.: E. Fromont, 1910; Jobert

Antar, a play in five acts by the Arab poet Chékry-Ganem, with incidental music by Rimsky-Korsakov partially reorchestrated by Ravel, probably in 1910. The music includes selections from Rimsky-Korsakov's *Antar* and *Mlada,* fragments of *Antar* reorchestrated by Ravel, and songs by Rimsky-Korsakov (Opus 4 and Opus 7), orchestrated by Ravel. The songs have not been recovered.
Autog.: Archives of Editions Alphonse Leduc, 59 pp. (55 pp. in the hand of a copyist, 4 pp. in Ravel's hand)
Ed.: Unpublished; parts available for rental
First Perf.: Gabriel Pierné conducting the Colonne Orchestra, February 12, 1910, Odéon Theater (*Comœdia,* February 12 and 13, 1910)

Schumann, *Carnaval,* orchestrated for Vaslav Nijinsky, probably in 1914
Autog.: MAT, fragmentary, consisting of c. 60 pp., comprising four complete sections: "Préambule," "Valse allemande," "Paganini," and "Marche des 'Davidsbündler' contre les Philistins." The full autog. formerly in the private collection of Mme Romola Nijinsky has not been traced.
Ed.: Salabert & A.R.I.M.A., 1975 (of the four above-mentioned sections)
First Perf.: Vaslav Nijinsky and his troupe, London, Palace Theatre, March 2, 1914

Chabrier, *Menuet pompeux,* orchestrated for the Ballets Russes in 1919
Autog.: Private collection, 12 pp., s. & d. April, 1919. Prov. Serge Lifar
Ed.: Enoch, 1937
First Perf.: Ballets Russes, Ernest Ansermet, conductor; choreography, Léonide Massine; scenery and costumes, José-Maria Sert; London, Alhambra Theatre, July 18, 1919

CATALOGUE OF WORKS

First Perf. in the concert hall, Albert Wolff conducting the Pasdeloup Orchestra, March 21, 1936

Mussorgsky, *Tableaux d'une exposition* (Pictures at an Exhibition), orchestrated in 1922
Autog.: Boosey & Hawkes, London, 98 pp., s. & d. May, 1922. (Nos. 1–9, pp. 1–79; No. 10, pp. 1–19. The date of May, 1922, applies only to the final part of the score, "La grande porte de Kiev," which was the first piece to be transcribed. The remainder of the work was completed by the early fall of 1922. The autog. contains many corrections in pencil by Ravel together with many blue crayon markings in another hand, and was used as a conductor's score.
Ed.: Edition Russe de Musique, 1929; Boosey & Hawkes
First Perf.: Serge Koussevitzky, conductor, Concerts Koussevitzky, October 19, 1922, Paris Opéra

Debussy, "Sarabande" and *Danse,* orchestrated in 1922
Autog.: KOCH, "Sarabande," 9 pp., s. & d. November, 1922; *Danse,* 32 pp., s. & d. December, 1922. Prov. Mme D. Jobert-Georges
Ed.: Jobert, 1923
First Perf.: Paul Paray conducting the Lamoureux Orchestra, March 18, 1923, Salle Gaveau

II. Miscellaneous Works, Compositions Not Recovered, Sketches, and Fragments

Chopin, *Les Sylphides,* orchestrated for Vaslav Nijinsky, probably in 1914
  Autog.: Not traced
  First Perf.: Vaslav Nijinsky and his troupe, London, Palace Theatre, March 2, 1914 (*The Times,* February 25 and March 3, 1914)
Delage, Sonatine (incomplete). Corrections in blue pencil by Ravel
  Autog.: MDBN, MS. 17519, 6 pp.
Mendelssohn, The complete works for piano solo and the piano concerti, Dur., 9 vols., 1915–18. Maurice Ravel, editor
Mussorgsky, *Khovanshchina,* orchestrated by Rimsky-Korsakov, partially re-orchestrated by Ravel and Stravinsky in 1913. Unpublished
  Autog.: KOCH, 40 pp. Prov. Serge Lifar. Full score, for orchestra, of two sections of Ravel's orchestration of Mussorgsky's unfinished opera. Contains 167 measures from Act I (episode between the Scribe and the People of Moscow), and 124 measures from Act II (Kuzka's Song).

First Perf.: Ballets Russes, June 5, 1913, Théâtre des Champs-Elysées (*Comœdia,* June 5 and June 7, 1913)

Saint-Saëns, *La Jeunesse d'Hercule,* reduction for piano and analysis by Ravel, apparently as a school assignment.

    Autog.: MDBN, MS. 17649, 8 pp.

Satie, Preludes to *Fils des étoiles,* orchestrated by Ravel in 1911

    Autog. and First Perf.: Not traced (The orchestration is mentioned in a letter from Satie to his brother, dated April 11, 1911.)

Ravel harmonized a Corsican lullaby in 1896. See *Music Student* (November, 1917), plate opposite p. 93.

Ravel, *La Parade,* for piano, c. 1898. Based on a scenario by Antonine Meunier of the Paris Opéra, this work was apparently written for interpretive dancing in the home.

    Autog.: MDBN, MS. 16939, 17 pp.

Ravel, *Callirhoé,* a cantata submitted as a preparatory exercise for the Prix de Rome in January, 1900

    Autog.: Not traced

Ravel, Prelude and Fugue, submitted for the composition prize in January, 1901

    Autog.: Not traced

Ravel, *Semiramis,* a cantata submitted for the composition prize in January, 1902

    Autog.: Not traced

Ravel, *Le Portrait de l'Infante* [The Portrait of the Infanta]. Comp. 1923. Based on a scenario by Henry Malherbe, this ballet is set in Madrid about 1670.

    Autog.: Private collection, 25 pp., 11 pp. for piano solo, the remainder being excerpts from the printed scores of the *Pavane pour une Infante défunte,* the "Alborada del gracioso," and the *Rapsodie espagnole.* The MS. is unpublished, and the ballet was apparently never performed. (See Orenstein, *A Ravel Reader,* letter 226, pp. 245–46.)

Sketches and fragments in the private collection of Mme Alexandre Taverne

Title	pp.
L'Eventail de Jeanne (two pianos)	1
Noël des jouets	1
Rêves	1
L'Indifférent	1
Chopin, Etude Opus 10, No. 11 (orchestration)	1
Mazurka	1
Barcarolle	1
Mussorgsky, La Chambre d'enfants	1
Sur l'eau (voice and orchestra)	1

CATALOGUE OF WORKS

Title	pp.
Chanson écossaise (voice and piano)	1
Les Patineuses (voice and piano)	1
Prelude to *Intérieur* (Maeterlinck)	1
Sketch of a development section of a trio (Symphony)	1
Couperin, Forlane (transcribed by Ravel)	2
Sonatine (first movement only)	2
Variations on a theme by Grieg (Peer Gynt)	3
Variations on a theme by Schumann (Chorale, Opus 68)	3
Perpetuum mobile (finale of Sonata for Violin and Piano)	3
Zaspiak-Bat	3
Rapsodie espagnole (orchestra)	3
Le Ciel est, pardessus le toit (voice and piano, poem by Verlaine)	4
Piano Concerto in G major	5
Beethoven, orchestrations of fragments of piano sonatas	5
String Quartet	6
Don Quichotte à Dulcinée	7
Albéniz, Rondeña (orchestration)	8
Beethoven, Symphonies 8 and 9 (analysis by Ravel, apparently as a school assignment)	8
Chansons madécasses	8
Waltz in D major (a piece of juvenilia)	8
Boléro (for orchestra and for two pianos)	9
Soupir (instrumental parts copied out separately)	10
Alborada del gracioso (orchestra)	10
La Valse (orchestra)	15
La Cloche engloutie (voice and piano)	15
Daphnis et Chloé: Daphnis's Dance (orchestra)	17
Le Tombeau de Couperin (piano)	22
Suite for two pianos (the first piano is lacking)	22
L'Enfant et les sortilèges (voice and piano)	25
School assignments: figured bass exercises, counterpoint assignments, scales, ranges of orchestral instruments, etc.	c. 30
Trio (almost complete)	40
Ma Mère l'Oye (orchestra)	42
Mussorgsky, Pictures at an Exhibition (orchestra)	45
L'Heure espagnole (almost complete; voice and piano)	60

Sketches and fragments in the Robert Owen Lehman Collection
(Prov. of these sketches: the collection of Georges Van Parys)

	pp.
Passacaille (Trio)	1
Chopin, Etude Opus 10, No. 11 (orchestration)	1
Farfadets	1
Fugato	1
La Nonne maudite	1
Rapsodie espagnole (two pianos)	3
Chabrier, Menuet pompeux (orchestra)	4
Le Tombeau de Couperin (for orchestra)	16
Le Tombeau de Couperin (for piano)	21

KOCH

Four-part fugue on a subject by Henri Reber,
dated May 31, 1900. Prov. Manuel Rosenthal   4 pp.

SML	pp.
Transcription for piano of Beethoven's Coriolanus overture	1
Sonata for Violin and Cello	1
School assignments	1
Sketches for *Morgiane* [?]	1
Chansons madécasses	2

The following four album leaves are in the Charles Alvar Harding Collection, on deposit at the Pierpont Morgan Library. Prov. Louise Alvar, at whose London home these gatherings took place.

1) [Sonata for Violin and Cello], 1 p., the first four measures of the fourth movement, s. & d. June 30, 1922. Also on the album leaf are musical quotations signed by Arthur Bliss (from *A Colour Symphony*) and Ralph Vaughan Williams.

2) [L'Enfant et les sortilèges], "La Tasse," 1 p., four measures of music, s. & d. June 5, 1925. Text begins: "Keng-ça-fou, Mah-jong." Also on the album leaf is a musical quotation signed by Georges Auric (from *Les Fâcheux*) and an autograph sentiment signed by Hugo von Hofmannsthal.

3) [L'Enfant et les sortilèges], 1 p., the opening two measures of the opera, s. & d. London, October 20, 1923. Also on the album leaf are autograph sentiments signed by George Moore and Paul Valéry.

4) [La Valse], 1 p., 5 measures of music (the violas, beginning four measures after rehearsal no. 9, Durand orchestral score), s. & d. April 17, 1923. Also on the album leaf are a musical quotation signed by Lord Berners (from *Le Carrosse du Saint Sacrement*), and autograph sentiments signed by Joseph Conrad and Arnold Bennett.

[Le Tombeau de Couperin, piano, Forlane], KOCH, 1 p., 3 measures of music (measures 61–63), s. & d. November, 1922. Also on the album leaf is an ink drawing of Ravel by Robert Kastor.

APPENDIX B

Historical Recordings (1912-1939)

COMPILED BY JEAN TOUZELET

The gramophone seems to me a marvelous instrument. Moreover, it assures music of a complete and meticulous immortality.

CLAUDE DEBUSSY (1904)

NOTE: The lifetime of Maurice Ravel paralleled the birth of the phonograph and the earliest developments in the recording industry. From acoustical disks and perforated piano rolls to electrical disks, the quality of sound reproduction made important strides during the opening decades of the twentieth century. From a historical viewpoint, it is clear that Ravel was the first composer to have virtually all of his major works recorded during his lifetime. It will be observed that the composer not only recorded his works but also supervised a number of recordings, all of which are of great historical interest. The many rare piano rolls and recordings listed in this appendix may be heard at the following institutions:

France: Phonothèque Nationale, Paris
       Bibliothèque Nationale, Département de la Musique, Paris
Great Britain: British Institute of Recorded Sound, London
United States: Library of Congress, Washington, D.C.
               Rodgers and Hammerstein Archives, Lincoln Center for the Performing Arts, New York
               Yale Collection of Historical Sound Recordings, Yale University Library, New Haven, Conn.

247

The following catalogue lists recordings devoted to Ravel's music from 1912 to 1939. It is as exact and as complete as possible. Following the catalogue is a list of colleagues and acquaintances of the composer who recorded his works after 1939. The works are presented, as in Appendix A, in chronological order by date of composition, then by date of recording. The dates given are those of the recording or of its appearance, while the dates in brackets could not be verified and are therefore approximations. If the performer is Ravel or a colleague of his, the name is in italics. If no performer is listed, no name appears on the label of the piano roll or of the recording. A recording issued in different countries will bear several references which do not claim to be exhaustive. In principle, the first of these references corresponds to the country of origin and to the given date.

Abbreviations:
R Perforated Piano roll, 88 notes, unless otherwise indicated
AD Acoustical Disk, 78 r.p.m.[1]
ED Electrical Disk, 78 r.p.m.[1]
M A recording reissued on LP before 1975
Fr France
Ger Germany
GB Great Britain
US United States

Principal Sources:
Private collection of Jean Touzelet of piano rolls and disks
F. F. Clough and G. J. Cuming, *World's Encyclopedia of Recorded Music,* London, 1952
R. D. Darrell, *The Gramophone Shop Encyclopedia of Recorded Music,* New York, 1936
Phonothèque Nationale, Paris
Office de Radiodiffusion Télévision Française
International Piano Archives, New York
Musique et Instruments, Paris, 1910–29
L'Edition Musicale Vivante, Paris, 1928–34
Revue des Machines Parlantes, Paris, 1929–37
Revue Pleyel, Paris, 1923–27
Musique, Paris, 1927–30
The Musical Courier, New York, 1919–25
The Musical Observer, Disc-Roll Review, New York, 1920–21
The Musical Digest. New York, 1925–30
The Musical Times, Disc and Roll Review, London, 1921–39
The Gramophone, London, 1923–39

---

[1] With the exception of Columbia records issued before 1928 and of Pathé-Art, recorded at 80 r.p.m. All the disks in this catalogue are laterally cut.

Die Musik, Berlin, 1927–39
Various catalogues (1903–39)

Menuet antique

1920   R   Piano
L'Edition Musicale Perforée (Fr), Aeolian (Fr), and Odéola (Fr) RA1802
1930   ED   Orchestre Symphonique, *Piero Coppola,* conductor
30 cm. Gramophone (Fr) W1074, Victor (US) 11133
1930   ED   Orchestre Lamoureux, *Albert Wolff,* conductor
30 cm. Polydor (Fr) 566032, (Ger) 66972, Brunswick (US) 90099

Sainte

[1913]   R   Transcription for piano
Aeolian, Pianola (GB, US) TL22263
1921   R   Transcription for piano
L'Edition Musicale Perforée (Fr), Aeolian (Fr), and Odéola (Fr) RA3377
1936   ED   M   Pierre Bernac, baritone; *Francis Poulenc,* piano
25 cm. Gramophone (Fr) DA4891

Epigrammes de Clément Marot
I) "D'Anne qui me jecta de la neige"
II) "D'Anne jouant de l'espinette"

[1913]   R   Transcription for piano
Aeolian, Pianola (GB, US) TL22311/2
1920   R   Transcription for piano
L'Edition Musicale Perforée (Fr), Aeolian (Fr), and Odéola (Fr) RA1782/3
1927   II   ED   *Paule de Lestang,* soprano, *Paule de Lestang,* harpsichord
25 cm. Gramophone (Fr) K5338

249

Pavane pour une Infante défunte

[1912] R   Piano
Aeolian, Pianola (GB, US) TL21204
1913   R   65 notes   *Rudolph Ganz,* piano
Solodant (Ger) 14748
1920   R   Piano
L'Edition Musicale Perforée (Fr), Aeolian (Fr), and Odéola (Fr) RA2813
1921   AD   Orchestre des Concerts Touche, Francis Touche, conductor
30 cm. Gramophone (Fr) W356, L548
1922   R   M   *Maurice Ravel,* piano
Duo-Art (GB, US) 084
1923   R   Transcription for cello and piano
L'Edition Musicale Perforée (Fr), Aeolian (Fr), and Odéola (Fr) RA20945
1925   R   *Maurice Dumesnil,* piano
Pleyela (Fr), Aeolian (Fr), and Odéola (Fr) AP5269
1925   AD   New Queen's Hall Light Orchestra, Frank Bridge, conductor
30 cm. Columbia (GB, Fr) L1605
[1926] R   *E. Robert Schmitz,* piano
Ampico (US) 65473H
1928   R   Transcription for violin, viola, cello, flute (*Louis Fleury*), oboe, clarinet,
horn, and piano
Pleyela (Fr), Aeolian (Fr), and Odéola (Fr) AC9201
1928   ED   Orchestre Symphonique du Gramophone, *Piero Coppola,* conductor
30 cm. Gramophone (Fr) W871, (GB) D1564
1928   ED   Berlin Philharmonic Orchestra, *Albert Wolff,* conductor
30 cm. Polydor (Ger, Fr) 66726, (Fr) 516649, Decca (GB) CA8230, Brunswick (US) 90149
1928   ED   Edmond Mahieux, saxophone
25 cm. Odéon (Fr) 165345
1928   ED   Myra Hess, piano
25 cm. Columbia (US) 157M, 4082M
[1928] R   Leonadis Leonardi, piano
Welte-Mignon (US) X6669
1929   ED   Orchestre Colonne, *Gabriel Pierné,* conductor
30 cm. Odéon (Fr) 123617, Columbia (US) G67785D
1930   ED   Georges de Lausnay, piano
30 cm. Pathé-Art (Fr) X5507
1930   ED   *André Asselin,* violin, with piano accompaniment
30 cm. Gramophone (Fr) L804
1931   ED   Yvonne Curti, violin; Maurice Faure, piano
30 cm. Columbia (Fr) DFX82
1931   ED   Association des Concerts Poulet, Gaston Poulet, conductor
25 cm. Parlophone (Fr) 29011

1932   ED   Orchestre Symphonique, *Pedro A. de Freitas-Branco,* conductor
30 cm. Columbia (Fr) LFX259; (GB) LX196; (US) 68066D
1939   ED   The Lamp Is Low (arrangement of the *Pavane*), Tommy Dorsey and His Orchestra
25 cm. Victor (US) 26259

Jeux d'eau

[1912]   R   Piano
Aeolian, Pianola (GB, US) TL20183; 65 notes, L2459
[1913]   R   Suzanne Godenne, piano
Welte-Mignon (Ger) 2931
1917   AD   Benno Moiseiwitsch, piano
30 cm. Gramophone (GB) 05581, (GB, Fr) D58
1919   R   *E. Robert Schmitz,* piano
Duo-Art (US) 6199
[1919]   R   Benno Moiseiwitsch, piano
Ampico (US) 57836
1920   R   Piano
L'Edition Musicale Perforée (Fr), Aeolian (Fr), and Odéola (Fr) RA1799
1921   AD   *Alfred Cortot,* piano
30 cm. Victor (US) 74659, 6065, Gramophone (GB, India) 05657, (GB, Fr, Holland) DB643
[1923]   AD   Walter Gieseking, piano
30 cm. Homocord (Ger) 1-8446
1925   R   *Suzie Welty,* piano
Pleyela (Fr), Aeolian (Fr), and Odéola (Fr) AP8746
1926   R   Suzanne Godenne, piano
Pleyela (Fr), Aeolian (Fr), and Odéola (Fr) AP8747
1928   ED   *Robert Casadesus,* piano
25 cm. Columbia (Fr) D13054, (US) 1864D, 2080M
1928   R   *E. Robert Schmitz,* piano
Ampico (US) 69383H
1928   ED   *Madeleine de Valmalète,* piano
30 cm. Polydor (Fr, Ger) 95176
[1928]   R   Austin Conradi, piano
Welte-Mignon (US) C6605
1929   ED   Léon Kartun, piano
25 cm. Odéon (Fr) 166166
1929   ED   Marie-Thérèse Brazeau, piano
30 cm. Polydor (Ger, Fr) 27094, Brunswick (US) 90113

1929   ED   Benno Moiseiwitsch, piano
       30 cm. Gramophone (GB) D1648
1932   ED   *Alfred Cortot*, piano
       30 cm. Gramophone (GB, Fr) DB1534, Victor (US) 7729

String Quartet

I Allegro moderato   Très doux
II Assez vif   Très rythmé
III Très lent
IV Vif et agité

1917   I,III,IV   AD   London String Quartet (Albert Sammons, Thomas W. Petre,
       H. Waldo-Warner, C. Warwick-Evans)
       30 cm. Columbia (GB) L1038, L1163
1927   ED   *International String Quartet (André Mangeot,* Boris Pecker, Frank
       Howard, Herbert Withers)
       30 cm., National Gramophonic Society (GB) 78/81
1928   ED   Quatuor Capet (Lucien Capet, Maurice Hewitt, Henri Benoit, Camille
       Delobelle)
       30 cm. Columbia (Fr) D15057/60
1929   ED   Quatuor Krettly (*Robert Krettly,* R. Costard, F. Broos, A. Navarra)
       30 cm. Gramophone (Fr) W975/7, Victor (US) 9799/801
1930   I   ED   Quatuor Guarneri (Daniel Karpilowsky, Moritz Stromfeld, Boris
       Kreyt, Walter Lutz)
       30 cm. Polydor (Ger) 67127, (Fr) 95321
1931   ED   Virtuoso Quartet (Marjorie Hayward, Edwin Virgo, Raymond Jeremy,
       Cedric Sharpe)
       30 cm. Gramophone (GB) C2268/71
1934   ED   Léner Quartet of Budapest (Eugen Léner, Smilovits, Roth, Hartman)
       30 cm. Columbia (GB) LX270/3, (US) 68270/3D, (Argentina) 264983/6
1934   ED   Quatuor Pro-Arte (Alphonse Onnou, Laurent Halleux, Germain
       Prévost, Robert Maas)
       30 cm. Gramophone (Fr, GB) DB2135/8, Victor (US) 14569/72
1934   ED   *Quatuor Galimir de Vienne (F. Galimir,* A. Galimir, R. Galimir, M.
       Galimir) *Maurice Ravel,* conductor.
       30 cm. Polydor (Fr) 516578/80, (Ger) 27329/31, Decca (GB) LY6105/7,
       Brunswick (US) 90411/3
1937   ED   *Quatuor Calvet (Joseph Calvet,* Daniel Guillevitch, Léon Pascal, Paul
       Mas)
       30 cm. Gramophone (Fr) DB5025/8

Shéhérazade
I "Asie"
II "La Flûte enchantée"
III "L'Indifférent"

[1913] R Transcription for piano
Aeolian, Pianola (GB, US) TL22265/7
1921 R Transcription for piano
L'Edition Musicale Perforée (Fr), Aeolian (Fr), and Odéola (Fr) RA3418/20
1929 II,III ED Suzanne Cesbron-Viseur, soprano; Orchestre, *Gustave Cloez,* conductor
25 cm. Odéon (Fr) 188630, Decca (US) 20537
1929 ED *Marcelle Gerar,* soprano; Orchestre, *Piero Coppola,* conductor
30 cm. Gramophone (Fr) W993 (I)
25 cm. Gramophone (Fr) P790 (II, III)
1938 II (in English) ED Rose Walter, soprano; Orchestra, Walter Goehr, conductor
25 cm. Columbia (GB) DB1785, (US) DB1301

Sonatine
I Modéré
II Mouvement de menuet
III Animé

1913 I,II R M *Maurice Ravel,* piano
Welte-Mignon (Ger) C2887
1920 R Piano
L'Edition Musicale Perforée (Fr), Aeolian (Fr), and Odéola (Fr) RA1779/81
1923 R *Mieczyslaw Horszowski,* piano
Pleyela (Fr), Aeolian (Fr), and Odéola (Fr) AP8156/8
1925 II R Marthe Girod and Alexandre Angot, piano 4 hands
Pleyela (Fr), Aeolian (Fr), and Odéola (Fr) E8294
1925 AD Mark Hambourg, piano
30 cm. Gramophone (GB) D1001
1927 ED Kathleen Long, piano
30 cm. National Gramophonic Society (GB) 81 and 87
1928 II ED Lucie Caffaret, piano
30 cm. Polydor (Fr, Ger) 95051
[1928] II R *Dimitri Tiomkin,* piano (issued privately without serial number)
Ampico (US) NI2; roll reissued in 1973

1931   ED *Alfred Cortot,* piano
       30 cm. Gramophone (Fr, GB) DB1533/4, Victor (US) 7728/9
1931   II ED A. Herbert, violin, with piano accompaniment
       25 cm. Gramophone (Ger) EG1754
1932   II ED Elsie Hall, piano
       25 cm. Gramophone (Australia) EA1127
1932   ED *Franz Josef Hirt,* piano
       25 cm. Gramophone (Ger) EG1762/3, (GB) B4127/8
1938   II (transcription by Léon Roques) ED Georg Kulenkampff, violin, with piano accompaniment
       25 cm. Telefunken (Ger, Fr) VA2653

Miroirs

    I "Noctuelles"
   II "Oiseaux tristes"
  III "Une Barque sur l'océan"
  IV "Alborada del gracioso"
   V "La Vallée des cloches"

[1912] V R Piano
       Aeolian, Pianola (GB, US) TL21117; 65 notes, L2859
[1914] I,II,III,IV R Piano
       Aeolian, Pianola (GB, US) TL22710/3; 65 notes, II only, L2863
1922   II R M *Maurice Ravel,* piano
       Duo-Art (GB, US) 082
[1924] II,V R Piano
       Pleyela (Fr), Aeolian (Fr), and Odéola (Fr) M7153/4
1926   IV ED Orchestra of the Berlin State Opera, Otto Klemperer, conductor
       30 cm. Polydor (Ger) 66463, Brunswick (US) 80012
1928   IV ED Orchestre Symphonique du Gramophone, *Piero Coppola,* conductor
       30 cm. Gramophone (Fr) W955, (GB) D1594, Victor (US) 9702
1928   V ED *Franz Josef Hirt,* piano
       25 cm. Gramophone (Ger) EG815
[1928] II R *Dimitri Tiomkin,* piano (issued privately without serial number)
       Ampico (US) NI2; roll reissued in 1973
1929   II,V ED Eliane Zurfluh-Tenroc, piano
       30 cm. Gramophone (Fr) W1031
1929   V R M *Maurice Ravel,* piano
       Duo-Art (GB, US) 72750

1930 IV ED Eliane Zurfluh-Tenroc, piano
      30 cm. Gramophone (Fr) W1097
1930 IV ED *Marcelle Meyer,* piano
      25 cm. Columbia (Fr) LF11
1931 IV ED Orchestre des Concerts Straram, *Walther Straram,* conductor
      30 cm. Columbia (Fr) LFX185, (US) 68077D, (Japan) JW56
1933 IV ED Carlo Vidusso, piano
      25 cm. Gramophone (Italy) HN152
1935 IV ED Carmen Guilbert, piano
      30 cm. Pathé (Fr) PAT23
1935 IV ED Carlo Zecchi, piano
      25 cm. Telefunken (Ger) A1947, Ultraphone (Fr) BP1469
1935 IV ED Minneapolis Symphony Orchestra, Eugene Ormandy, conductor
      30 cm. Victor (US) 8552, Gramophone (GB) DB2459
1938 V ED Boris Zadri, piano
      30 cm. Pathé (Fr) PAT104
1939 V ED Walter Gieseking, piano
      30 cm. Columbia (GB) LX772, (Fr) LFX580, (Australia) LOX509
1939 V ED Walter Gieseking, piano
      30 cm. Columbia (GB) LX772, (Fr) LFX580, (Australia) LOX509
1939 IV ED Walter Gieseking, piano
      25 cm. Columbia (GB) LB53, (US) 17137D, (Ger) LW24, (Australia) LO29

Cinq Mélodies populaires grecques
      I "Chanson de la mariée"
      II "Là-bas, vers l'église"
      III "Quel galant m'est comparable"
      IV "Chanson des cueilleuses de lentisques"
      V "Tout gai!"

[1913] R Transcription for piano
        Aeolian, Pianola (GB, US) TL22245/9
1920 R Transcription for piano
      L'Edition Musicale Perforée (Fr), Aeolian (Fr), and Odéola (Fr) RA3388/92
1935 II,III,V ED Pierre Bernac, baritone; Jean Doyen, piano
      25 cm. Ultraphone (Fr) BP 1435

Introduction et Allegro

[1913] R Piano 4 hands, transcription by Léon Roques
        Aeolian, Pianola (GB, US) TL22454
1924   AD *Miss G. Mason,* harp; *Robert Murcie,* flute; *H. P. Draper,* clarinet;
        . and String Quartet (*Woodhouse, Dinsey, Tomlinson, James*), *Maurice Ravel,*
        conductor.
        30 cm. Columbia (GB) L1518/9, (US) 67091/2D
1925   R *Carlos Salzedo,* piano (accompaniment only)
        Duo-Art (US, GB) 11838
1929   ED John Cockerill, harp; *Robert Murcie,* flute; Charles Draper, clarinet;
        and the Virtuoso Quartet (Marjorie Hayward, Edwin Virgo, Raymond
        Jeremy, Cedric Sharpe)
        30 cm. Gramophone (GB) C1662/3, Victor (US) 9738/9
1931   ED Denise Herbrecht, harp and ensemble; *Piero Coppola,* conductor
        30 cm. Gramophone (Fr) L903/4
1938   ED M *Lily Laskine,* harp; *Marcel Moyse,* flute; Ulysse Delecluse,
        clarinet; and the *Quatuor Calvet* (*Joseph Calvet,* Daniel Guillevitch, Léon
        Pascal, Paul Mas)
        25 cm. Gramophone (Fr) K8168/9, Victor (US) 4509/10

Histoires naturelles

   I   "Le Paon"
   II "Le Grillon"
   III "Le Cygne"
   IV "Le Martin-Pêcheur"
   V   "La Pintade"

[1913] R Transcription for piano
        Aeolian, Pianola (GB, US) TL22283/7
1920   I R Transcription for piano
        L'Edition Musicale Perforée (Fr), Aeolian (Fr), and Odéola (Fr) RA2224
1929   I,II,IV ED M *Jane Bathori,* mezzo-soprano, *Jane Bathori,* piano
        30 cm. Columbia (GB) D15179
1931   ED *Elsa Ruhlmann,* soprano; *Piero Coppola,* piano
        25 cm. Gramophone (Fr) K6396/7 (II,IV,V)
        30 cm. Gramophone (Fr) L907 (I,III)
1939   ED Suzanne Stappen, soprano; Marius-François Gaillard, piano
        25 cm. Odéon (Fr) 188903/5

Vocalise-Etude en forme de Habanera (*Pièce en forme de Habanera*)

1929 ED   Horace Britt, cello; Joseph Adler, piano
        25 cm. Columbia (US) 2081D, 192M, 3944X
1929 ED   Jules Viard, saxophone; Charles Grigaut, piano
        25 cm. Pathé (Fr) X9800, Salabert (Fr) 975
1929 ED   *Maurice Maréchal,* cello; Maurice Faure, piano
        25 cm. Columbia (Fr) D13101, (US) 2446D
1929 ED   Guilhermina Suggia, cello, with piano accompaniment
        25 cm. Gramophone (GB) DA1065
1929 ED   Mieczyslaw Münz, piano
        25 cm. Homocord (Ger) 42885, Decca (US) 20301
1930 ED   Madeleine Marcelli-Herson, cello; Lucien Petitjean, piano
        25 cm. Gramophone (Fr) K5741
1930 ED   Marcel Darrieux, violin, with piano accompaniment
        25 cm. Odéon (Fr) 166197
1930 ED   André Lévy, cello, with piano accompaniment
        25 cm. Odéon (Fr) 166233
1930 ED   Lucienne Radisse, cello, with piano accompaniment
        25 cm. Odéon (Fr) 166065
1931 ED   Maurice Dambois, cello; Fernand Goeyens, piano
        25 cm. Columbia (Fr) D13100
1931 ED   Roger Boulmé, cello, with piano accompaniment
        25 cm. Sonabel (Fr) 12075
1932 ED   Léon Zighera, violin, with piano accompaniment
        25 cm. Decca (Fr) T138
1932 ED   Madeleine Marcelli-Herson, cello; Denise Herbrecht, piano
        25 cm. Gramophone (Fr) K6617
1933 ED   Mischa Elman, violin; Caroll Hollister, piano
        25 cm. Victor (US) 1592
1935 ED   Lucienne Radisse, cello; Jean Doyen, piano
        25 cm. Ultraphone (Fr) AP1506
1937 ED   *Joseph Szigeti,* violin; Nikita de Magaloff, piano
        30 cm. Columbia (GB) LX575, (US) 68922D, (Australia) LOX323

Sur l'herbe

[1913] R   Transcription for piano
        Aeolian, Pianola (GB, US) TL22305
1921 R   Transcription for piano
        L'Edition Musicale Perforée (Fr), Aeolian (Fr), and Odéola (Fr) RA3415

1932 ED *Elsa Ruhlmann,* soprano; *Piero Coppola,* piano
25 cm. Gramophone (Fr) K6397
1936 ED M Pierre Bernac, baritone; *Francis Poulenc,* piano
25 cm. Gramophone (Fr) DA4891

Rapsodie espagnole
I "Prélude à la nuit"
II "Malagueña"
III "Habanera"
IV "Feria"

[1913] R Transcription for piano 4 hands
Aeolian, Pianola (GB, US) TL22467/70
1920 I,II,III R Transcription for piano
L'Edition Musicale Perforée (Fr), Aeolian (Fr), and Odéola (Fr) RA2724/6
1929 ED Grand Orchestre Symphonique, *Piero Coppola,* conductor
30 cm. Gramophone (Fr) W1029/30, Victor (US) 9700/1
1931 ED L'Association Artistique des Concerts Colonne, *Gabriel Pierné,* conductor
30 cm. Odéon (Fr) 123770/1, Decca (US) 25321/2, Odéon (Ger) 07882/3, (Argentina) 177218/9
1933 ED Orchestre Lamoureux, *Albert Wolff,* conductor
30 cm. Polydor (Fr) 566166/7, (Ger) 67052/3, Decca (GB) CA8174/5, Brunswick (US) 90340/1
1935 ED Philadelphia Orchestra, Leopold Stokowski, conductor
30 cm. Victor (US) 8282/3, Gramophone (Fr, GB) DB2367/8

L'Heure espagnole

1929 ED *Jeane Krieger,* soprano; Louis Arnoult, tenor; J. Aubert, baritone; Raoul Gilles, tenor; Hector Dufranne, bass; Orchestre, *Georges Truc,* conductor (complete recording)
30 cm. Columbia (Fr, GB) D15149/55, (US) 68838/44D (set OP14).
1931 excerpts ED *Fanny Heldy,* soprano; Louis Morturier, bass; Pierre Favreau, tenor; Orchestre, *Piero Coppola,* conductor
30 cm. Gramophone (Fr, GB) DB1512 (scenes 17 and 18).

Gaspard de la nuit
I "Ondine"
II "Le Gibet"
III "Scarbo"

1920 I,II R Piano
L'Edition Musicale Perforée (Fr), Aeolian (Fr), and Odéola (Fr) RA1784/5
1922 II R M *Maurice Ravel,* piano
Duo-Art (GB, US) 0219
1922 I AD Mark Hambourg, piano
30 cm. Gramophone (GB) D644
[1924] I R Walter Gieseking, piano
Welte-Mignon (Ger) 3831
1926 R Marius-François Gaillard, piano
Pleyela (Fr), Aeolian (Fr), and Odéola (Fr) E8968/70
1927 I R Jacques Jolas, piano
Ampico (US) 67043H
[1928] I R Katherine Bacon, piano
Welte-Mignon (US) C6825
1937 I ED Walter Gieseking, piano
30 cm. Columbia (GB) LX623, (Fr) LFX539, (Australia) LOX354
1937 ED Jean Doyen, piano
25 cm. Gramophone (Fr) DA4906/7 (I,II)
30 cm. Gramophone (Fr) DB5043 (III)
1939 II ED Walter Gieseking, piano
30 cm. Columbia (GB) LX772, (Fr) LFX580, (Australia) LOX509
1939 III ED Walter Gieseking, piano
30 cm. Columbia (GB) LX813, (Ger) LWX282, (Australia) LOX432, (US)
set X141 (I,II,III)

Ma Mère l'Oye
I "Pavane de la Belle au bois dormant"
II "Petit Poucet"
III "Laideronnette, Impératrice des pagodes"
IV "Les Entretiens de la Belle et de la Bête"
V "Le Jardin féerique"

[1913] R Piano 4 hands
Aeolian, Pianola (GB, US) TL22389/93
[1917] II Pipe Organ Roll
Aeolian (US) 927

1920   R   Piano
L'Edition Musicale Perforée (Fr), Aeolian (Fr), and Odéola (Fr) RA1794/5
1922   AD   Grand Orchestre Symphonique du Gramophone, Albert Coates, conductor
30 cm. Gramophone (GB) D708/9, (Fr) W456/7, Victor (US) 55170 and 55175
1922   III,V   AD   Hallé Orchestra, Sir Hamilton Harty, conductor
30 cm. Columbia (GB) L1418
1923   I,III—II,V   AD   The Aeolian Orchestra, *Cuthbert Whitemore,* conductor
30 cm., Vocalion (GB) J04019 and D02121—J04022 and D02123
1924   I,II—III,V   AD   Orchestre Artistique Chantal
30 cm. Chantal (Belgium) 2123—2124
1925   R   Marthe Girod and Alexandre Angot, piano 4 hands
Pleyela (Fr) Aeolian (Fr), and Odéola (Fr) E8292/3
[1927]   III,IV   R   *Walter Damrosch* and Polly Damrosch, piano 4 hands
Duo-Art (US, GB) 7189-4
1928   ED   New York Symphony Orchestra, *Walter Damrosch,* conductor
30 cm. Columbia (US) 67343/5D (set M74), (GB, Fr) 9516/8 (Ger) CS1063/5
1929   ED   L'Association Artistique des Concerts Colonne, *Gabriel Pierné,* conductor
30 cm. Odéon (Fr) 123546/7, Parlophone (GB) 20066/7, Decca (US) 25319/20
1929   ED   Orchestre Pasdeloup, *Désiré-Emile Inghelbrecht,* conductor
30 cm. Pathé-Art (Fr) X5485/7
1929   III,IV   ED   Le Trigentuor Lyonnais, *Charles Strony,* conductor
30 cm. Gramophone (Fr) L750
[1929]   I,III   R   Guy Maier and Lee Pattison, piano 4 hands
Welte-Mignon (US) C7544
1930   ED   Boston Symphony Orchestra, *Serge Koussevitzky,* conductor
30 cm. Victor (US) 7370/1
1931   II   ED   Orchestre Symphonique de Paris, *Pierre Monteux,* conductor
30 cm. Gramophone (Fr) W1108
1933   ED   Orchestre de la Société des Concerts du Conservatoire, *Piero Coppola,* conductor
30 cm. Gramophone (Fr, GB) DB4898/9, Victor (US) 13482/3, (set M693)
1933   ED   Orchestre Lamoureux, *Albert Wolff,* conductor
30 cm. Polydor (Fr) 566161/2, Brunswick (US) 90342/3
1935   I   ED   Victor Orchestra, Bruno Reibold, conductor
25 cm. Victor (US) 24784
1939   ED   Columbia Broadcasting Symphony Orchestra, Howard Barlow, conductor
30 cm. Columbia (US) 69753/4D (set X151), (GB) DX994/5

Chants populaires

    I "Chanson espagnole"
   II "Chanson française"
 III "Chanson italienne"
 IV "Chanson hébraïque"

1917 IV AD Alma Gluck, soprano, Efrem Zimbalist, violin, with orchestral accompaniment arranged by Pasternack
      25 cm. Victor (US) 87519-3003 Gramophone (Fr) 713360, (GB, Fr) DA448
1929 I,II,IV ED Charles Panzéra, baritone, with piano accompaniment
      25 cm. Gramophone (Fr) P795 (I,II)
      30 cm. Gramophone (Fr) W990 (IV)
[1930] IV ED Sara Goldstein, contralto, with piano accompaniment
      25 cm., Odéon (Ger, Fr) 199388
1932 IV ED M *Madeleine Grey,* mezzo-soprano, with piano accompaniment
      25 cm. Polydor (Fr) 561075, (Ger) 62706, Decca (GB) PO5066, Brunswick (US) 85022

Valses nobles et sentimentales

1913 R M *Maurice Ravel,* piano
      Welte-Mignon (Ger) C2888
[1913] R Piano
      Aeolian, Pianola (GB, US) TL22195/9
1920 R Piano
      L'Edition Musicale Perforée (Fr), Aeolian (Fr), and Odéola (Fr) RA1790/3, RA1796
1934 ED Orchestre de la Société des Concerts du Conservatoire, *Piero Coppola,* conductor
      30 cm. (Fr, GB) DB4935/6, Victor (US) 11727/8

Daphnis et Chloé

    Suite I—"Nocturne, Interlude, Danse guerrière"
    Suite II—"Lever du jour, Pantomine, Danse générale"

[1914] R Transcription for piano of the complete ballet score
      Aeolian, Pianola (GB, US) TL22514/8-TL22548/9
1928 II R *Gustave Samazeuilh,* piano (transcription by the performer)
      Pleyela (Fr), Aeolian (Fr), and Odéola (Fr) TR10367/9

1930 II ED Boston Symphony Orchestra, *Serge Koussevitzky,* conductor
      30 cm. Victor (US) 7143/4, Gramophone (Fr) W1084/5, (GB) D1826/7
1930 II ED Orchestre des Concerts Straram, *Philippe Gaubert,* conductor
      30 cm. Columbia (Fr) LFX41/2, (GB) LX105/6, (US) 67827/8D (set X32), (Ger) LWX253/4
1934 I ED Orchestre de la Société des Concerts du Conservatoire, *Piero Coppola,* conductor
      30 cm. Gramophone (Fr, GB) DB4930, Victor (US) 11882

Deux Mélodies hébraïques
   I "Kaddisch"
   II "L'Enigme éternelle"

1928 I ED M. Lewandowski, baritone, with piano accompaniment
      30 cm. Homocord (Ger) 4-8799
1929 I ED Charles Panzéra, baritone, with piano accompaniment
      30 cm. Gramophone (Fr) W990
1929 I ED *Nina Koshetz,* mezzo-soprano, with orchestral accompaniment
      30 cm. Gramophone (GB, Fr) DB1205
1931 I ED *Dolorès de Silvera,* mezzo-soprano; Maurice Faure, piano
      30 cm. Columbia (Fr) RFX14
1932 ED M *Madeleine Grey,* mezzo-soprano, with piano accompaniment
      25 cm. Polydor (Fr) 561075, (Ger) 62706, Decca (GB) PO5066, Brunswick (US) 85022
1936 I ED Yehudi Menuhin, violin; Marcel Gazelle, piano
      30 cm. Gramophone (Fr, GB) DB2873, Victor (US) 15887

Trio

1931 ED Henri Merckel, violin; Madeleine Marcelli-Herson, cello; Eliane Zurfluh-Tenroc, piano
      30 cm. Gramophone (Fr, GB) DB4803/5, Victor (US) 11243/5 (set M129)

Trois Chansons pour chœur mixte sans accompagnement
   I "Nicolette"
   II "Trois Beaux Oiseaux du Paradis"
   III "Ronde"

1930 I ED Les Chanteurs de Saint-Gervais, *Paul Le Flem,* conductor
    25 cm. Gramophone (Fr) P823
1934 ED Les Chanteurs de Lyon, Léon Vietti, conductor
    30 cm. Columbia (Fr) DFX181, (GB) DX849, (US) 9136M
1935 I,III ED La Chorale Jean Pesnaud, Jean Pesnaud, conductor
    25 cm. Ultraphone (Fr) AP1438
1938 ED Les Chanteurs de Lyon, E. Bourmauck, conductor
    30 cm. Columbia (Fr) RFX68

Le Tombeau de Couperin

Piano	Orchestra
I "Prélude"	I "Prélude"
II "Fugue"	II "Forlane"
III "Forlane"	III "Menuet"
IV "Rigaudon"	IV "Rigaudon"
V "Menuet"	
VI "Toccata"	

1920 R Piano
    L'Edition Musicale Perforée (Fr), Aeolian (Fr), and Odéola (Fr) RA1798,
    RA1800/1
1922 VI R M *Maurice Ravel,* piano
    Duo-Art (GB, US) 086
1922 III,V AD *Charles Scharres,* piano
    30 cm. Gramophone (Fr) L297
1923 III,IV AD The Aeolian Orchestra, *Cuthbert Whitemore,* conductor
    30 cm. Vocalion (GB) J04044 and D02139
1925 III,IV AD Orchestre Artistique Chantal
    30 cm. Chantal (Belgium) 2131
1926 I,II AD The Aeolian Orchestra, Stanley Chapple, conductor
    30 cm. Vocalion (GB) K05225
1927 R Mlle M. Brillot, piano
    Pleyela (Fr), Aeolian (Fr), and Odéola (Fr) E10129/32
1928 IV ED *Victor Staub,* piano
    25 cm. Odéon (Fr) 166045
[1928] IV R Dorothy Miller Duckwitz, piano
    Welte-Mignon (US) B6786
1929 VI ED Léon Kartun, piano
    30 cm. Odéon (Fr) 171069

1930   III   ED   Orchestre de la Société des Concerts du Conservatoire, *Philippe Gaubert,* conductor
30 cm. Columbia (Fr, GB) D15208, (US) 67637D

1931   ED   Orchestre de la Société des Concerts du Conservatoire, *Piero Coppola,* conductor
30 cm. Gramophone (Fr) W1163/4, (GB) D2073/4, Victor (US) 11150/1 and 12320/1

[1932]   I,IV   ED   Nathalie Radisse, piano
25 cm. Odéon (Sweden) D1003

1933   ED   *Madeleine de Valmalète,* piano
25 cm. Polydor (Fr) 522754/5, Decca (GB) PO5088/9, Brunswick (US) B85027/8
30 cm. Polydor (Fr) 516577, Decca (GB) LY6079, Brunswick (US) B90337

1935   VI   ED   Alexandre Borovsky, piano
30 cm. Polydor (Ger) 27342, (Fr) 516612, Fonit (Italy) 91109

1935   III   ED   **Arthur Rubinstein, piano**
30 cm. Gramophone (GB, Fr) DB2450

1938   VI   ED   Boris Zadri, piano
30 cm. Pathé (Fr) PAT104

La Valse

1927   ED   Orchestre Symphonique, Albert Coates, conductor
30 cm. Gramophone (GB) AB233/4, (Fr) W758/9, Victor (US) 9130/1

1927   ED   Orchestre de la Société des Concerts du Conservatoire, *Philippe Gaubert,* conductor
30 cm. Columbia (Fr, GB) 12502/3, (GB) L2245/6, (US) 67384/5D

1931   ED   Orchestre Lamoureux, *Albert Wolff,* conductor
30 cm. Polydor (Fr) 566068/9, (Ger) 67016/7, Brunswick (US) 90186/7

1931   ED   Orchestre Symphonique de Paris, *Pierre Monteux,* conductor
30 cm. Gramophone (Fr) W1107/8

1931   ED   Boston Symphony Orchestra, *Serge Koussevitzky,* conductor
30 cm. Victor (US) 7413/4, Gramophone (GB) DB1541/2

Berceuse sur le nom de Gabriel Fauré

1930   ED   Marcel Darrieux, violin, with piano accompaniment
25 cm. Odéon (Fr) 166322

Ronsard à son âme

1934 ED *Martial Singher,* baritone; Orchestre, *Piero Coppola,* conductor (*recorded in Ravel's presence*)
25 cm. Gramophone (Fr, GB) DA4866, Victor (US) 4405

Tzigane

1929 ED *Lucien Schwartz,* violin; Lucien Petitjean, piano
30 cm. Gramophone (Fr) W1033
1932 ED *Zino Francescatti,* violin; Maurice Faure, piano
30 cm. Columbia (Fr) LFX191, (GB) LX258, (US) 68102D, (Argentina) 264967
1933 ED Yehudi Menuhin, violin; Arthur Balsam, piano
30 cm. Gramophone (GB, Fr) DB1785, Victor (US) 7810
1934 ED *Jascha Heifetz,* violin; Arpad Sandor, piano
30 cm. Victor (US) 8411

L'Enfant et les sortilèges

1928 "Five o'clock" ED Orchestre Symphonique du Gramophone, *Piero Coppola,* conductor
30 cm. Gramophone (Fr) W871 (GB) D1564 Victor (US) 9306 (label on the American pressing only: "Dream of a naughty boy," Continental Orchestra)
1928 "Five o'clock" R *Henri Gil-Marchex,* piano (transcription by the performer)
Pleyela (Fr), Aeolian (Fr), and Odéola (Fr) E10370
[1931] Duo de la théière et de la tasse, L'arithmétique ED *Livine Mertens,* soprano; Henri Marcotty, tenor
25 cm. Columbia (Fr) LF96
1931 "Five o'clock" ED Jules Viard, saxophone; Godfroy Andolfi, piano
25 cm. Pathé (Fr) X98043

Chansons madécasses
I "Nahandove"
II "Aoua!"
III "Il est doux . . ."

1932   ED   M   *Madeleine Grey,* mezzo-soprano, accompanied by piano, flute, and cello; *Maurice Ravel,* conductor
25 cm. Polydor (Fr) 561076/7, Brunswick (US) 85032/3

Boléro

1930   ED   Grand Orchestre Symphonique, *Piero Coppola,* conductor (*recorded in Ravel's presence*)
30 cm. Gramophone (Fr) W1067/8, Victor (US) 13659/60 (set M793)
1930   ED   M   Orchestre Lamoureux, *Maurice Ravel,* conductor (recorded several days after the preceding)
30 cm. Polydor (Fr) 566030/1, (Ger) 66947/8, Decca (GB) CA8015/6, Brunswick (US) 90039/40
1930   ED   Orchestre du Concertgebouw d'Amsterdam, *Willem Mengelberg,* conductor
30 cm. Columbia (GB) LX48/9, (Fr) LFX90/1, (US) 67890/1D
1930   ED   Boston Symphony Orchestra, *Serge Koussevitzky,* conductor
30 cm. Victor (US) 7251/2 (set M352), Gramophone (GB) D1859/60, (Italy) AW175/6
1930   ED   Victor Orchestra, Nathaniel Shilkret, conductor
25 cm. Victor (US) 22571
1930   ED   Leo Reisman and His Orchestra
25 cm. Victor (US) 64316 (matrix); recording not released
1931   R   Morton Gould, piano
Ampico (US) 71043
1931   ED   Jack Payne and His B.B.C. Dance Orchestra
30 cm., Columbia (GB) DX273, (Fr) DFX98, (Ger) DWX1596
1932   ED   Morton Gould, piano
25 cm. Victor (US) 24205
1933   R   *Rudolph Ganz,* piano
Duo-Art (US, GB) 74728
1934   ED   *Jacques Fray* and Mario Braggiotti, two pianos
25 cm., Victor (US) 24563, Gramophone (GB) B8264
1934   ED   Hal Kemp and His Orchestra
25 cm., Brunswick (US) 41566-6629, Decca (GB) F5189

1934 ED Odéon Theatre Orchestra
25 cm. Parlophone (GB) R1930

1934 ED Grand Orchestre Symphonique, Paul Minssart, conductor
25 cm. Odéon (Fr) 250746, Parlophone (GB) R1995

1934 ED Harold Ramsay Rhythm Symphony
25 cm. Decca (GB) F5236, Polydor (Fr) 524230

1934 ED Joseph Muscant and the Troxy Broadcasting Orchestra
25 cm. Regal-Zonophone (GB) MR1431, Idéal (Fr) 12786

1935 ED *Larry Adler,* harmonica, with orchestral accompaniment
25 cm. Columbia (GB) DB1516, (US) 35515

1935 ED George Scott-Wood, piano-accordion, with guitar, bass, and drums
25 cm. Gramophone (GB) BD319

1936 ED Jack Hylton and His Orchestra
25 cm. Gramophone (GB) BD393, Victor (Canada) 28833

1937 ED London Symphony Orchestra, Walter Goehr, conductor
30 cm. Gramophone (GB) C2914, Victor (US) 36214

1937 ED Boston Pops Orchestra, Arthur Fiedler, conductor
30 cm. Victor (US) M12174/5 (set M552), Gramophone (GB) C2954/5, (Switzerland) FKX36/7, (Ger) EH1109/10, (Hungary) AN859/60

1938 ED Ray Ventura and His Collegians
30 cm. Pathé (Fr) PAT115

1938 ED Les 2 Cavallis, accordions
25 cm. Odéon (Fr) 279493

1939 ED Le Grand Orchestre Georges Tzipine avec le Grand Orgue de Cinéma du Gaumont-Palace
25 cm. Odéon (Fr) 281326

[1939] ED Al Bollington, organ
25 cm. Gramophone (GB) BD630

Concerto pour la main gauche

1938 ED *Jacqueline Blancard,* piano; Orchestre Philharmonique de Paris, *Charles Münch,* conductor
30 cm. Polydor (Fr) 566192/3 (Ger) 67192/3, Decca (GB) X204/5, Fonit (Italy) 91077/8, Vox (US), set 168

1939 ED M *Alfred Cortot,* piano; Orchestre de la Société des Concerts du Conservatoire, *Charles Münch,* conductor
30 cm. Gramophone (Fr, GB) DB3885/6, Victor (US) 15749/50 (set M629)

Concerto en sol majeur pour piano et orchestre

1932 ED M *Marguerite Long,* piano; Orchestre Symphonique, *Pedro A. de Freitas-Branco,* conductor (see Orenstein, *A Ravel Reader,* pp. 535–36)
30 cm. Columbia (Fr) LFX257/9, (GB) LX194/6, (US) 68064/6D (set M176), Odéon (Ger) O-9413/5

Don Quichotte à Dulcinée
   I "Chanson romanesque"
   II "Chanson épique"
   III "Chanson à boire"

1934 ED *Martial Singher,* baritone; Orchestre, *Piero Coppola,* conductor (*recorded in Ravel's presence*)
25 cm. Gramophone (Fr, GB) DA4865/6, Victor (US) 4404/5
[1936] I,II ED Marex Liven, baritone, with piano accompaniment
25 cm. Polydor (Ger, Fr) 524189

Nocturnes
Debussy (Ravel)
   II. "Fêtes"

1935 ED M Josef and Rosina Lhévinne, two pianos
25 cm. Victor (US) 1741

Prelude à l'Après-midi d'un faune
Debussy (Ravel)

1911 R *Sir Henry Joseph Wood,* piano 4 hands
Aeolian, Pianola Autograph, 88 notes (GB, US) TL35001
[1912] R Piano, 4 hands
Aeolian, Pianola (GB, US) TL21033; 65 notes, T16603
1920 R Piano, 4 hands
L'Edition Musicale Perforée (Fr), Aeolian (Fr), and Odéola (Fr) DE757

Tableaux d'une exposition
(Pictures at an Exhibition)
Mussorgsky (Ravel)

1930 ED M Boston Symphony Orchestra, *Serge Koussevitzky,* conductor
30 cm. Victor (US) 7372/5 (set M102), Gramophone (GB, Fr) DB1890/3
1931 ED Orchestra of the Berlin State Opera, Alois Melichar, conductor
30 cm. Polydor (Ger, Fr) 27246/9, Decca (GB) LY6053/6, Brunswick (US)
B90333/6
1933 ED Extract: "Tuileries" Victor Orchestra, Bruno Reibold, conductor
25 cm. Victor (US) 24778

"Sarabande"
Debussy (Ravel)

1930 ED Boston Symphony Orchestra, *Serge Koussevitzky,* conductor
30 cm. Victor (US) 7375, Gramophone (GB, Fr) DB1893

Danse
Debussy (Ravel)

1931 ED Boston Symphony Orchestra, *Serge Koussevitzky,* conductor
30 cm. Victor (US) 7414, Gramophone (GB, Fr) DB1542
1932 ED Orchestre de la Société des Concerts du Conservatoire, *Piero Coppola,*
conductor
30 cm. Gramophone (Fr, GB) DB4680

Colleagues and Acquaintances of the Composer Who Recorded His Works after 1939

Larry Adler, harmonica
Ernest Ansermet, conductor
Jacqueline Blancard, piano
Robert Casadesus, piano
Gaby Casadesus, piano
Alfred Cortot, piano
Jeanne-Marie Darré, piano
Lucette Descaves, piano
Roger Désormière, conductor
Georges Enesco, conductor
Henriette Faure, piano
Jacques Février, piano
Pierre Fournier, cello
Zino Francescatti, violin
Pedro A. de Freitas-Branco, conductor
Wilhelm Furtwängler, conductor
Felix Galimir, violin
Vladimir Golschmann, conductor
Marcel Grandjany, harp
Clara Haskil, piano
Jascha Heifetz, violin
Désiré-Emile Inghelbrecht, conductor
Serge Koussevitzky, conductor
Lily Laskine, harp

Yvonne Lefébure, piano
Marguerite Long, piano
Jean Martinon, conductor
Willem Mengelberg, conductor
Marcelle Meyer, piano
Pierre Monteux, conductor
Charles Münch, conductor
Paul Paray, conductor
Emile Passani, piano
Vlado Perlemuter, piano
Francis Poulenc, piano
Manuel Rosenthal, conductor
Arthur Rubinstein, piano
Vittorio De Sabata, conductor
E. Robert Schmitz, piano
Martial Singher, baritone
Joseph Szigeti, violin
Jacques Thibaud, violin
Arturo Toscanini, conductor
Alfred Wallenstein, conductor
Beveridge Webster, piano
Paul Wittgenstein, piano
Albert Wolff, conductor

Selected Bibliography[1]

Ackere, Jules Van. *Maurice Ravel*. Brussels: Elsevier, 1957.

Akeret, Kurt. *Studien zum Klavierwerk von Maurice Ravel*. Rapperswil: Gasser & Co., 1941.

Alajouanine, Théophile. "Le Naufrage d'un génie." *Opéra de Paris,* 15 (n.d.), 18–20.

—— "Aphasia and Artistic Realization." *Brain,* 71(3) (Sept., 1948), 229–41.

Ansermet, Ernest, and J.-Claude Piguet. *Entretiens sur la musique*. Neuchatel: Editions de la Baconnière, 1963.

Aubin, Tony, et al. *Maurice Ravel*. Paris: Les Publications Techniques et Artistiques, 1945.

Auric, Georges. "L'Enfant et les sortilèges." *Les Nouvelles Littéraires,* April 11, 1925.

Berkeley, Lennox. "Maurice Ravel." *ADAM,* 41 (404–6) (1978), 13–17.

Bernard, Robert. *Les Tendances de la musique française moderne*. Paris: Durand & Co., 1930.

Bizet, R. "Ma Mère l'Oye." *L'Intransigeant,* January 28, 1912.

—— "L'Heure espagnole." *L'Intransigeant,* May 17, 1911.

Boulez, Pierre. "Trajectoires: Ravel, Stravinsky, Schoenberg." *Contrepoints,* 6 (1949), 122–42.

Bruyr, José. *Maurice Ravel*. Paris: Plon, 1950.

Cahiers Maurice Ravel. Nos. 1–4 (1985–1989).

Calvocoressi, M. D. *Musicians Gallery: Music and Ballet in Paris and London*. London: Faber & Faber, 1933.

—— "Les 'Histoires naturelles' de M. Ravel et l'imitation Debussyste." *La Grande Revue* (May 10, 1907), pp. 508–15.

—— "Le Mariage, par Moussorgsky." *Bulletin Français de la S.I.M.,* 4 (Dec. 15, 1908), 1284–90.

—— "Aux concerts—Mme. Olénine." *Comœdia Illustré,* 3 (Jan. 15, 1911), 244–45.

—— "Maurice Ravel." *Musical Times,* 54 (1913), 785–87.

---

[1]See also the Selected Bibliography in Orenstein, *A Ravel Reader,* pp. 619–24.

—— ''When Ravel Composed to Order.'' *Music and Letters*, 22 (Jan., 1941), 54–59.

—— Ravel's Letters to Calvocoressi.'' *Musical Quarterly*, 27 (Jan., 1941), 1–19.

Carraud, Gaston. ''Une Barque sur l'océan.'' *La Liberté*, Feb. 5, 1907.

—— ''Société Nationale—M. Maurice Ravel.'' *La Liberté*, Jan. 15, 1907.

—— ''La Rapsodie espagnole.'' *La Liberté*, March 17, 1908.

—— ''Gaspard de la nuit.'' *La Liberté*, Jan. 12, 1909.

—— ''L'Heure espagnole.'' *La Liberté*, May 21, 1911.

—— ''Daphnis et Chloé,'' *La Liberté*, June 11, 1912.

Catalogue de l'œuvre de Maurice Ravel. Paris: Fondation Maurice Ravel, 1954.

Chailley, Jacques. ''Musique française,'' *La Revue Musicale* (April, 1946), pp. 96–103.

—— ''Une Première Version inconnue de 'Daphnis et Chloé' de Maurice Ravel.'' In *Mélanges Raymond Lebègue*. Paris: Nizet, 1969, pp. 371–75.

Chalupt, René, and Marcelle Gerar. *Ravel au miroir de ses lettres*. Paris: Robert Laffont, 1956.

Chalupt, René. ''Théâtre de l'opéra-comique—L'Heure espagnole.'' *La Phalange*, 6 (June, 1911), 555–56.

—— ''Les Grands Concerts.'' *La Phalange* (Feb. 1913), pp. 188–89.

—— ''Maurice Ravel.'' *Les Ecrits Nouveaux* (Dec., 1918), pp. 312–19.

Chantavoine, Jean. ''L'Heure espagnole.'' *La Revue Hebdomadaire*, 20 (June 24, 1911), 579–80.

—— ''La Musique française en 1912.'' *L'Année Musicale*, 2 (1912), 227–32.

—— ''La Musique française en 1913.'' *L'Année Musicale*, 3 (1913), 283–89.

Collaer, Paul. ''L'Esprit de la musique française.'' *La Revue Musicale*, 20 (July–Dec., 1939), 79–85.

Collet, Henri. ''Un Livre de Rimsky et un livre de Cocteau—Les cinq Russes, les six Français et Erik Satie.'' *Comœdia*, Jan. 16, 1920.

Constant, Pierre. ''Le Conservatoire national de musique.'' *La Revue Musicale*, 3 (July 15, 1903), 313–34.

Cooper, Martin. *French Music*. London: Oxford Univ. Press, 1951.

Coppola, Piero. *Dix-Sept Ans de musique à Paris*. Lausanne: F. Rouge, 1944.

Cortot, Alfred. *La Musique française de piano*. 3 vols. Paris: Editions Rieder, 1932.

Coveille. ''Prix de Rome.'' *Le Matin*, May 21 and 22, 1905.

Deane, Basil. ''Renard, Ravel and the 'Histoires naturelles.' '' *Australian Journal of French Studies*, 1 (1964), 177–87.

Delahaye, Michel. "Neuf lettres de Maurice Ravel à Marguerite Baugnies de Saint-Marceaux." *Revue internationale de musique française*, 24 (Nov., 1987), 10–37.

Demuth, Norman. *Ravel*. London: J. M. Dent, 1947.

Downes, Olin. ''Maurice Ravel, Man and Musician.'' *New York Times*, Aug. 7, 1927.

—— ''Mr. Ravel Returns.'' *New York Times*, Feb. 26, 1928.

Dumesnil, René. *Portraits de musiciens français*. Paris: Plon, 1938.

Durand, Jacques. *Quelques Souvenirs d'un éditeur de musique*. Paris: Durand & Co., 1924.

Falla, Manuel de. ''Notes sur Ravel.'' Trans. Roland-Manuel. *La Revue Musicale* (March, 1939), pp. 81–86.

Fargue, Léon-Paul. *Maurice Ravel*. Paris: Domat, 1949.

Fauré, Gabriel. ''L'Heure espagnole.'' *Le Figaro*, May 20, 1911.

Feuilles Libres, Les. ''Hommage à Léon-Paul Fargue.'' Special Issue, 8 (June, 1927).

Février, Jacques. ''Les Exigences de Ravel.'' *Revue Internationale de Musique* (April, 1939), pp. 893–94.

Fragny, Robert de. *Maurice Ravel*. Lyon: Editions et Imprimeries du Sud-est, 1960.

—— ''Les Inédits de Maurice Ravel.'' *Concorde—Hebdomadaire Républicain, Politique et Littéraire*, April 11, 1946.

Gauthier-Villars, Henri. "Pierre Lalo contra Ravel—Louis Laloy pro Ravel." *Mercure de France* (June 1, 1907), pp. 528–31.

Gheusi, P.-B. "Boléro de M. Maurice Ravel." *Le Figaro,* Nov. 24, 1928.

Goldbeck, F. "Don Quichotte à Dulcinée." *La Revue Musicale,* 16 (Jan., 1935), 42–43.

Goss, Madeleine. *Bolero; The Life of Maurice Ravel.* New York: Henry Holt, 1940.

Guadagnino, Luigi. "Teatro raveliano." *La Scala,* 126 (May, 1960), 24–28.

Gubisch, Nina. "Le Journal inédit de Ricardo Viñes." *Revue internationale de musique française,* 1(2) (June, 1980), 154–248.

Guichard, Léon. "Jules Renard et Ravel." *Résonances,* 126 (Nov., 1964), 8–10.

Gutiérrez, Mariano Pérez. *La Estética Musical de Ravel.* Madrid: Editorial Alpuerto, 1987.

Hammond, Richard. "Maurice Ravel." *Modern Music,* 5 (Jan.–Feb., 1928), 20–23.

Harris, Donald. "Ravel Visits the *Verein:* Alban Berg's Report." *Journal of the Arnold Schoenberg Institute,* 3(1) (March, 1979), 75–82.

Honegger, Arthur. "Théâtres de musique: L'Enfant et les sortilèges." *Musique et Théâtre,* 3 (April 15, 1925), 5.

Hugo, Valentine. "Trois souvenirs sur Ravel." *La Revue Musicale* (Jan., 1952), pp. 137–46.

Indy, Vincent d'. "Concerts Lamoureux—Le Bon Sens." *S.I.M.,* 8 (Nov., 1912), 56–58.

Inghelbrecht, D.-E. "Les Arts et la vie—La Musique—Ravel." *La Revue de France,* 18 (March 1, 1928), 118–26.

Jankélévitch, Vladimir. *Ravel.* Paris: Editions du Seuil, 1956.

Jean-Aubry, Georges. *La Musique française d'aujourd'hui.* Paris: Perrin & Co., 1916.

—— "Profils perdus—Maurice Ravel." *Le Censeur Politique et Littéraire,* July 20, 1907.

—— "Maurice Ravel." *Chesterian,* 19 (1938), 65–69.

Jourdan-Morhange, Hélène. *Ravel et nous.* Geneva: Editions du Milieu du Monde, 1945.

Klingsor, Tristan. "Les Musiciens et les poètes contemporains." *Mercure de France* (Nov., 1900), pp. 430–44.

Koechlin, Charles. "Les Tendances de la musique moderne française." In A. Lavignac and L. de la Laurencie, *Encyclopédie de la musique et Dictionnaire du Conservatoire.* Paris: Delagrave, 1925. 2me partie, pp. 56–145.

Lalo, Pierre. "Concert à la Société Nationale de Musique: M. Ravel." *Le Temps,* June 13, 1899.

—— "Le Concours du Prix de Rome en 1905; Le Cas de M. Ravel." *Le Temps,* July 11, 1905.

—— "La Suite pour piano." *Le Temps,* Jan. 30, 1906.

—— "Quelques Ouvrages nouveaux de M. Ravel et le Debussysme. L'Art Debussyste et l'art de M. Debussy." *Le Temps,* March 19, 1907.

—— "Encore le Debussysme. Une Lettre de M. Ravel." *Le Temps,* April 9, 1907.

—— "La Guerre des deux sociétés." *Le Temps,* Aug. 31, 1910.

—— "L'Heure espagnole." *Le Temps,* May 28, 1911.

—— "Daphnis et Chloé." *Le Temps,* June 11, 1912.

—— "L'Heure espagnole." *Le Temps,* Feb. 3, 1922.

Laloy, Louis. *La Musique retrouvée.* Paris: Plon, 1928.

—— "Les Réformes du Conservatoire." *Le Mercure Musical,* 1 (Oct. 15, 1905), 451–53.

—— "Le Mois—Concerts, Société Nationale—Histoires naturelles, de Jules Renard, par Maurice Ravel." *Mercure Musical et Bulletin Français de la S.I.M.,* 3 (Feb. 15, 1907), 155–57.

—— "Musique nouvelle—Maurice Ravel." *Mercure Musical et Bulletin Français de la S.I.M.,* 3 (March 15, 1907), 279–82.

—— "Société Nationale—Gaspard de la nuit." *La Grande Revue,* 13 (Jan. 25, 1909), 395–96.

—— "Les Partis musicaux en France." *La Grande Revue* (Dec. 25, 1907), pp. 790–98.

273

——— "Claude Debussy et le Debussysme." *S.I.M.*, 6 (Aug.–Sept., 1910), 507–19.

——— "Wagner et les musiciens d'aujourd'hui—Opinions de MM. Florent Schmitt et Maurice Ravel." *La Grande Revue*, 13 (May 10, 1909), 160–64.

Landowski, Wanda A. L. *Maurice Ravel*. Paris: Editions Ouvrières, 1950.

Lecherbonnier, Bernard. "La Sensibilité de Parny." Paris, La Sorbonne, 1966 (unpub. thesis).

Léon, Georges. *Maurice Ravel*. Paris: Seghers, 1964.

Lesure, François. " 'L'Affaire' Debussy-Ravel—lettres inédites." In *Festschrift Friedrich Blume*, Kassel: Bärenreiter, 1963, pp. 231–34.

Lesure, François, and Jean-Michel Nectoux. *Maurice Ravel, 1875–1975*. Paris: S.A.C.E.M., 1975. [A selection of contemporary writings and iconography honoring the centenary of Ravel's birth.]

——— *Maurice Ravel*. Paris: Bibliothèque Nationale, 1975. [A catalogue of the Ravel exhibition (367 items) held at the Bibliothèque Nationale in 1975.]

Liess, Andreas. "Maurice Ravel." *Österreichische Musikzeitschrift*, 5 (March–April, 1950), 41–44.

Lockspeiser, Edward. *Debussy: His Life and Mind*. 2 vols. London: Cassel, 1962.

Long, Marguerite. *Au piano avec Maurice Ravel*. Paris: Julliard, 1971.

Machabey, Armand. *Maurice Ravel*. Paris: Richard-Masse, 1947.

Malipiero, Riccardo. *Maurice Ravel*. Milan: Istituto d'alta cultura, 1948.

Marnat, Marcel. *Maurice Ravel*. Paris: Fayard, 1986.

Marnold, Jean. "Un Quatuor de Maurice Ravel." *Mercure de France* (April, 1904), pp. 249–51.

——— "Schéhérazade." *Mercure de France* (July, 1904), pp. 241–43.

——— "Le Scandale du Prix de Rome." *Mercure de France* (June 1, 1905), pp. 466–69.

——— "Le Scandale du Prix de Rome." *Le Mercure Musical*, 1 (June 15, 1905), 155–58, and (July 1, 1905), 178–80.

——— "Conservatoriana." *Le Mercure Musical*, 1 (Oct. 1, 1905), 396–402.

——— "Concerts Engel-Bathori: Œuvres de Maurice Ravel." *Mercure de France* (Jan. 16, 1908), pp. 336–39.

——— "La Société Musicale Indépendante." *Mercure de France* (April 16, 1910), pp. 723–24.

——— "Opéra-Comique: L'Enfant et les sortilèges." *Mercure de France* (March 15, 1926), pp. 701–04.

Mauclair, Camille. "Les Symbolistes et leur musiciens." *Revue de Paris*, 43 (March 15, 1936), 285–301.

Méry, Jules. "Avant-Première—L'Enfant et les sortilèges." *Le Petit Monégasque*, March 21, 1925.

Milhaud, Darius. *Notes sans musique*. Paris: Julliard, 1949.

Morris, Reginald O. "Maurice Ravel." *Music and Letters*, 2 (1921), 274–83.

Musical. "Ravel." Special Issue, 4 (June, 1987).

Myers, Rollo H. *Ravel*. London: G. Duckworth, 1960.

Narbaitz, Pierre. *Maurice Ravel*. Côte Basque, 1975.

Nectoux, Jean-Michel. *Fauré*. Paris: Editions du Seuil, 1972.

——— "Maurice Ravel et sa bibliothèque musicale." *Fontes artis musicae*, 24 (1977), 199–206.

Nichols, Roger. *Ravel*. London: Dent, 1977.

——— *Ravel Remembered*. London: Faber and Faber, 1987.

Noske, Frits. *French Song from Berlioz to Duparc*. 2d ed. Trans. Rita Benton. New York: Dover, 1970.

Onnen, Frank. *Maurice Ravel*. Stockholm: Continental Book Co., 1947.

Orenstein, Arbie. "L'Enfant et les sortilèges: Correspondance inédite de Ravel et Colette." *Revue de Musicologie*, 52, No. 2 (1966), 215–20.

—— "Maurice Ravel's Creative Process." *Musical Quarterly*, 53 (Oct., 1967), 467–81.

—— "Some Unpublished Music and Letters by Maurice Ravel." *Music Forum*, 3 (1973), 291–334.

—— "Ravel's Letters to Charles Koechlin." *ADAM*, 41 (404–6) (1978), 20–25.

—— "Ravel and Falla: An Unpublished Correspondence, 1914–1933." In E. Strainchamps, M. R. Maniates, and C. Hatch, eds., *Music and Civilization: Essays in Honor of Paul Henry Lang*, pp. 335–49. New York: W. W. Norton, 1984.

—— "La Correspondance de Maurice Ravel aux Casadesus." *Cahiers Maurice Ravel*, 1 (1985), 113–42.

—— *Maurice Ravel: Lettres, Écrits, Entretiens*. Paris: Flammarion, 1989.

—— *A Ravel Reader*. New York: Columbia University Press, 1990.

Perlemuter, Vlado, and Hélène Jourdan-Morhange. *Ravel d'après Ravel*. 5th ed. Lausanne: Editions du Cervin, 1970.

Petit, Pierre. *Ravel*. Paris: Hachette, 1970.

Photiadès, Constantin. "Maurice Ravel." *Revue de Paris*, 45 (March, 1928), 213–27.

Pilarski, Bohdan. "Une Conférence de Maurice Ravel à Houston (1928)." *Revue de Musicologie*, 50 (Dec., 1964), 208–21.

Poulenc, Francis. *Moi et mes amis*. Paris: La Palatine, 1963.

—— "Le Cœur de Maurice Ravel." *La Nouvelle Revue Française* (Jan. 1, 1941), pp. 237–40.

Prunières, Henry. "L'Enfant et les sortilèges à l'opéra de Monte Carlo." *La Revue Musicale* (April 1, 1925), pp. 105–09.

—— "Les Concerts—Trois Chansons Madécasses de Maurice Ravel." *La Revue Musicale*, 7 (July 1, 1926), 60–62.

—— "Trois Silhouettes de musiciens—César Franck, Saint-Saëns, Maurice Ravel." *La Revue Musicale*, 7 (Oct. 1, 1926), 225–40.

—— "Ravel: Concerto pour la main gauche." *La Revue Musicale* (Feb., 1933), pp. 127–28.

Ravel, Maurice. "Concert Lamoureux." *Revue Musicale de la S.I.M.*, 8 (Feb. 15, 1912), 62–63.

—— "Concerts Lamoureux." *Revue Musicale de la S.I.M.* (March, 1912), pp. 50–52.

—— "Les 'Tableaux symphoniques' de M. Fanelli." *Revue Musicale de la S.I.M.* (April, 1912), pp. 55–56.

—— "La Sorcière à l'opéra-comique." *Comœdia Illustré*, 5 (Jan. 5, 1913), 320–23.

—— "Fervaal—poème et musique de Vincent d'Indy." *Comœdia Illustré*, 5 (Jan. 20, 1913), 361–64.

—— "A propos des Images de Claude Debussy." *Les Cahiers d'Aujourd'hui* (Feb., 1913), pp. 135–38.

—— "Au Théâtre des Arts." *Comœdia Illustré*, 5 (Feb. 5, 1913), 417–20.

—— "Boris Godounoff." *Comœdia Illustré*, 5 (June 5, 1913), n. pag.

—— "A L'Opéra-Comique." *Comœdia Illustré*, 6 (Jan. 20, 1914), 390–91.

—— "Parsifal—version française d'Alfred Ernst." *Comœdia Illustré*, 6 (Jan. 20, 1914), 400–03.

—— "Les Nouveaux Spectacles de la saison russe—Le Rossignol." *Comœdia Illustré*, 6 (June, 1914), 811–14.

—— "Les Mélodies de Gabriel Fauré." *La Revue Musicale*, 3 (Oct., 1922), 22–27.

—— "Contemporary Music." *Rice Institute Pamphlet*, 15 (April, 1928), 131–45.

Revue Musicale, La. "Maurice Ravel." Two Special Issues. April, 1925, and Dec., 1938.

Roland-Manuel. *Maurice Ravel et son œuvre*. Paris: Durand & Co., 1914.

—— *Maurice Ravel et son œuvre dramatique*. Paris: Les Editions Musicales de la Librairie de France, 1928.

—— *A la gloire de Ravel*. Paris: Editions de la Nouvelle Revue Critique, 1938.

—— *Ravel*. Paris: Gallimard, 1948.

—— "Maurice Ravel." *L'Echo musical*, 2 (Feb. 5, 1913), 1–3.

—— "Maurice Ravel." *La Revue Musicale*, 2 (1921), 1–21.

—— "Théâtre de l'opéra-comique—L'Enfant et les sortilèges." *Le Ménestrel* (Feb. 5, 1926), pp. 60–61.

—— "Maurice Ravel et la jeune musique française." *Les Nouvelles Littéraires* (April 2, 1927), pp. 1–2.

—— "Le Génie de Maurice Ravel." *Temps Présent*, Jan. 7, 1938.

—— "Réflexions sur Ravel." *La Grand Revue*, 42 (April, 1938), 40–44.

—— "Une Esquisse autobiographique de Maurice Ravel." *La Revue Musicale* (Dec., 1938), pp. 17–23.

—— "Maurice Ravel à travers sa correspondance." *La Revue Musicale* (Jan.–Feb., 1939), pp. 1–7.

—— "Lettres de Maurice Ravel et documents inédits." *Revue de Musicologie*, 38 (July, 1956), 49–53.

Rolland, Romain, and Richard Strauss. *Correspondance, fragments de journal*. Paris: Albin Michel, 1951.

Rorem, Ned. "Historic Houses: Maurice Ravel at Le Belvédère." *Architectural Digest*, 43(9) (Sept., 1986), 182–88 and 212.

Roy, Jean. *Maurice Ravel: Lettres à Roland-Manuel et à sa famille*. Quimper: Calligrammes, 1986.

Sannemüller, Gerd. "Ravels Stellung in der französischen Musik." In *Hans Albrecht in Memoriam*. Kassel: Bärenreiter, 1962, pp. 251–56.

Schmitt, Florent. "Une Belle Exécution de la sonate pour violon et violoncelle de Maurice Ravel." *Le Temps*, Jan. 8, 1938.

Segalla, Paul. "Ravel's Songs." *Monthly Musical Record*, 85 (Dec., 1955), 264–69.

Séré, Octave. *Musiciens français d'aujourd'hui*. Paris: Mercure de France, 1911.

Sérieyx, A. "Salle Erard—Société Nationale." *Le Courrier Musical*, 10 (Feb. 1, 1907), 77–78.

Seroff, Victor. *Maurice Ravel*. New York: Henry Holt, 1953.

Sert, Misia. *Misia*. Paris: Gallimard, 1952.

Shattuck, Roger. *The Banquet Years*. London: Jonathan Cape, 1958.

Stravinsky, Igor. "Maurice Ravel est mort." *L'Intransigeant*, Dec. 29, 1937.

Stuckenschmidt, H. H. *Maurice Ravel*. Frankfurt am Main: Suhrkamp Verlag, 1966.

Szmolyan, Walter. "Maurice Ravel in Wien." *Österreichische Musikzeitschrift*, 30(3) (March, 1975), 89–103.

Tappolet, Willy. *Maurice Ravel: Leben und Werk*. Olten: O. Walter, 1950.

—— "Maurice Ravel 'der Baske.' " *Schweizerische Musikzeitung*, 95 (Nov., 1955), 421–24.

Vaughan Williams, Ursula. *R.V.W.: A Biography of Ralph Vaughan Williams*. London: Oxford Univ. Press, 1964.

Veen, Jan van der. "Problèmes Structuraux chez Maurice Ravel." In *Bericht über den siebten internationalen Musikwissenschaftlichen Kongress*, Köln, 1958. Kassel: Bärenreiter, 1959, pp. 289–90.

Vuillemin, Louis. "L'Heure espagnole." *Comœdia*, May 20, 1911.

—— "Daphnis et Chloé." *Comœdia*, June 10, 1912.

Vuillermoz, Emile, et al. *Maurice Ravel par quelques-uns de ses familiers.* Paris: Editions du Tambourinaire, 1939.
—— "En l'an 2012." *Revue Musicale de la S.I.M.* (August–Sept., 1910), pp. 520–29.
—— "Les Théâtres—L'Heure espagnole—Thérèse—Le Martyre de Saint Sébastien." *Revue Musicale de la S.I.M.*, 7 (June 15, 1911), 65–70.
—— "Les Théâtres—La grande saison de Paris." *Revue Musicale de la S.I.M.* (June 15, 1912), 62–68.
—— "Maurice Ravel." *Les Cahiers d'Aujourd'hui,* 10 (1922), 196–98.
—— "L'Enfant et les sortilèges." *Excelsior,* Feb. 3, 1926.
—— "Ravel's New Piano Concerto." *Christian Science Monitor,* Feb. 13, 1932.
—— "La Carrière et la fin du grand musicien." *Excelsior,* Dec. 29, 1937.
—— "Défendons Ravel." *Candide,* Jan. 13, 1938.
Wolff, Stéphane. *Un Demi-siècle d'Opéra-Comique (1900–1950).* Paris: Editions André Bonne, 1953.
—— *L'Opéra au Palais Garnier (1875–1962).* Metz: Imprimerie Maisonneuve, 1962.

UNSIGNED OR INITIALED INTERVIEWS AND REVIEWS

"Les 'Histoires Naturelles' de M. Maurice Ravel." *La Revue Musicale de Lyon,* 7 (Feb. 27, 1910), 612–17.
"The Art of Maurice Ravel." *The Times,* Dec. 20, 1913.
"M. Maurice Ravel contre M. de Diaghilew." *Comœdia,* June 18, 1914.
"L'Heure espagnole." *The Times,* July 25, 1919.
"Ravel and Modern Music." *Morning Post,* July 10, 1922.
"Het Fransche Muziekfeest." *De Telegraaf,* Sept. 30, 1922. [The French music festival. In Dutch.]
"Ravel as Conductor." *The Times,* April 16, 1923.
"Maurice Ravels Ankomst." *Berlingske Tidende,* Jan. 30, 1926. [Maurice Ravel's arrival. In Danish.]
"Skandinaviskt inflytande på fransk komposition." *Svenska Dagbladet,* Feb. 9, 1926. [Scandinavian influence on French composition. In Swedish.]
"Entretien avec Ravel." *La Revue Musicale* (March, 1931), pp. 193–94.
"Tien opinies van M. Ravel." *De Telegraaf,* April 6, 1932. [Ten opinions of M. Ravel. In Dutch.]

Index

Ackere, Jules Van, 148, 160

Adélaïde, ou le langage des fleurs, 65, 156, 175, 176, 177, 231

Adénis (Adénis-Colombeau), Edouard: Prix de Rome text (*Alcyone*) and Ravel entry, 37, 37*n*, 151, 153, 223

Adénis (Adénis-Colombeau), Eugène: Prix de Rome text (*Alcyone*) and Ravel entry, 37, 37*n*, 151, 153, 223

Adler, Larry, 270

Alain-Fournier (Henri-Alban Fournier), 75

Alajouanine, Dr. Théophile, 105*n*

A la manière de . . . , 68, 181, 232

Albéniz, Isaac, 23, 31; *Iberia,* 98

"Alborada del gracioso," 49, 50, 101, 136*n*, 140, 159, 160, 167, 224-25; orchestral transcription, 75, 160, 225; see also *Miroirs*

Alcyone, 37, 151, 153, 223

Alheim, Mme Marie Olénine d', 63, 63*n*, 230

Alheim, Pierre d', 63*n*

Alkan, Charles: Etude, Opus, 76, No. 1, 202*n*

Alvar, Louise, 92

Alvina-Alvi, Mme, 69, 233

Alyssa, 38, 151, 153, 223

American music, 3-4, 82-83; and Ravel, 95, 97-98; *see also* Jazz

"D'Anne jouant de l'espinette," 19, 23, 149-50, 222; see also *Epigrammes de Clément Marot*

"D'Anne qui me jecta de la neige," 22-23, 149, 192, 222; see also *Epigrammes de Clément Marot*

Ansermet, Ernest, 127; and Ravel, 107, 110, 214, 241, 270

Antheil, George, 82, 83

Anthiôme, Eugène, 14, 15

"Aoua!," 91, 195, 196*n*, 197, 203, 237-38; see also *Chansons madécasses*

Apaches (group), 28-29, 30, 40, 41, 159; and Ravel, 28-29, 30, 40, 48, 49, 58, 83

Aranyi, Jelly d', 85, 88, 236.

Arbós, Enrique, 98

Arnold, Billy, 83*n*

"Asie," 40, 148, 156, 157, 224; see also *Shéhérazade* (song cycle)

Association Française d'Expansion et d'Echanges Artistiques, 95

Astruc, Gabriel, 155*n*, 223

Aubert, Louis, 62*n*, 86*n*, 88*n*, 93; and Ravel, 64, 231, 233, 241

Aubry, Pierre, 41, 41*n*

Aulnoy, Marie-Catherine, Comtesse d': Ravel's use of tale in *Ma Mère L'Oye,* 172, 173

Auric, Georges, 60n, 239; and Ravel, 31, 73n, 80, 83, 113-14, 245; see also *Les Six*

L'Aurore, 44, 151, 152, 226

Babaïan, Marguerite, 41, 41n, 49n, 225, 230

Bach, Johann Sebastian, 20, 98, 121, 217

Bakst, Leon, 40, 61, 231

Balakirev, M. A., 16, 25, 49, 63n: *Islamey*, 58, 170

Ballade de la Reine morte d'aimer, 17, 131, 139-40, 171, 220, 230

Ballets Russes, *see* Diaghilev, Serge (and the Ballets Russes)

Bardac, Raoul, 32, 33

"Une Barque sur l'océan," 49, 50, 159, 160, 171, 224-25; orchestral transcription, 50-51, 137n, 160, 225; see also *Miroirs*

Bartók, Béla, 3, 78, 84, 218; and Ravel, 74, 97, 110, 121, 125, 190

Bathori, Mme Jane (Jean-Marie Berthier), 23, 23n; and Ravel, 23, 87, 227; Ravel performed by, 23, 50, 52, 54n, 68, 91, 92, 93n, 226, 227, 232, 237, 238, 256

Baudelaire, Charles, 3, 126, 128; Ravel's interest in, 16, 18, 77, 117, 123n, 126, 128n; Ravel's use of epigraph, 142, 220

Bax, Sir Arnold, 82

Les Bayadères, 27, 150, 152, 222

Beecham, Sir Thomas, 68

Beethoven, Ludwig van, 30, 82; influence of, 3, 31, 123n, 126; and Ravel, 25, 121, 122, 123, 123n, 126, 134, 210; Sonata Opus, 13, 183; Eighth Symphony, 210

Beissier, Fernand, 34n; Prix de Rome text (*Myrrha*) and Ravel entry, 34-35, 36, 36n, 151, 153, 222

Bellenot, Philippe: *Un Début*, 89n

Bellini, Vincenzo, 124, 152

Benedictus, Edouard, 28, 48

Bennett, Arnold, 246

Berceuse sur le nom de Gabriel Fauré, 85, 86, 92, 192, 235, 264

Berg, Alban, 125, 125n

Bériot, Charles de, 14, 15, 16, 17, 227

Berkeley, Lennox, 112

Berlioz, Hector, 33n, 43, 82; and Ravel, 114, 121, 123, 136

Berners, Gerald Tyrwitt, Lord, 246

Bertelin, Albert, 35, 37

Bertrand, Aloysius: Ravel's *Gaspard de la nuit* based on poetry by, 58-59, 170, 228; see also *Gaspard de la nuit*

Bizet, Georges, 33n, 123, 168; *Carmen*, 30, 123

Blancard, Jacqueline, 270

Bliss, Arthur, 245

Bloch, Ernest: Suite for Viola and Piano, 92; and Ravel, 125, 125n

Blondel, Albert, 45n, 226

Blum, Léon, 30, 113

Boceta, Joaquín, 28

Le Bœuf sur le toit, 83-84

Bogue-Laberge, 95n

Boléro, 94, 98-99, 100, 101, 103, 105, 136, 136n, 200-01, 204, 239, 266-67

Bolero (film), 99

Bonnard, Pierre, 41, 164

Bonnet, M. and Mme, 75

Bonniot, Edmond, 67

Borlin, Jean, 187, 234

Borodin, Alexander, 58, 106; and Ravel, 16, 125, 178-79; Ravel pastiche in the style of, 68, 181, 232; *Prince Igor*, 178-79

Boschot, Adolphe, 56

Boston Symphony Orchestra, 86n; Ravel performed by, 94, 95, 96, 260, 262, 264, 266, 269

Boulanger, Lili, 83, 86

Boulanger, Nadia, 3-4

Brahms, Johannes: Casella pastiche, 68; and Ravel, 102n, 121; Symphony in D Major, 121, 122

Braque, Georges, 60n, 84

Bréville, Pierre de, 21, 23

Buffon, Georges-Louis Leclerc, Comte de, 162, 162n

Burns, Robert: Ravel's setting ("Chanson écossaise") of poem by, 175, 230

Busser, Henri, 65; *Les Roses pleurent*, 39n

Les Cahiers d'Aujourd'hui, 106n-107n

Callirhoé, 26, 243

Calvocoressi, Michel D., 28, 41, 44n, 48, 49n, 58; and Ravel, 29, 39, 41, 48, 49, 49n, 83, 101-02, 225; on Ravel, 32, 49-50, 52, 119, 121; Ravel, correspondence, 84, 200-01

Canudo, Ricciotto: Ravel's *Frontispice* to poems by, 75, 75n, 188, 188n, 234

Caplet, André, 28, 35, 36, 36n, 62n, 67, 88n; *Dans la fontaine*, 39n; Prix de Rome, 153, 153n

Carol, King of Romania, 103

Carraud, Gaston: on Ravel, 32, 53, 57, 58, 59, 61, 106n-107n

Carré, Albert, 55, 56

Casadesus, Robert: and Ravel, 87, 108, 172, 251, 270

Casadesus, Mme Robert (Gaby), 85, 270

Casals, Pablo, 30, 110

Casella, Alfredo, 3, 41, 65, 68, 181, 199; and Ravel, 68, 79, 181; Ravel performed by, 92, 222, 232, 233, 235, 237

Casella, Mme Alfredo, 66

Cercle Musical, 54, 226

Cervantes, 103-04; see also *Don Quichotte à Dulcinée*; *Don Quixote*

Chabrier, Emmanuel, 20n, 53, 126, 131, 163, 168; and Ravel, 16, 17, 22, 123, 124, 124n, 126, 136, 138, 140, 150, 166; *Trois Valses romantiques*, 16; Ravel pastiche in the style of, 68, 181, 232; *Menuet pompeux*, orchestral transcription by Ravel, 124n, 141, 241-42; *Le Roi malgré lui*, 100n; *Bourrée fantasque*, 140; *Dix Pièces pittoresques*, "Idylle," 150; *España*, 166

Chadeigne, Marcel, 18, 28

Chaliapin, Feodor, 54, 60n; *Don Quixote* (film), Ibert songs for, 103, 104, 104n; and Ravel, 103, 110, 206n

Chanson du rouet, 20, 22, 22n, 138, 145-46, 147, 203, 221

Chansons madécasses, 23, 91, 92, 121, 126, 132, 137, 138, 138n, 139, 195-97, 203, 237-38, 266

Chants populaires, 63, 174-75, 230, 261; "Chanson hébraïque" ("Mejerke mein Suhn"), 88, 175, 230; "Chanson espagnole," 174-75, 206, 230; "Chanson française," 175, 230; "Chanson italienne," 175, 230; "Chanson écossaise," 175, 230-31

Charles-René, 11

Charlot, Jacques, 75, 234

Charpentier, Mme Raymond, 86n, 235

Chausson, Ernest, 20n, 23, 31; *Poème de l'amour et de la mer*, 122n

Chevillard, Camille, 30n, 80, 234

Chopin, Frédéric, 29, 139, 217; and Ravel, 14, 15, 49, 68-69, 119, 124, 124n, 126, 127, 134, 136, 146, 202n, 205, 242; Ballade in F minor, 15; *Les Sylphides*, orchestration by Ravel, 68-69, 242; and Debussy, 73n, 126, 217; Etudes, transcription by Godowsky, 292n; *Berceuse*, 205

Cinq Mélodies populaires grecques, 29, 41, 41n, 59, 161, 174, 208, 225, 255; transcriptions of accompaniments by Rosenthal, 108n, 225

Clémenceau, Paul, 83

Clémenceau, Mme Paul, 83, 233

La Cloche engloutie, 10n, 48, 50, 54, 72, 160, 209-10

Cocteau, Jean, 41, 60n, 83n, 84, 119; and Ravel, 80, 126

Coiffier, Marguerite: Prix de Rome text (*Alyssa*) and Ravel entry, 38, 38n, 151, 153, 223

Colette (Sidonie-Gabrielle Colette), 24, 78, 93n, 193; and Ravel, 21, 111; Ravel's *L'Enfant et les sortilèges* based on libretto by, 78-79, 89, 90, 138, 193, 209, 210, 236-37; see also *L'Enfant et les sortilèges*

Collet, Henri, 80

Colonne, Jules-Edouard, 30n, 58, 227

Colonne Orchestra, 30, 30n, 57-58, 82, 106; Ravel performed by, 48, 51, 57, 106, 225, 227, 236, 240, 241, 250, 258, 260

Comœdia, 70, 80, 90

Comœdia Illustré, 16, 29

Concertgebouw Orchestra, 86, 266

Concerto for the Left Hand, 100, 101, 102, 104-05, 108, 121, 131, 136, 189, 202-03, 204, 205, 239, 267

Concerto in G Major (for piano and orchestra), 100, 101-02, 102n, 103, 105, 136, 202, 202n, 203-05, 240, 268

Concerts Colonne, see Colonne Orchestra

Concerts du Conservatoire, see Société des Concerts du Conservatoire

Concerts Lamoureux, see Lamoureux Orchestra

Concerts Pasdeloup, see Pasdeloup Orchestra

Condillac, Etienne de, 113
Conrad, Joseph, 246
Conservatoire, 26, 44, 44n, 48; Ravel, 12-17 passim, 19, 20, 24-28, 30, 33-39 passim, 42-45, 47, 48, 48n, 68, 77, 118, 132n, 150-53, 209; Dubois as director, 26, 44; Fauré as director, 44, 48; see also Prix de Rome; Société des Concerts du Conservatoire
Il Convegno, 86
Coolidge, Mrs. Elizabeth Sprague, 91, 92, 237
Copland, Aaron, 83, 130, 131n
Coppola, Piero: Ravel conducted by, 107, 236, 249, 250, 253, 254, 256, 258, 260, 261, 262, 264, 265, 266, 269
Le Coq, 80
Cortot, Alfred, 11, 40, 58; on Ravel, 17-18, 143n; Intermèdes, 40; Ravel performed by, 40, 224, 251, 252, 254, 267, 270
Couperin, François, 65, 136, 185, 186, 217, 218; see also Le Tombeau de Couperin
Le Courrier Musical, 49-50, 64-65, 73n, 124n
Croiza, Claire, 86
Cruppi, Mme Jean, 55, 55n, 226, 228
"Le Cygne," 29n, 53, 162, 164, 226-27; see also Histoires naturelles
Czerny, Karl: Ecole de la main gauche, Opus 399, 202n; 24 Etudes pour le main gauche, Opus 718, 202n

Daily Telegraph, 102n, 200-01
Daphnis et Chloé, 8, 9, 48, 60-61, 66, 68, 69-70, 84, 99, 101, 108, 135, 136, 137, 139, 152, 177-79, 180, 183, 184, 215n, 215-16, 231-32, 261-62; orchestral suites from, 61, 215, 216, 231, 261-62
Darré, Jeanne-Marie, 270
Debussy, Claude, 2, 4, 8, 20n, 21, 60n, 64, 65, 80, 82, 86, 124n, 126, 127, 151-52, 168, 247; influence of, 3, 4, 29, 30, 31, 32, 66, 127; and Satie, 3, 16-17, 31, 78n, 126; Diaghilev and the Ballets Russes, 3, 31, 60n, 61, 127; Prélude à l'Après-midi d'un faune, 3, 31, 61, 127, 241, 268-69; Pelléas et Mélisande, 8, 28, 32, 37, 66, 157; and Viñes, 21, 32, 49n, 159; and Ravel, 25, 31-33, 39, 40, 42, 49n, 51, 51n, 53, 62, 67, 85, 89, 92, 106n-107n, 110, 114, 119, 121,
126-27, 138, 141, 155, 157, 159, 190, 235, 241, 242, 268-69; La Mer, 30n, 127; "Jardins sous la pluie," 32; Pour le piano, 32; "Soirée dans Grenade," 32; Pierre Lalo on, 32, 107n; Nocturnes, 33, 127, 241, 268; Prix de Rome, 33n; Dans le jardin, 39n, 156; "Poissons d'or," 49n; "Reflets dans l'eau," 49n; D'un cahier d'esquisses, 49n, 62, 159; Louis Laloy, correspondence, 53; Jacques Durand, correspondence, 53, 67; Durand and Company, 67, 67n; Trois Poèmes de Stéphane Mallarmé, 67, 126, 180; Fêtes galantes, 67n; Préludes, 67n; Casella pastiche, 68; Chopin works edited by, 73n; Danse, orchestral transcription by Ravel, 85, 89, 92, 242, 269; orchestral transcription by Ravel, "Sarabande," 85, 89, 92, 242, 269; Images, 106n-107n; and Chopin, 126, 217; Estampes, 127; L'Ile joyeuse, 127; Proses lyriques, "De Fleurs," 141; La Fille aux cheveux de lin, 146; Voiles, 147; Quartet, 155; Children's Corner, 173, 192, 200; Trois Chansons de Charles d'Orléans, 184
Debussy, Mme Claude, 85
Decombes, Emile, 11
Dédale 39, 100n
Defauw, Désiré, 87n
Delage, Maurice, 9, 28, 29, 58, 88n; Ravel, correspondence, 10, 50, 72; and Ravel, 29, 48, 49, 83, 98, 107, 112, 119, 225, 230, 242; Conté par la mer, 61n; Quatre Poèmes hindous, 68; Sonatine, 242
Delage, Mme Maurice (Nelly): and Ravel, 48, 87, 91, 98, 107
Delannoy, Marcel, 107n, 126, 239
Delius, Frederick: Margot la Rouge, transcription by Ravel, 37-38, 240
Delteil, Joseph: Ravel's opera based on Jeanne d'Arc, 100
Désormière, Roger, 93, 104, 234, 238, 270
Deux Mélodies hébraïques, 69, 77, 182, 233, 262; orchestral transcription, 76, 233
Diaghilev, Serge (and the Ballets Russes), 54, 60, 60n, 69n, 83; Prélude à l'Après-midi d'un faune, 3, 31, 61, 127; and Stravinsky, 3, 60n, 66, 66n, 78, 205, 242-43; Daphnis et Chloé, 9, 48, 60-61, 66, 69-70, 177, 231-32; Boris Godunov, 60n; The Firebird, 66;

Petrushka, 66, 205; *Khovanshchina*, 66, 66*n*, 242-43; *Menuet pompeux*, 124*n*, 141, 241-42; *La Valse* originally planned for, 76, 77-78, 114

Diderot, Denis, 128*n*

Doire, René, 124*n*

Don Quichotte à Dulcinée, 103-04, 105-06, 108, 205-06, 240, 268

Don Quixote (film), 103, 104, 104*n*

Doucet, Clément, 84

Downes, Olin, 96-97

Dreyfus, Alfred, trial, 1, 30

Dreyfus, Fernand, 75

Dreyfus, Mme Fernand, 75, 75*n*

Dron, Marthe, 20, 220-21

Dubois, Théodore, 26, 35, 44, 64, 132*n*; and Ravel, 26, 27, 38, 42

Dubost, Mme Jeanne, 93, 238-39

Dukas, Paul, 3, 31, 60*n*, 78*n*, 88*n*, 122*n*; *La Péri*, 65

Dumesnil, René, 148*n*

Duncan, Isadora, 22

Duparc, Henri, 20*n*, 49*n*, 65, 122*n*

Dupont, Gabriel, 35, 36

Durand, Auguste, 49, 50, 67

Durand, Jacques, 75, 93; and Ravel, 49; and Debussy, 53, 67; Ravel, correspondence, 75-76, 89, 119, 119*n*, 128*n*, 207

Durand and Company, 29, 73*n*; and Ravel, 8, 49, 49*n*, 50*n*-51*n*, 67, 73, 93, 107; concerts sponsored by (1910-13), 67, 67*n*; concerts sponsored by (1927), 93, 238

Durey, Louis, 80, 83, 112, 218*n*; see also *Les Six*

Durony, Geneviève, 62, 62*n*, 229

Ecorcheville, Jules, 54, 59, 59*n*-60*n*

Edwards, Alfred, 29*n*, 45, 46, 48

Edwards, Mme Alfred (Misia), *see* Sert, Mme José-Maria

Einstein, Albert, 83

Elman, Mischa, 30, 257

Enesco, Georges, 3, 20, 86*n*; Ravel performed by, 19, 93, 238, 270

L'Enfant et les sortilèges, 10*n*, 78-79, 89-90, 91-92, 135, 136, 138, 152, 193-95, 201, 202, 209, 210, 236-37, 265

"L'Enigme éternelle," 69, 76, 182, 233; see also *Deux Mélodies hébraïques*

"Entre cloches," 19, 20, 21, 142-43, 143*n*, 149, 220-21; see also *Sites auriculaires*

Epigrammes de Clément Marot, 19, 21, 22-23, 26-27, 64, 138, 149-50, 162, 192, 222, 249

Erard Company (Maison Erard), 45, 45*n*, 81, 126

Espagnat, Georges d', 41

L'Eventail de Jeanne, 93, 238-39; Ravel's "Fanfare," 93, 136, 200, 238-39

Exoticism, interest in and influence of: International Exposition (1889), 11, 131, 139-40, 183; Ravel, 11-12, 40, 107, 114, 131, 142, 147, 157

Falla, Manuel de, 2, 3, 28, 60*n*, 78*n*, 218; and Ravel, 8-9, 99, 100*n*, 121, 125, 126

"Fanfare," 93, 136, 200, 238-39

Fargue, Léon-Paul, 28; Ravel's *Rêves* to poem by, 23, 29, 93, 198, 238; on Ravel, 29, 84, 118; and Ravel, 49, 83, 225; *Les Feuilles Libres* issue honoring, 93, 93*n*; Marcel Raval on, 198, 198*n*

Faucigny-Lucinge, Prince Jean-Louis de, 83

Fauré, Gabriel, 2, 3, 20*n*, 21, 23, 31, 54, 62, 62*n*, 67, 80, 86, 165; and Ravel, 13, 19, 20, 26, 27-28, 31, 33, 39, 42, 49, 64, 123, 124, 135, 136*n*, 138, 141, 145, 223 (see also *Berceuse sur le nom de Gabriel Fauré*); as teacher, 13, 19, 20, 21, 26, 27-28, 30, 33, 39*n*, 86*n*, 120; as director of Conservatoire, 44, 48; Ballade for Piano and Orchestra, 58; *La Chanson d'Eve*, 62; Ravel, correspondence, 62, 82, 86; Schumann works edited by, 73*n*; *Dolly*, 136*n*; Verlaine set to music, 141; Sonata for Violin and Piano, 145; *Nell*, 146

"Feria," 166, 167-68, 227; see also *Rapsodie espagnole*

Ferroud, Pierre-Octave, 91*n*, 238

Les Feuilles Libres, 93, 93*n*

Février, Jacques, 87, 108, 142*n*, 270

Le Figaro, 55-56

"La Flûte enchantée," 40, 156, 157, 224; see also *Shéhérazade* (song cycle)

Fokine, Michel, 60, 61, 231

Francescatti, Zino, 92, 265, 270
Franck, César, 3, 20n, 23, 30, 31, 40, 82; and
   Ravel, 16, 19, 64, 121, 122, 145; *Symphonic
   Variations,* 58; Symphony, 106, 121, 122;
   Sonata for Violin and Piano, 145
Franc-Nohain (Maurice-Etienne Legrand), 30,
   54n; Ravel's *L'Heure espagnole* based on
   libretto by, 54-55, 56, 57, 168, 169-70, 209,
   228; see also *L'Heure espagnole*
Freitas-Branco, Pedro de, 102, 250, 270
Freund, Marya, 79, 84
Fried, Oskar, 79
Frontispice, 75, 143n, 188, 234
Furtwängler, Wilhelm, 103, 270

Galimir, Felix, 270
Gallois, Victor-Léon, 33n
Ganz, Rudolph, 123n, 229, 250, 260
Garban, Lucien, 29, 32; Ravel, correspon-
   dence, 36, 66, 105, 208n; and Ravel, 83,
   91n, 105, 107, 206, 236
Gaspard de la nuit, 37, 48, 49n, 58-59, 121,
   123n, 135, 139, 160, 170-72, 200, 202,
   228-29, 259; "Scarbo," 136n, 140, 170,
   171-72; "Le Gibet," 142, 170, 171, 172,
   201, 203; "Ondine," 170, 171, 172
Gaudin, Pascal, 75, 234
Gaudin, Pierre, 75, 234
Gauley, Marie-Thérèse, 89, 89n, 236
Gauthier-Villars, Henry (Willy), 23, 24, 27
Gédalge, André, 19, 20n; and Ravel, 13,
   19-20, 26, 42, 50n, 233; as teacher, 13,
   19-20, 26, 131, 134
Georges, Alexandre, 63, 63n
Gerar, Marcelle: and Ravel, 87, 89, 98, 113,
   235; Ravel performed by, 88, 236, 253
Gershwin, George, 97, 125, 125n, 204, 205;
   Rhapsody in Blue, 125n
Ghys, Henry, 11, 11n, 14n
"Le Gibet," 142, 170, 171, 172, 201, 203,
   228, 229; see also *Gaspard de la nuit*
Gide, André, 2, 3, 41, 84
Gieseking, Walter, 125n; Ravel performed by,
   136n, 251, 255, 259
Gil-Marchex, Henri: and Ravel, 87, 172, 207;
   Ravel performed by, 114, 236, 265
Glazunov, Alexander, 16, 54
Godebska, Ida, 83; Ravel, correspondence, 9,

9n, 54n, 76-77, 89, 112; and Ravel, 41-42,
   48, 54, 62n, 66, 83, 87, 224, 232
Godebska, Mimie, 42, 62, 113, 229
Godebska, Misia, *see* Sert, Mme José-Maria
Godebski, Cipa, 83; and Ravel, 29n, 41-42,
   48, 54, 62n, 66, 83, 87, 224, 232; Ravel,
   correspondence, 72, 110, 122n
Godebski, Jean, 42, 42n, 62, 113, 229
Godowsky, Leopold, 202n
Golschmann, Vladimir, 83, 88, 270
Gounod, Charles: Prix de Rome, 33n; *Faust,*
   83, 181; and Ravel, 123, 124, 152, 181;
   Philémon et Baucis, 124; *Venise,* 124
Granados, Enrique, 125
Grand Prix de Rome *see* Prix de Rome
Un Grand Sommeil noir, 17, 121, 141, 146,
   203, 220
Les Grands Vents venus d'outremer, 54, 165,
   203, 227
Gravollet, Paul (Paul Barthélémy Jeulin), 39,
   39n, 156; Ravel's *Manteau de fleurs* to poem
   by, 39, 156, 158, 223-24
Grey, Madeleine: Ravel performed by, 77, 98,
   99, 100, 108, 233, 261, 262, 266; and Ravel,
   87
Grieg, Edvard, 15, 25, 124n; *Peer Gynt,*
   Ravel's variations on a theme, 11
"Le Grillon," 52, 162, 164, 226-27; see also
   Histoires naturelles
Grovlez, Gabriel, 49n, 224, 229
Gunsbourg, Raoul, 89, 237

"Habanera," 16, 17, 20, 21, 32, 130, 135,
   142, 166, 167, 220-21, 227; orchestral
   transcription, 142, 142n; see also *Rapsodie
   espagnole; Sites auriculaires*
Hahn, Reynaldo, 11, 60n, 65, 171
Haour, Pierre, 29, 79
Hardy-Thé, 26, 222
Haskil, Clara, 270
Hatto, Jane, 40, 224
Hauptmann, Gerhardt: Ravel's *La Cloche
   engloutie* based on libretto by, 50, 51n, 209,
   210; see also *La Cloche engloutie*
Haydn, Franz Joseph, 59n-60n; Ravel's
   Menuet sur le nom d'Haydn, 59, 59n, 100,
   101, 174, 230; *The Seasons,* 164
Heger, Robert, 104n, 239

Heifetz, Jascha, 110, 265, 270
Hérold, A. Ferdinand, 50, 50n, 51n, 76, 209
Hettich, A. L., 165
L'Heure espagnole, 48, 54-57, 59, 68, 84, 89, 101, 114, 131, 135, 138, 157, 160, 163, 168-70, 171, 177, 193, 194, 208, 228, 258
Heymann Quartet, 39, 223
Hindemith, Paul, 83, 100n, 125n, 199, 218
Histoires naturelles, 23, 33, 48, 51-55 passim, 57, 59, 64, 79, 88n, 138, 157, 162-65, 168, 194, 226-27, 256; "Le Cygne," 29n, 53, 162, 164; "Le Grillon," 52, 162, 164; "Le Martin-Pêcheur," 52, 147, 162, 164; Rosenthal orchestration of accompaniment, 108n; "Le Paon," 162, 163-64; "Le Pintade," 162, 163, 164
Hoérée, Arthur, 91n
Hofmannsthal, Hugo von, 245
Honegger, Arthur, 19, 80, 83, 88n, 98, 165; and Ravel, 80, 80n, 88, 90, 107n, 125n; Pacific 231, 86n; Pierre Lalo on, 107n; Quatre Chansons pour voix grave, 141, 141n; see also Les Six
Horowitz, Vladimir, 110
Hugard, Mme Jeanne, 65, 229
Hugo, Jean, 100
Huré, Jean, 62, 65
Huysmans, Joris Karl, 16

Ibert, Jacques, 19, 83, 83n, 165, 238; Prix de Rome, 33n; and Ravel, 88, 126, 218n; Don Quixote (film), music for, 104
Icare, 100n
"Il est doux . . . ," 195, 197, 237-38; see also Chansons madécasses
"L'Indifférent," 40, 156, 157, 162, 224; see also Shéhérazade (song cycle)
Indy, Vincent d', 3, 20n, 21, 30, 31, 54, 60n, 67, 73; Second String Quartet, 20; and Ravel, 23, 31, 52, 121, 122, 123n, 126; Tableaux de voyage, 26-27; and Schola Cantorum, 30, 31; as teacher, 31, 53, 122n, 126; Mirage, 39n, 156; on Ravel, 40, 42, 61; Istar, 65; Casella pastiche, 68; Saugefleurie, 121, 122
Inghelbrecht, Désiré-Emile, 28, 64, 187; Ravel conducted by, 108, 232, 234, 260, 270

International Exposition (1889), 11, 131, 139-40, 183
International Society for Contemporary Music, 100, 100n
Introduction et Allegro, 45, 54, 67n, 96, 99, 101, 157, 162, 256

Jazz, interest in and influence of, 83, 84, 199; Ravel, 79, 83n, 84, 97, 112, 131, 136, 139, 194, 194n, 198, 199, 201, 202, 203, 205
Jean-Aubry, Georges, 23; and Ravel, 52, 53n, 85, 92, 165-66, 185
Jeanne d'Arc, 100
Jeux d'eau, 20, 29, 32, 36-37, 44, 119, 130-31, 132, 136, 154, 158, 160, 164, 171, 191, 213-14, 222-23, 251-52
Jobert, Jean, 85
Jourdan-Morhange, Mme Hélène, 88, 93n; and Ravel, 85, 86n, 87, 93n, 108, 195, 235, 238

"Kaddisch," 69, 76, 182, 233; see also Deux Mélodies hébraïques
Karsavina, Thamara, 60, 61, 231
Kastor, Robert, 246
Kindler, Hans, 85, 91, 92, 237
Kiriac, D., 26
Klingsor, Tristan (Arthur Justin Léon Leclère), 28, 29, 40, 156-57, 157n; Ravel's Shéhérazade to poems by, 29, 40, 156, 209, 224 (see also Shéhérazade); and Ravel, 110, 233
Kodály, Zoltán, 3; and Ravel, 64, 65, 74, 121, 125, 190; Duo for Violin and Cello, 190
Koechlin, Charles, 20, 23, 65, 86n; and Ravel, 52, 61, 106; Société Musicale Indépendante, 61, 62, 62n
Koussevitzky, Serge, 83, 86, 86n; Ravel conducted by, 94, 96, 242, 260, 262, 264, 266, 269, 270
Kreisler, Fritz, 97
Kunc, Aymé, 37n; Prix de Rome, 33n, 35, 37, 37n, 153, 153n

Laberge, Bernard, 95n, 113
Lacretelle, Jacques de, 108
Ladmirault, Paul, 28, 86n
La Fontaine, Jean de, 111, 218
Lalo, Edouard, 21n, 168; Le Roi d'Ys, 58

Lalo, Pierre, 21n, 66; on Ravel, 21, 24-25, 32, 39-40, 42, 43-44, 50, 52-53, 57, 58, 61, 137n, 147, 148-49; Ravel on, 32, 106n-107n; on Debussy, 32, 107n; on the Conservatoire, 44n; on Milhaud, 80n, 107n; on Honegger, 107n

Laloy, Louis, 41n, 44n, 48, 53, 54; on Ravel, 40n, 50, 52, 53, 59; Faure's *Dolly* adapted for stage by, 136n

Lamoureux, Charles, 30n

Lamoureux Orchestra, 30, 30n, 82, 121; Ravel performed by, 80, 99, 220, 231, 234, 239, 240, 242, 249, 258, 260, 264, 266

Laparra, Raoul, 20, 39, 39n; *La Habanera*, 39n; *L'Illustre Fregona*, 39n; Prix de Rome, 153, 153n; *Sur l'herbe*, 166

Larbaud, Valéry, 41

Laskine, Lily, 107, 256, 270

Lazzari, Sylvio, 23

Leconte de Lisle, Charles Marie, 3, 146, 156; Ravel's *Chanson du rouet* to poem by, 20, 145-46, 221; see also *Chanson du rouet*

Le Flem, Paul, 41n

Lehár, Franz: *Die blaue Mazur*, 79

Leleu, Jeanne, 62, 62n, 229, 232

Le Masle, Robert, 108

Lenepveu, Charles, 35, 36, 37n, 43, 44

Lenormand, René, 132-34, 132n

Léon, Paul, 42-43

Léopold, King of Belgium, 92

Leprince de Beaumont, Mme Marie: Ravel's use of tales in *Ma Mère l'Oye*, 172, 173

Leroux, Xavier, 36

Lestang, Mme Paule de, 49n, 224, 249

Lévy, Claude, 98, 99

Leyritz, Léon, 88, 107

La Liberté, 90; see also Carraud, Gaston

Lifar, Serge, 83

Liszt, Franz, 49n, 98, 168, 189; and Ravel, 119, 124, 135, 136, 152, 154, 170, 187, 192, 202; *Les Ideals*, 124n-125n; *Les Jeux d'eau à la Villa d'Este*, 154; *Transcendental Etudes*, 170

Loeffler, Charles: *Cantique au soleil*, 92

Long, Marguerite, 62n, 75, 76; Ravel performed by, 76, 102, 103, 105, 234, 240, 268, 270

Loty, Maud, 91n

Maeterlinck, Maurice, 72, 72n

Mahler, Gustav, 3, 84, 122n; Second Symphony, 30n

Maison du Lied, 63, 63n

"Malagueña," 58, 166, 167, 227; see also *Rapsodie espagnole*

Mallarmé, Stéphane, 2, 3, 20, 29, 29n, 129, 218; and Ravel, 16, 18, 19, 126, 143, 179, 221 (see also *Trois Poèmes de Stéphane Mallarmé*); Ravel's *Sainte* to poem by, 19, 143, 221 (see also *Sainte*); and Debussy, 67, 126, 186; Wallace Fowlie on, 121n, 180; Poe translated by, 128; Renard on, 179

Ma Mère l'Oye, 41-42, 48, 62, 62n, 79, 87, 92, 101, 106, 125n, 136, 137, 139, 161, 172-73, 208n, 229-30, 259-60; as ballet, 65, 146, 172, 173, 229-30; orchestral transcriptions, 136n, 172, 173, 229

Manteau de fleurs, 39, 156, 158, 223-24

Maré, Rolf de, 187, 234

Maréchal, Maurice, 85, 98, 235, 257

Marès, Roland de: Ravel's *Ballade de la Reine morte d'aimer* to poem by, 17, 139, 220; see also *Ballade de la Reine morte d'aimer*

Marliave, Joseph de, 75, 234

Marnold, Jean, 47; on Ravel, 32, 40, 40n, 52; and Ravel, 40n, 47, 48, 229; Ravel, correspondence, 45, 71, 73, 134-35, 188

Marot, Clément, 149; Ravel's *Epigrammes de Clément Marot* to poems by, 19, 21, 22-23, 149, 222; see also *Epigrammes de Clément Marot*

"Le Martin-Pêcheur," 52, 147, 162, 164, 226-27; see also *Histoires naturelles*

Massenet, Jules, 30, 33n, 35; and Ravel, 36, 124, 124n, 138, 141, 146, 152; *Thérèse*, 56

Massine, Léonide, 77, 241

Mathias, Georges: *Allegro symphonique*, 15

Mathot, A. Z., 50n, 62n, 181

Le Matin, 29n

Matinée de Provence, 151, 152, 223

Matisse, Henri, 2, 60n, 110

Matsa, Pericles, 41

"Mejerke mein Suhn," 63, 88, 230; see also *Chants populaires*

Mendelssohn, Felix, 82; and Ravel, 14, 15, 16, 123, 135, 135n; Capriccio in B minor, 15; Ravel's edition of piano works, 73, 242;

Violin Concerto, 123, 135*n*, 162

Le Ménestrel, 24, 93*n*

Mengelberg, Willem, 86, 266, 270

Menuet antique, 17, 19, 21, 130, 131, 136, 141, 158, 186, 220, 249; orchestral transcription, 141, 150, 220

Menuet sur le nom d'Haydn, 59, 59*n*, 100, 174, 230

Mercure de France, 40; on Ravel, 21, 40; receptions, 29

Le Mercure Musical, 44*n*, 49*n*

Messager, André, 21, 49*n*, 54

Messiaen, Olivier, 83

Meunier, Antonine: Ravel's *La Parade* based on scenario of, 22*n*, 243

Meyer, M. and Mme Jacques, 107

Meyer, Marcelle, 77

Meyerbeer, Giacomo, 30, 83

Mihalovici, Marcel, 83, 112

Milhaud, Darius, 3, 19, 60*n*, 80, 83, 83*n*, 84, 199, 239; and Ravel, 80, 80*n*, 107*n*, 108, 121, 126, 218*n*; Pierre Lalo on, 80*n*, 107*n*; *Les Malheurs d'Orphée,* 80*n*, 126; Liszt and Schubert orchestrated by, 98; *Les Choéphores,* 126; see also *Les Six*

Miroirs, 37, 48, 49-50, 95, 127, 132, 135, 159-61, 224-25, 254-55; "Oiseaux tristes," 29, 49, 49*n*, 50, 159-60; "Alborada del gracioso," 49, 50, 75, 101, 136*n*, 140, 159, 160, 167; "La Vallée des cloches," 49, 50, 142-43, 143*n*, 149, 159, 160-61, 171; "Une Barque sur l'océan," 49, 50-51, 137*n*, 159, 160, 171; "Noctuelles," 49, 159, 160

Mompou, Federico, 93*n*

Monte Carlo Opera, 89-90, 236-37

Monteux, Pierre: Ravel conducted by, 60-61, 101, 231, 260, 261, 270; and Ravel, 101, 110

Moore, George, 246

Morand, Paul, 83, 103, 104, 104*n*; Ravel's *Don Quichotte à Dulcinée* to poems by, 103, 104, 206, 240; see also *Don Quichotte à Dulcinée*

Moreau, Léon, 91

Moreau, Luc-Albert, 88, 196*n*

Morgiane, 103, 107, 209

Morning Post, 69, 127, 127*n*

Mortier, Robert, 49*n*

Mortier, Mme Robert (Jeanne), 48, 49*n*

Moscheles, Ignaz: Third Piano Concerto, 11

Mouveau, Georges, 28

Mozart, Wolfgang Amadeus, 30, 82, 106, 126, 217; and Ravel, 16, 20, 92, 102, 117-18, 119-20, 123, 123*n*, 124, 126, 135, 136, 202*n*, 204; Fortieth Symphony, 92; Piano Concerto in C Minor, 204

Münch, Charles, 108, 267, 270

Mussorgsky, Modest, 54, 63, 63*n*, 126; and Ravel, 53, 55, 66, 66*n*, 86, 100, 119, 125, 126, 136*n*, 137, 138, 163, 242-43, 269; *Nursery,* 53, 173; *Marriage,* 55, 163; *Boris Godunov,* 60*n*; *Khovanshchina,* Ravel and Stravinsky reorchestration of Rimsky-Korsakov, 66, 66*n*, 242-43; *Pictures at an Exhibition,* orchestral transcription by Ravel, 86, 100, 136*n*, 137, 242, 269

Myrrha, 34-35, 36, 36*n*, 151, 153, 222

"Nahandove," 195, 196*n*, 196-97, 237-38; see also *Chansons madécasses*

Natanson, Alexandre, 30

Natanson, Thadée, 29*n*, 30, 51

National League for the Defense of French Music, 73-74

Neue Freie Presse, 79*n*, 235, 239

New York Philharmonic, 99

New York Times, 96-97, 104*n*, 125*n*

"Nicolette," 184, 195, 233; see also *Trois Chansons pour chœur mixte sans accompagnement*

Nijinsky, Vaslav, 69*n*; and Ravel, 60, 61, 68-69, 110, 231, 241, 242

Nijinsky, Mme Romola, 111

"Noctuelles," 49, 159, 160, 224-25; see also *Miroirs*

Noël des jouets, 23, 49, 50, 161, 226

Les Nouvelles Littéraires, 80*n*, 107*n*

La Nuit, 151, 152, 223

"Nuit en gondoles," 21

Obouhov, Nicolas, 112; *Le Livre de vie,* 107

"Oiseaux tristes," 29, 49, 49*n*, 50, 159-60, 224-25; see also *Miroirs*

Olénine, Alexander, 63, 63*n*

"Ondine," 170, 171, 172, 228; see also *Gaspard de la nuit*

Opéra (Paris), 8, 30, 83, 93n, 238; Ravel performed by, 57, 84, 98, 99, 228, 236, 238, 239, 242; bust of Ravel by Leyritz, 88

Opéra-Comique: Ravel performed by, 48, 55, 57, 90, 91, 228

Orchestre Symphonique de Paris, 101; Ravel performed by, 101, 104, 239, 260, 264

Pabst, Georg W., 104

Paganini, Nicolò, 192

Painlevé, Paul, 83, 113, 233

"Le Paon," 162, 163-64, 226-27; see also *Histoires naturelles*

La Parade, 22n, 243

Paray, Paul: Ravel conducted by, 105, 106, 240, 242, 270

Parny, Evariste-Désiré de, 91, 195; Ravel's *Chansons madécasses* to poems by, 91, 138, 195-96, 196n, 237-38; see also *Chansons madécasses*

Pasdeloup, Jules-Etienne, 30n

Pasdeloup Orchestra, 30, 30n, 82; Ravel performed by, 77, 105, 107, 225, 233, 234, 236, 242, 260

"Pavane," 137-38, 173; see also *Ma Mère L'Oye*

Pavane pour une Infante défunte, 22, 37, 64, 150, 158, 181, 195, 203n, 205, 222, 250-51; orchestral transcription, 63, 103, 150, 222

Périer, Jean, 41n, 57, 228

Perlemuter, Vlado, 93n, 270

Pernot, Hubert, 41, 41n, 161, 174

Perrault, Charles: Ravel's use of tales in *Ma Mère l'Oye*, 172-73

Pessard, Emile, 14, 15, 17

Petit, Abbé Léonce, 28

Piano concerti, see Concerto for the Left Hand; Concerto in G Major

Picasso, Pablo, 2, 60n, 84, 93n, 110, 188n

Pierné, Gabriel, 30n, 93; Ravel conducted by, 225, 236, 241, 250, 258, 260

"La Pintade," 162, 163, 164, 226-27; see also *Histoires naturelles*

Piston, Walter, 83

"Placet futile," 66, 67, 128-29, 179, 180, 181, 232; see also *Trois Poèmes de Stéphane Mallarmé*

Poe, Edgar Allan, 117, 128, 129; and Ravel, 16, 21, 97, 117, 118n, 121n, 126, 128-29, 170, 171

Polignac, Princess Edmond de, 22, 48, 222

Le Portrait de l'Infante, 243

Poulenc, Francis, 2, 3, 202, 239; Diaghilev and the Ballets Russes, 60n, 77-78; and Ravel, 80, 83, 108, 142, 218n, 249, 258, 270; see also *Les Six*

Prélude, 68, 181, 232

"Prélude à la nuit," 166-67, 227; see also *Rapsodie espagnole*

Prix de Rome, 33n, 33-34, 77; (1900), 26, 27, 33n, 150, 152, 222; (1901), 33-36, 36n, 151, 152, 153, 222; (1902), 33n, 37, 151, 152, 153, 223; (1903), 38-39, 39n, 151, 152, 153, 223; (1905), 33n, 42-45, 47, 48, 53, 151, 152, 226

Prokofiev, Sergei, 2, 60n, 84, 100n, 205, 218; and Ravel, 108, 110

Pro Musica Society, 95

Prunières, Henry, 78; works commissioned for *La Revue Musicale*, 78, 78n, 85, 86, 86n, 88, 88n, 235-36; on Ravel, 90, 92, 102n, 104, 104n

Puccini, Giacomo, 30, 125, 125n, 195; *Tosca*, 125n

Rabaud, Henri, 48n, 102n, 136n

Rachmaninov, Sergei, 54

Rameau, Jean Philippe, 29, 186, 218

Rapsodie espagnole, 8-9, 48, 54, 57, 58, 79, 96, 131, 136, 142, 166-68, 227-28, 258; see also "Habanera"

Raunay, Mme Jeanne, 62

Raval, Marcel, 93, 198, 198n

Ravel, Edouard (brother), 8, 10, 59, 71-72, 109; and Ravel, 9, 10, 75, 77, 98, 107, 108; Ravel, correspondence, 94, 95-96

Ravel, Edouard (uncle), 9, 81

Ravel, Joseph (Pierre Joseph), 8, 9-10, 54, 59, 109; and Ravel, 16, 54, 54n, 168; portrait of, by Desboutin, 81

Ravel, Mme Joseph (Marie Delouart), 8, 9, 10, 59, 113; and Ravel, 8, 9, 10, 72, 74, 75, 76-77, 112, 189; ill health and death, 74, 75, 109; portrait of, by Edouard Ravel, 81

Ravel, Maurice (Joseph Maurice): World War I, 1, 70-75 *passim*, 186, 189; as pianist (performer and accompanist), 3, 14*n*, 22, 26, 29, 49*n*, 50, 54*n*, 56, 62, 64, 67*n*, 69, 77, 93, 93*n*, 101, 102-03, 113, 221, 222, 226, 227, 232, 233, 235, 236, 238, 241, 252, 256, 266, 268 (*see also* concerts and concert tours *below*); as conductor, 3, 23, 50, 65, 67*n*, 79*n*, 87, 92, 95, 99, 101-05 *passim*, 113, 220, 221, 226, 231, 232, 239, 240, 252, 256, 266, 268 (*see also* concerts and concert tours *below*); birth, 8; and mother, 8, 9, 10, 72, 74, 75, 76-77, 112, 189; Spanish music, interest in and influence of, 8, 16, 17, 103, 107, 111*n*, 125, 131, 135, 139, 142, 160, 168, 201, 204, 206 (*see also* "Alborada del gracioso"; *Boléro; Don Quichotte à Dulcinée;* "Habanera"; *Rapsodie espagnole*); Basque culture and music, interest in, 8, 48, 72*n*, 83, 100-01, 111, 112, 114, 131, 135, 145, 204*n*, 206; religion, 8, 113; childhood and early life, 8-12 *passim,* 130, 131; and brother, Edouard, 9, 10, 75, 77, 98, 107, 108; and father, 10, 16, 54, 54*n*, 168; piano, study of, 11, 12, 15-16; Russian music, interest in and influence of, 11-12, 16, 25, 26, 54, 105, 119, 125, 126, 131, 149, 177, 178; composition, study of, 11, 13, 14-15, 17, 19-20, 26, 27-28, 30, 33, 47-48, 132*n*; exoticism, interest in and influence of, 11-12, 40, 107, 114, 131, 142, 147, 157 (*see also Chansons madécasses; Shéhérazade*); and Conservatoire, 12-17 *passim,* 19, 20, 24-28, 30, 33-39 *passim,* 42-45, 47, 48, 48*n*, 68, 77, 118, 132*n*, 150-53, 209; piano, study of (at Conservatoire), 14, 15, 16, 17, 19, 47, 118; literary interests, 16, 19, 81, 111 (*see also* Baudelaire; Mallarmé; Poe; Verlaine); on music, 16, 29, 30-31, 97-98, 117-26 *passim,* 157-58, 217; clothes, interest in, 18, 42, 111; characteristics and personality, 18-19, 21, 22, 42, 46, 47, 81, 110-14, 163; humor, sense of, 18-19, 22, 54, 81, 111, 168; on his own music, 19-20, 24, 25, 31, 37, 52, 55-56, 60, 101, 132-34, 142, 159, 161, 165-66, 175-76, 178, 188, 194, 196, 200-01, 207, 208-09; criticism of, 20-21, 23-27 *passim,* 31, 32, 35-40 *passim,* 41*n*, 42, 43-44, 49, 49*n*, 52-53, 54, 56-57, 58, 59, 61, 64, 65, 68, 73*n*, 79, 80, 84-88 *passim,* 88*n*, 90, 92, 93, 93*n*, 94, 96-97, 99-100, 102-03, 104, 106, 164; bells and clocks (in music), 21, 140, 170, 171 (see also *Ballade de la Reine morte d'aimer; La Cloche engloutie;* "Entre cloches"; "Le Gibet"; *L'Heure espagnole;* "La Vallée des cloches"); Prix de Rome (1900), 26, 27, 150, 152, 222; and *Apaches,* 28-29, 30, 40, 48, 49, 58, 83; as teacher, 29, 36*n*, 58, 64, 93, 112, 119-20, 137, 157-58; Prix de Rome (1901), 33-36, 36*n*, 151, 152, 153, 222; Prix de Rome (1902), 37, 151, 152, 153, 223; water (in music), 37, 160 (see also *Gaspard de la nuit; Jeux d'eau; Miroirs*); Prix de Rome (1903), 38-39, 39*n*, 151, 152, 153, 223; folk songs, interest in and use of, 41, 138 (see also *Chants populaires; Cinq Mélodies populaires grecques; Deux Mélodies hébraïques*); descriptions of, 42, 111; Prix de Rome (1905), 42-45, 47, 48, 53, 151, 152, 226; monogram, 45; concerts and concert tours, 59, 64, 68, 79, 83, 85-104 *passim,* 205 (*see also* as conductor; as pianist *above*); health, 65-66, 71, 74-75, 100, 102*n*, 102-08 *passim,* 112; pastiches, 68, 131, 135-36, 139, 140, 174, 181 (see also *A la manière de . . . ; Menuet antique; Menuet sur le nom d'Haydn*); Hungarian music, interest in and influence of, 74, 121, 125, 190, 191, 192; Prix de Rome, 77; awards, citations, and honors, 77, 77*n*, 80, 92, 98, 99, 100-01, 103, 110; jazz, interest in and influence of, 79, 83*n*, 84, 97, 112, 131, 136, 139, 194, 194*n*, 198, 199, 201, 202, 203, 205; painting of, by Tanzy, 81; Le Belvédère, 81, 87-88, 111; animals, interest in, 81, 111, 113, 114, 160 (see also *L'Enfant et les sortilèges; Histoires naturelles;* "Oiseaux tristes"; "Trois Beaux Oiseaux du Paradis"); bust of, by Leyritz, 88; trip to North America, 93-98 *passim,* 205; brother, Edouard, correspondence, 94, 95-96; American music and orchestras, 95, 97-98 (*see also* jazz *above*); on critics, 106, 106*n*-107*n*; trip to Spain and North Africa,

107; death and burial, 108, 109; writing style, 111; musicians and composers aided by, 112, 113; children, interest in, 113, 114 (see also *L'Enfant et les sortilèges; Ma Mère l'Oye; Noël des jouets*); musical aesthetics, 117-29; dance and dance rhythms, interest in and use of, 131, 134-35, 142, 150, 177, 201, 206 (see also *Boléro; Daphnis et Chloé; L'Enfant et les sortilèges;* "Habanera"; *Ma Mère l'Oye; Menuet antique; Menuet sur le nom d'Haydn; Pavane pour une Infante défunte; Le Tombeau de Couperin; Tripatos; La Valse, Valses nobles et sentimentales*); piano works and piano used in composition, 135-36, 209; orchestrations, 136-38; vocal works, 138-39; death (in music), 146, 171, 189, 203, 203*n*; creative process, 207-16; influence of, 218, 218*n*; catalogue of works, 219-40; transcriptions of works of others, 240-43; recordings, 247-70

Ravel family, 9, 10, 12, 12*n*, 59
Reber, Henri, 132*n*
Régnier, Henri de, 3, 30, 154; Ravel's *Les Grand Vents venus d'outremer*, 54, 165, 203, 227; Ravel's use of quotations, 154, 175, 223
Renard, Jules, 55, 179; *Histoires naturelles* and Ravel work based on, 51*n*, 51-52, 161, 162*n*, 162-63, 164, 226; see also *Histoires naturelles*
Renoir, Pierre Auguste, 2, 8, 29*n*, 186, 218
La Républicaine, 85
Respighi, Ottorino, 101
Révelot, Mme, 81, 107
Rêves, 23, 29, 93, 198
La Revue Blanche, 29*n*, 29-30, 40
La Revue Musicale: on Ravel, 40*n*, 102*n*, 104, 104*n*; Debussy issue and Ravel work, 78, 78*n*; Fauré issue and Ravel work, 85, 86, 86*n*, 235; Ronsard issue and Ravel work, 85, 88, 88*n*, 235-36; Gédalge on melody, 131
Revue Musicale de la S.I.M., 56-57, 121-22, 124*n*-125*n*; Haydn issue and Ravel work, 59*n*-60*n*, 230
Rhené-Baton (René Baton), 77, 225, 233, 234
Riéra, Santiago, 15-16
Rieti, Vittorio, 60*n*
Rimsky-Korsakov, Nikolai, 3, 11, 25, 40, 54, 58, 66*n*, 82, 168; and Ravel, 16, 49*n*, 66*n*,

125, 136, 148, 149, 166, 167, 241, 242; *Shéhérazade*, 40, 61, 136, 148; *Antar*, 49*n*, 241; piano concerto, 49*n*; *La Nuit de Noël*, 58; *Snégourotchka*, 58; *Capriccio espagnol*, 136, 166; *Mlada*, 136, 241
Roger-Ducasse, Jean Jules, 20, 37, 39*n*, 62*n*, 80, 86*n*, 93, 227; Three Etudes for Piano Four Hands, 20
Roland-Manuel (Alexis Manuel Lévy), 64*n*, 83, 88*n*, 239; on Ravel, 52, 111, 113*n*, 131-32, 143*n*, 146, 148*n*, 169-70, 218*n*; and Ravel, 64, 83, 88, 112, 117, 119, 120, 139, 140, 175-76, 178, 185; Ravel, correspondence, 67, 71, 72, 76, 77, 78, 128-29
Roland-Manuel, Mme, 83, 88
Roland-Manuel, Claude, 86, 235
Rolland, Romain, 41*n*, 42-43, 47, 54
"Ronde," 185; see also *Trois Chansons pour chœur mixte sans accompagnement*
Ronsard, Pierre de, 88*n*, 192
Ronsard à son âme, 85, 88, 138, 192, 199, 203, 235-36; orchestral transcription, 107, 236
Ropartz, J. Guy: Psalm 136, 23, 24, 25
Rosenthal, Manuel, 83; and Ravel, 88, 93, 100*n*, 112, 119, 120, 137, 157-58, 209, 236, 270; and Ravel, transcriptions of, 107, 108*n*, 206, 225, 236
Rouché, Jacques, 65, 78, 84, 100, 229, 238
Roussel, Albert, 31, 41, 49*n*, 78, 83, 86, 88*n*, 93, 165, 239; and Ravel, 83*n*, 122*n*
Rubinstein, Arthur, 30, 264, 270
Rubinstein, Ida, 83; and Ravel, 98, 99*n*, 103, 107, 201, 239
Ruhlmann, François, 57, 228
Russian music, interest in and influence of, 3, 16, 29, 54, 126, 131; Ravel, 11-12, 16, 25, 26, 54, 105, 119, 125, 126, 131, 149, 177, 178

Sabata, Vittorio De, 89*n*, 236, 270
Sachs, Léo, 64, 65
Sainte, 19, 138, 143-44, 221, 249
Saint-Marceaux, Mme René de, 21, 48*n*-49*n*; and Ravel, 20*n*, 21-22, 48, 49*n*, 224; Ravel, correspondence, 22, 45-46, 60
Saint-Saëns, Camille, 2, 20*n*, 35, 65, 67, 73, 82, 124, 124*n*; and Ravel, 15, 64, 102, 119, 123-24, 125*n*, 135, 136, 202*n*, 204; on

Ravel, 36, 36*n*, 124*n*; *La Jeunesse d'Hercule*, 124; *Phaéton*, 124; *Six Etudes pour la main gauche*, 202*n*
Samazeuilh, Gustave, 85, 98, 204*n*, 261
Sargent, Sir Malcolm, 103
Satie, Erik, 3, 16, 31, 41, 60*n*, 64, 65, 131; and Debussy, 3, 16-17, 31, 78*n*, 126; and Ravel, 3, 16-17, 18, 21, 31, 64, 80, 123, 124, 126, 138, 139, 143, 173, 205, 232, 243; *Parade*, 126, 205; *Prélude de la porte héroïque du ciel*, 143; *Sarabandes*, 143; *Gymnopédies*, 173, 205; Preludes to *Fils des étoiles*, orchestration by Ravel, 243
Sauguet, Henri, 60*n*, 126, 127
"Scarbo," 136*n*, 140, 170, 171-72, 228, 229; see also *Gaspard de la nuit*
Scarlatti, Domenico, 136, 186
Schmitt, Florent, 3, 19, 28, 49*n*, 62*n*, 64, 67, 78*n*, 86, 86*n*, 93; and Ravel, 23-24, 59, 122*n*, 232, 239; Prix de Rome, 33*n*; *La Tragédie de Salomé*, 65
Schmitz, E. Robert, 95, 250, 251, 269, 270
Schoenberg, Arnold, 3, 79, 83, 84, 132*n*; *Pierrot Lunaire*, 66, 84, 179, 196; and Ravel, 74, 110, 121, 125*n*, 125-26, 138, 179, 190, 196; *Gurrelieder*, 79
Schola Cantorum, 30, 31, 61
Schubert, Franz, 98, 122, 152; *Unfinished Symphony*, 58; and Ravel, 123, 134, 152, 175; *Gretchen am Spinnrade*, 146
Schumann, Robert, 65, 122; Ravel's variations on a chorale, 11; and Ravel, 11, 14, 14*n*, 15, 68-69, 124, 124*n*, 152, 241; Sonata in G Minor, 14; Andante and Variations for Two Pianos, 14*n*; Piano Quartet in E♭, 14*n*; Sonata in F♯ Minor, 14*n*; *Fantaisie*, 15; *Carnaval*, orchestral transcription by Ravel, 68-69, 124*n*, 241; works edited by Fauré, 73*n*; *Kinderszenen*, 173; *Romanze*, Opus 28, No. 2, 183
Scott, Cyril, 82
Scriabin, Alexander, 54; Prelude and Nocturne, Opus 9, 202*n*
Selva, Blanche, 26-27
Semiramis, 36*n*, 243
Sérénade grotesque, 17, 140, 220
Sérieyx, Auguste, 53
Sert, José-Maria, 29*n*, 241
Sert, Mme José-Maria (Misia Godebska Natanson Edwards), 29*n*, 45; and Ravel, 29, 29*n*, 45, 46, 48, 77, 227, 234
Séverac, Déodat de, 3, 28, 31, 49*n*, 122*n*
Shéhérazade (song cycle), 29, 32, 38, 39, 40, 40*n*, 92, 101, 106, 127, 132, 138*n*, 147, 148, 149, 156-58, 162, 224, 253
Shéhérazade, overture to, 20, 23-26, 40, 131, 136, 147-49, 154*n*, 208, 221
Sibelius, Jean, 125, 125*n*
Siloti, Alexander, 49*n*
Si morne!, 20, 121, 146-47, 165, 203*n*, 221
Singher, Martial: Ravel performed by, 105-06, 107, 236, 240, 265, 268, 270
Sites auriculaires, 17, 19, 20-21, 24, 26, 31-32, 142-43, 208, 220-21; "Entre cloches," 19, 20, 21, 142-43, 143*n*, 149; see also "Habanera"
Les Six, 3, 80, 83*n*, 84, 126, 127; see also Auric, Georges; Durey, Louis; Honegger, Arthur; Milhaud, Darius; Poulenc, Francis; Tailleferre, Germaine
Société des Concerts du Conservatoire, 30, 83, 260, 261, 262, 264, 267, 269
Société des Concerts Français, 59
Société Musicale Indépendante (S.M.I.), 61-62; concerts by, 62, 64-65, 66, 68, 78*n*, 82-83, 86*n*; Ravel performed by, 62, 64-65, 66, 68, 69, 72, 76, 85, 85*n*, 86*n*, 98, 231-35 *passim*
Société Nationale de Musique, 20*n*, 62, 83; concerts by, 20, 20*n*, 23, 26, 30, 40, 122*n*; Ravel performed by, 20, 20*n*, 23, 26-27, 31, 40, 43, 49, 52, 59, 61, 221-30 *passim*
Society of Authors, Composers, and Music Publishers, 49
Society of Phonic Arts and Sciences, 101
Sonata for Violin and Cello, 78, 84-85, 86, 131, 182, 190-91, 198, 211, 235
Sonata for Violin and Piano (1897), 19, 144-45, 155, 221
Sonata for Violin and Piano (1923-27), 86, 88, 88*n*, 92-93, 93*n*, 96, 145, 194, 198-200, 202, 238
Sonatine, 29, 39, 48, 49, 49*n*, 59, 95, 96, 100, 135, 135*n*, 152, 157, 158-59, 161, 186, 187*n*, 212-13, 224, 253-54
Sordes, Paul, 28, 29, 49, 225
"Soupir," 66, 67, 179-80, 181, 203, 232; see also *Trois Poèmes de Stéphane Mallarmé*

Spanish music, interest in and influence of, 131; Ravel, 8, 16, 17, 103, 107, 111n, 125, 131, 135, 139, 142, 160, 168, 201, 204, 206; *see also* "Alborada del gracioso"; *Boléro; Don Quichotte à Dulcinée;* "Habanera"; *Rapsodie espagnole*

Straram, Walther, 83, 98, 239, 255

Strauss, Johann, 76, 79, 188

Strauss, Richard, 3, 84, 100n; *Symphonia Domestica,* 30n; and Ravel, 54, 119, 120, 121, 125, 125n, 136, 177; *Salome,* 54, 125n; *Feuersnot,* 55; *Till Eulenspiegel,* 125n, 136; *Don Juan,* 136

Stravinsky, Igor, 2, 29, 78n, 83n, 84, 126, 131n, 199; Diaghilev and the Ballets Russes, 3, 60n, 66, 66n, 78, 205, 242-43; *The Firebird,* 66; and Ravel, reorchestration of Mussorgsky's *Khovanshchina,* 66, 66n, 242-43; *Le Sacre du printemps,* 66, 67, 84, 135; *Poèmes de la lyrique japonaise,* 66, 68; and Ravel, 66, 77, 78, 108, 110, 114, 126, 177, 232; Ravel on, 66, 121, 125, 125n, 204; *Petrushka,* 66, 205; *Symphony of Psalms,* 86n; *Oedipus Rex,* 125n; *Le Rossignol,* 125n; *Un Grand Sommeil noir,* 141, 141n

String Quartet (Quatuor), 20, 32, 37, 38, 39-40, 54n, 64, 96, 106, 155-56, 157, 158, 166, 182, 183, 190, 223, 252

"Surgi de la croupe et du bond," 66n, 67, 126, 179, 180-81, 232; *see also Trois Poèmes de Stéphane Mallarmé*

Sur l'herbe, 54, 165-66, 180, 227, 257-58

Swedish Ballet, 79, 83, 187, 234

Synnestvedt, Magnus, 28, 48, 49n

Szigeti, Joseph, 96, 270

Tabuteau, Maurice, 28-29

Tailleferre, Germaine, 80n, 88, 112, 218n; see also *Les Six*

Tansman, Alexandre, 83; and Ravel, 88, 94, 97, 112, 125n

Tchaikovsky, Peter Ilyitch, 121

Le Temps, 90; *see also* Lalo, Pierre

Terrasse, Claude, 30

Teyte, Maggie, 67n

Théâtre du Châtelet, 8

Théâtre du Vieux-Colombier, 80, 83

Thibaud, Jacques, 30, 87, 270

Thomas, Ambroise, 14, 26

Thomasset, Louise, 41, 225

Thomson, Virgil, 83

The Times (London), 82, 87, 88n

Le Tombeau de Couperin, 70, 72, 75, 76, 135, 136, 141, 152, 185-87, 210-11, 212, 234, 263-64; orchestral transcription, 76, 101, 185, 234; as ballet, 79, 79n, 185, 234

Toscanini, Arturo, 99, 114, 270

Tout est lumière, 151, 152, 222

Trio, 48, 70, 72, 72n, 73n, 135n, 145, 182-84, 191, 204-05, 233, 262

Tripatos, 59, 174, 230

"Trois Beaux Oiseaux du Paradis," 184, 203, 233; see also *Trois Chansons pour chœur mixte sans accompagnement*

Trois Chansons pour chœur mixte sans accompagnement, 73, 152, 184-85, 233-34, 262-63; "Nicolette," 184, 194; "Trois Beaux Oiseaux du Paradis," 184, 203; "Ronde," 185

Trois Poèmes de Stéphane Mallarmé, 23, 48, 66, 67, 68, 79, 132, 138, 138n, 144, 179-81, 232; "Placet futile," 66, 67, 128-29, 179, 180, 181; "Soupir," 66, 67, 179-80, 181, 203; "Surgi de la croupe et du bond," 66n, 67, 126, 179, 180-81

Trouhanova, Natasha, 65, 231

Turina, Joaquín, 3, 83, 89, 125

Tzigane, 86, 88, 92, 131, 192-93, 198, 200, 236, 265; orchestral transcription, 89, 192, 236

Valéry, Paul, 3, 29, 30, 41, 93n, 119, 246

"La Vallée des cloches," 49, 50, 142-43, 143n, 149, 159, 160-61, 171, 224-25; see also *Miroirs*

La Valse, 29n, 72, 76-80 *passim,* 86, 87, 89, 92, 101, 106, 119, 121, 134, 135, 136, 177, 188-89, 195, 197, 203, 208n, 214, 234-35, 264

Valses nobles et sentimentales, 48, 49n, 64, 65, 67n, 119, 132-34, 136, 162, 175-77, 181, 189, 195, 208, 231, 261; as ballet (*Adélaïde, ou le langage des fleurs*), 65, 156, 175, 176, 177, 231; orchestral transcription, 175, 176, 177, 231

Varèse, Edgard, 97

Vaughan Williams, Ralph, 3, 58, 82, 218; and Ravel, 58, 69, 76, 112, 119, 120-21, 125, 125n, 131, 245

Vaughan Williams, Mrs. Ralph, 59

Verhaeren, Emile: Ravel's *Si morne!* to poem by, 20, 146, 221; see also *Si morne!*

Verlaine, Paul, 3, 16, 29; Ravel's *Un Grand Sommeil noir* to poem by, 17, 141, 220 (see also *Un Grand Sommeil noir*); Ravel's *Sur l'herbe* to poem by, 54, 166, 227 (see also *Sur l'herbe*); Fauré, Honegger, and Stravinsky works based on, 141, 141n; Laparra work based on, 166

Villa-Lobos, Heitor, 110

Villiers de l'Isle-Adam, Comte Philippe de, 16

Vincent, Clovis, 108, 108n

Viñes, Ricardo, 21, 23, 28, 48n-49n; on Ravel, 13, 18, 39n, 124n; and Ravel, 16, 18, 19, 20, 21, 37, 41, 49, 49n, 59, 91, 214, 220, 221, 222, 223, 225, 229; and Debussy, 21, 32, 49n, 159

Vocalise-Etude en forme de Habanera, 54, 165, 181, 227, 257

Vuillermoz, Emile, 28, 61, 62n; on Ravel, 56-57, 102-03, 163

Wagner, Richard, 3, 30, 58, 82, 83, 84, 107n, 123, 123n, 125; and Ravel, 16, 121, 122, 123, 123n, 125, 126, 138, 141, 152, 200; Casella pastiche, 68; and Debussy, 126, 200; *Tristan und Isolde*, 132, 141, 200

Wallenstein, Alfred, 270

Weber, Carl Maria von, 15, 124, 152; *Le Spectre de la rose*, 61

Webern, Anton, 125, 125n

Webster, Beveridge, 98, 111, 172, 270

Weekly Critical Review, 39

Whiteman, Paul, 97

Widor, Charles-Marie, 60n, 136

Wiener, Jean, 83, 83n, 84

Wittgenstein, Paul, 100, 100n; and Ravel, 100, 101, 104, 104n, 239, 270

World War I, 1-2; Ravel, 1, 70-75 *passim*, 186, 189

Wurmser, Lucien, 64, 65

Youmans, Vincent: *Tea for Two*, 194

Zaspiak-Bat, 72, 72n, 204n

Zay, Jean, 108-09

Zogheb, Robert de, 108

Zweig, Stefan, 83

A CATALOG OF SELECTED
DOVER BOOKS
IN ALL FIELDS OF INTEREST

A CATALOG OF SELECTED DOVER
BOOKS IN ALL FIELDS OF INTEREST

CONCERNING THE SPIRITUAL IN ART, Wassily Kandinsky. Pioneering work by father of abstract art. Thoughts on color theory, nature of art. Analysis of earlier masters. 12 illustrations. 80pp. of text. 5⅜ × 8½.   23411-8 Pa. $3.95

ANIMALS: 1,419 Copyright-Free Illustrations of Mammals, Birds, Fish, Insects, etc., Jim Harter (ed.). Clear wood engravings present, in extremely lifelike poses, over 1,000 species of animals. One of the most extensive pictorial sourcebooks of its kind. Captions. Index. 284pp. 9 × 12.   23766-4 Pa. $11.95

CELTIC ART: The Methods of Construction, George Bain. Simple geometric techniques for making Celtic interlacements, spirals, Kells-type initials, animals, humans, etc. Over 500 illustrations. 160pp. 9 × 12. (USO)   22923-8 Pa. $9.95

AN ATLAS OF ANATOMY FOR ARTISTS, Fritz Schider. Most thorough reference work on art anatomy in the world. Hundreds of illustrations, including selections from works by Vesalius, Leonardo, Goya, Ingres, Michelangelo, others. 593 illustrations. 192pp. 7⅛ × 10¼.   20241-0 Pa. $8.95

CELTIC HAND STROKE-BY-STROKE (Irish Half-Uncial from "The Book of Kells"): An Arthur Baker Calligraphy Manual, Arthur Baker. Complete guide to creating each letter of the alphabet in distinctive Celtic manner. Covers hand position, strokes, pens, inks, paper, more. Illustrated. 48pp. 8¼ × 11.
24336-2 Pa. $3.95

EASY ORIGAMI, John Montroll. Charming collection of 32 projects (hat, cup, pelican, piano, swan, many more) specially designed for the novice origami hobbyist. Clearly illustrated easy-to-follow instructions insure that even beginning papercrafters will achieve successful results. 48pp. 8¼ × 11.   27298-2 Pa. $2.95

THE COMPLETE BOOK OF BIRDHOUSE CONSTRUCTION FOR WOOD-WORKERS, Scott D. Campbell. Detailed instructions, illustrations, tables. Also data on bird habitat and instinct patterns. Bibliography. 3 tables. 63 illustrations in 15 figures. 48pp. 5¼ × 8½.   24407-5 Pa. $1.95

BLOOMINGDALE'S ILLUSTRATED 1886 CATALOG: Fashions, Dry Goods and Housewares, Bloomingdale Brothers. Famed merchants' extremely rare catalog depicting about 1,700 products: clothing, housewares, firearms, dry goods, jewelry, more. Invaluable for dating, identifying vintage items. Also, copyright-free graphics for artists, designers. Co-published with Henry Ford Museum & Green-field Village. 160pp. 8¼ × 11.   25780-0 Pa. $9.95

HISTORIC COSTUME IN PICTURES, Braun & Schneider. Over 1,450 costumed figures in clearly detailed engravings—from dawn of civilization to end of 19th century. Captions. Many folk costumes. 256pp. 8⅜ × 11¾.   23150-X Pa. $11.95

THE INFLUENCE OF SEA POWER UPON HISTORY, 1660–1783, A. T. Mahan. Influential classic of naval history and tactics still used as text in war colleges. First paperback edition. 4 maps. 24 battle plans. 640pp. 5⅜ × 8½.
25509-3 Pa. $12.95

THE STORY OF THE TITANIC AS TOLD BY ITS SURVIVORS, Jack Winocour (ed.). What it was really like. Panic, despair, shocking inefficiency, and a little heroism. More thrilling than any fictional account. 26 illustrations. 320pp. 5⅜ × 8½. 20610-6 Pa. $7.95

FAIRY AND FOLK TALES OF THE IRISH PEASANTRY, William Butler Yeats (ed.). Treasury of 64 tales from the twilight world of Celtic myth and legend: "The Soul Cages," "The Kildare Pooka," "King O'Toole and his Goose," many more. Introduction and Notes by W. B. Yeats. 352pp. 5⅜ × 8½. 26941-8 Pa. $8.95

BUDDHIST MAHAYANA TEXTS, E. B. Cowell and Others (eds.). Superb, accurate translations of basic documents in Mahayana Buddhism, highly important in history of religions. The Buddha-karita of Asvaghosha, Larger Sukhavativyuha, more. 448pp. 5⅜ × 8½. , 25552-2 Pa. $9.95

ONE TWO THREE . . . INFINITY: Facts and Speculations of Science, George Gamow. Great physicist's fascinating, readable overview of contemporary science: number theory, relativity, fourth dimension, entropy, genes, atomic structure, much more. 128 illustrations. Index. 352pp. 5⅜ × 8½. 25664-2 Pa. $8.95

ENGINEERING IN HISTORY, Richard Shelton Kirby, et al. Broad, nontechnical survey of history's major technological advances: birth of Greek science, industrial revolution, electricity and applied science, 20th-century automation, much more. 181 illustrations. ". . . excellent . . ."—Isis. Bibliography. vii + 530pp. 5⅜ × 8¼.
26412-2 Pa. $14.95